Learning for Work

Learning for Work

How Industrial Education Fostered Democratic Opportunity

CONNIE GODDARD

UNIVERSITY OF
ILLINOIS PRESS
Urbana, Chicago, and Springfield

Publication was supported by a grant from the Howard D. and Marjorie I. Brooks Fund for Progressive Thought.

© 2024 by the Board of Trustees
of the University of Illinois
All rights reserved
1 2 3 4 5 C P 5 4 3 2 1
∞ This book is printed on acid-free paper.

Library of Congress Cataloging-in-Publication

DataNames: Goddard, Connie, 1943– author.
Title: Learning for work : how industrial education fostered democratic opportunity / Connie Goddard.
Description: Urbana : University of Illinois Press, 2024. | Includes bibliographical references and index.
Identifiers: LCCN 2024003675 (print) | LCCN 2024003676 (ebook) | ISBN 9780252046049 (hardcover) | ISBN 9780252088148 (paperback) | ISBN 9780252047220 (ebook)
Subjects: LCSH: Manual training—United States—History. | Technical education—United States—History. | Vocational education—United States—History. | Chicago Manual Training School—History. | Manual Training and Industrial School for Youth (Bordentown, N.J.)—History. | State Normal and Industrial School (Ellendale, N.D.)—History.
Classification: LCC LB1596.U6 G64 2024 (print) | LCC LB1596.U6 (ebook) | DDC 370.1130973—dc23/eng/20240403
LC record available at https://lccn.loc.gov/2024003675
LC ebook record available at https://lccn.loc.gov/2024003676

*For Luke and his cousins,
Gwendolyn and Gabriela*

"Mente atque manu ad virtutem"

> The most colossal improvement which recent years have seen in secondary education lies in the introduction of the manual training schools; not because they will give us a people more handy and practical . . . but because they will give us citizens with an entirely different intellectual fibre.
>
> They occupy the pupil in a way most congruous with the spontaneous interests of the age.
>
> —William James
> Talks to Teachers, 1899

Contents

Acknowledgments xi
Preface: Learning How the Work of the World Is Done xiii

1. Through Mind and Hand to Manhood 1
2. Learning and Doing Arrives in Chicago 28
3. Joining Hands and Heads on the Midway 59
4. A "Star of Hope" Defines Industrial Education 91
5. The People's School on the Prairie and How It Grew 126
6. Agency and Efficiency: Manual Training Becomes Vocational Education 159

   Epilogue: Lessons on Education and Work from Bordentown and Ellendale 197

Notes 209
Bibliography 249
Credits 269
Index 271

Acknowledgments

There is a lifetime of people to thank for helping me bring this story to life. I cannot name them all, but I do want to acknowledge the men who were the immediate catalyst for my taking the project on. In 2013, I had an opportunity to teach composition and history to students at the state prison in Rahway, New Jersey. It was a rewarding experience, one that led me to ask why they were in there while I was free to come and go. This book addresses that question, so thanks to all of you for leading me to ask it.

Soon after that experience, I learned about the Manual Training and Industrial School in Bordentown, further south in New Jersey, and of John Dewey's influence on it. Why had I, as a student of his works, not heard of it before? This book addresses that question as well.

Thus, I want to thank John Medley, MTIS class of 1954 and keeper of the school's records; he has been generous with his time, his memories, and insights into why the school was such a special place. Thanks are due as well to Sheila Gregory Thomas, granddaughter of the school's second principal, who shared family papers with me and supported this endeavor.

Also essential to the writing of this book is Ken Smith of Ellendale, North Dakota. He has not only helped bring into being a museum of local history but has brought into virtual being records of the town, of its Normal and Industrial School, and of Dickey County that surrounds both. These materials transported me half a continent away and over a century back in time to reconstruct the history of the school, so thanks, Ken; this book could not have become what it has without your efforts and assistance.

Among others who deserve special thanks are William Schubert, my doctoral advisor, and curriculum historian William Wraga. Both have led me to books and articles essential to telling this story and offered valuable feedback as it moved through the writing process. Another special thank you is due fellow writer Louise Knight; early on, she suggested that I look into the brief but significant history of the Society for Promoting Manual Labor in Literary Institutions. Learning of the society's goals and the extent to which they influenced the schools I studied led me to tell a distinctive story. I am very grateful to all three. Thanks are due as well to historian John Rury; though we view industrial education rather differently, he has otherwise long been a source of valuable advice.

I am also grateful to the research staff at the Monmouth County Library; if I could not locate something I needed, you all could. Thanks, also, to the staff at the New Jersey State Library and at the State Archives in Trenton; they led me to valuable resources. Similar thanks are due to several people at the University of Chicago Special Collections Research Center and the Chicago History Museum.

There are many others to thank as well—members of the History of Education Society, the Country Schools Association of America, the John Dewey Society, the Society of Midland Authors, the Society for Historians of the Gilded Age and Progressive Era, plus local groups such as a branch of the Campaign to End the New Jim Crow, the AAUW, and the T. Thomas Fortune Cultural Center. You all have enabled me to revivify a neglected aspect of our collective history. And many, many thanks to Martha Bayne at the University of Illinois Press, who saw that a book on "learning and labor"—the university's motto—deserved a place on the Press's list. Thanks, Martha, for choosing a trio of readers whose comments vastly strengthened the manuscript. And thanks as well to the numerous other people at the Press who helped bring this book into being. Often unsung, but always essential. I appreciated good advice and guidance along the way.

Several friends and family members have read parts of the manuscript and been frank in their comments, pointing to overlong sentences, overuse of dashes, and questionable assertions. Fellow wordsmith Helen Gagel is chief among the latter; thanks for your honest critiques. Special thanks as well to the Suffragists Speak troupe and to Holmdel hikers for challenging questions and exercise along the way.

For unlimited support and encouragement, as well as a room of my own, I thank Jerry Schreiber; all three have nourished the project beyond measure.

Preface

Learning How the
Work of the World Is Done

> The school that elevates labor and honors the laborer, the school that trains man in his natural elements, the school that not only instructs but educates, not only teaches how to think but how to do—the secret of the progress of civilization.
> —Ina Randall, 1901
> "Industrial Training in the Schools" Graduation Oration, North Dakota Manual Training School

> Through the years, our academic and trade training were graced with an all-Black cadre of teachers and staff educated at the best institutions. They were at MTIS to, in turn, educate an all-Black student body who otherwise might not . . . have had an academic opportunity . . . What we received was a solid academic education and a trade sufficient for going on to college or pursuing a livelihood in one's chosen vocation.
> —Arthur Symes, 2016
> Class of 1953, Manual Training and Industrial School, Bordentown, New Jersey

Books most often come with back stories of their own; this one is no exception. Its tale might be told through the evolution of its title, which began as the Deweyan "learning to do," thus rooting the story in the philosophy of John Dewey. When that became too limiting, the title was briefly "schooling hands and heads," which was dismissed as suggesting a grade-school textbook. The next choice was "revisiting industrial education," which worked in several ways, but an early reviewer suggested that it sounded too dull for the story told. When the University of Illinois Press took an interest in the book, "learning and labor" became the working title: not only is the book about how the two activities are intertwined, but the words are the university's motto. Though maintaining that literal connection had considerable value, "labor" connoted a history of unions, so the title became *Learning for Work*, with "for" implying how work is done in the world as well as the academic, practical, and behavioral skills needed for a person to assume a rewarding place in the workforce.

Through illustrating how industrial education was practiced at a variety of schools during the Progressive Era, this book argues that these programs provided learning experiences for young people that enriched their opportunities to participate fully in a rapidly industrializing economy. Thus, industrial education extended the benefits of a democratic education to a broader swath of American society rather than limiting those benefits through providing the less privileged with an inferior education. Further, *Learning for Work* sets the development of industrial education in the context of how both schools and workplaces changed from the early years of the republic and then on through the years when the United States became the world's leading industrial economy. As the nineteenth century opened, educators on both sides of the Atlantic realized that academic work needed to be complemented by manual work, an idea that went through various manifestations over several decades. Then, in the 1870s, engineering schools in particular needed a means of teaching tool use to secondary students; to do so, they adopted manual training programs. As the century turned, educators and a wide variety of reformers sought a means for encouraging 12- and 13-year-olds to remain in school; manual work was seen as such a means. A decade later, the concern extended to broadening the young persons' awareness of their work and their world—called "industrial intelligence"—before their imagination was curtailed by the monotony of a factory job. Further, acquiring good work habits, many believed, encouraged good citizenship. The argument was that industrial education benefitted both students and society at large.

As noted in this book's epigraph, the influential philosopher William James—mentor for John Dewey, W. E. B. Du Bois, and other public intellectuals of their day—saw manual training as a "colossal improvement," not only because it provided practical skills but because it would yield citizens of "an entirely different intellectual fibre." A few years later, a young woman graduating from a new manual training school in a small Dakota town made a similar comment. Five decades on, a young man studying at a

Figure 1. The great seal of the University of Illinois memorializes the union of learning and labor that led to its founding as Illinois Industrial University in 1867. Its establishment was an outcome of ideas articulated by Theodore Weld, Jonathan Baldwin Turner, and others in the decades before its charter.

school whose mission owed much to both Dewey and Du Bois experienced the mix of academic and practical courses that were at the core of manual and industrial education from the Progressive Era and beyond. Comments from both of them appear above.

Though this is a work of history, it was undertaken out of a conviction that industrial education—now more commonly known as career and technical education—is due for a rejuvenation. The pandemic that began in 2020 and its repercussions for higher education—a new focus on its cost and a reevaluation of its necessity—suggest that a study such as this is particularly timely.

The great seal of the University of Illinois includes not only the motto "Learning and Labor," but a book, a plow, an anvil, and a steam engine—representations of agriculture, science, and art. The school, founded in 1867 just after the end of the Civil War, was initially called Illinois Industrial University; it was to be a school for "industrial" or working people rather than for an elite, those for whom colleges had previously been intended. Jonathan Baldwin Turner, the industrious educator who pressured the Illinois legislature into establishing the university, is among those who play a role in *Learning for Work*. Born in New England, as were most of the men responsible for conceptualizing and implementing industrial education, Turner went west in 1833, one of many graduates of eastern colleges who during that decade took on "civilizing the wilderness"—of the Mississippi River valley—as a mission.

A biologist by training, Turner taught initially at Illinois College, a school founded in 1829; among its early students was a young man who would, four decades later, be one of those responsible for establishing the Chicago Manual Training School (CMTS). That school is the subject of chapter 1, which gets the story underway through providing the first published history of an institution that was influential in its time but is largely forgotten today. Among others who contributed to the origins of CMTS were Calvin Woodward of St. Louis. Remembered for promoting a curriculum that was half academic and half practical skills, Woodward is often regarded, if incorrectly, as the founder of the manual training movement. Among others significant to the origin of CMTS was a Chicago enthusiast by the name of Charles Ham; also unfortunately forgotten, he wrote an admirable history of technology that complemented Woodward's curriculum.

Chapter 2 looks back to the European roots of manual and industrial education, bringing Comenius, Pestalozzi, and a school in Switzerland called Hofwyl into the story before crossing the Atlantic again to consider the role of Theodore Weld. Remembered now as an ardent abolitionist, Weld in the 1830s headed a short-lived but influential organization called the Society for Promoting Industrial Education in Literary Institutions. Illinois College was one of many established on that model. Another strand discusses the origin of several technical institutes founded prior to the Civil War. For context, chapter 2 offers a brief history of work in the nineteenth century as it was transformed from tasks performed by independent yeomen and artisans to other tasks, often mechanized, performed by employees of others. The story then returns to Chicago, the nation's fastest growing city at the time and a center for corporate and educational innovation, as well as union militance.

The role of John Dewey in the evolution of industrial education is the chief topic of chapter 3. It explores his surprising neglect of CMTS after it became part of his department at the University of Chicago and his involvement, or lack thereof, in movements that complemented his "new education": the "new architecture" and the "new industrialism." Both contributed to Chicago's vitality during Dewey's decade in the city; both were instigated in part by his colleagues at the university. The chapter enriches the oft-told tale of Dewey's abrupt departure from Chicago by raising new questions about his work there. Dewey's substantial impact on industrial education, both as theorist and as advocate, comes up again in chapter 6.

Chapter 4 tells the story of New Jersey's Manual Training and Industrial School for Colored Youth (MTIS) and relays the impact of uniting learning and labor on its origins. Founded in 1886, the school owes something to Woodward as well as to the founders of Hampton and Tuskegee and, indirectly, to Weld and Turner. Though limited funding got the school off to a slow start, in 1894 it was acquired by the state of New Jersey and became as much a model as was CMTS.

Chapter 5 moves the story from semi-urban New Jersey and very urban Chicago out to North Dakota and the founding of the state's Manual Training School in 1899. In 1907, it became the Normal and Industrial School (the NI), combining ideas about the "new education" articulated by Dewey with those of Woodward and the state's greatest need: teachers for its rapidly growing population. The vitality of the ideas behind its founding are evident in the accomplishments of its early faculty and the role the school played in the lives of its graduates.

The concluding chapter focuses on programs in the city of Chicago and in cities across the state of Wisconsin; its point is to consider how the manual training movement became the movement for vocational education in the decade between 1910 and 1920. To do so, chapter 6 begins with a survey of past histories of industrial education and claims that too few were based on stories of actual schools and programs. As a consequence, these standard histories, written from the perspective of policies articulated on a national level, missed the value and significance of the programs covered in this book: courses that addressed the interests of a community's students and the needs of local industries.

The book's epilogue, "Lessons on Education and Work from Bordentown and Ellendale," opens by claiming that programs designed for these two different communities had a variety of similarities; chief among them is that they were designed to meet the specific needs of the people they served. It also suggests some needed research areas in the hope that this rather personalized history inspires studies of other local industrial education programs in order to tell a more positive history of industrial education—one that is relevant to the needs of today's students, communities, and industries.

In addition to these intellectual influences on *Learning for Work,* there are some very personal ones. Its immediate origin was my experience in the mid-2010s, teaching at a New Jersey state prison. A question inspired by that was how come those men—eager and intelligent as students—were on the "inside" and I was free to come and go? Among the possible answers is that as young men they'd not found a legitimate way to adequately support themselves, so they did it in ways that got them into trouble with the law. A successful businessman I met during this period once said to me: "I was fortunate. I learned to be a roofer before I went to prison, so I knew how to make a living once I got out." A book on "reskilling America" that I read then began with a related comment from a prison warden. Why, he asked, do we as a society wait until men wind up in prison before we give them a decent vocational education? So, this book set out to address his question.

Part of my response is the story of MTIS, which is also known as Bordentown. The school was closed in 1955, in the wake of *Brown v. Board of Education*. For a dozen years before that, it had been under attack from integrationists who called it a "Jim Crow" institution. That it may have been, but it also offered an education similar to that of CMTS, which was founded at around the same time. Both featured a curriculum that was half academic and half trade-related, as advised by Woodward and Ham. MTIS graduates were not only well prepared to enter college if that was their choice, but they were also prepared to make a living.

As a student of Dewey's work in Chicago, I was intrigued to learn that longtime MTIS principal William Valentine had, between his graduation from Harvard in 1904 and his 1915 arrival in Bordentown, headed a school for "colored youth" in Indianapolis. That year, it had received a laudatory review in *Schools of Tomorrow*, a 1915 book written by Evelyn Dewey with her father John Dewey. MTIS, I learned as I delved into its history, had also received favorable attention from both Booker T. Washington and W. E. B. Du Bois. Why then, I asked, would students of Dewey's work, or historians of education in general, be largely unaware of or critical of the school?

"Learning to do" was also a concept that dominated my childhood, both at home and at school. During the 1930s, my father established what he called a play club in suburban Chicago: its motto was "Doing to Learn and Learning to Do." The club's function was to take boys and girls of eight to fourteen or so on weekend outings to explore their surroundings: its wooded parks, beaches, and the city itself. On afternoons, club members went to a church basement where they learned to make stilts, scooters, and model ships—all of which they learned to use. Unlike too many of the men in my prison classes, I'd had a childhood that included a version of the play club in our basement workshop and backyard, with my father directing the learning experiences.

The elementary school I attended also owed its origin to Dewey and other progressive educators. Called Crow Island and located in a Chicago suburb, it had been built in 1940 and became, during the 1950s, the model for elementary school construction nationwide. As students we not only learned to do, we absorbed the embracing warmth of the natural woods and fibers that graced the building's design and construction, all inspired by Prairie Style architecture.

Whether or not that experience led, decades later, to my interest in progressive education, I cannot now say, but its precepts led to another question addressed in this book. Dewey, who had founded the Laboratory School in 1896, became in 1901 head of a sprawling School of Education at the University of Chicago; CMTS was one of its many components. Though it

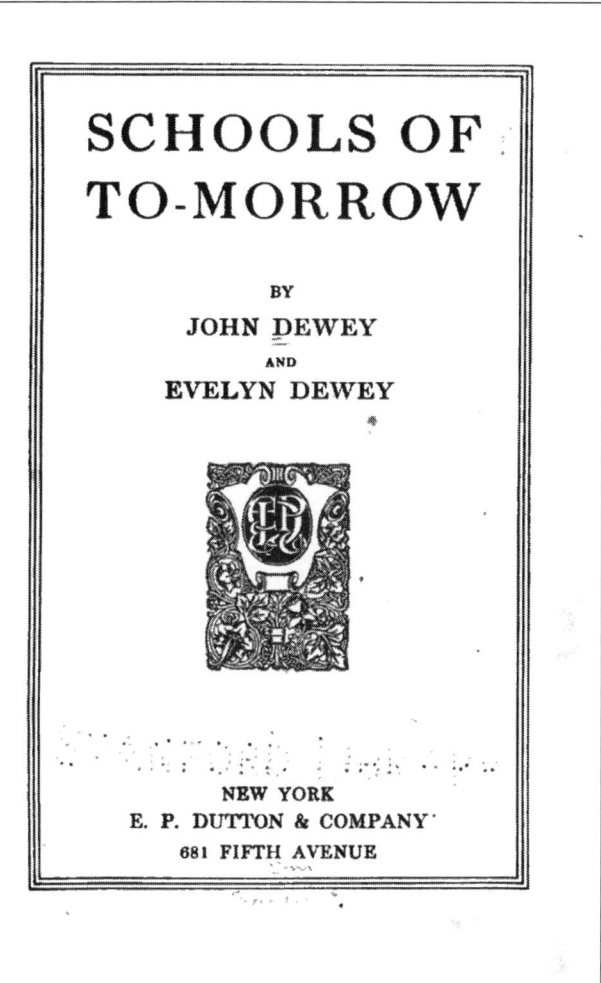

Figure 2. *Schools of Tomorrow*, published in 1915, was written by Evelyn Dewey under the auspices of her father John. In a chapter called "Education Through Industry," it described programs established in Chicago and other cities. Another chapter, "The School as Social Settlement," lauded the work of a school in Indianapolis headed by the man who would later preside over the Manual Training and Industrial School in New Jersey.

shared many characteristics with Dewey's lab school, he virtually ignored it. Why? I wondered.

Personal history led to my interest in the Normal and Industrial School, the subject of chapter 5. My mother, like my father, was the grandchild of Dakota homesteaders. The two, along with Crow Island, surely influenced my interest in the history of education. Mother's respect for the NI, her hometown of Ellendale, and the education she received there, led to another of this book's themes. Historians of education have tended to regard industrial education with considerable suspicion. Too often, it is dismissed as a product of Progressive Era condescension toward immigrants and other urban workers. Given my mother's affection for the NI, this was jarring; the school gave her, at the minimal price her farming parents could afford, the means to a job with growth potential in Chicago, a city with far more opportunities than were available in her hometown.

As I learned when delving into the NI's history, it provided the same for many hundreds of the school's other graduates. Opened in 1899 as the Manual Training School, it also attracted talented faculty and students, as is apparent in the 1901 commencement oration of one. Most graduates became teachers, often of domestic arts and manual training; many went on to acquire more education and many also moved on to the West Coast. In this, Ellendale's NI was very similar to Bordentown's MTIS: both provided students, largely at state expense, the possibility of a life far less constrained by the limitations their parents had faced, thus providing opportunities for fuller participation in a democratic society.

A positive attitude toward industrial education, I concluded, was influenced as much by personal experience as by what actually went on in classrooms. As the granddaughter of farmers and a student in a school characterized by active, practical learning, I was distressed by the negative attitude toward industrial education reflected in standard books on the topic. At some point, I decided that one's own childhood experience influenced one's attitude as much as the facts of the matter. In his introduction to *School to Work,* the late (and lauded) historian of curriculum Herbert Kliebard noted his skepticism about the virtue of lessons in the dignity of work and its character-building attributes. He recalled instead seeing his own father return from day after day of unrewarding work in New York's garment district, exhausted and dispirited by the boredom of his job. Later, when teaching at a vocational high school whose students came mainly from impoverished families, Kliebard was appalled at the mediocre academic education and substandard training for jobs that no longer existed his students received.

Figure 3. In 1901 Ina E. Randall, a young woman graduating with the first class from the Manual Training School in Ellendale (later, the NI), gave a quite extraordinary oration, one abounding with quotations from Cicero to John Ruskin. Some of it suggests that among her sources was a book by Chicago's Charles Ham.

Given those experiences, Kliebard's negativity is understandable, but the popularity of his book and others has had an unfortunate impact on how today's historians of education regard industrial education. In the minds of Turner and Weld, Woodward and Chicago's Charles Ham, manual labor and industrial training had a noble purpose for individuals and numerous benefits for society as a whole. Even if it did not turn out to be the "solution to social and industrial problems," as Ham predicted, it did manage to educate rich and poor alike; in particular, it gave the latter opportunities they otherwise would not have had. But this message seldom comes through in the studies of vocational education published since the 1960s. This need to "revisit" industrial education is addressed in chapter 6.

This closing chapter also covers the work and influence of Chicago's Ella Flagg Young, whose half century with the city's schools culminated with being superintendent from 1909 to 1915. From 1899 until 1904, she was on the faculty at the University of Chicago. Like her colleague John Dewey, she had a positive regard for manual work. For her, it was an important part of the curriculum and made a substantial contribution to democratic opportunity—so long as it was properly designed and delivered. Both Young and Dewey had grown up in close connection to the work of farmers and tradesmen, mechanics and metalsmiths. Dewey, according to one of his daughters, felt he had learned more from visits to his grandparents' farm than he did in school. Young's early education was a product of work with her practical parents; she credited them for lessons in compassion and how to get essential work done.

W. E. B. Du Bois, on the other hand, had an early experience with the "trade schools" to which young Black boys with an independent streak were sent. Though a wise high school principal saved his most gifted student from such a fate, it surely influenced some of Du Bois's skepticism toward much of what passed as "practical" education for his fellows. This, along with Du Bois's interactions with Dewey and other educators, is covered in chapter 4.

The title of chapter 6, "Agency and Efficiency," also demonstrates how the book has evolved. Called at first "agency *versus* efficiency," its intention was to describe how manual training became vocational education, a process that took place between 1900 and 1920, and to claim that the movement respected student volition—what "agency" implies—rather than "efficiency," a pejorative term to some historians of education. But adhering to this conventional understanding of "efficiency" ran up against what I was learning from my reading: Young, for example, often employed the term to describe programs she endorsed in Chicago. So, too, did some of her contemporaries, including heads of equally admirable programs in Wisconsin and North Dakota.

While weighing the accuracy of placing "agency"—which I view as enabling students to become, in Dewey's famous phrase "masters of their own industrial fate"—in opposition to "efficiency," I arrived at a new understanding of the latter term. In his 2022 book on Dewey, intellectual historian Michael Knoll discusses how the idea of "social efficiency" evolved between the 1890s and 1920. It describes how these words could describe both programs endorsed by Dewey—or "humanitarian" efficiency—and those advocated by, for example, David Snedden—or "utilitarian" efficiency.

With that distinction in mind, chapter 6 continued on its intended course, but "versus" became "and," with "humanitarian" understood. The chapter begins by suggesting that the history relayed in standard books on industrial education has been determined more by policy pronouncements from above than by the programs developed and implemented on the ground level in actual schools. Conventional wisdom is that industrial education, in addition to being aimed at the less advantaged, "failed" because the various interests—manufacturers, labor unions, educators—involved in the movement could not agree on just what ought to be taught in such programs. But, as histories of labor demonstrate, technology was moving too fast for any curriculum to keep up. Hence the significance of small-scale programs intended for specific communities.

Some historians of the movement have suggested that there are few studies of actual industrial education programs; this book fills that gap. It not only provides histories of CMTS, MTIS, and the NI that are not available elsewhere, it also incorporates the connected stories of programs in Wisconsin and New Jersey, plus some in St. Louis, Cleveland, Milwaukee, and Philadelphia. While hardly providing a thorough summation, through its review of programs for rural students, for those in semi-urban areas, and for others in major cities, *Learning for Work* attempts to offer some balance. It also accomplishes something no other study of which I am aware has done—it incorporates an industrial education program for Black students into the story of those attended largely by whites.

By analyzing the work of Ella Flagg Young, chapter 6 regards vocational education as designed to teach students "how the work of the world is done" (to borrow a phrase from Evelyn Dewey). Young's intention was to keep students "going on to higher grades," not to train them for specific jobs. Though her considerable accomplishments are widely known, her prominence as an advocate for vocational education is not. Further, *Learning for Work* offers an alternate view of Dewey's accomplishments, one influenced not only by my study of CMTS but by the work of Michael Knoll, who has cast a skeptical eye on some Dewey-related hagiography.

Thus, *Learning for Work* revisits not only industrial education but the careers of several noted educators associated with it. As schooling's role in preparing young people for their lives and work is undergoing considerable reevaluation, my hope is that this book can make a timely and useful contribution to discussions about education and work, or at least how they might impact my grandchildren's generation.

Learning for Work

CHAPTER 1

Through Mind and Hand to Manhood

> The acquisition of industrial skill should be the means of promoting the general education of the pupil: the education of the hand should be the means of more completely and more efficaciously educating the brain.
>
> —Felix Adler, 1883

The brief life of the Chicago Manual Training School (CMTS), the decades between its widely heralded opening in 1884 and its loss of identity twenty years later, belies its influence on several similar institutions that opened around the country in the 1880s and 1890s. Established shortly after the pioneering schools in St. Louis and Cambridge, the Chicago school was the first to be independent; the others were preparatory institutions for Washington University and Massachusetts Institute of Technology. Names associated with CMTS still resonate in Chicago. Marshall Field donated its initial funding, and George Pullman secured the architect for its first building. Richard T. Crane, a leading manufacturer of plumbing supplies, was a member of its first board; one of Chicago's first public manual training schools still bears his name. N. K. Fairbank, another early board member, is recalled in the name of Fairbank Court along the Chicago River. Famed educator Francis W. Parker, who in 1883 arrived in Chicago to lead its Normal School, employed practices associated with manual training in his widely emulated curriculum; two Chicago schools still bear his name.

Thinking CMTS might become the nucleus for a school of technology, William Rainey Harper had the University of Chicago acquire it in 1897. John Dewey, one of the new university's most prominent appointments, somewhat reluctantly took charge of CMTS in 1901 when Harper thought that it, along with Parker's practice school at the Normal and Dewey's Laboratory School, might all merge into one grand institution. That did not happen, but the name of H. H. Belfield, the founding director of CMTS, lives on as a building now occupied by the Laboratory School, a successor to the pedagogical experiment Dewey had founded in 1896.

Though its new building, at the bustling intersection of Michigan Avenue and Twelfth Street, was not yet finished, the Chicago Manual Training School began holding classes in February 1884. Two years earlier, in March 1882, members of the city's elite Commercial Club had decided such a school was necessary. Over the next year, its members—Field, Pullman, Crane, and others—raised $200,000 to establish it; a principal, called the director, was hired, and seventy-plus boys were accepted for its first class. On the evening of June 19, in that year of 1884, the new director Henry Holmes Belfield, a veteran of the city's rapidly growing school system, gave his inaugural address to members of the club. The school's Latin motto was *"mente atque manu ad virtutem"*—through mind and hand to manhood—and Belfield's address made clear what was meant by this.[1] He began his remarks by claiming that "the problem of education is ever new" and the "ever-changing conditions of modern life" demand a "broader culture." For too long, he argued, "have education and the knowledge of books been regarded as synonymous; whereas literary culture is only a part of education."[2]

Belfield's address described this "new education" as the "training of the brain and of the body, the just and harmonious development of every organ." Neglecting one or the other results in only a partial education, he argued, whether for the athlete or the scholar. Though man is a "tool-using animal," tools used in the school had heretofore been confined to the pen and the pencil. But the manual training school was going to change that—its "distinctive feature" is not only the education of the mind, but "of the hand as the agent of the mind."[3] It was the intertwining of learning and labor.

Belfield's audience that evening included, in addition to students and their parents, members of the Commercial Club who had shepherded the school into existence. The club, established in 1877 and composed of the most select among the businessmen who had turned the city into an industrial and commercial powerhouse in the years since the Civil War, took a strong interest in preparing the city's youngsters for its workforce, hence their initial interest in the school. E. W. Blatchford, a club member and president of the school's board of trustees, had made his fortune producing lead-based products for the plumbing and printing industries; he would in 1887 help found the city's Newberry Library. Field and Pullman were members of the school's board. Adding to the evening's importance was the presence of John Eaton, then U.S. commissioner of education. Blatchford had called the assembly to order by expressing pleasure that this experiment in the new education could, after less than a year in existence, present a class of graduates.[4]

Figure 4. The motto and logo for CMTS, as it appeared on the cover of the school's catalog for 1886–1887. The Latin was translated as "Through mind and hand to manhood"; the lathe and anvil pictured represent fundamental skills CMTS imparted to its students.

After outlining what this first class—of its seventy or so members, only a few were graduating—had learned since the school opened in February, Belfield told his audience that spending two hours per day in the school's workshop did not detract from their interest in books, but instead stimulated it. An hour in the shop "develops as much mental strength as an hour devoted to Virgil or Legendre," he said, referring to the Latin poet and the French mathematician. Every school hour, "whether spent in the classroom, the drawing-room, or in the shop, is an hour devoted to intellectual training," he said. And the students' comprehension of the "essential branches of knowledge" will be as superior to that of the man who has actually seen "the grandeur and beauty of the Alps" is to that of one who has "merely read of them."[5]

Buttressing his argument with comments from Felix Adler, then famed for having begun the Workingmen's School in New York City, Belfield claimed that by moving between classroom and shop, students will "experience a new zest and relish for their school duties, and every faculty will be brighter and keener.... They learn in half-time what others learn in full-time." A classical education, Belfield continued, quoting yet another enthusiast, "'neglects all the powers of some minds, and some of the powers of all minds.'" Further, he asked, "would you give a boy classical training by confining him to the declension of Latin nouns, or the conjugation of Greek verbs. Would daily, hourly repetition of the multiplication tables be regarded as a mathematical education?" No, he replied. The mind of the "Training School pupil is kept constantly alert; when one principle is mastered, he passes to another, his shop exercises being as carefully systematized as are his exercises in

Algebra." Quoting Adler again, he said, "The acquisition of industrial skill should be the means of promoting the general education of the pupil: the education of the hand should be the means of more completely and more efficaciously educating the brain."[6]

Further, this new education benefitted not only the individual pupil but society as a whole: every boy born into the world should be able to support himself in some honest way. In addition to having that ability, manual training school graduates would learn to respect the work of the bookkeeper, the artisan, or the inventor equally; further, they will resist being used as mere tools by their employers. Belfield then referred to a study sponsored by Commissioner Eaton to the effect that educated workers were far more valuable to their employer than were the ill-educated or illiterate. Relying next on arguments made by William Torrey Harris, who would soon replace Eaton as U.S. commissioner of education, he said: "An uneducated workman will be thrown aside to perish in an almshouse." Belfield repeated the truism that "there are but three ways of getting a living, by working, by begging, by stealing, and a boy [who] is not educated to support himself by working, is condemned to be a mendicant or a rogue."[7]

These were arguments sure to please the members of the Commercial Club who had donated the money to build the school—it would be preparing a labor force whose members knew not only how to study and to work but had practical skills as well. The school either had or shortly would have not only well-equipped carpentry shops but lathes, a blacksmith shop, various kinds of machinery, and a sixty-horsepower engine, all of which the students would learn to operate.[8] Parents who had paid thirty dollars for their sons to attend that first quarter should also be confident that it was money well spent. Their boys had not only fit themselves for the further pursuit of knowledge, they had learned "to convey to others many of [their] thoughts in the most ancient and expressive of languages, the language of drawing." Belfield ended his remarks by commending the "public spirit" and "noble philanthropy" of the school's board of trustees, claiming that their venture was being watched with interest throughout the land. The school's existence, and its sponsorship by the city's leading men of business, "has given an impetus to this new education which is felt, literally and actually, from the Atlantic to the Pacific."[9]

Eaton, who had begun his distinguished career as a school principal and then as a chaplain during the Civil War, had also been responsible for managing camps to which newly freed slaves had fled; he would later work with the Freedmen's Bureau.[10] He was equally enthusiastic about the promise of the Chicago Manual Training School. A reporter in attendance recorded Eaton as commending the trustees for "placing the manual portion on an equal level with other branches of study." He said that Chicago, with its half-million people, had not started the training school movement any too soon. "Some of the vast moneys derived from industries should be expended for the establishment of schools for the learning of skilled labor."[11]

After the speeches, attendees had an opportunity to tour the school, which would be completed over the summer. Several of the business leaders who attended the inauguration had had earlier tours of the school, including one on February 4 that year, when the first classes were held in the partially constructed building.[12] In addition to Marshall Field, whose retail and wholesale operations were one of the city's largest employers, others attending that winter day were Edson Keith, who headed a major wholesale dry-goods firm; Nathaniel Fairbank, whose firm produced lard and soap as byproducts of the meatpacking industry; and Charles Ham, an attorney whose articles in the *Chicago Tribune* and *Inter Ocean* had encouraged the Commercial Club to establish the school.

An event the previous September—the laying of the building's cornerstone—was even more auspicious. Its attendees included "a large number of ladies and gentlemen" and such distinctive personalities as "Long John" Wentworth, mayor of Chicago when it first asserted its coming dominance in the 1840s; Francis Parker, the charismatic trainer of teachers; A. C. Bartlett, whose wholesale hardware firm had become rich supplying Union troops during the Civil War; and William Frederick Poole, then the city's librarian who would in 1887 join with Blatchford to establish the private Newberry Library.[13]

In his remarks on that day in September 1883, Blatchford noted that, unlike polytechnics in the United States and abroad, CMTS would not teach specific trades but prepare students for a career in rapidly growing mechanical fields. He also made a plea for support from others. Though members of the Commercial Club had been generous in providing for the building and its equipment, plus supporting a three-year curriculum, it wanted to ensure "future growth" through "co-operation in this work from fellow citizens." Blatchford announced the extensive contents of the cornerstone as he deposited them—annual reports from several other educational institutions, national and local board of trade reports, plus a half-dozen newspapers.

Remarks by Francis Parker warmly commending the "system of instruction" at the school were followed by those from T. W. Bicknell, president of the National Education Association. He had come from Boston to endorse the school on the NEA's behalf: "Mind and matter exist for each other" for the highest possible development of the individual, he said. The school would be a combination of "two specific purposes—directive agency and practical skill." Though this all took place on September 23, the article noted that the building, with an 8,500 square-foot footprint, was expected to be completed by January 1. The Michigan Avenue side would be devoted to academic work; that on Twelfth Street (in 1919, it became Roosevelt Road) would contain the carpentry, blacksmith, and machine shops. The machinery was anticipated to cost $40,000.

Making Large Plans for the "City of the Century"

The assemblage of talent and money behind the CMTS was representative of Chicago's brash self-confidence at the time. That "nobody had ever built a city like this before" remains a comment Chicagoans take legitimate pride in—only a dozen years had passed between the 1883 cornerstone laying and the Great Chicago Fire of 1871. Rebuilding the city had attracted architects like Louis Sullivan, who arrived in 1873 and would define the art and engineering of the skyscraper over the next decade. As the book titled *City of the Century* noted: "the average age of the Chicago architect of 1880 was just under 30" and by 1886 the city would be "the world's center of architectural experimentation."[14] Among these young architects was Solon Spencer Beman, who had been lured to Chicago in 1879 by George Pullman; at twenty-six, he was commissioned to design the company town to house workers at Pullman's Palace Car Company. Beman would be thirty when he received the commission for the Manual Training School.[15]

Beman's design reflects the solidity of the then-popular Romanesque Revival style, while its Gothic details add a certain graceful lightness. The speed of the building's construction—four months from cornerstone to occupancy—suggests the energy behind structures rising in the city at the time. A basement slightly below grade with arched windows for letting in light was topped by two identical stories also with arched windows. A Gothic style prevails on the third story, as on the fourth with its dormer windows under a steeply pitched roof; this top floor was designed to be a museum and exhibition space. The imposing entranceway rose all four stories to a tower from which, a drawing suggests, a banner flew. Faced with brick and terra cotta, the building at the time took its place among Chicago structures of distinction.[16]

As Chicago's architects transformed the city's physical appearance, some of the businessmen behind the manual training school had transformed the city's economy in the years since the Civil War. George Pullman was one; he first made his mark on the city in 1859 by raising some of the city's buildings out of the swampy muck in which their foundations were set; later he would devise both the elegant sleeping car associated with his name and, in 1881, inaugurate the nation's first substantial company town. Though

Figure 5. An 1887–1888 catalog for CMTS included this line drawing of the school, reportedly done by a student. The building, constructed in three months during the fall of 1883, faced Twelfth Street, a mile south of the Loop. Its architect, Solon Spencer Beman, had earlier designed Pullman, the company town south of Chicago.

Pullman's obdurate refusal to deal with a railway workers strike in 1894 would forever discredit his name, attributes of Pullman the town—warmth and order, healthful cleanliness, schools, and recreational facilities (but no saloons)—suggest a social vision that led to Pullman's support for the manual training school. According to a family biography of a Prairie Avenue neighbor William Hibbard, he along with Pullman and Field would occasionally walk the mile or so north to the city center, passing by the site of the school on the way.[17] Field, not only the city's most successful merchant, had also seen his wealth grow through heavily investing in real estate. His commitment of $20,000 at the Commercial Club's initial meeting to discuss the school launched its fundraising efforts; soon the fund had $100,000, or half what was felt needed to sustain it for its first few years.[18]

Attending that March 1882 Commercial Club meeting, a Saturday evening dinner at the elegant Palmer House, were many of the city's most prosperous men of business. They were there to hear remarks by Charles Ham, an attorney who had been actively promoting manual training, and an ally in his efforts named Augustus Jacobson. A few days later, the *Chicago Tribune*—in whose pages Ham had been proselytizing for the manual training idea—carried speeches delivered by Ham and Jacobson that evening. The article's subtitle proclaimed that a manual training school was "The Only Way to Fill the Void Caused by the Death of the Apprenticeship System."[19] Ham and Jacobson, an introduction to their talks noted, had "painstakingly investigated the subject from all points of view." Many of the arguments made were likely familiar to the audience, but Ham's words tend to make the obvious refreshing: "Skilled labor digs iron-ore from the earth, endows it with genius, and magnifies its value a million-fold." Skill is the "addition of labor to intelligence"; skilled labor houses, clothes, and feeds mankind, but too many products that American comforts depended upon were produced in Europe, while the United States was providing only raw materials. "We are exchanging the products of unskilled labor for the products of skilled labor at a ruinous rate," he argued. "We are bartering muscle for thought," and such put the future of the nation's esteemed political institutions at risk.[20]

Thus, the "question for the evening" was "how can we increase the supply of skilled labor?" The solution, according to Ham, was to educate the laborer "by training not only his brain but his eye and his hand." And how might this be done? By looking at the example set two years earlier in St. Louis when, following the leadership of Calvin Woodward, it opened a school of manual training. After describing the school's course of study, its virtues, and its costs, Ham asserted that its benefactors there had so quickly perceived the school's value that they raised sufficient funds to expand it and to provide scholarships for needy students. The school's success, Ham continued, was partially due to adapting a method developed in Russia that "solved the problem of tool instruction"; further, it was much more suited to a system of popular education than was the trade-schools system in other European countries. "The mechanic arts should be taught as the sciences are, through a graded series of exercises," a laboratory method, Ham said. America's current system of education was inadequate because it "crams the brain with isolated facts" and offers too few opportunities to assimilate them. "What is needed in education is that the brain should be taught a new mode of expression through the hand—drawing, the short-hand language of modern science, and the cunning of familiarity with mechanical tools." In conclusion, Ham added one of his verbal flourishes: "without [tools] man is nothing, but with which he is all."

Jacobson's comments augmented those of Ham by comparing manual training to other modes of teaching the young. "The manual training school has stepped in to supply the want caused by the end of the apprenticeship system"; it does this by teaching no trade "but the rudiments of all." With older methods, such as fathers teaching sons, skill grew only arithmetically. But when teaching a variety of skills—the more modern approach—growth is geometric. Further, skilled people are efficient people and efficient people are bent upon improving their condition, i.e., acquiring more skills. The benefits of manual training were to society as a whole: "to ensure the peace and safety of the country, there is no means so efficient as that of teaching the young how to earn their daily bread." Either invest more money in education or waste it on soldiers and policemen: "it is better, and cheaper, to spend our money in training good citizens than in shooting bad ones," Jacobson claimed.[21]

The *Tribune* article included no comments from Calvin Woodward, but were he there, he could have added remarks he did make at a National Education Association meeting the following summer. In recounting the history of the St. Louis school, which opened as a preparatory school for Washington University in 1879, Woodward noted his debt to some farsighted businessmen who supported his effort financially; he quoted one as saying the school was his best investment in St. Louis thus far.[22] The school's initial cost was $63,400 for a first class of one hundred students, but, he argued, such schools could no more be self-supporting than could a medical school; for both mechanics and surgeons, mental and manual training were complementary.

By the gathering's close that March evening, $65,000 had been raised, tripling Field's commitment.[23] By the 1880s, Chicago had overtaken St. Louis, its earlier rival as the dominant metropolis of the middle west, but the city's leading industrialists still might not have wanted to be outdone—it too would have a manual training school. A year later, in April 1883, the Chicago Manual Training School Association was incorporated, and a board of trustees chosen. E. W. Blatchford, who would speak at the cornerstone laying the following September, was its president. Richard T. Crane, whose pipe and plumbing firm supplied central heating systems for the city's skyscrapers, was its vice president. Field was treasurer, and William A. Fuller, a lumber merchant whose firm produced window sashes and doors, was secretary. Other members were coffee dealer John W. Doane and Nathaniel K. Fairbank, whose firm repurposed by-products of the city's slaughter houses; others included dry-goods merchant Edson Keith and George Pullman.[24]

Together, according to the *Encyclopedia of Chicago History*, four of these men—Field, Keith, Fuller, and Pullman—employed around 11,000 people in the mid-1880s.[25] In the census of 1880, the city's population was 503,185; it had grown by over 200,000 since the fire of 1871; roughly three-fourths of these people had either been born abroad or were the children of immigrants.[26] The city's boundaries in the mid-1880s ran from four miles north of the center (State and Madison streets) to four miles south and six miles west. By 1890, the city would annex several suburban neighborhoods, so that it stretched further north to Evanston and west to Oak Park; the 1889 addition of Hyde Park to the south nearly doubled the city's geographic size.[27] In 1880, the city's public school system had nearly 60,000 pupils in the elementary grades; just over 1,000 attended high school. A decade later, after the annexations, the city's population had doubled as well—to over a million people; there were then 131,000 students in grades one to eight and nearly 3,000 in the city's three high schools.[28]

The rapid growth of Chicago's population, and of the industries that supported them, had in the 1880s led to a period of extraordinary upheaval, particularly labor unrest—a labor historian has claimed that the number of strikes, large and small, exceeded in "number, breadth, intensity, and national importance" those of any other U.S. city.[29] As industries grew, so did labor's resistance to corporate authority and repression; some of the fiercest battles were fought during the 1880s, in part a product of the city's large number of immigrants from Germany, a part of Europe in which education fostered political independence, if not necessarily opportunities for advancement.[30] Though addressing labor unrest was not among the justifications given in contemporaneous speeches for establishing the manual training school, it was likely on the minds of Commercial Club members. And it was definitely on the mind of Charles Ham. His compellingly exhaustive argument in its favor appeared in 1886 in the form of an extensively researched, annotated, and indexed volume called *Manual Training: The Solution of Social and Industrial Problems*.[31]

Other educational and social ventures during the decade included the arrival in January 1883 of Francis Parker, who would make the fledgling Cook County Normal School into a nationally noted center of what he called "illustrative teaching," an instructional method that relied heavily upon the use of pictures and models, concrete examples, and practical experiences—the school demonstrated methods that its teachers-in-training were expected to put to use in their own classrooms.[32] A decade earlier, Parker had studied in Germany, where he had been exposed to the Froebelian idea that learning best took place through direct experience with objects and their use. In addition to serving as an additional impetus for manual training, these ideas also inspired the kindergarten movement, which like the former had taken root in St. Louis during the 1870s.

In the fall of 1883, Elizabeth Harrison and other early childhood educators founded the Chicago Kindergarten Club, which would advocate the establishment of programs for young children and their mothers, again relying on learning through creative use of objects. By the decade's end, this had become one of the nation's prominent kindergarten training schools.[33] Among Harrison's supporters was another innovator, Jane Addams; in 1889, along with Ellen Gates Starr, she opened the doors of Hull House a mile west of where CMTS stood. Its instructional programs, support for labor, children's activities, and ethnic clubs—particularly encouraging the crafts immigrants brought with them from home—shared many of the progressive impulses behind both manual training and kindergartens.[34] All of them—Parker, Harrison, and Addams—enjoyed the support of Chicago's cadre of activist women; all, including Starr, would figure in the development of the manual training movement and of CMTS in particular.

Chicago in the 1880s also witnessed extraordinary growth in its meatpacking, lumber—it was still rebuilding after the fire—and publishing industries. It had earlier become the nation's rail center, and in 1883, a group of railroad executives had established a nationwide system of standard time zones to facilitate dependable scheduling. In 1887, Sears, Roebuck and Company, utterly dependent on the railroads, got its start. Precedent-setting buildings such as the elegant Rookery (1888) and the awesome Auditorium (1889), both of which still stand, were constructed during the 1880s. By the decade's end, Chicago began to agitate for the privilege of hosting the Columbian Exposition initially planned for 1892; the boasts of its promoters earned for the city the sobriquet "windy." Truer to Chicago's plans for itself was a comment attributed to the architect for the White City, Daniel Burnham: "Make no little plans; they have no magic to stir men's blood . . . Make big plans; aim high in hope and work, remembering that a noble, logical diagram once recorded will never die . . . Let your watchword be order and your beacon beauty."[35]

Though Burnham does not figure in the history of the Chicago Manual Training School, the vision that inspired him drove the founders of the school as well.

The Principal, the Proselytizer, and the Philanthropist

When CMTS began offering classes in February 1884 in its unfinished building, its principal Henry Holmes Belfield, whose actual title was director, may have felt that this was a job for which he'd been preparing much of his life. And the school's two other chief supporters, E. W. Blatchford and Charles Ham—the proselytizer—seem to have agreed. Though born in Philadelphia in 1837, Belfield had been raised in eastern Iowa. Autobiographical notes written when he was near retirement claimed that he had wanted to attend the University of Michigan, but that was an expense his family could not afford, so he attended what was then called Iowa College near his home along the Mississippi in Davenport—the school later became Grinnell and moved west toward the center of the state. Of his life as a student, Belfield wrote that there was no gym and no clubs, as "life was too serious." The students' day began at four in the morning, when they would feed pigs, milk cows, and saw wood for the stove. Classes were held during the day; studying had to be done at night.[36]

These experiences, according to Joseph Rathnau, another Chicago educator who has written extensively about Belfield and worked as a vocational educator himself, provided the "foundations necessary and essential for him to develop a philosophy of manual training." The essentials were acquiring an intellectual discipline and the practical skills necessary to living a productive life.[37] Working one's way through college by helping to maintain its physical facilities was not uncommon at the time; further, such combining of learning and labor offered a less-noted impetus for the manual training movement.[38]

Upon graduating from Iowa College as valedictorian in 1858, Belfield moved north to the city of Dubuque, where he taught briefly before becoming superintendent of its schools. After two years, he moved back to Davenport where he both taught and acquired a master's degree from another local college. Some of his salary, he wrote, went to help support his family.[39] During the Civil War, he joined an Iowa regiment, fought in several battles, and was captured; he spent part of the war in a prison camp in South Carolina. At the war's end, he moved to Chicago where he served as principal of two elementary schools; in 1875, he became principal of the city's North Division High School, one of its three secondary institutions—as noted earlier, at the time, only one thousand Chicago students continued on to attend a public high school. He was also named to head the Chicago Evening High School, which offered instruction in bookkeeping, mathematics, mechanics, and drawing. Its students were young men working in technical pursuits during the day.

According to his own report, this was the first time Belfield had been involved with industrial education, but apparently it agreed with him. It perhaps inspired his writing textbooks, which he did with the needs of children unable to continue their education after elementary school in mind.[40] Rathnau reported that, in 1872, Belfield had proposed to the Chicago Board of Education that it incorporate some manual training into the public schools, but his proposal was "met with derision."[41] Among those opposed to the idea was the then-superintendent of the Chicago Public Schools, George Howland, a classically educated man well-regarded by his colleagues, according to one who later wrote about the founding of a club in Howland's honor.[42] Belfield, reminiscing about his hiring, claimed that Howland maintained that "there was no intellectual training in the training of the hand." But Belfield also wrote that Howland later retracted those words.

When Blatchford went looking for candidates to head the new manual training school in 1883, Belfield also recounted, he was directed to the North Division High School. Another educator had told Blatchford that the school's principal, Belfield, was the only one capable of handling the job. Friends, the principal later wrote, advised him against taking it. But Belfield stated that "I had been for twelve years advocating the training of boys in the mechanic arts. I did not intend to let slip the opportunity to put my theories into practice. And I have never regretted it. It gave me the opportunity to broaden my own life as well as to help propagate a broader education in this country and in others."[43]

Through running a successful school for the next decade and a half, Belfield did propagandize for manual training, but Charles Ham was far more active in spreading that particular gospel. He did not leave a set of personal papers to tell his story, as Belfield did, but his 400-page tome on how manual training could solve social and industrial problems testifies to his broad knowledge, his values and commitments, plus his remarkable ability to articulate them with clarity and persuasiveness.[44] Aside from his books, articles in the *Tribune* and the *Inter Ocean*, plus a lengthy paper published in 1890 by what became Columbia's Teachers College, the available record of his life is an obituary published in 1902. He was born on a farm near Concord, New Hampshire, in 1831, and worked as a railroad clerk while studying law on his own. In 1856, he moved to Chicago and was eventually admitted to the bar with only an informally acquired education; between 1860 and 1866, he had a law partnership with Melville Fuller, who would from 1888 until 1910 serve as chief justice of the U.S. Supreme Court. Ham served as appraiser for the Port of Chicago from 1871 until 1885, during which time he also became a journalist and highly visible advocate for manual training. In 1890, he was appointed to the federal Board of General Appraisers; he served as its president from 1897 until 1902, at which point he apparently became ill. He died in October that year, near the home of his daughter in Montclair, New Jersey.[45]

Though an obituary for Ham claims that he was an expert on tariffs, he today deserves note for his vision of what a manual training school might be—it was, as the subtitle for his chief work proclaimed, "the solution of social and industrial problems." The detailed curriculum, historical background, and sociological rationale expounded in two editions of his book offer evidence of wide-ranging research and progressive convictions. First published in 1886 and then brought out again in 1900, the preface to the latter tells of the book's initial reception and complexities. This suggests in part why it might have so little notice today: the message and the manner of its delivery were overwhelming in detail; so was the messenger's self-confidence.[46] The book's twenty-six chapters—these are substantially identical in both editions—begin with nine that appear to describe the actual Chicago Manual Training School. They describe its drawing and engine rooms; laboratories for carpentry, founding, and forging; and another for machine tools. Reading these, it is easy to be seduced by the argument that all these practical skills can be taught along with an appreciation of their historical evolution, for that is what the chapters lay out. Apparently, as Ham admitted in the 1900 preface, the curriculum described was for an imagined school, not the real one that Belfield and the Commercial Club had brought into being; in the 1900 edition, the title of the first chapter was changed to "The Ideal School." The first edition, Ham wrote, had become available in all English-speaking countries, and despite some criticism, had received largely positive reviews.[47]

Following that initial group of nine chapters are seven more expounding the intellectual and moral effects of manual training, the power of the trained hand, and the "Prime Necessity" for educating women, all with justifications from history. This section ends with a chapter titled "Power of Steam and Contempt of Artisans"—why is it, Ham asked, that the aristocracy had for millennia felt themselves superior to those who farmed their fields, designed their buildings, and fought their wars? Then come three chapters contrasting "automatic" versus "scientific" education—i.e., traditional rote learning contrasted with the practical, hands-on curriculum Ham as author advocated. The next five chapters explain "Education and the Social Problem," moving from ancient Egypt to modern America, again showing that Ham's sympathies lay with those who developed the skills essential to doing the real work of any society. The last chapter offers the "History of the Manual Element in Education"; here one actually gets a brief history of the real Chicago Manual Training School, enmeshed in commentary on the mid-nineteenth century schools that had preceded and, more recently, followed it.

If the first edition was an exhaustive treatment of its subject, the 1900 edition was even more so. There's an additional chapter on developments between 1883 and 1898, plus some additional footnotes added in response to criticisms. But more valuable is its Appendix, which includes twelve tables listing all of the nation's manual training programs at the time; among them those in public and private high schools, charity schools, normal schools, and "Schools for the Colored Race," plus notes on state laws, and nearly twenty pages summarizing programs in Europe. Indicative of Ham's progressive views are quotations from John Stuart Mill and Mary Wollstonecraft on the education of women—in order for men and woman to live together as equals, they must be associated in education, he wrote.[48] Elsewhere in the manuscript, Ham commented on the need to make equal education available to the descendants of former slaves.

Another addition to the 1900 edition is an introduction by Francis Parker, then still principal of the Chicago Normal School.[49] Both he and Ham referred to the close connection between kindergartens and manual training schools—Ham in fact claimed that he was using both terms, along with "the new education" as "equivalent." Though Parker was a teacher educator and not specifically involved with kindergartens, he was an early proponent of progressive education, a movement that incorporated schools represented by all three of Ham's "equivalent" terms. Parker noted the "value of the work of the hand in the building of the brain," and Ham's "fervid patriotism," which caused him to regard the new education as necessary to the evolution of a democracy. After commending Ham for inspiring the establishment of other manual training programs, Parker reiterated one of Ham's favorite points: "Manual Training gives a true dignity to labor" and predicted that it would quickly assume a "higher place in the hearts of the people."[50]

However essential were the high-minded conviction of Charles Ham the propagandist and the practical experience of Belfield the principal, it's possible that the Chicago Manual Training School would not have come into being were it not for the contacts and the reputation of E. W. Blatchford, president of the school's board for the fifteen years between its founding and its acquisition by the University of Chicago. (Blatchford's full name was Eliphalet Wickes, and it speaks to his religious commitments; the name's Hebrew meaning is "God has judged.") Born in 1826 and the son of a minister, he'd grown up in Chicago and attended Illinois College (which had been founded, as was Belfield's alma mater, by missionaries from New England colleges).[51] He built a firm that manufactured essential components of ammunition used during the Civil War as well as lead products for the building and printing industries. An early member of the Commercial Club, Blatchford also served on the board of the Chicago Theological Seminary, missionary societies, and the Art Institute. He was essential as well to the establishment of the Newberry Library, on whose board he served from its beginning in 1887 until his death in 1912.[52]

A man of consequence, Blatchford's guidance was apparently heeded by other members of the board. When, in the summer of 1883, they discussed whether the school's program should be of two or three years, some members felt that the former would be sufficient; as Belfield reported, they argued that all courses not related to mechanics could be eliminated. Then Blatchford reminded them that "the object of the school was to develop a boy and produce not only a good mechanic, but a good and well-informed man." He reminded fellow members of Calvin Woodward's advice that no more than two hours per day should be spent on mechanics; the rest should be devoted to academic work. Belfield's advice was sought, and he told the group of an investigation done by the U.S. commissioner of education John Eaton, which supported a "superior intellectual discipline for mechanics." Blatchford and Belfield were apparently persuasive, as the trustees then voted for a three-year program.[53]

By November, the school had issued circulars announcing its planned opening in February 1884. Applicants needed to be fourteen years of age, have "good moral character," and pass an examination on "arithmetic through fractions," English composition and spelling, plus geography. The course of study would include academic subjects, plus an hour per day of drawing and two of shop work. Several dates were given when potential students could apply to Mr. Belfield.[54] Ham recounted that when school opened in February, 72 students had been selected out of 130 applicants. He also restated the school's object as given in its articles of incorporation: "Instruction and practice in the use of tools," along with instruction in standard secondary subjects. Students' time, as far as possible, was to be divided "equally between manual and mental exercises."[55]

Though the school building was not quite ready, in addition to classrooms, it already contained two dozen cabinet-maker's benches, numerous high-quality lathe tools, a 52-horsepower Corliss engine, two boilers, plus a variety of other essential tools. Further, the American Electrical Society had donated a "valuable scientific library" of five hundred volumes, the Blatchford Literary Society had donated books and periodicals, plus the city librarian—William Frederick Poole, a friend of Blatchford—had offered access to its collection "on unusually favorable conditions." In sum, this school (after Francis Bacon's own heart) "sprang from the brain of a number of plain, practical business men, full-armed, as Minerva from the brain of Jupiter."[56]

The Pupils and Their Program

When the Chicago Manual Training School opened its doors in 1884, few secondary schools contained more than wooden desks, textbooks, a wall map, and blackboards. This new school would be different; when it was incorporated in 1883, its founders defined its purpose as follows:

Instruction and practice in the use of tools, with such instruction as may be deemed necessary in mathematics, drawing, and the English branches of a high school course. The tool instruction as at present contemplated shall include carpentry, wood turning, pattern making, iron chipping and filing, forge work, brazing and soldering, the use of machine shop tools, and such other instruction of a similar character as may be deemed advisable to add to the foregoing from time to time, it being the intention to divide the working hours of the students, as nearly as possible, equally between manual and mental exercises.[57]

Meeting such an ambitious set of objectives proved a challenge. Belfield and the trustees, with prodding and guidance from Charles Ham, attempted to accomplish them with a well-equipped facility, careful selection of students, a coherent curriculum, and competent faculty to realize it. Over the school's first five years, the student body tripled in size, the faculty doubled, and by 1889, CMTS revenues equaled its expenses. Belfield commented that the school's initial success was due to its ability to adapt its program as it grew in size and its independence.[58] A 1967 history of the school claimed that "Mr. Belfield guided the school into one of the most influential high schools of the manual training era . . . [and] was able for a while to work with independence and freedom that is rarely known in secondary schools."[59] But, by 1890, despite accolades from educators nationwide, it became apparent that the program was more demanding than its setting could support. Further, during the 1890s, competing schools, both public and private, were established, and several trustees considered turning CMTS over to another institution. But in its first decade, the school provided a model that many other cities wanted to emulate.

One of the reasons for the school's early success was its carefully selected body of students. Though manual training has often been associated with reformatories, CMTS made it known that it was not to be "an asylum for indolent [or] incompetent" boys.[60] However, as the founders recognized and as Charles Ham would note in his 1886 book, "Young men, without an adequate education and no industrial skill, were prone to violence in the street."[61] Some scholarships were offered, which could hold a few boys from such a fate, but this manual training school would not be regarded as a reformatory.

The test for admission, for example, indicates standards so stringent that ill-educated boys would not be admitted. The arithmetic test instructs students to "transcribe work sufficient to show processes" by which they changed fractions to decimals, then divided a decimal number by a fraction, and a series of word problems dealing with money, area, and the amount of materials needed for a particular project. The ten multi-part geography questions included naming the five most populous U.S. cities "in order"; knowing on what bodies of water Cairo and Calcutta were located; knowing the principal coal and iron regions of the United States; and being able to compare the height of the Alps versus the Rockies. The language questions asked students to correct the grammar in five sentences, to turn a five-line poem into prose, to describe the parts of speech, and to write an essay on Chicago.[62] In a later catalog, Belfield claimed that lack of preparation was the reason why some boys had been denied admission and why others, once admitted, had failed to do satisfactory work.[63] Some few students were possibly dismissed due to "impropriety in conduct."[64]

The seventy-two students admitted in the first class, of February 1884, had come mainly from Chicago Public Schools, most directly from grammar grades. Only eight had attended private schools; five were employed. Their parents' occupations were given, too—a third were "mechanics"; a dozen were professionals; the rest in manufacturing and businesses of various kinds—one owned a billiard hall.[65] A list of students with their home addresses published in 1887 indicates that most came from the city of Chicago itself; only a few came from suburban communities.[66] Students' surnames suggest that they were drawn from the city's middle-class population at the time, mainly Anglo-Saxon and Scandinavian; a few names suggest Irish or Jewish origin. In the summer of 1886, a discussion about "the admission of colored boys" resulted in a decision to do so, but there is no record of whether any ever attended.[67] A newspaper article, likely written by Ham, noted the number of prominent families who had enrolled their boys in the school.

The second CMTS catalog, for the academic year 1884–1885, noted that sixty-six students remained from the previous year (and thus became the "middle class"), and that eighty additional students had enrolled for that fall's junior, or first year, class.[68] By the following academic year, 1885–1886, enrollment had grown to 155 students: twenty-eight remained in the senior class, forty-six in the middle class, and there were seventy-seven juniors. Four were called "special students."[69] The next catalog, for 1886–1887, suggests that though the school was still attracting new students, attrition was substantial: enrollment had grown to 190, with ninety-eight students in the junior class, fifty-nine in the middle, but only thirty-three in the senior class, less than half of those who had enrolled two years earlier.

In February 1885, the school began to produce a newsletter called *Hand and Brain*; its first issue offered a history of the school, information for prospective parents and students, and several pages of advertisement. A following issue, in May, was of only four pages; it included extracts from an address Belfield had given, a list of evening activities, comments on student work, and answers to questions "asked orally or by mail almost daily": no, the school teaches no specific trade nor is it a boarding school; students do not make products for sale and they are discouraged from "amus[ing] themselves by making gimcracks"; yes, visitors were welcome at any time. Potential students need not to have graduated from an elementary program so long as they could pass the entrance examination; the next one would be held on June 30.[70]

Tuition for the school increased as students progressed through the program. It was $30 per term for juniors, $40 for the middle class, and $50 for seniors. (By way of comparison, a middle-class professional income at the time was $3,000 per year.) In addition, students were to supply their own pens and textbooks, aprons and overalls.[71] Tuition had been increased by 1887 to $40, $50, and $60 per term.[72] Some "worthy boys" were offered scholarships which were paid by the trustees. An article about the school in *Scientific American* claimed that tuition for twenty pupils admitted in the fall of 1886 had their tuition paid by Commercial Club members.[73] A later study of the school stated that nineteen graduating seniors in 1889 had received some scholarship assistance. More tuition assistance became available the following year after manufacturer and philanthropist John Crerar, who had joined the board in 1884, left the school an endowment of $50,000, some of which was expected to go for scholarships.[74]

Belfield often commented on the difficulty of finding suitable faculty members. The initial catalog's list of faculty included five in addition to Belfield: the two handling academic subjects both held master's degrees; the two doing wood and iron work held bachelor's degrees; the man teaching drawing held a master's degree from a normal school in Massachusetts. Belfield by this time had acquired a PhD, apparently an honorary one granted in 1878 by Iowa College, his alma matter.[75] For the second year, an additional faculty member was added; two years later there were nine. A Frank Bennett, at the time serving in the U.S. Navy, was lent to the school during its third year.[76] The following year, he was replaced by an Ira Hollis.[77] But the faculty was not growing in number as the student body grew in size; in 1888, when the school had 202 students, it had only eleven faculty members.

Part of the challenge, Belfield wrote, is that the work at CMTS was "peculiarly difficult"; he had a high regard for teachers, particularly those who could do their work well, but those with technological competence and academic knowledge were not easy to find, particularly if one was also required to be a good teacher—the faculty needed to be composed of more than just skilled mechanics: "Teaching is an art and the highest success in it demands more than the simple knowledge of the matter to be taught," he wrote in

1885.[78] Among his life-long goals, Belfield later said, was to "elevate the character of the teachers' calling, which demands for its complete success the exercise of patience, judgment, tact, and enthusiasm of the highest order."[79]

If the school had difficulty finding sufficient well-qualified faculty, it was not for want of a magnificently well-equipped facility, a credit to the generosity of the Commercial Club. By the fall of 1884, the building was complete. Its basement included a forge and a Corliss steam engine (a recent invention that provided reliable temperature control), plus boiler rooms. The first floor contained academic classrooms and administrative offices, the second floor was for woodworking, the third floor had classrooms for drawing; the fourth was for displays of student work and projects in progress.[80] A report on the school carried by *Scientific American* offered more detail: the woodworking room contained dozens of carpenter's benches and lathes, saws, planes, and a grindstone. The foundry had two furnaces, crucibles, troughs, trowels, "and other apparatus, so that sixty boys can work at once." The forge contained two dozen forges and anvils, "and all the other tools required to turn clean skinned youths into the sootiest of blacksmiths." The machine shop had engine lathes, drills, vises, chisels, files, "and other tools—enough for thirty-two amateur machinists."[81]

The forty-week school year began on the first Monday of September and ended at graduation in late June; a spring quarter began in January and ended in March; there was a three-week break between the first two quarters.[82] In their first year, the "junior" students took standard academic classes in mathematics, physiology and geography, English language and literature; equally important, they also studied the "universal language of drawing." Shop work was carpentry, including care and use of tools and a lathe. In the middle year, students studied geometry and physics, literature and history. The drawing classes became more elaborate, featuring "Orthographic Projection and Shadows," making exact measurements, and the graphic representation of machinery. Shop work moved on to metals: molding, casting, forging, welding, and soldering. Mathematics for seniors included trigonometry and higher algebra (even a bit of bookkeeping); continuing language study included literature, civics, political economy, plus some Latin or French. In the drawing classes, students were expected to build a machine from their carefully measured drawings and learn something of "architectural perspective." In the machine shop, seniors did more drilling and planing; plus, they learned to manage and care for the steam engines and boilers in the school's basement.[83]

Facility in learning to use this equipment was gradual: in their first year, boys made picture frames and tables (including those they ate on in the basement dining room), and then they moved on to the foundry and blacksmith

Figure 6. An eight-horsepower engine created by students in the Class of 1887; it was based on a design done by the head of the school's machine shop. It also appeared in the CMTS 1887–1888 catalog.

shop where they produced hammers and screwdrivers ("no better . . . can be found in Chicago than those made by the lads," claimed a review). In their senior year, students got into the machine shop, where, beginning with detailed drawings, they designed and put together a steam engine.[84] Prior to graduation, the boys also had to write an essay; some of these were read at the graduation ceremony. Those by the fifty-one members of the class of 1889 included several on various manifestations of electricity; others on railroads, including one on air brakes and another on wheels; transportation also figured in the two on steam navigation and flying machines; some essays were about processes and materials: Bessemer and cement, glass, gold, glucose. Even those in traditional subjects suggest a technological bent: machine guns, the Brooklyn Bridge, lighthouses. On the other hand, some students wrote about ideas such as socialism and the influence of Chaucer.[85]

Although the school's enrollment was growing, the numbers were strongest in each year's entering class. By the fall of 1886, there were 190 students, but half of them were the juniors, or in the first-year class. Belfield surely was aware of the high attrition but was reluctant to lower admission standards. An undated "Circular to Parents and Guardians" suggests an alternate response: a quite demanding set of expectations presented in writing for both students and parents. Pupils had not only to master the same amount of academic work as did students in "the best high schools";

in addition, they were required to devote one hour per day to drawing and two hours to shop work. As the school day left little time for the preparation of academic lessons, the rest needed to be learned at home; "any attempt to secure good results without at least three hours of faithful study at home will prove disastrous," Belfield wrote in the circular. Parents were responsible for supervising their boys, rather than let them be governed by "the demands of society [which] conflict with those of the school." Unsatisfactory progress was "justly attributable to the waste of precious hours in frivolous amusement and trashy literature."[86]

Such preachments, however sincere they were, had not accomplished their supposed purpose—that of encouraging entering students to remain until they had graduated. However, the demanding curriculum did impress admission staff at leading schools of technology. Belfield noted that Purdue University, Cornell's Sibley School of Engineering, the Massachusetts Institution of Technology, and a few other schools would accept CMTS graduates on the basis of their diploma alone.[87]

The school's first graduation ceremony had taken place in June 1884, but those students had matriculated for only five months and there is no record of what they went on to do. Catalogs for the next several years did provide such information. The twenty-seven students who graduated in June 1886 had two-plus years of experience at CMTS, and their plans thus indicate what work the school had prepared them to do. Nine of the graduates continued their education—mainly at MIT and Cornell. Four others went directly to work at family firms, three joined architecture or engineering firms, a few others were apparently hired by firms headed by school trustees.[88] The size of the class of 1887 suggests that attrition continued—only twenty-two received diplomas; four others were given certificates. Eight students headed for Cornell, MIT, and Purdue; five to other colleges. A half-dozen went to work for hardware or railroad firms; nothing was listed for four of the students, and one was headed for Europe.[89] By 1888, there were twenty-eight graduates and four who received certificates.[90] An 1894 summary of graduates' occupations appears in a set of later catalogs; of nearly four hundred graduates, ninety-seven attended schools of technology, thirty-six others studied literature and law; fifty-four worked for manufacturing firms, mainly as draftsmen; forty were employed as engineers or in architectural firms; and eighty-one worked as clerks or salespeople.[91]

That the class of 1889 had fifty-one graduates indicates that the school had made some changes in direction. Admission requirements given in the catalog for the academic year 1887–1888 suggest that they were somewhat less demanding than they had been when the school opened; further, the school appeared to be admitting students in the middle and senior classes, rather than insisting they begin as juniors. Deportment was emphasized, and tuition had risen by 25 percent.[92]

E. W. Blatchford's annual report, given in June of 1886 to school trustees, hints at challenges the school had thus far faced. The difficulty of acquiring a faculty of "men who combined the qualities of the mechanic and the teacher" was one; another was parental expectations—some apparently assumed that the shop work would be recreational rather than instructional. Blatchford remained optimistic, however; as he told his fellow trustees: many "favorable results [had been] thus far realized," but they needed to recognize that they are "far short of our desires and efforts." True to his role as a philanthropist with a mission—he was on the board of several religious organizations—Blatchford looked not only to the benefits their education had for individual students but the "perpetuating power" of their potential contributions to the city of Chicago.[93]

According to newspaper reports about CMTS between 1887 and 1890, the school undertook several outreach efforts; an annual lecture series on American history established in 1888 had become so popular that it was moved from the school to a large church and then to the Central Musical Hall in its first three years. Some faculty members offered short courses at the YMCA and a church school. In 1888, CMTS fielded football and baseball teams that played other schools (CMTS boys won at both, but not at cricket, another sport they participated in). A sign that the school wanted to attract more college-bound students was hiring a woman to teach Latin. Reports of the annual exhibitions of student work held at graduation time attracted, according to one story, a thousand people. One exhibition featured an ornamental wrought-iron gate for the school, which included the CMTS monogram. It had been designed by a member of the faculty but executed by students in the middle class between 1888 and 1890.[94] Other work was equally impressive; an 1890 report from the Illinois State Fair claimed that the student work "astonished" attendees: "The people could not believe that the artistic work in wood and iron have been done by boy mechanics."[95]

In 1887, alumni of the school began holding annual banquets at graduation time; the number of attendees grew each year—ninety attended in 1890, a goodly proportion of its graduates at the time. The outreach efforts, and possible changes in admission requirements and the curriculum, were paying off: Belfield told attendees in 1888 that applications were up 50 percent over what they had been the previous year.[96] By 1890, enrollment had increased to 278 students, of which forty-eight were graduating.[97] Two Chicago newspapers carried lengthy articles in late June of 1890 about a banquet given by a school supporter named John B. Clark. Members of the Commercial Club sat at a head table; 281 attended, including students, faculty, and trustees. Unable to

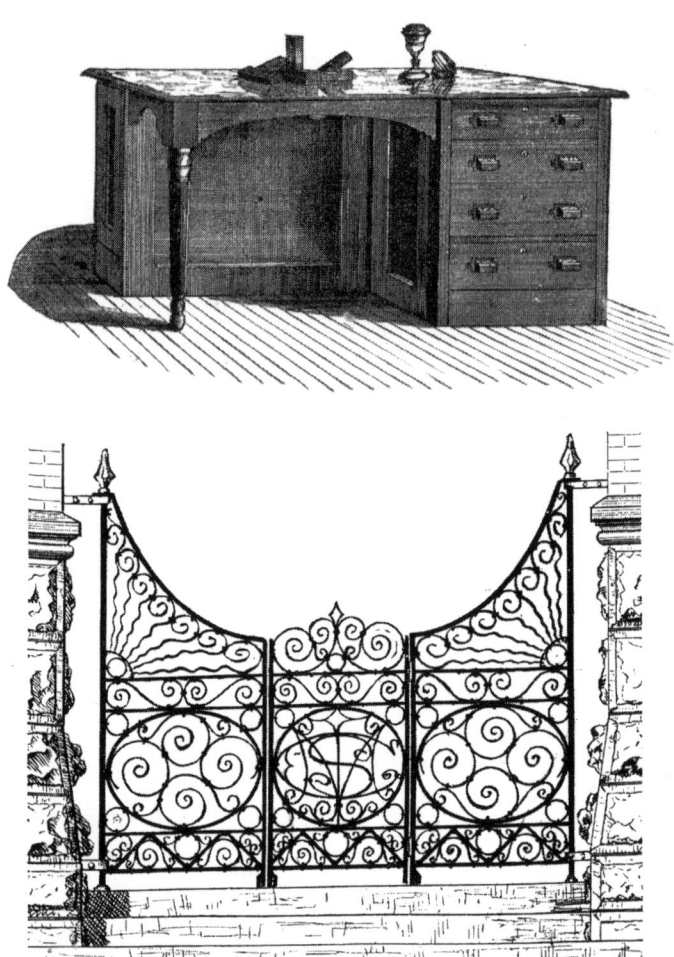

Figure 7. CMTS's catalog for 1887–1888 included these two images, with drawings that illustrate student work in carpentry and metalworking. The desk was made by members of the first-year class under faculty supervision; the wrought iron gate, which includes the CMTS initials, was designed by an instructor and fabricated by students.

attend, Charles Ham had sent a letter of regard. Belfield told the gathering that the school's graduates would not be "future magistrates and law givers, but merchants and manufacturers."[98] The 1927 study of the school stated that a writer who examined entries in *Who's Who* for 1926–1927 found that four graduates from the years 1886–1890 were listed; this was an impressive figure, according to the writer.[99]

Accolades and Opportunities

By the mid-1880s, Belfield was recognized nationally as an expert on manual training programs. In February of 1885, he spoke before the Wisconsin State Teachers Association; in December that year, accompanied by Charles Ham and Augustus Jacobson, he went to help inaugurate the manual training school opening in Toledo, Ohio.[100] By 1886, when Ham's book was published, manual training programs were being established nationwide. In July of the following year, several dozen influential Chicagoans undertook a major effort to name Ham a "school inspector" for the city, the term then used for board of education members; it was not successful, but the campaign took dozens of column inches of newsprint—and the number of signatories suggest that Ham's campaign on behalf of manual training had won him numerous supporters.[101]

In the summer of 1887, the schools of Racine, Wisconsin, hired a CMTS graduate to run a program that would "keep the boys off the street" during vacation. It was, according to the high school principal, wildly successful. As he wrote of it, the lessons were those Ham and Belfield had tried to instill at the school in Chicago:

> The purpose of the work was not to give them [the students, boys from nine to fourteen] a start for the carpenter's trade but to train them in accuracy of thought and action, to secure habits of neatness and orderly arrangement of tools and materials, and to stimulate them to do eager and independent thinking.[102]

Also during that summer, Belfield had been called to the Santee Agency in Nebraska to render his opinion on the manual training program there, for both girls and boys; though his comment about the school working a "wonderful transformation" among the youth would be questioned today, he did come out strongly against a federal regulation that aimed at banning the use of Native American languages in classrooms.[103]

In 1888, Belfield was asked for a contribution to the first issue of a series called Educational Monographs, which were published by the Industrial Education Association in New York, a program that would a few years later become Teachers College at Columbia University. As a sign of Belfield's stature, the other contributor to this first issue was Daniel Coit Gilman, president of the newly established Johns Hopkins University, one of the nation's first institutions dedicated to graduate education. Gilman's article, "A Plea for the Training of the Hand," discussed the attributes of these, mankind's essential tools, and principles for incorporating their use at all levels of schooling. Manual skills enhanced intellectual powers, Gilman argued.[104] Belfield directed his attention toward "Manual Training in the Public School," a controversial issue at the time. It was, he argued, not only practical and desirable, it developed "physical health" and "mental vigor": "We seek intellectual training through the eye and hand," he claimed, and for all students, not just those headed for work in the trades. "If every professional man were also a mechanic, he would be a stronger man professionally than he is now." Manual work in the schools would also encourage youth to remain there longer.[105]

Despite his initial resistance, Chicago superintendent of schools George Howland heeded the pleas made by Gilman, Belfield, and others. In his annual report for the year 1887, Howland noted the public-school program in manual training that had opened that year just west of the downtown area. Students at other high schools took their regular classes in the morning, and then traveled in the afternoon to the manual program for classes in drawing and tool use. About seventy-five boys participated during the program's first year. Then, when the city annexed several other areas and schools, this became impractical, so the English High and Manual Training School was established in another building a few blocks west. It offered a three-year course and enrolled around 260 students. Several other programs, both public and private, would be established in Chicago during the following decade.[106]

By the late 1880s, newspaper stories about CMTS were no longer treating it as a novelty—as yet another "big plan" emanating from the boastful, bustling city. But, in addition to competition from the public schools, CMTS was becoming a financial drain on the members of the Commercial Club. After breaking even in 1889, CMTS returned to running a deficit of $3,000 to $4,000 per year for the next several years.[107] Belfield was struggling with how to redefine the school without hampering its distinctive accomplishments and curricula. In 1893, CMTS developed a four-year program, with the first year considered preparatory. That fall, the school began to offer three separate programs: one in technology, one in general business, and a third college preparatory.[108] The other manual training programs established in the city put additional pressure on CMTS to maintain its distinctiveness.

Other changes were brewing in the city as well. In January of 1890, Belfield appeared before the newly established World's Fair Committee to give a talk on the subject of trade schools.[109] The glories and contradictions of the resulting 1893 Columbian Exposition justified the extravagant claims made by its boosters—writer Henry Adams said that through it he had glimpsed the future, and its landscaping launched the City Beautiful movement nationwide (though visionary architect Louis Sullivan claimed its neoclassicism had set architecture back several decades). Countries around the world brought displays while crusading journalist Ida B. Wells wrote about why American Negroes were excluded.[110] The fair had attracted 26 million entrants, in numbers, roughly a third of the nation's population at the time.

But the national depression that began as the fair was underway resulted in the 1894 Pullman Strike—workers in the "ideal" community George Pullman had built around his far south side factory resisted his order that their rents would not be lowered though their wages were. The conflict caused the new American Railway Union to stop trains from running nationwide, which led to federal troops being called in—stopping the trains meant stopping the mail, which interrupted interstate commerce.[111] Chicagoans like Jane Addams were appalled at Pullman's lack of sympathy for his workers. In the middle of the strike, her new friend John Dewey arrived to join the faculty at the University of Chicago, which was being built along the fair's border.

Then, as the century turned, Belfield and Dewey, along with Francis Parker, were all colleagues in a program envisioned as a dynamic School of Education based at the new university. The venture would prove not to be successful, but its brief existence provides a compelling chapter in the long history of efforts to combine learning with labor. The role of the Chicago Manual Training School in this unrealized ambition has been little told, but it is best understood in the context of nearly three centuries of programs designed for the coeducation of hands and heads. To this history, our discussion of industrial education now turns.

CHAPTER 2

Learning and Doing Arrives in Chicago

> It would be difficult to find a better exemplification of scientific education than a course of training which exercises simultaneously the powers of both body and mind, a course which with every fresh burden put upon the mind puts new vitality into the body.
> —Charles Ham, 1886

The grand scheme behind the Chicago Manual Training and Industrial School—through brain and hand to manhood—might well be found in what was known as the "mission to the wilderness": lofty ambitions for a new nation as articulated by an evangelical movement often called the Second Great Awakening. Beginning around the 1825 opening of the Erie Canal in upstate New York, which greatly eased transportation to what would soon be known as the Middle West, adventuresome young men, mainly New Englanders and often graduates of Yale College or Andover Seminary, headed west, beyond the new states of Ohio and Indiana, toward the Mississippi. Inspired by reformist fervor and known to history as either the Yale Band or the Andover Band, these volunteer missionaries ventured out to the prairies with the intention of establishing colleges to "civilize" the communities filling with pioneers—and manual labor was the means for such civilizing.[1]

Both E. W. Blatchford, the dedicated head of CMTS's board of trustees, and Henry Belfield, its first director, were graduates of these colleges. Blatchford, the minister's son, attended Illinois College, located between the Mississippi and the state's capital in Springfield.[2] Established in 1829, its first president was Edward Beecher, son of the noted evangelist Lyman Beecher and a founder of the Society for Promoting Manual Labor in Literary Institutions; Blatchford, an 1845 graduate, attended during the last few years of Beecher's administration and was surely influenced by the then-popular idea that college students should do agricultural and maintenance work to help sustain their school.³ Belfield, a decade younger than Blatchford, recounted in his autobiography the responsibility to care for cows and pigs while a student at Iowa College.⁴ Such labor was common at the time, particularly in the new colleges springing up on the prairies in the decades prior to the Civil War. Both men approached their work at CMTS with a missionary zeal, likely imparted to them by these early experiences.⁵

Such schooling of the hands and the head, or combining learning with doing, was, during the nineteenth century, not uncommon. Though its origins date to the seventeenth century in Europe, the movement in the United States evolved from manual labor in the 1830s to manual training in the 1870s to industrial education around the century's turn to vocational education by 1915. That mental and manual labor were mutually reinforcing influenced the kindergarten movement, the development of manual training curricula in secondary schools nationwide, both Hampton and Tuskegee institutes, the Laboratory School at the University of Chicago—and the Chicago Manual Training School.⁶

Beginning with their European origins, such schools can be represented in several different ways: there were manual labor seminaries for young men preparing for the ministry, charity schools and reformatories for youth in need of firm guidance and the means to make a living, mechanics institutes such as Rensselaer, plus those that were products of the Freedmen's Bureau. Soon after came the manual training schools in St. Louis and Chicago and similar institutions designed to prepare boys (and girls) of the middle classes for higher education or employment, and various philanthropic schools such as Chicago's Jewish Manual Training School and Armour Institute. Some were influenced by the Arts and Crafts Movement that sought to counteract the inhumane aspects of the Industrial Revolution. Most all of them were infused with the idea that honest labor dignifies those who do it, and that practical skills were as essential to becoming a full human being as knowledge of literature and the natural sciences.⁷

Charles Ham's enthusiastic 1886 telling of how manual training was the solution to social and industrial problems may have been the earliest published history of such programs, but perhaps not the most systematic and inclusive.⁸ That honor should go to two volumes on the history of manual and industrial training written by Charles A. Bennett. Published in 1926 and 1937, the first volume covers the history up to 1870 and the other 1870 to 1917.⁹ Bennett had begun his career heading manual training programs in St. Paul, Minnesota, then helped develop the manual training program at Teachers College in New York. In 1897, he joined Bradley Institute in Peoria, Illinois, which had been established as a junior college for the University

Figure 8. Charles Bennett, who established this magazine in conjunction with the University of Chicago, had managed manual training programs in Minnesota and New York before joining Bradley Institute in Illinois. In addition to editing this journal, Bennett also wrote two extensive histories of manual education in the United States and abroad.

of Chicago. Bennett later established a publishing company that would for decades bring out a magazine called *Manual Training*.[10] Bennett's books are the most comprehensive, with extensive lists of contents, excerpts from dozens of reports written by originators of such programs, and chronological charts comparing developments in Europe and the United States.

Another valuable reference is Lewis R. Anderson's *History of Manual and Industrial Education,* published in 1926 as a textbook.[11] Anderson, a professor of pedagogy at what was then Michigan Normal College in Marquette, also includes an extensive list of contents, plus chapter summaries, and a useful index. Both Anderson and Bennett begin their histories in the Renaissance and note that education for anyone other than male members of an elite was the exception until the middle of the eighteenth century. Titles of the first three chapters in Bennett's first volume aptly summarize his treatment: labor and learning, the relation between things and thoughts, and hand training as a means of mental development. Ham's history begins with the Egyptians and Greeks, and repeatedly points out that elites, quite wrongfully to his mind, disdained manual labor.

Learning Things by the Doing of Them

More recent histories of manual training in the United States trace its origin to a Russian exhibit at the Philadelphia Centennial Exposition in 1876, but the idea that heads and hands should be schooled together attracted adherents at least two centuries earlier. A Moravian minister and educator named John Amos Comenius, considered the father of modern education, promoted ideas in the mid-seventeenth century that would be associated with kindergartens and manual training schools two hundred years later.[12] Learning by doing may not have originated with Comenius, but his dictum "Let those things that have to be done be learned by doing them" may have articulated it most succinctly.[13]

In his rather grand manner, Charles Ham described these European antecedents when discussing the origins of the Chicago school:

> This is the school of the future; the school that is to dignify labor . . . where the brain informs the muscle . . . where the mind, the eye, and the hand constitute an invincible triple alliance. This is the school that Locke dreamed of, that Bacon wished for, that Rousseau described, and that Comenius, Pestalozzi, and Froebel struggled in vain to establish.[14]

The kindergarten, the institution Friedrich Froebel *is* credited with establishing, "fills a place in the educational field entirely unoccupied until [his] time," Ham wrote. It decidedly was not "a convenient asylum for the children of mothers who desire to be relieved of their care," as some thought. It was the precursor to the manual training school: "for as the child is father of the man, so the kindergarten is father of the manual training school." In the words of Froebel, both were dedicated to "the harmonious growth of the whole being."[15] Further, as Ham wrote, "Intelligence is the basis of character," and "manual training tends to correct vicious mental impulses."[16]

The value of connecting manual labor with schoolwork had been noted on the American side of the Atlantic since before the Revolutionary War, when Chicago was little more than a languid stream spilling its waters into Lake Michigan. Schooling hands and heads together was perhaps first promoted in the colonies by Benjamin Franklin at both charitable and higher academies in the 1750s, but it was enthusiastically endorsed by his fellow Philadelphian Benjamin Rush.[17] Rush himself had actually prepared for study at what became Princeton in one of the "log colleges" that proliferated around the Delaware River Valley beginning in the 1740s. In writing of his own preparatory education, Rush told of the "school" he had attended in the 1760s. His widowed mother had determined that the best situation for her fatherless sons would be with an uncle, a minister and later a president of Princeton, who with his wife ran a rural boarding school for two dozen students in nearby Maryland. In addition to their daily lessons in the classics, scripture, and "good breeding," the boys had a course in "practical agriculture": all the "boarders shared in the harvest and haymaking." In addition to being both "pleasant and useful," these exercises "begat health," Rush wrote with admiration.[18]

Comenius himself may have inspired other schools established in Pennsylvania at the eighteenth century's turn. Rush reported on Moravian schools located outside of Philadelphia: though they did not adopt the sort of industrial training advocated by Comenius, they did feel that students might receive the physical education they needed through vocational training rather than in sports and games.[19] At the time—the early 1800s—some educators were beginning to address students' need for physical exercise to complement their book learning, and this was particularly so in the seminaries preparing young men for the ministry. Was the solution a gymnasium program in conjunction with studying, or should students be urged to do real work—of the kind that could help maintain the schools' facilities—producing food, doing carpentry and cleaning?

During the 250 years between Comenius's explication of a methodology based on the nature of children rather than theology and the opening of manual training schools, philosophers, pedagogues, and social reformers developed ideas on how heads, hands, and hearts could "put the whole boy to school," a phrase popularized by Calvin Woodward in the 1880s. The social background of those to be educated kept expanding along with the definition of education—schools would bring in outcast and abandoned children as well as those of merchants and artisans; seminaries would prepare clerics for their role and teachers for theirs. At least in Europe and North

America, the use of manual labor to complement reading and recitations in the education process increased as did the number and backgrounds of students to be educated. By 1700 or so, German princes supported theologians who valued the use of the vernacular in schools and laid the foundation for a system that would be emulated in dozens of lands. Scotland recognized that a literate population was essential to developing a thriving economy; Presbyterian clerics brought the idea to the middle colonies to complement the Puritan conviction that a literate population would be best prepared to combat "that old deluder Satan." Benjamin Franklin and Thomas Jefferson decreed that a people could not be both ignorant and free, so developed systems of popular education that would buttress the new nation against tyrannies domestic and foreign. By the 1830s, Horace Mann in Massachusetts began advocating a "common school" that would unite the children of the wealthy and the less so in a common purpose. His idea, to one extent or another, was carried across the northern tier of states to the Mississippi and beyond, into North Carolina and Kentucky, even if it would be decades before the idea prevailed elsewhere in the South.

Hofwyl to Weld and Labor for Taming the Wilderness

The early nineteenth century, the decades of the Second Great Awakening, were also those in which manual labor schools began to flourish on both sides of the Atlantic, in the wake of reforms popularized by the Swiss educator Johann Heinrich Pestalozzi. For him, every human being had a right to an education and society had an obligation to provide it. He was particularly concerned about the poor; they deserved to have an education—of the head, heart, and hands—that would enable them to make a living.[20] In addition to the schools Pestalozzi established, these ideas influenced several others; most influential were Hofwyl in Switzerland, those in upstate New York and Ohio, the New Harmony Colony in Indiana, and others in the Midwest and beyond.[21]

Philipp von Fellenberg, the founder of Hofwyl, was a fellow Swiss whose father was a friend of Pestalozzi. Through him, Fellenberg became interested in education, and in 1799 he acquired an estate near Bern known as Hofwyl; there, over the next forty years, he would develop an innovative set of schools based on learning by doing through farming and handicrafts. One school sought to elevate the poor, another to provide a secondary education for local youth, and a third attracted children of wealthy families.[22] Among his primary concerns was greater harmony among different classes of society, and his ideas quickly gained wide currency in Europe. Fellenberg believed that healthy societies depended on preparing students for more efficient and intelligent performance of the duties relevant to their station in life, and he placed special emphasis on those at the extreme ends of the social spectrum. He was concerned that children from poor families would be able to earn a living, but he also wanted children of the wealthy to appreciate the challenges and efforts of the less fortunate.

These novel ideas—and that they had been realized in an actual school—were soon known not only in Europe, but in the United States as well.[23] Among its admiring students was Robert Dale Owen, the Scottish-born founder, with his father, of the utopian New Harmony community in Indiana. Owen, after having become a U.S. citizen, was elected to the Indiana legislature and then to the U.S. Congress; there he was instrumental in establishing the Smithsonian Institution. In 1865, the *Atlantic* magazine published Owen's account of his education at Hofwyl.[24] Other Americans either visited or attended the schools; one, a chemistry professor by the name of John Griscom, stopped there on an 1818–1819 journey to Europe, and on his return tried to convince New York's Public School Association to start a school based on what he had seen at Hofwyl.[25] A Georgian named George Dent had attended Hofwyl as well and was taken by its ideals. When, in 1850 or so, he and his wife inherited a rice plantation near the coast, home also to several hundred enslaved people, they renamed it Hofwyl-Broadfield.[26]

Fellenberg's ideas were, during the 1820s, incorporated into programs at seminaries in Maine, Massachusetts, and elsewhere, but most prominently at Oneida, near Utica, New York; its founder was a minister by the name of George Washington Gale, who would later establish a similar school in Illinois.[27] Concerned that the rapidly developing "west"—then Ohio to the Mississippi—was in need of "taming," leading evangelicals recognized that they had to provide a clergy strong of mind and of body. Oneida Academy, established in 1827, was a manifestation of this concern, as were the Yale and Andover bands that had established the alma maters of Blatchford and Belfield. Oneida quickly attracted young men of conviction and determination, among them the reformist theologian Horace Bushnell and Henry Stanton, soon to marry Elizabeth Cady, who would later be noted as a leading feminist.[28] Most prominent was Theodore Weld; a decade later, he would become one of the nation's leading abolitionists. Vigorous both intellectually and physically, and possessed of immense oratorical skills, Weld personified the school's mission.[29] Students rose before dawn for devotions, then tended to the school's fields and livestock; after their classwork and studies, they did another stint at the manual labor that supported both them and the school.[30]

Oneida's ability to attract young men of piety and moral purpose persuaded supporters, such as the young president of Illinois College Edward

Figure 9. Theodore Weld, pictured here, was a forceful advocate for the educational attributes of useful work and for abolition. In the early 1830s, he served as general agent for the Society for Promoting Manual Labor in Literary Institutions, an idea that influenced the founding of both CMTS and Hampton Institute.

Beecher, to extend the idea. Thus was founded, in 1831, the Society for Promoting Manual Labor in Literary Institutions. Funded by the philanthropist merchants Arthur and Lewis Tappan, they engaged Weld as its agent. His task was to survey similar institutions on both sides of the Ohio River and report on characteristics that made them successful.[31] In Weld's mind, manual labor had a beneficial effect on every aspect of man's existence—it was God's plan that mind and body would work together to produce character and purpose. Such work also promoted "habits of industry, independence, and originality." Additionally, it would aid "republican institutions" by promoting a greater sense of equality among students from different stations in life.[32] The manual labor model, Weld admitted, did have some limitations, such as the students were often too tired to pursue theological studies and too unskilled for their efforts to produce sufficient income to support a school. But Weld was certain that better program design and management could ameliorate these deficiencies.[33]

Weld also suggested that the recently established Lane Theological Seminary in Cincinnati would be an excellent site for another manual labor school, one which would enable "poor but earnest young men" to train for the "westward ministry."[34] Whether this mission to the wilderness might succeed would not be known because disputes about slavery during 1834, led by Weld, caused its trustees to ban such discussion from the campus, which led to a rapid exodus of students. Several relocated northeast to equally new Oberlin, which initially adopted the manual labor idea but abandoned it for the reasons Weld had warned about.[35] Lane continued as a Presbyterian seminary for a while, under its president Lyman Beecher and professor Calvin Stowe, respectively father and husband of Harriet Beecher Stowe. In 1852, her famous book would be published; it was based on research Weld would undertake in the late 1830s, after he had departed Ohio.[36]

Though largely ignored in the years prior to the Civil War, some higher education for women became available around the same time. Another Beecher sister, Catherine, had established the Hartford Female Academy in 1823. It was one of a half-dozen or so such schools, some secondary, some college level, established during the following decade. One, Mount Holyoke College, opened in 1837, was founded on the idea that women, even of the lower and middling classes, deserved a rigorous education, and it made such schooling possible via a system in which students were responsible for housekeeping and food preparation.[37] Charles Ham, with typical vigor, gave a chapter to the "prime necessity" of educating women, because they were "designed to teach" and needed higher education in order to do it well.[38]

Schools spawned by Pestalozzi and Fellenberg served not only pastors in training and young men of privilege, but orphans and pauper children in Europe and the United States.[39] Often called industrial reform schools, they were established to provide homeless children with a stable environment and a way to make a living rather than abandon them to a life of crime. St. George's Fields in England somewhat resembled the log colleges Benjamin Rush extolled; a husband and wife team took in a dozen boys to provide them with an elementary education and instruction in a useful trade. John Griscom, who suggested a Hofwyl-like school in New York, visited St. George's in 1818.[40] By the 1850s, there were dozens of "ragged schools" in London; promoters saw them as the only way some children could remain honest and have enough to eat.[41]

Industrial reform schools were established in the United States as well; the first may have been on Randalls Island in New York in 1824. Prisons also used manual labor as a means of employing the time of their wards; men (and women) working at a useful task were less likely to indulge in evils such as gambling. Bennett claimed that, by 1850, when the manual labor movement had spent its force in theological seminaries, advocates turned to setting them up in prisons and correctional facilities for the young. The idea was to focus on character development rather than retributive justice. Activities might lead to acquiring the skills of a tailor, a cobbler, or a cook, but the emphasis was on socially acceptable behavior, not learning a trade.[42]

In January of 1836, Calvin Stowe, a noted Biblical scholar as well as other accomplishments, married Harriet Beecher, the president's daughter; a few months later he embarked on an extensive trip to Europe.[43] Professor Stowe, who also was a staunch advocate for public education, had been asked by the Ohio legislature to learn about schools there. His *Report on the Elementary Education in Europe* was widely circulated upon his return.[44] While in Prussia, he was particularly impressed by the schools' focus on instruction in drawing. That, and the large number of German draftsmen in the Cincinnati area, encouraged the establishment in 1840 of a two-year course in drawing in the city's public schools, making it the first school in the United States to teach this, often called an alternate universal language.[45]

Learning and Labor

The Prussian course in drawing was only one manifestation of another trend toward more courses in various kinds of handwork that had been underway in Europe since the time of Comenius. By the early 1800s the trend—more mechanics than just manual labor—became popular in the United States.[46] A General Society of Mechanics and Trades, organized in New York in 1820, offered courses and a library or reading room; two years later, the Franklin Institute opened in Philadelphia. Similar institutions were organized in Baltimore, Boston, and Cincinnati over the following decade. Some focused on practical courses for the children of mechanics; others on advancing the basic skills of working men. As some leaders felt their members knew too little math and science to learn from the lectures given, the institutes began to offer a combination of liberal and practical courses.

Schools with similar intentions that opened in rural areas were often called lyceums. One, the Gardiner Lyceum in Maine, founded in 1823, was based on the idea that learning chemistry and the laws of mechanics was insufficient; students needed to learn practical applications of those laws. The school, which was supported by gifts, tuition, and some grants from the state legislature, also featured a manual labor component. These lyceums, according to Bennett, gained widespread support and were a means of building up America's reputation as the land of popular education for the acquisition of "useful knowledge."[47]

Rensselaer Polytechnic Institute, established in 1824 in Troy, New York, was another innovative school in this tradition. Though it did not follow the Fellenberg model of requiring manual labor of its students, it did focus on practical experiences with useful knowledge. According to its founder, its purpose was "instructing persons . . . in the application of science to the common purposes of life."[48] Initially, according to Bennett, open to both the sons and the daughters of mechanics, its courses applied the sciences to agriculture and domestic economy, the arts and manufacturing. As it also attracted students who had already attended other colleges, it has been considered the nation's first graduate school.[49] One of these graduate students was George Washington Gale Ferris Jr. Born in Galesburg, Illinois, and named after the founder of not only the town but Oneida Institute, he would gain acclaim as the inventor of the Ferris Wheel, which dominated the grounds of Chicago's Columbian Exposition in 1893.

Thus, the movement toward manual work in the years prior to the Civil War, and its related focus on useful knowledge, influenced numerous institutions as the growing nation's needs demanded a more broadly educated populace; practical subjects and experiences were increasingly offered to complement classical studies. The lines between and among academies, secondary schools, colleges, and universities were far less clear than they would be later. In the Midwest, Jonathan Baldwin Turner, a classically trained botanist who taught with Edward Beecher at Illinois College, instigated a movement that resulted in the establishment of Illinois Industrial University in 1867. As part of his argument for such an institution, he noted that society was divided into two classes that are cooperative, not antagonistic, a professional class and an industrial one; 95 percent of the populace belongs to the latter. But it, too, deserves an opportunity to apply existing knowledge to their pursuits. In his terms, they are the "thinking laborers"; the professionals the "laborious thinkers." Turner's efforts, and those of like-minded colleagues, added momentum to the push for what became land-grant colleges via the 1862 Morrill Act.[50] In 1885, the Illinois Industrial University whose founding Turner had instigated was renamed the University of Illinois; its motto: learning and labor.

Massachusetts Institute of Technology and Cornell University, another early land-grant institution—and two schools that would welcome graduates of the Chicago Manual Training School on the basis of their diplomas alone—opened respectively in 1861 and 1865.[51] MIT would, in the midst of its second decade, lead the development of the next step to be taken in the schooling of

Figure 10. Jonathan Baldwin Turner, pictured in this undated photograph, migrated to Illinois in the 1830s as part of the manual labor movement that led to the founding of many colleges, particularly in the Midwest. He is recalled as promoting the idea that doers should also be thinkers and thinkers, doers.

hands and heads. These programs are best understood in the context of the changes the economy and the workforce were undergoing at the time.

"An Escalator in Perpetual Motion"

In one of his several books about technology and education published in the 1970s and 1980s, Arthur Wirth, who was also a biographer of John Dewey, commented that "We lack as yet a probing study of the manual training phenomenon which would relate it meaningfully to broader social-intellectual contexts."[52] Among those broader contexts is how labor changed during the nineteenth century. An impetus behind the establishment of mechanics institutes and schools such as Rensselaer was the rapid development of technology, the topic that had fascinated Charles Ham. His focus, though, was on the inventors of the new technology rather than on the workers, skilled and less so, who turned this technology into products from farm machinery to household furnishings to new shoes. In *Artisans into Workers*, historian Bruce Laurie, writing a century later, offered a brief but compelling history of how laboring men (and women) responded to these technological changes during the nineteenth century. Prior to the mid-1800s, Laurie recalled, entrepreneurial-minded men, workers and yeomen alike, felt they could rise through America's dynamic and open society as on a perpetually moving escalator.[53] Mid-century and beyond, that process became far more complicated.

The nation, which had begun as one of self-sufficient farmers and artisans of varied talents, was in the process of a transformation as states and cities spread to the Mississippi River and beyond. The nation's prevailing ideology, influenced by the prevailing theology of evangelical Protestantism, had been that one should earn one's bread by the sweat of one's brow, which was possible in the small-scale workshops where workers not only made but sold and distributed, on a local level, the products of their labor. The mechanics institutes and lyceums that sprang up in towns and cities across the land, though largely in the North, were a response to demands from those workers who wanted to acquire new technical skills so as to board that escalator—and to assume a higher position in society than that to which they were born. Benjamin Franklin, still influential decades after his death, had preached usefulness, and the elevation of work was an "ethos that permeated life and manners," wrote David Rodgers in another study of labor in the nineteenth century, *The Work Ethic in Industrial America*.[54]

American society as a whole was imbued with the individualistic spirit of the entrepreneur; self-employed artisans and experienced journeymen were able to make a decent living or start their own businesses. Self-sufficient, these men (and the women whose work complemented their efforts) made much of their own equipment, using locally available materials and expertise. Then, states and the federal government encouraged expanding opportunities for industries large and small by building canals and enacting tariffs to protect domestic manufacturing. Growth was interrupted by an economic slump in the 1830s, the decade in which Weld and others were pushing manual labor as a means of improving one's condition through higher education. Self-reliant independence became a luxury some small-scale craftsmen and factory workers could no longer afford, so a "militant minority" of organizers responded to workers' needs for more equitable wages and better working conditions by advocating collective action through unionization.[55] The men and women who had staffed the workshops that dominated manufacturing at the beginning of the century found themselves forced, by an expanding economy, to be employees of ever-larger factories. No longer self-sufficient, they were wage earners sharing the products of their labor with often-distant employers.

The self-improvement era of the antebellum mechanics institutes and schools supported by the manual labor of its students had come to an end.

Workingmen's parties formed along with a national General Trades Union; factory workers were discovering that their needs differed from those of the merchants and manufacturers who employed them. The paternalism of the small-scale factory owner was replaced by the self-interest of industrialists who pushed the division of labor; the typical worker became a semi-skilled machine operator with limited autonomy. At the mid-point of the nineteenth century, roughly half of the nation's workers were employees. Then came the Civil War. Its need for military equipment forced manufacturing firms to intensify the move toward mechanization; railroads capable of moving raw materials and finished products long distances replaced canals and locally maintained toll roads.

After the war, unionized workers increasingly fought back against regimentation, loss of independence, and poor wages through strikes large and small, both peaceful and violent. The invention of machines that replaced handwork intensified mechanization in both the North and the South. The subdivision of labor increased in rapidly expanding industries such as textiles, machine-making, meatpacking, and railcar construction. Still, most workers did not belong to unions; membership may have peaked to a third of all workers just before the postwar panic of 1873.[56] Despite an economic slowdown, labor agencies continued recruiting workers from abroad and sent them off to logging camps and iron mines; class divides grew; new immigrants unfamiliar with American customs could be employed to break strikes. "Captains of industry" adopted Social Darwinism to justify repressive tactics; the federal government and the courts sided with them rather than with workers. The Gilded Age witnessed the fraying of the American fabric; the escalator seemed no longer in motion. Mechanization had challenged the traditional connection between work and virtue, skill and art.

National organizations such as the idealistic Knights of Labor endeavored to mend these frays; socialist parties formed though they had little lasting appeal for American workers. By the mid-1880s, their fixation with remaking industrial capitalism was eclipsed by the more effective efforts of the American Federation of Labor. Led by immigrant, intellectually minded Samuel Gompers, who studied history and politics with like-minded coworkers, the AFL quickly absorbed other, smaller trade unions nationwide. Recalled for "pure and simple unionism"—bettering conditions for workers in the here and now—and for opposing strikes likely to activate government repression, the AFL saw its membership quadruple between 1897 and 1903.[57]

Some state and federal initiatives toward workers and unions during the Gilded Age indicated concern particularly for the "mechanicalized" laborer, to use the term Rodgers employed while discussing the monotony of factory jobs during the era. One was the appointment of Massachusetts attorney

Carroll D. Wright as the nation's first commissioner of labor, a post he was given in 1885 after undertaking extensive studies of the factory system in his home state. Wright, according to Rodgers, even saw some virtue in the structure and regimentation of modern factory jobs, calling them a "mental escalator" that could lift the minds of laborers who had previously worked in squalid conditions at home.[58] Whatever the case, Wright was sought after as a statistically minded expert for the next two decades. He served as a conciliator in major strikes of the time, was a professor of statistics and social economics at a trio of leading universities, and in 1902 wrote a book titled *Some Ethical Phases of the Labor Question.*

A question that emerges as a result of reviewing the changing role of workers during the nineteenth century is why there has been little scholarly interaction between histories of labor and histories of industrial education.[59] If three different categories of workers emerged—the common laborers valued for their strength; the machine tenders or operatives needed for repetitive tasks in factories; and the skilled craftsmen who designed, managed, and repaired the machines—might educational programs of the era have catered to one or the other? Lawrence Cremin, in his *The Metropolitan Experience*, covered an aspect of this question in a section titled "Places of Work." Before reviewing various means of introducing research-based agricultural education to farmers north and south, he noted the decreasing percentage of the nation's workers who were involved in farming—from half of the nation's work force in 1870 to a third by the century's turn. The number of wage-earners in factories grew substantially during the same period—from 2.7 million in 1880 to 4.5 million in 1900, some of which was a result of population growth in general.[60] (For some context, the nation's population grew from 50 million in 1880 to 76 million in 1900.)

While common laborers in factories or logging camps had limited schooling and needed little or no training for their work, the same was only somewhat true of the machine operators, but the skills needed for their tasks could be learned in a few weeks. Skilled craftsmen had tended to acquire their competence through apprenticeships, entry to which was controlled by craft unions. Getting onto an escalator—whether one to board on one's own initiative or that which factory regimentation might impose—had become a far more complex process as the century ended than when it began. Plus, there may have been more than one escalator. However many, the process was gathering considerable attention from educators, particularly as the century was nearing its end. Chicago, the nation's fastest growing major city, was also home to many of its largest manufacturing concerns, and to its militant unions, so it is no surprise that it would have generated considerable interest in industrial education.[61]

"How Powerless Mere Words Are in the Presence of Things"

Arthur Wirth, in making his comment about works on manual education that failed to connect it to a broader social context, also cited a few noted studies of secondary education during the Progressive Era and beyond that did so. Among them was Lawrence Cremin's 1964 *Transformation of the School*, which approached the topic as ideas set in motion during the 1880s and 1890s by Dewey and others. Wirth noted Charles Ham's 1886 *Manual Training* but paid it little attention, calling Ham an "enthusiast" for the movement. Cremin commends Ham's efforts, but in a footnote.[62] Neither likely read Ham's paeon to manual training, which also appears in few bibliographies. One could argue that Ham's intention was to produce, if not the "probing study" Wirth said was missing, a detailed survey of great leaps in industrial development. He began with the potter's wheel and eventually got to the Bessemer process and Corliss engine, and he indicated their relationship to an ideal manual training curriculum.[63] Ham's work may have been ignored because, according to Charles Bennett, he had antagonized educators at an 1888 meeting of the National Education Association with harsh criticism of public schools.[64] Neglecting Ham's work is unfortunate because, in addition to its history of tool use and inventions, *Manual Training* sets its subject in a solid historical and intellectual context.

The book's preface is based on a paper Ham read in 1879 before the Chicago Philosophical Society titled "Inventive Genius, or an Epitome of Human Progress." Right off, he wrote, he "realized the force of [Francis] Bacon's remark that 'the real and legitimate goal of the sciences is the endowment of human life with new inventions and discoveries.'" He then claimed that tools are "the great civilizing agency of the world" and credited Thomas Carlyle with the observation that "Man without tools is nothing; with tools he is all." Education, Ham asserted, "is the development of all the powers of man to the culminating point of action," the power to do something useful for one's fellows. However, he continued, these ideas were not new. They had been earlier formulated by Comenius, Jean-Jacques Rousseau, Pestalozzi, and Herbert Spencer; Froebel "had tried to carry them into practical application in the schoolroom," but with limited success. Ham then claimed:

> It remains for the age of steel to show how powerless mere words are in the presence of things, and so to advocate for a radical reform in educational methods.

That last remark, or the need for radical reform, may have had him in trouble with the schoolmasters, but that should not diminish the power of his

Figure 11. Charles Ham, whose profile appears here, articulated the idea that manual training was an essential aspect of education. His 1886 history of technology contributed to the curriculum at CMTS; the 1900 version of that book includes an extensive compilation of manual training programs around the world at the time. This etching appeared as a frontispiece for that version; it was based on an earlier photograph.

assertions, such as "tool practice is highly promotive of intellectual growth" and fosters "the upbuilding of character." Tools have, as Ham's contents list claims, not only "majesty" but intellectual and moral benefits. And, making a claim that he would reiterate throughout his book—that the aim of manual training is to "redeem manual labor from the scorn of the ages of slavery, and, in the end, to render the skilled laborer worthy of a high social distinction." In this lies the solution to social and industrial problems, he insisted.[65]

Ham's preface veers from the theoretical to the practical by crediting the work of men commonly connected with the origins of manual training, such as MIT's John Runkle, Calvin Woodward of St. Louis, and their mutual debt to Victor Della Vos, head of the Imperial Technical School in Moscow. That standard story begins, famously, with a display at the 1876 Centennial Exposition Philadelphia—an exhibit from Moscow that led to new programs at both MIT and Washington University. As Runkle told the story in a letter to Ham: "almost the first thing I saw was . . . graded models for teaching" tool use. "In an instant" he realized that the problem he had been trying to solve became clear in his mind—these mechanical arts could be taught "just as we teach chemistry and physics," with a form of step-by-step laboratory instruction.[66]

The idea behind the models that Della Vos had on display was how to teach mechanical arts rather the way drawing is taught, as a succession of steps gradually increasing in difficulty. Further, in the student workshops the focus was on instruction; students would only be admitted to the school's shops for actual production and construction after they had acquired the necessary skills—school workshops at the time often supported themselves through student labor. However, Della Vos insisted that instruction be separate from production. The pedagogical problem that Runkle felt the "Russian method" helped him solve was how to more efficiently teach basic tool use, so that students could quickly move into more advanced courses requiring those skills. MIT added these instruction shops within a year, and in 1878, Runkle got permission from MIT's trustees to expand these shops into a secondary-level School of Mechanic Arts.[67]

Though Runkle is often credited with first recognizing the value of this Russian system, Calvin Woodward made the most use of it, not only at Washington University in St. Louis, but through the impact its program had on others nationwide. Runkle saw the system's practical attributes; Woodward incorporated a version of them into a larger pedagogical framework that had the power to address a host of pedagogical problems. Among his concerns was that the youth seeking entry to his university program were largely unfamiliar with the use of basic tools. He wrote of his pedagogy in two major books, published in 1887 and 1890. They included the text of several addresses he gave on the subject, his history of manual training and its results in St. Louis and elsewhere, plus dozens of "Exercises in Woods and Metals," numerous illustrations, and his "Reply to Criticisms," of which there would be many.[68] Like Ham, Woodward was philosophical about the virtues of manual training. In an 1878 address, he too quoted Carlyle on the value of tool use: the knowledge of material things was as necessary to the development of the intellect as knowledge of the abstract, he said. Therefore, there should be the coeducation of mind and hand.[69]

Born in Massachusetts and a graduate of Harvard, Woodward had quickly become a popular professor of mathematics upon his move to Washington University. Shortly after his arrival in 1865, he became dean of its O'Fallon Polytechnic Institute, a school of mechanics similar to those founded elsewhere in previous decades. During the 1870s, he was also a member of the St. Louis board of education; one of his chief concerns then and in later years was students' exodus from school before they were ready to be self-supporting in some honorable way.[70] He had analyzed the shortcomings of the schooling students were getting compared to the needs of a growing city. In an 1873 address, he laid out what he meant by this. Noting the strengths and weaknesses of American education—and the inferiority of American products compared to those of Europe—he claimed that manual work was being neglected in schools: "It trains boys not to be better craftsmen but to be unwilling to do any craft." Polytechnics such as the one in Worcester, MA, were preparing boys for "the duties of an active life" and the common schools needed to move in the same direction: "as every boy should be taught to swim, to row, to ride ... so should he be taught to use the ax, the saw, the plane and the file." However, "unless labor has more than dignity, we are not likely to be very zealous in seeking it." The "world judges us by what we can do," he concluded.[71]

Combining Skillful Hands with Cultured Minds

Frustrated by O'Fallon students' inability to use even basic tools, Woodward had worked out a series of exercises that instructed them in their use. Thus, "the Russian exhibit at Philadelphia was less of a surprise to me than it was to many," he wrote a few years later.[72] Nevertheless, he used the attention Runkle's new School of Mechanic Arts received to solicit support for a Manual Training School, which would be a secondary-level adjunct to Washington University. In an 1879 prospectus, Woodward lamented that the nation was importing too many of its skilled laborers; the new school would help correct that but do so without simply directing students into the lines of work their fathers did. Thus, regardless of their family's social standing, students would be immersed not only in the acquisition of mechanical skills, but with that acquisition gain a "willingness to recognize skill in his fellows."[73] In this, the St. Louis school would practice an intention Fellenberg had for Hofwyl decades earlier: the financially privileged should recognize the contributions of others without such advantages.

Promoting his vision for the school, Woodward said that its three-year course of instruction would be "about equally divided between mental and manual exercises.... The change from recitation to shop ... will be agreeable and healthful, keeping both mind and body fresh and vigorous." Students will learn "the nature, theory, and use" of the seven basic hand tools: the ax, saw, plane, hammers, square, chisel, and file [291]. They will study "materials and processes" but not make items for sale, so as not to compete with local industries. "Thus, without teaching one trade, we teach the essential mechanical principles of all" [294]. The school opened its doors in September 1880 with fifty students; three years later, it enrolled over two hundred; its facilities kept expanding as did its graduating classes.[74] Over its front door appeared the school's famous motto:

> Hail to the skillful, cunning hand!
> Hail to the cultured mind!
> Calling for the world's command,
> Let them be here combined.

As the St. Louis school grew, so did its influence. Visitors abounded; over the next few years, similar schools opened not only in Chicago and Toledo, but in Baltimore and Philadelphia and smaller cities, especially in the center of the country. Both Runkle and Woodward argued that manual training belonged not only in secondary schools, but at all levels of public education. In Runkle's words: schooling should "better fit all for that sphere of life in which they are destined to find their highest happiness and well-being."[75] Woodward wrote in 1881 that a manual training school would "bring out into clear relief those very aptitudes which ought to control the destiny of the boy."[76] As Runkle resigned as MIT president in 1880 and returned to his work in mathematics and astronomy, Woodward became the prominent spokesperson for this new education. In an 1883 address to fellow educators, he claimed that among the fruits of manual training were that boys stayed in school longer, that it enhanced their intellectual and moral development, and that it enabled sounder judgment. By raising the cultural profile of the laborer, it could solve labor problems.[77] Few St. Louis graduates actually became laborers, however; as with those of Chicago's manual training school, they became managers, merchants, and manufacturers, along with draftsmen. Of those who continued their education, most became engineers; others were educators and attorneys.[78]

Thus, Ham's claim that manual training could solve social problems by elevating the status of industrial workers was overly optimistic. Despite the efforts of Pestalozzi, Turner, and others to bring the classes, or the workers and the thinkers, together, manual work in schools did not usher in a halcyon era of sustainable cooperation between workers and their corporate employers. However, as industrial education programs in public schools, some in cooperation with labor unions and with employers, began to expand after 1890, more young people were persuaded to remain in school, even if only on a temporary basis, after age fourteen. So, the aims of Ham and Woodward were eventually realized, even if not on the scale they might have wished.

The Union of Teaching and Working

Most of the early manual training programs were established by private entities, were at the secondary level, and were for boys. An exception to the latter two, and one that seemed to owe nothing to Woodward, was the Workingmen's School in New York City, which opened in 1880 as a charity, but with the idea of inspiring the public schools to establish similar programs. A distinctive institution, it was founded by Felix Adler, the son of a prominent rabbi, and it provided a free kindergarten, an elementary program with a strong manual component, a technical secondary program for students with particular promise, plus evening classes for others. It admitted girls and aimed to impart not only skills, but "mind-education" that emphasized the moral over the intellectual.[79] Aspects of Adler's program, which united teaching and working, continue as the Ethical Culture Fieldston School in New York City.

Woodward's vision that manual training belonged on the same plane as other school subjects had not immediately won over other educators. Some skeptics who heard his first address, in 1882, to the National Education Association (NEA) ridiculed the idea, claiming it would kill the basic principles of public education. One, in a particularly cutting remark, claimed that there "is no information stored up in the plow, hoe handle [or] steam engine; but there is information stored in books."[80]

By 1884, opinions had begun to change. The NEA met that year in Madison, Wisconsin; Woodward organized a session on industrial education and attracted several noted speakers, among them Augustus Jacobson, a chief supporter of Chicago's school, Felix Adler of New York City, and John Ordway, who headed the School of Mechanic Arts in Boston. All endorsed Woodward's efforts, if for different reasons: Jacobson claimed that "The wealth of a nation depends upon skill" and that educated laborers could more quickly acquire skills. Adler's argument was less practical: art and handwork were elements of culture and belonged in the public school. Ordway summarized similar developments in Europe.[81] At the time, his name was associated with an analogous movement in Scandinavia. Known as sloyd, it began as a means of improving handicrafts, both in rural communities and in schools. Aimed at developing grace and dexterity, sloyd was based on a carefully organized set of exercises and enjoyed a period of vogue in the United States.[82]

Philadelphia could claim to be the first, if not the only, large system to incorporate manual training into all levels of its classes, from the kindergarten to the high school, and it began to do so in 1884. An 1889 publication describing its components was introduced with a particularly graceful essay on "The General Question of Manual Training" written by the superintendent James MacAlister. The program's goal was to bring the schools "more into harmony with existing social conditions," he wrote [5], and thus meet the "supreme end of education . . . the harmonious development of all the powers of a human being" [6]. In addition to a manual training high school, the system offered industrial arts classes for boys and girls in the elementary grades, plus sewing and cookery classes for girls. These classes, he believed, so stimulated pupils' general intelligence that time in the "work-shops more than compensates for the amount of text-book work that it supplants" [8]. Such work had greater relevance to the community's social needs; while schools were not to train "mere breadwinners," they must give students the "power to hold their own in the struggle of life" [10]. Beyond that, schools had a role to play in resolving the "struggle between labor and wealth" by bringing thought and labor together: "to make every worker a thinker and every thinker a worker" [11]. Manual training, by ridding the schools of "antiquated and useless work" would encourage more children to spend more time in school—which would be to their benefit.[83]

While the Philadelphia program was uniquely comprehensive, it was not wholly unique. The 1900 edition of Charles Ham's book compiled manual training programs in public and private institutions from kindergartens through colleges. By his count, thirty-one cities had established public secondary-level manual training programs by 1890; nearly as many cities had them at the grammar-school level. They were located in seventeen different states, mainly in the Northeast and Midwest. The number of secondary students in public school programs alone was roughly 6,500.[84] In his *Transformation of the School*, Cremin, citing a 1889–1890 U.S. Bureau of Education Report, wrote that "thousands of boys and girls [were] studying carpentry, metal and machine work, sewing, cooking, and drawing" in over three dozen cities.[85]

Though "manual training" had expanded beyond Woodward's original concept, the issue was the "crux of the most vigorous pedagogical battle of the eighties," Cremin continued.[86] Two of the most intriguing arguments, pro and con, were offered at the decade's end by two men who would, as the century turned, be among the nation's most prominent educators: Nicholas Murray Butler, then head of the New York College for the Training of Teachers, argued in its favor; William Torrey Harris, long Woodward's sparring partner as superintendent of St. Louis schools, argued against. Although their addresses were not point-counterpoint, they illustrate how one phenomenon can be interpreted as meaning two very different things.

The Psychology of Coeducating Hands and Minds

The different routes Harris and Butler took to their preeminent positions might have influenced the stands they took on the union of hands and minds. Butler's "Argument for Manual Training" appeared as an address given in March 1888; Harris's "Psychology of Manual Training," also an address to a group of prominent educators, was given a year later. At the time, Butler was in the midst of a national debate about the sort of preparation teachers needed to have for a job that was undergoing vast changes in complexity and responsibility. Harris, who spent the 1880s teaching philosophy in Connecticut, was in time and distance far removed from the daily challenges teachers faced. Butler's talk dealt with immediate reality; that of Harris with a metaphysical one. Their differing backgrounds might have suggested otherwise.

A generation younger than Harris, Butler had taken a royal road into educational leadership. After receiving a PhD in philosophy from Columbia in 1884, he spent a year in Germany and there realized his calling—the scientific study of educational theory. He returned to Columbia to teach and was soon known for popular lectures on education. These attracted the attention of the Industrial Education Association, which had been founded in 1880 as the Kitchen Garden Association, a philanthropic venture that aimed at ameliorating slum conditions through classes for young children and their mothers. Hired as the association's president early in 1887, Butler further changed its focus from tactile exercises for young children to teacher preparation. Soon known as Teachers College, this new venture was to be neither a trade school nor a normal; it would be a professional school offering courses on psychology, history, and science. It quickly became a "mecca for educational pilgrims," according to its future president Lawrence Cremin, bringing in a host of compelling speakers—such as Chicago's Francis Parker and Charles Ham—and getting its message out through leaflets and monographs and a journal, including the *Educational Monographs* series. With the institution's distinctive role well-established, Butler resigned in 1891 and returned to Columbia.[87] By 1902, he headed both the university and the National Education Association.

Harris took a distinctively novel route to educational leadership. Though a graduate of Phillips Academy in Andover, he dropped out of Yale after two years and moved to St. Louis to teach prior to the Civil War. The thriving city had a strong German community, and Harris's friends among its members led him to see history as a Hegelian process of contending forces leading to synthesis. In 1867, he founded the *Journal of Speculative Philosophy* and was the Hegelians' guiding spirit. The following year he became St. Louis superintendent of schools, in which role he championed the kindergarten and the city's growing industrialization.[88] Cremin described Harris's career as "a remarkable marriage of the intensely idealistic philosopher and the eminently practical schoolman."[89] His pedagogy transformed the common school into a system that could meet the conflicting demands of the emerging urban society. This might suggest an affinity for the manual training school; instead, he was largely critical of its aims and assumptions, in part because he saw no way in which manual work could do the more important work of the mind. In 1889, Harris became the U.S. commissioner of education; like Butler, he appeared frequently at meetings of the NEA.

Published one year before Harris's "Psychology," Butler's "Argument" focused on the practical rather than the theoretical.[90] Education, beginning with Comenius and on through Froebel to Woodward, means something different to every age. For the current one the kindergarten was at one end and the manual training school at the other [380]. Both rest on a sound pedagogical principle because learning through the hands and the eyes—the senses—is mental training of importance equal to what is learned through thought alone. (Nevertheless, he complained, "sense-training is accorded but a narrow corner of the schoolroom" [382]). However, despite its value as a means of education, manual training is not an end in itself; public schools ought not to be turning out carpenters or cooks, but boys and girls trained to take their own part in life.

Drawing on recent discoveries about the central nervous system, Butler differentiated between the receptive and the expressive powers, and praised the study of drawing as one of the latter—a boy who can draw a three-dimensional cube knows far more about it than one who can merely repeat its definition [386]. He bemoaned the fact that parents valued mental work over manual labor and noted that active manual training in schools was increasingly important given that the country was fast becoming an urban rather than a rural society; skills the young would acquire growing up on a farm cannot so easily be acquired in a city [391–93]. Asking whether the school has "kept pace with civilization," Butler argued that the negative seemed true until manual training came along. Still, it was meeting with "no little opposition" and "considerable misrepresentation." However, the movement had "run the gauntlet"; it was based on the new science of the mind, and it better prepared students for contemporary life and citizenship [395].

In his "Psychology," Harris disputed most of Butler's contentions, if only indirectly—there is no ad hominem in either.[91] Acknowledging that educators tended to be conservative, Harris claimed that while schools ought not neglect students' spontaneity, their chief role was to guide them into control over their impulses; school's role was to prepare students for their social role. "The ideal standard of progress," he argued, "is found in the form of government which secures the greatest degree of individual development while not losing the centralized power of the whole" [5]. The Pestalozzian idea of harmony between body and soul, or hands and minds, was "dangerous" because it ignored the "great distinction between our higher and lower faculties, between our faculties that are means to ends" and those that are "ends in themselves" [7]. And thus, he came to the "essential idea of education": it is "the preparation of the individual for reciprocal union with society" [8].

Manual training, learning from objects, even sloyd, had some value, but because it is based on "sense-perception"—the sort of learning an infant does—it has a limited role in school [9–11]. "Man" becomes educated by "withdraw[ing] his attention from the external world of the senses" and attending instead to the principles and causes that have been discovered in ages past. It is a "false psychology" that tells us "we derive all our knowledge from sense perception" [12]. We learn only through thought, not through the senses. What Butler saw as an essential aspect of schooling, Harris saw as something to avoid: "It is not desirable," he argued near the conclusion of his address, "that children be taught that rough hand labor is itself as honorable as the elaborative toil of thought which gives direction to the hand" [20].

Though Harris's speculation about the value of education to the individual and society enabled him to guide school systems of both a growing city and the nation as a whole, this address suggests that he knew students more in the abstract than as individuals—a historian of the St. Louis schools suggested that Harris was more interested in how students could fit into the city's economy than whether or not they stayed in school.[92] Woodward, an agitator in the system Harris was trying to rationalize, saw students as individuals whose senses needed an education along with their minds. In his 1890 book, Woodward countered arguments the philosopher turned superintendent had made: Harris's famed "windows to the soul" of arithmetic, geography, history, grammar, and literature via books alone worshiped the ancient and ignored the modern.[93] "Book learning," Woodward argued, "neglects some of the faculties of all minds and nearly all of some minds." Schools needed to be "pruned of worthless appendages" and "enriched with judicious additions" [38]. Rather than these five windows of a classical education, Woodward proposed an alternative course of study for secondary schools: mathematics, literature, sciences, drawing, plus tools and processes [48]. Instead of assuming that all knowledge of nature and human life resides in books, Woodward claimed that students needed more personal experience, more action, more interest: "more of growth, less of absorption" [45].

In the same book, Woodward responded directly to an 1889 report on the "Educational Value of Manual Training" that Harris and three others had written. Woodward's detailed and impatient rebuttal suggests that the report's writers had spent little time actually visiting manual training schools or reviewing their curricula. Instead, they based their objections on the consequences to children who grew up without the benefit of even a rudimentary education—the direction in which they apparently thought manual training was moving the schools. Assuming that Woodward's charge about the report's inaccurate portrayal of manual training has some validity, the report hardly seems a credit to Harris. Again, quoting Cremin, Harris was "the great consolidator . . . who ultimately rationalized the institution of the public school."[94] But did he, in his concern for the soul of American society, fail to appreciate the needs of its individual bodies?

Coeducating Hands and Minds in Chicago

In a paper published in the *Educational Monograph* series edited by Nicholas Murray Butler at the New York College for the Training of Teachers, Charles Ham issued another indirect challenge to Harris's unfavorable conception of manual training. Called "The Co-education of Mind and Hand," it covers much the same ground as his 1886 book, but far more succinctly.[95] The new education is "the union of thought and action," Ham argued [121]. Beginning with Plato's disdain for manual labor and the useful arts, he claimed that it is through technology that civilization advances: the hand is "the mind's rudder, its balance-wheel" [122]; "the mind devises, and the hand executes" [125]; and "mental and manual combined is the most potent of educational forces" [130]. Rounding up Comenius, Pestalozzi, Ruskin, Spencer, and others in support of his points, Ham asserted that "industry, talent, and genius" are "the triple powers that move the modern world" [132] and that the workshop is as necessary to the common school as the laboratory is to the university [137]. It is "through the hand that man has spanned the great gulf between barbarism and civilization" [141]. Morality and character are both outcomes of this co-education; prisons are full of men who never learned to work. As the essay concludes: "there is but one high road to character—unselfish industry. Idleness is hideous; work is sublime" [150].

Instructed for nearly two decades by Ham's imprecations in the city's lecture halls and newspapers, Chicago's educators and philanthropists heeded his pleas. Though Ham moved to Washington, DC, in 1890, his influence continued. During the following decade, several manual training schools were established, many headed by men who echoed Ham's ideas. An 1891 newspaper article about them carries the subhead: "Importance of Reciprocity in Mental and Manual Studies Conclusively Established."[96] Featured in the article is the Jewish Manual Training School, located south of Hull

House and close to the famed Maxwell Street market of immigrant peddlers. Arriving as principal in 1890 was Gabriel Bamberger, brought by philanthropists from the Workingmen's School in New York. Soon after opening, the Chicago school had over a thousand students from kindergarten through eighth grade. According to the article, it was designed to inculcate "ideas of industry, morality, and cleanliness, and deportment." Its programs also included night classes for working adults in subjects such as bookkeeping and dressmaking, as well as "Americanization" and English as a foreign language. All might be considered courses for students who wanted to board the escalator mentioned by Laurie.

In 1892, meatpacker Philip Danforth Armour provided an endowment of $1.4 million for an Armour Institute, to be located near the stockyards, or about three miles south of Hull House. Through educating "head, hand, and heart," it aimed to be "the greatest institute for manual training, science, and art in the country." This would be a "school good enough for the richest" but would "reach out to the poorest," as well. Classes would not be free, but "affordable," and would welcome girls as well as boys with courses in drawing, "liberal culture," and domestic sciences.[97] As tuition at Armour Institute may have been half that of CMTS, it quickly offered substantial competition.[98]

In September 1896, yet another such school opened. Named Lewis Institute in honor of the man whose $1.6 million endowment made it possible, this was a secondary school and a junior college in one.[99] Located on the city's west side, it offered courses in science, technology, literature, and domestic economy.[100] In the spring of its first year, the institute's principal claimed it had "exceeded all expectations," welcoming seven hundred students in day and night programs. It aimed to provide a "broad foundation" for all students, because through "education for both trades and professions lies the solution to social discontent," he said, repeating a claim of Charles Ham.[101] Eventually, however, Lewis began to focus more on college-level academics than on manual training; it had several distinguished graduates over the next few decades—they would include musician Benny Goodman and noted journalist Arthur Krock.

The Chicago Public Schools' commitment to manual training continued. In 1897, the system's superintendent Albert Lane told a reporter that the city had fifteen centers teaching manual training, plus programs in grammar schools that together gave over six thousand students some manual training experience. Of the program's origin, he said: "Our object was to let the city trained boys discover that they had some ability and aptitude in this line." Though he noted that one of the programs' objectives was to help high school students find their way into "good paying positions," the schools' overall goal was "to train all the powers of the child and to develop his own special powers . . . so that he may know . . . what line of work to undertake."[102] Providing students with skills through which they could make their own decisions was the goal. At the normal school, which the city took over from the county that year, director Francis Parker, in the same article, agreed with Lane that the public school's priority was not to direct students into particular trades, but to teach them to do work: "Manual training assists a pupil greatly to find his particular vocation in life," Parker said.

Gabriel Bamberger, like his mentor Felix Adler in New York, took a broad, social view of his school's purpose. "The modern world forgets that labor with the hands is a blessing. We educate our children to be lawyers, doctors, bookkeepers, or clerks," thus ignoring the old maxim about honest labor being a blessing. "A large part of the unemployed today have not been trained to labor . . . and do not know how to do any kind of skilled work," Bamberger said. Instead, through the union of teaching and working, schools should teach children "to love work, to see the pleasure in it."

This mix of programs in Chicago—public and private, kindergarten through college—was representative of developments in manual training nationwide during the 1890s. Calvin Woodward's concept of a school that taught no trade but skills useful in all was likely more stringently followed in Chicago because of Charles Ham's influence; elsewhere, it was also applied to programs more puffery than structured pedagogy. Businessmen, Lawrence Cremin argued in summing up programs that were established around the county, wanted more trade training to free themselves from union-dominated apprenticeships; students on their part were less concerned about "dignifying manual labor" than about escaping it themselves through some "higher" calling.[103]

Ham, ever the enthusiast, claimed in 1900 that over the previous fifteen years, "a great wave of educational awakening [had] swept over the country." Led by reformers such as Chicago's Francis Parker and James MacAlister, who had moved on to become president of Philadelphia's Drexel Institute, the "new education" had become "an aggressive force openly demanding recognition." The victory, however, was not completely satisfactory.[104] Ham's tabulations indicate that seventy-two more cities had added manual training programs to their public high schools during the 1890s, bringing the total to 103.[105] Given that only 10 percent of the nation's six million youth ages fourteen to seventeen even attended high school, this was hardly the radical reform Ham had prophesied.[106] Further, even this had serious shortcomings as "the progress . . . has not been very satisfactory in quality."[107]

CMTS Loses Its Novelty and Its Backers

If Ham's observation was that manual training had not created an educational utopia nationwide by the century's turn, his friend Henry Belfield had more serious concerns on his mind during the 1890s; the combination of competition and continuing deficits forced him to redefine the school early in the decade, making its curriculum less the idealized mix of manual and mental lessons reinforcing each other. Though the March 1891 Chicago *Inter Ocean*'s lengthy feature about the city's manual training programs had lauded the "reciprocity in mental and manual studies," that claim proved increasingly aspirational as students and families actually reacted to it.[108] The decade began with enrollment at CMTS peaking at 339 for the 1891–1892 school year, but there was still considerable attrition: 156 students in the junior (or entering) class that year, 108 in the middle class, and 71 seniors; 68 students would actually graduate that spring; 2 received certificates.[109] Thus, half of the entering students dropped out before completing the program. CMTS first responded by offering a "preparatory" year in 1893, presumably so that it could continue keeping admission standards high without losing enrollment; the first year would provide better preparation for admission than the public schools were able to do. As noted, CMTS had begun to offer three separate programs: in technology, in business, and the third a standard secondary curriculum; Latin was added that fall as well.[110] In 1891, CMTS tuition had increased to $80, $100, and $120 per term, a substantial outlay when other manual training and college preparatory programs in the city were free.[111]

Newspaper notices about the school and its activities continued to decline in number and length during the decade; most announced scores of school teams—with alumni support, CMTS had joined area baseball and football leagues. In February 1894, the *Chicago Tribune*—a major backer while Charles Ham had promoted the manual training idea a decade earlier—ran a brief article about the school's tenth anniversary, which was celebrated with a talk by its early enthusiast Augustus Jacobson on the value of industrial training; his comments were echoed by two graduates. Belfield's remarks at the event advertised the value of a CMTS education: "The school was not designed to fit boys for the university, but to prepare them for active life. Its course of study, however, accomplishes both these results, since about two-fifths of the graduates continue their studies in higher institutions," the account recorded.[112] A 1927 study of the school summarized occupations for the class of 1893 as follows: one-third went immediately on to college, mainly to schools of technology; one-quarter were employed in technology-related work, as machinists, electricians, and draftsmen; another quarter were employed as clerks and salesmen. Very few went into the law, medicine, or teaching.[113]

In June 1894, CMTS graduated its largest class—sixty students. Commencement exercises included the annual tour for the public, which attracted one thousand people. For it, seventy-five students, dressed in overalls, demonstrated the carpentry and metal work they did.[114] One student project received considerable attention—a member of that graduating class had designed a tower clock, a complex piece of machinery that struck hours and quarter hours. Constructed by younger students in a metal-work class, it weighed 150 pounds.[115] The clock, which was also displayed in a major furniture manufacturer's showroom, was both a credit to the school and likely a disappointment. One report claimed that it was to be placed in a library endowed with a $440,000 gift from CMTS trustee John Crerar; his estate also gave the school the only endowment it was to have—$50,000, which it received in 1894. Crerar left similar amounts to several other institutions, including an orphan asylum and a training school for nurses.[116] On reading that, Belfield might have wished that Crerar had been more generous to CMTS; at any rate, a 1895 report stated that the clock would instead go into an addition to the CMTS building.[117]

That addition was never built. After 1894, the number of graduates decreased yearly, dropping to forty-eight in 1900.[118] CMTS faced considerable competition from schools that charged far less tuition. Though lingering effects of the 1894 depression meant that the public system opened no new programs, the ones already established were free. Belfield, who claimed that a great part of his school's early success was the freedom and independence with which he was able to operate, realized that, lacking an endowment, the school needed to affiliate with another institution. In the spring of 1896, he wrote to Blatchford, who still chaired his board of trustees. He described three alternatives: one, remaining independent wasn't really an option as the Commercial Club wanted to relieve itself of responsibility for the school; another was affiliation with the city system, which Belfield dismissed as "obnoxious" because of the city's politics; and the third was affiliation with the new University of Chicago.[119]

Fortunately for the Commercial Club, early in 1896, William Rainey Harper, the university's president, began courting CMTS and its assets, then $200,000 in property and facilities plus $50,000 in endowment. Harper did so thinking that the school could form the nucleus of a technology program at the University of Chicago.[120] Belfield's response was cautious; he urged Blatchford to hold the transfer until the university had actually established a school of technology.[121] But by May, the absorption had begun to take place. The university's trustees were concerned about whether they were obligated to maintain the school in its then-current form; Belfield had a similar concern, though his was to maintain the school's distinctiveness and independence.[122]

The acquisition was announced during the CMTS commencement ceremony in mid-June 1896. The *Tribune* report, titled "Harper's New Gift," stated that the Commercial Club felt the school's long-term interest would be best served by affiliation with a "permanent" institution, where it could "expand and grow to a larger usefulness." Harper announced the acquisition to university students at chapel service. "This is the beginning of our new department of technology," he was reported to have said. "The manual training school will be used as a preparatory school" for the new program. Until then, the "same curriculum will continue in use and the present corps of teachers will be retained."[123] CMTS would for the time remain in its building at Michigan Avenue; the formal transfer would take place a year later.

Neither institution got all of what it wanted, and the University of Chicago never started a school of technology or engineering. Hindsight, or fancy, suggests CMTS's fate might have been more secure had it been associated with another movement that captured the city's attention as the century turned—that of a multifaceted fascination with handicrafts. Influenced by Thomas Carlyle and John Ruskin, two of Ham's guides, the Arts and Crafts Movement, which in many ways complemented that of manual training, attracted considerable attention in Chicago. Given similarities of interest and attracting support from many of the same people, these two complementary movements had much to learn from each other. That did not happen, nor did any collaboration between Belfield and John Dewey, who in the summer of 1894 arrived in Chicago to join the faculty at Harper's university. The details of that missed opportunity add more drama to the oft-told tale of Dewey's decade in Chicago; they are the subject of the next chapter.

CHAPTER 3

Joining Hands and Heads on the Midway

> If [the past] were wholly gone and done with, there would be only one reasonable attitude toward it. Let the dead bury their dead. But knowledge of the past is key to understanding the present. . . . The true starting point of history is always some present situation with its problems.
> —John Dewey, *Democracy and Education*, 1916

The years between Henry Belfield's 1888 talk on manual training in the public schools and one John Dewey would give early in 1904 on the significance of the School of Education at the University of Chicago were years of promise, great accomplishment, and eventual disappointment for the educational institutions with which both are closely identified—Belfield's Chicago Manual Training School and Dewey's Laboratory School. In January of 1896, Dewey established what was to be one of the most noted educational ventures of his time; a year later, Belfield would see his once-lauded school absorbed into the University of Chicago and begin to lose its identity. Although both schools were rooted in the ideas of Comenius, Pestalozzi, and Froebel, neither the institutions nor the individuals involved were able to reinforce each other's considerable strengths and build a thriving institution that could outlast them. Why they found no common purpose is particularly intriguing because, a decade after he left Chicago, Dewey became a highly visible advocate for the sort of combined academic and industrial training program that Belfield had established. Adding intrigue to the flawed union of the two schools was the promise of another contemporary development, that of the Arts and Crafts Movement, which in Chicago got its start at Hull House in 1897, the year the university formally acquired the Chicago Manual Training School. Some enthusiasts for arts and crafts conceptualized a "new industrialism" to complement the new education both Dewey and Belfield were associated with. Its ideas, particularly as articulated by architect Frank Lloyd Wright, carried with them a potential for rejuvenating manual training; that, too, did not happen.

Chicago was, during these years, a hothouse for innovations in education. It had actually been so since the 1870s when some of the city's women of privilege had embraced the kindergarten movement. With the establishment of Dewey's school at the University of Chicago—on its own, a hothouse for intellectual ideas—the city became home to a real laboratory for the study of pedagogy. To adapt some of Dewey's own words, at his school, students were guided to blaze their own trail through the subject matter; other programs, according to Dewey, tended to provide a map, with the routes already marked out. The curriculum dreamt of by Charles Ham and implemented by Henry Belfield was of the latter type. Belfield may never have appreciated this difference, and Dewey—already taxed by administrative duties for which he was ill-suited—lacked the patience to explain.

The tale of Dewey's abrupt departure from Chicago in 1904 has often been told, but considering it in light of his apparent neglect of a distinctive manual training school, and of the union between art and labor imagined by proponents of arts and crafts, adds a new dimension to the story. So, too, does the latter's campaign for a "new industrialism," which added the idea of agency—or self-fulfillment—to the necessity for earning a living. This chapter explores those connections.

The years of Dewey's work in Chicago were momentous for the city as well. Though the decade of the 1890s ended Chicago's role as Donald Miller's *City of the Century*, it began a period that another writer dubbed the "Chicagoization of America": institutions and ideas about them generated in Chicago—social welfare, publishing, education, juvenile justice, professional organizations, architecture and city planning—came to define twentieth century urban America, he argued.[1] The city continued to grow, incorporating neighboring communities in 1889 that doubled its size, including the once-suburban village of Hyde Park where the university would be located. Writers Eugene Field and Finley Peter Dunne began newspaper columns in the language of ordinary people and thus established Chicago as a center for vernacular journalism and a distinctive literary style. Reformers took on crooks and politicians, often one and the same. The Democratic national convention of 1896—held in the Chicago Coliseum a few blocks from the Manual Training School building—wrested control of the party from an Eastern elite, empowering immigrants and farmers and workers in a new political consensus. Dewey and his colleague Ella Flagg Young, soon to be called the city's "education stateswoman," articulated the democratization of education; she demonstrated it in her managerial style. The companies known as Sears Roebuck and Montgomery Ward democratized merchandizing, aided by the railroads that spread goods and produce throughout the nation. Chicago was, as it would later be romanticized by poet Carl Sandburg, the "stormy, husky, brawling, City of the Big Shoulders."

The new University of Chicago, rising along the Midway left by the Columbian Exposition, was to be an urban university, engaged with the challenge of defining the urban culture the city and the nation were rapidly developing. Fundraising for it began in 1890, aided not only by John D. Rockefeller's endowment but by Marshall Field's gift of land on which its Hyde Park campus would be built.[2] Led by the indefatigable William Rainey Harper, whose astonishing career had begun only fifteen years earlier as a twenty-year-old PhD and professor of Hebrew, the university officially opened in 1892. Intent on building a university that would quickly rival leading institutions in the United States and in Europe, Harper attracted a host of the nation's leading scientists, philosophers, and humanists who would establish new fields such as sociology and the "science" of pedagogy. Among them was John Dewey, who at only thirty-five had already made a name for himself; he arrived in Chicago during the summer of 1894 to head the university's new department of philosophy, psychology, and pedagogy. The mark that his ideas, and how they were actualized into actions and institutions, would make on the city and on the nation's schools for the next century and beyond has seldom been rivalled.

A Hothouse for Innovations in Education

If the manual training movement was an initial step in defining the "new education," a book published a year before Dewey's arrival in Chicago had brought considerable attention to the deficiencies of the "old education." Written by a young physician turned muckraking journalist named Joseph Mayer Rice, the book offered a tour of the nation's schools that found them seriously wanting: instruction was heartlessly mechanical and delivered by ill-prepared teachers, discipline was harsh and arbitrary, corruption and favoritism ruled boards of education. Published initially as a series of articles in an influential reform-minded periodical called *The Forum*, Rice's criticisms appeared as a book in 1893. They attracted a great deal of attention as well as negative feedback—the author was a reformer with an agenda. His report focused on abuses and thus supported his allies' goal of ridding the nation's schools of political meddling.[3] One of the few schools that did merit praise from Rice was the practice program of the Cook County Normal School headed by the charismatic Francis W. Parker. It approached an "educational ideal" in part because its teachers conducted their work "on purely psychological principles" that inspired both pupils in the model school and the normal students who did their practice teaching there. In its science program, young pupils worked in a garden to observe how plants grew, along with absorbing other lessons about botany, chemistry, and geology.[4] When, in 1895, Dewey's family joined him in Chicago, two of his children attended Parker's model school.

John Dewey was very much the sort of rising eminence President Harper was attracting to the campus rising on the Midway. Born in 1859 in Burlington, Vermont, Dewey had attended school there, then taught high school for two years in Pennsylvania prior to enrolling in a graduate program at Johns Hopkins University in Baltimore. His friendship there with leading Hegelian George Sylvester Morris led to his joining his mentor on the faculty at the University of Michigan. While in Ann Arbor, he became involved in assessing high schools in the state, determining whether or not their programs were sufficiently strong to merit their graduates' admission to the university; this along with becoming a parent himself after marrying the vigorous and intellectually gifted Alice Chipman in 1886 led to his growing interest in education.[5]

While teaching high school, Dewey had determined, according to one of his friends, that his "life task" was "reconciling ethics with physiology," or the moral with the material sciences. As a graduate student, he found Hegelian metaphysics gave him a sense of "unity, of things flowing together." But, the friend continued, his work at Michigan, and interacting with people who were not philosophers, had led Dewey to become more interested in what he called "instrumental logic"—the means by which people think out ways of getting what they want. And thus, "the problems of philosophy [became] thoroughly mixed up in his mind with the problems of education." His wrestling with these issues, combined with a facility for getting his thoughts onto paper and into print, led to numerous publications and, because of his growing following, an ability to go after what he wanted from President Harper.[6] Among those requests were invitations for two colleagues, one from Michigan and the other from Minnesota, to join Dewey. Thus, with others on the Hyde Park faculty, they constituted a group widely thought to be the most brilliant assemblage of pioneering scientists and humanists ever gathered at a new university.[7]

The city was, during Dewey's years in Chicago, not only a hothouse for educational ideas, it also stirred controversies. Harper ran the university as an aggressive entrepreneur but, in the minds of some, was attempting to impose his management prowess on the city's public-school system as well. He served on the board of education from 1896 until 1898, after which time he was appointed to education commissions run by federations that wanted to address the problems raised in Rice's book. One, organized by Chicago's mayor with support from the city council, spent a year doing research, consulting with other university presidents but with few if any actual teachers. It sought to remove the schools from political control and to centralize authority in the office of superintendent. Known as the Harper Report, it was not popular and was widely dismissed as "elitist" by parents and others most directly involved with the schools. Numerous efforts to turn its recommendations into state law failed over the next decade.[8]

Though Belfield had been among Chicago's most noted educators prior to the arrival of Harper and Dewey, his fame was eclipsed by that of those more visible personalities during the 1890s. E. W. Blatchford, long supportive of the Chicago Manual Training School, had turned his attention to establishing the Newberry Library, though he did speak at the school's 1897 commencement, along with the university's pioneering sociologist Albion Small.[9] Belfield, in acquiescing to his school being acquired by the university, hoped it might result in the needed endowment. That did happen, but only indirectly and not until 1901; by that time, it was of little benefit to maintaining his school's distinction. Until the century's turn, Belfield was able to operate CMTS with relative freedom, meeting only occasionally with Harper and the university comptroller. In June 1897, Harper asked Belfield to attend the university's commencement ceremony; when the school director told the university president that he lacked an academic gown, the latter found one to lend him.[10] At some point during that year, Belfield and his wife journeyed out to Pasadena, California, home to the recently established Throop School of Technology. He was offered its presidency, but declined, a decision he said later that he came to regret.[11] Two decades later, the Pasadena school would evolve into the California Institute of Technology.

Francis Parker, another of Chicago's noted educators during the 1880s, also felt threatened during the 1890s, if for different reasons. The Cook County Normal School he had made famous ran afoul of those who regarded adequate training for schoolteachers an expensive indulgence. Beginning in 1894, the county government wanted to close the school, arguing that it was paying for education the city's teachers did not need. The Chicago board of education was urged to take it over, but some of its members also objected, not only to the normal school's necessity but to Parker's charisma and independence. Parker called on influential friends to urge the transfer from county to city; among them was John Dewey who defended him in a published letter. "I do not believe there is a single step which would do as much for Chicago's schools," Dewey wrote late in 1895. The city should take advantage of this opportunity "in the line of progress." Not to do so would "take a step backward educationally."[12]

Among Parker's influential friends was Anita McCormick Blaine, an heir to the farm equipment fortune and the widowed mother of a boy enrolled during 1896 at the normal school's model kindergarten. She was to play a pivotal role in the fate of all three schools—that of Parker's normal school, Belfield's CMTS, and Dewey's laboratory. In 1898, she served on an education committee along with Harper, which resulted in her committing to a $5,000 annual donation to support a college for teachers under the university's umbrella.[13] With additional donations, this became an extension program located in the Fine Arts Building on Michigan Avenue in downtown Chicago.[14] Though she had chosen Parker's model school for her son over Dewey's school in the fall of 1896, Blaine was attracted to Dewey's experiment as well, and in April of 1899, she hosted a series of lectures he gave. These became the first three chapters of *The School and Society*, which has remained in print since its initial publication in 1900.[15] That year, Blaine also underwrote the establishment of a school for Parker, where he could continue to do his work, free from harassment by the city's board of education. In 1900, this became the Chicago Institute. Founded as both a teacher training and a practice school, it initially operated out of rented space on the city's North Side while Blaine's trustees tried to rein in some of Parker's expensive plans. In 1901, the trustees would be "rescued" from these by President Harper, who proposed that the institute instead be established, with Blaine's money, under the university's umbrella.[16]

A Laboratory for the Study of Pedagogy

Even before he hired Dewey to head a department that was to include pedagogy on the same plane as philosophy, Harper had been interested in establishing a graduate school of education. The 1894–1895 *University Register* listed this, describing as its aim "to train competent specialists for the broad and scientific treatment of educational problems." Dewey's program would be concerned with inquiry; it would offer advanced courses to people who had already established themselves as leaders of school systems. Essential to the education theory to be studied as philosophy and psychology was a pedagogical laboratory where these principles could be tested and demonstrated. This laboratory was to bear the same relationship to the pedagogical work as similar laboratories did to biology, physics, and chemistry.[17]

In January of 1896, the University Elementary School was established as an adjunct to Dewey's department. Somewhat grudgingly, Harper and the university trustees agreed to subsidize it with a grant of $2,500, an amount that was never adequate; thus, a parents' association agreed to contribute whatever was needed to keep the school going. It was an experiment upon which "more eyes were fixed" than upon any other elementary school in the county, according to a history of the university's first decade.[18] Largely unexplored in the numerous books and articles about the school in the decades since its establishment is whether it bore a resemblance to the laboratory workshops that had attracted similar attention when John Runkle and Calvin Woodward first promoted their manual training programs nearly twenty years earlier.[19] They had used the same rationale in arguing for their programs: they were to be laboratories for instructing students in tool use. Dewey's experiment also shared commonalities with the workshops Charles Ham had conceptualized and Henry Belfield established at the Chicago Manual Training School. Whether Dewey himself ever made the connection is not known, and Ham was no longer in Chicago to make a connection for him.

This pedagogical laboratory school also shared guiding principles with other contemporary proposals. Seeming almost to anticipate ideas with which Dewey and his faculty would experiment, Nicholas Murray Butler in his 1887 *Argument for Manual Training* had pointed to the "unity of principle" under the kindergarten and the manual training school: "both recognized the manual and expressive powers as well as the [receptive] and assimilative powers," he claimed. Remaining to be decided was "whether for some peculiar reason it could not be applied" in the primary and grammar school.[20] The Dewey school can be viewed as an experiment that aimed to accomplish that purpose.

At the time he wrote his *Argument*, Butler was moving what had been a philanthropic kindergarten program—the Kitchen Garden Association—into being a teacher preparation program. In starting his talk, Butler had noted the work of Comenius "to proscribe manual training as part of the curriculum" and that of Rousseau, who saw the value of manual training's "influence on the growth of the pupil, mental as well as physical."[21] The Dewey school, "or the 'Do-y School,'" his friend Max Eastman noted, had as a "chief slogan" to "learn by doing,"[22] which echoed the dictum of Comenius: "Let those things that have to be done be learned by doing them." What worried Dewey, according to teachers who worked with him, was the increasing gap between "the capacities of the child and the information of the adult." In their world then, experience in a traditional school alone, they claimed, could not fill this gap: "Learning was then being more and more divorced from doing."[23]

The most exhaustive history of the school Dewey established in 1896 was written by two of those dedicated teachers, the Camp sisters, Katherine and Anna, more commonly known by their married names: Mayhew and Edwards. Though not published until thirty years after the school as an experimental laboratory had ended, the book offers not only their memories, but quantities of documents written at the time, plus comments Dewey wrote to accompany its publication. Growth for all involved, pupils as well as teachers, was one of the fundamental ideas underlying the school, Mayhew and Edwards wrote in their preface. Dewey, in his introduction, said the same: "The school whose work is reported in this volume was animated by a desire to discover in administration, selection of subject-matter, methods of learning, teaching, and discipline how a school could become a cooperative community while developing in individuals their own capacities and satisfying their own needs," their own growth.[24]

In their "General History" of the school, the authors noted that it was an "undertaking" that aimed to work out a school system as "an organic whole from the kindergarten to the university" and that it was to be a "laboratory" for the departments of philosophy, psychology, and education that "bore the same relation" as did a laboratory for departments in the sciences. It would exhibit and verify theoretical statements and principles as well as add to their sum [3].[25] The core of school activities, as Dewey explained in his own words, "was to be found in occupations, rather than in what are conventionally called studies." The idea of occupations, representing in some ways the collective intelligence of mankind, was selected because, through them, "education could prepare the young for the future social life" and they could do so "only when the school was itself a cooperative society on a small scale"[5]. Dewey's argument for this choice of occupations somewhat resembles the arguments Ham devised to support his concept of manual training—the essential skills the curriculum was to impart were taught along with the life work of the scientists and inventors responsible for each technological leap. History, Dewey wrote, was an "extension of the process of human invention and integration." The "controlling aim of the school, "was to discover and apply the principles" and to "utilize the methods by which mankind has collectively and progressively advanced in skill, understanding, and associative life" [6].

Though Dewey wrote these words forty years after establishing his experimental school, the similarity between them and those of Charles Ham's ideal manual training curriculum, articulated along with his history of technology in 1886, suggests a need for examination.[26] Though the Dewey school was the first time the ideas and principles advocated by Ham and Butler, and earlier by Runkle and Woodward, had been systematically implemented and recorded in an actual school for elementary students, these efforts were not wholly without precedent. Similar ideas had influenced the curriculum James MacAlister had endeavored to implement in the Philadelphia public schools during the 1880s (these were described in chapter 2). That the Dewey school's curriculum was based on occupations—as

Ham's was as well—is credited to graduate students in a seminar Dewey taught during the 1896–1897 school year. It was a course in logical theory, and the students—like many of those attracted to Dewey's program at the university—were practicing professionals; both worked in the child study department of the Chicago Public Schools. Though there is no record of a connection, both men may well have known of Ham's book as well as of the Chicago Manual Training School and all the attention it had received in the previous decade.[27]

Adding support to the suggestion that Dewey may have known something of Ham's work is a comment in a lecture on the social significance of the laboratory school courses, given in March 1902. The study of industries, he said, can be a great deal more than just manual labor: "They can be made to teach a broader view of the evolution of civilization down the avenues of history." Students can be made to trace steps in the evolution of machines and the power to run them.[28] This was the fundamental purpose of Ham's 1886 book.

That said, the differences were even more significant. *The Dewey School* notes that the early new educators recognized that the traditional "Three R's" alone could not educate a child, so they added content like nature study, geography, and manual training to an already overburdened curriculum; these threatened to swamp the students who were their chief concern. Then along came Dewey "with his new vision of the school" as a "social environment" that gave "continuity and direction" to school activities. His ideal viewed education as "*a freeing of individual capacity in a progressive growth directed to social aims*" (italics in original). The school became "intermediary between the home and the community"; thus, the fundamental "activities of the home" became the "activities of the school" and were ever widened out to the community. Students did "things to and with others" for a purpose they understood and thus did willingly. The "by-product" was "*the development by the child of his own method of learning*" (italics in original).[29]

So, though there was a shared focus on occupations and manual activities, the curricula of Charles Ham and Calvin Woodward lacked fundamental aspects of Dewey's program—both the social aims of the school and the emphasis on self-initiated activity. Another difference was in their conceptions of "harmony." This idea was significant to advocates of manual training, but they conceived it as the harmonious development of all the student's powers: emotional, intellectual, moral, and physical. Dewey recognized this difference; to him, the educational problem was "the harmonizing of individual traits with social ends."[30] (Dewey failed to include the physical powers, or manual skills, so important to manual training advocates, but that omission was likely accidental.)

During the first year of the University Elementary School, Dewey produced both "The Reflex Arc Concept in Psychology" and "Interest in Relation to Training of the Will," articles that provided psychological foundations for his experiment in education.[31] In January 1897, after the school had been in existence for a year, "My Pedagogic Creed" appeared, laying out Dewey's understandings about education, subject matter, method, schools and social progress,[32] topics he would take up in greater detail two years later in *The School and Society*. The significance of these articles, in comparing his pedagogical laboratory with the ideas behind manual training, is best approached by a comment Dewey made in describing the theory behind his "Chicago experiment" in the Mayhew and Edwards book. Referring indirectly to himself, he wrote that as the "head" of that school "was trained in philosophy and psychology, the work of the school had a definite relation in its original conception to a certain body of philosophical and psychological conception." His goal was an "underlying theory of knowledge" and the "necessity of testing thought by action,"[33] an aim that did not enter directly into the conceptions of Ham and Belfield.

Dewey's quest was dependent upon advances in psychology that were only discovered or widely known after the initial manual training curricula were devised—the word "psychology" does not even appear in the extensive index to Ham's 1886 book. For Dewey, the complex relationship between sensory impulses and resulting actions became the core of the theory of knowledge he was after; his "reflex arc" article was the "key to his thought" about the school, claimed an eminent historian of this effort.[34] Dewey's article, which built upon then-recent work done by pioneers of experimental psychology working mainly in Germany, took issue with the idea that a sensory stimulus resulted directly in a motor action. The theory of the reflex arc—or this led to that in a linear fashion—Dewey, claimed, had no "organic unity"; it "breaks continuity and leaves us nothing but a series of jerks." In his article, Dewey expanded on the understanding of the famous experiment in which a small child sees a lighted candle, touches it, is burned, and removes its hand. The experience for the child, Dewey argued, begins not with reaching for the candle but in looking; only then can it see the light. The hand's movement depends upon how well it is controlled by vision—the eye must be kept on the candle if the hand is to do its work. If the child is to learn from the experience of being burned—the reflex arc—it must retain the memory of the vision not just the sensation of being burned.[35] From this, Dewey theorized, the acquisition of knowledge is a circular process, which he termed "co-ordination" and became known as the organic circuit process.[36] Education for Dewey, as Mayhew and Edwards claimed, is a "continuous process" in which the individual "obtains a wider command of body and environment as tools of thought. . . . one experience acts in reference to another" leading to "an increase in the complexity of the activity." This is the fundamental way of growth, of education, at all stages of life.[37]

In his 1902 essay "The Child and the Curriculum," Dewey distinguished between the "logical and psychological aspects of education," which he also referred to in his theory of the Chicago experiment: the logical is the subject matter itself; the psychological its relation to the child. He then compared these to the "difference between the notes which an explorer makes in a new country, blazing a trail and finding his way"—this is the psychological, or subject matter as the child sees it—and "the finished map that is constructed after the country has been thoroughly explored." The trail is the child's journey when exposed to the subject matter—or, what Dewey and his colleagues aimed to discover in their pedagogical laboratory.[38] The map, in the construction provided here, is what Ham in theory and Belfield in practice offered in their manual training program. It was a top-down curricula—these are the seven basic tools and this is the process by which students can be taught to use them proficiently. Self-activity—students blazing their own trail through the subject matter—was essential to Dewey's concept of education, but it did not play a role in the curricula implemented by manual training enthusiasts.

Interaction and Ambivalence

If Dewey and Belfield had any significant interaction with each other between July 1897, when the university absorbed the Chicago Manual Training School, and 1901 when the latter came directly under Dewey's supervision, it is not evident in readily available historical records. Belfield makes no mention of Dewey or of the University Elementary School, and the one thesis undertaken to investigate the connection was unable to find any substantial interaction between them.[39] If Belfield saw a connection between his efforts and those of Dewey, he did not mention it in his Autobiographical Writings, nor do his family papers suggest that he saw one.[40] Similarly, Dewey made almost no mention of Belfield.[41] However, reports and articles Dewey wrote during this period indicate that he had a solid understanding of the movement's aims and principles.

In an 1897 report Dewey wrote of the "great importance attached to manual training" because through hands and eyes, children become familiar with the "materials and processes of ordinary life." Further, manual training cultivates "habits of industry and continuity . . . personal deftness and dexterity"; cooking, sewing, and carpentry were all valuable because they contributed to a study of materials and invention, history and geography, and numerical processes.⁴² These, he noted elsewhere, were principles established "a generation ago." However, manual training was never employed at the Laboratory School simply to teach children the use of tools: shop work had to be correlated with other studies as an integral part of the curriculum.⁴³ The director of the school's workshop, a man named Frank Ball, augmented this point: some manual-training teachers criticized the idea that all shop work be integrated into other studies: "They say that manual training loses its dignity" if treated as "subordinate" to other studies. Not so, Ball wrote, it is part of the child's education, and "by working in harmony with other departments, it becomes more so."⁴⁴

In another report that year, Dewey addressed a challenge Belfield mentioned frequently—the difficulty of finding manual training teachers equipped both to offer instruction in a particular skill and to do so in a pedagogically sound manner.⁴⁵ Dewey hoped that a solid relationship with CMTS might accomplish this:

> When the Manual Training School is definitely annexed to the University, and its location changed so as to be sufficiently in close contact with University work, it would be highly desirable to have it include special courses for training teachers in the direction of manual training. The introduction of this line of work in the public schools is hindered now more by the lack of properly training teachers than by any other thing.⁴⁶

He went on to note that the Training School for Teachers in New York—which had become Teachers College a few years earlier—was "the only college of rank now making this a specialty."⁴⁷

Despite his sympathy with the aims of manual training, some of Dewey's comments suggest that he had an ambivalent relationship with the movement, or with some of its advocates—and perhaps they with him. In October of 1899, the University of Chicago Press—publisher of *School and Society* and other works by Dewey—began to publish *Manual Training Magazine*, edited by Charles A. Bennett who would later write comprehensive histories of the movement. Dewey provided an article for the second volume, and he wrote about manual training's place in the elementary school. He offered theory, not practice—stating that psychology had made it unnecessary to defend the idea that hand and eye coordination contributed to training attention and imagination; learning to use tools thus was not an end in itself but a means to other ends. Tools are "agencies through which the child may be initiated into . . . the methods by which man gains control of nature." This "constructive activity" is useful in the extent to which it furthers the school's social aims.⁴⁸ Supporters of the magazine, its masthead claimed, included Belfield,

Calvin Woodward, and Charles Richards, who originated the course for manual training teachers at Teachers College noted above.[49]

Dewey's interest in manual training thus was as a means to the more substantive work of schooling—its social purpose. He also regarded it as an aspect of primary and elementary education more than of secondary; in this capacity it filled the gap between kindergarten and the manual training high school that Butler mentioned, that Woodward and others had asked for over the previous twenty years. Despite this, neither Dewey nor his school received a mention in the 1900 edition of Ham's book. A chapter titled "Progress of the New Education—1883–1898" makes no note of either, though it does mention MacAlister in Philadelphia and Francis Parker, plus it commends aspects of the "new education" such as its great usefulness in fostering greater equality among peoples. In addition, Parker wrote an introduction; in it, he mentioned Ham's contribution to furthering the establishment of other manual training schools in Chicago, such as the Lewis and Armour institutes and the Jewish Manual Training School, the latter two of which welcomed elementary-grade students. Ham's extensive appendices—a forty-page compilation of manual training programs, at all levels, public and private, in the United States and Europe—lists CMTS, Armour, Lewis, and three other schools in Chicago, including one at Hull House, but not the Dewey school by any of its names.[50] Given the thoroughness of Ham's compilations, this omission suggests questions no longer answerable.

Though Ham was working in Washington, DC, during the 1890s, he remained sufficiently in communication with past colleagues in Chicago that some information about the purpose and practices of Dewey's experimental school must have reached him. Perhaps its connection to manual training or its stability seemed too tenuous in 1899 when the appendix was being compiled. Leaving other possible reasons for the omission of Dewey's laboratory school aside, the latter's foundation was far more fully rooted in the relatively new science of psychology than was CMTS. Dewey's 1897 article "Ethical Principles Underlying Education" clarifies this. This, along with Dewey's other pieces that articulate what was fundamentally new about how he saw schooling in the life of the child and in society as a whole, suggests that he was grappling with questions that had not drawn the same amount of attention from either Ham or Belfield. CMTS was dedicated to providing an education that enabled young men to be productive citizens; for Dewey, that was insufficient. School, he claimed, "must be itself made into a vital social institution to a very much greater extent than obtains at present." And, he continued, it "cannot be a preparation for social life," because the "only way to prepare for social life is to engage in social life."[51] For Belfield and perhaps for Ham, schooling was preparation; the former's actions may have suggested that his understanding went beyond that, but not his writings.

Though it is evident that Dewey well understood the manual training movement, his brief mention of CMTS in his 1904 "Significance of the Chicago School of Education" suggests that he may have regarded its future role as more a school of technology, which is how Harper sold acquiring CMTS to his board of trustees. Whatever their differences were, it seems evident that Dewey and Belfield made no effort to work them out either before or after CMTS came directly under the former's administrative responsibilities in 1901.

During the late 1890s, as Dewey's influence was growing and Belfield's retreating, another notable movement got underway in Chicago—that of arts and crafts, which aimed at beautifying living spaces and humanizing workplaces. In June of 1897, just as CMTS was being formally absorbed into the university, a lengthy article titled "The Workshop" appeared in the *Chicago Inter Ocean*. It carried no byline, but its writer was familiar with the ideals of arts and crafts and made a clear connection between them and manual training. Beginning with a mention of the movement's English roots, the article claimed that it aimed to "join art and labor, to add pleasure to things of common use" while making sure that all men had work to do that was "neither wearisome nor overanxious." A "number of prominent Chicagoans" were looking into these ideas and wondering whether, given the many unemployed, then would be an "opportune time . . . for a trial of the guild workshops" advocated by the movement's English founders.[52]

Among the "prominent Chicagoans" interested in the movement was "Miss Ellen [Gates] Starr," widely known as the co-founder with Jane Addams of Hull House. Her interest was in "urging the application of art to industry" so that workers could bring art and design back into their work, attributes thought to have been pushed out by the factory system.[53] Later that year, Starr left Hull House to study bookbinding with one of the English masters, and her involvement with Hull House diminished, though she and Addams remained friends.[54] Among other noted Chicagoans quoted in the article were heads of several manual training schools—Gabriel Bamberger at the Jewish Manual Training School, the head of Armour Institute, Francis Parker, and Henry Belfield. Their comments all related to labor and manual training, not to handicrafts, which suggests that the connection was more an assumption of the writer than of those being interviewed, though in the case of Bamberger, it soon became evident.

That Dewey saw connections between the handwork done at the Laboratory School—which included sewing and carpentry, carding and spinning—and the movement for incorporating more arts and crafts into both labor and learning is conjectural but highly likely. A history of the movement claims that soon after its opening, his school "introduced arts and crafts" as an aspect of learning by doing; such parallel developments were inevitable.[55] Dewey did mention William Morris, one of its English founders, in an 1891 article, and sometime after 1902 he visited the Byrdcliffe colony in New York, which had been established by followers of Morris and John Ruskin, but neither represents a substantive connection.[56] In the fall 1897, the Chicago Arts and Crafts Society was organized at Hull House, perhaps in conjunction with a manual training program there; its first head, a man named George Twose, taught manual training in the Chicago Public Schools as well as woodworking at Hull House.[57] Jane Addams was a charter member of the society, and her friend John Dewey, as a frequent Hull House visitor, had to have been aware of it, as it rapidly attracted adherents.

Belfield's connection with arts and crafts is more conjectural, though also likely. A study of the origins of the manual training program in Toledo, which Belfield helped inaugurate in 1885, claims that manual training, by the century's turn, represented the "democratization of the Arts and Crafts Movement." Instructors in the Toledo program "clearly articulated" the connection between the two movements; their program would unite arts and craftsmanship to "create a demand for good things on the part of the public."[58] Whether direct or peripheral, the two movements thrived on many of the same ideas and appealed to many of the same people, particularly in Chicago. Advocates of the arts and crafts felt their priorities could revitalize the manual training movement—and they had novel means in mind to do so.

The New Education Meets the New Industrialism

Gracing the cover of a 1902 booklet called *The New Industrialism* is a woodcut of three flowers printed in a warm red and surrounded by three words: Labor, Art, Education. Evoking both its time and its topics, the woodcut was likely produced by a Chicago Arts and Crafts Society member, perhaps in a Hull House workshop. If, during the 1880s, manual training was an essential aspect of the new education that added handwork to head work in many of the nation's schools, as the nineteenth century turned into the twentieth arts and crafts emerged as a movement intended to fundamentally alter how both kinds of work were done. Adherents called this the "new industrialism." Through schools started by Parker, Belfield, Dewey, by kindergartner Elizabeth Harrison, and by Gabriel Bamberger, Chicago was a center for the new education; through the Arts and Crafts Society and an Industrial Art League, the city played host to proponents of the new industrialism. Though the new education did fundamentally alter schooling in the new century, the new industrialism failed to outlive its advocates. But as a set of social reforms that anticipated a new relationship between work and workers, it sought to deliver benefits of the manual training movement to the nation's labor force. Contents of *The New Industrialism* booklet covered "Labor" through remarks by Oscar Lovell Triggs, founder of the Industrial Art League; "Art" broadly conceived in those by architect Frank Lloyd Wright; and "Education" in those of Wilbur Jackman, a colleague of Parker and eventually of Dewey at the University of Chicago. The three talks, set in their Chicago context, describe how the new industrialism would have reconceptualized art and labor through education.[59]

In *Art and Labor: Ruskin, Morris, and the Craftsman Ideal in America,* historian Eileen Boris claims that Chicago had "the largest number of groups claiming allegiance to the example of Ruskin and Morris" and that the city "exemplified the diversity of the craftsman ideal."[60] John Ruskin, the mid-nineteenth century English Romantic writer and social critic credited with articulating the enthusiasms that brought arts and crafts as a set of aesthetic ideas into being, was for Charles Ham a source for his conception of the brain's dependence on the hands. "It is through the hand alone that ideas are realized into things," Ham wrote, crediting a comment Ruskin made in one of his essays that the "lips of man" could never teach a youth to "lay a brick level to its mortar."[61] William Morris, the English designer in whose workshops Ruskin's aesthetics took physical form as patterns (wallpaper and textiles) and print (*The New Industrialism* cover woodcut is Morrisonian), was not yet widely known in America while Ham was promoting his version of the new education. Boris argues that Morris "elaborated upon, and ultimately transformed Ruskin's views," especially those on the "interdependence of art and labor" and how both were related to the "overall state of society."[62] Impressed by his vision of how work was done in medieval guilds, Morris saw them a providing a model for a new economic system that would reform both the individual and the social order—this was the guild ideal noted in the 1897 *Inter Ocean* article.

In the 1890s, these ideas attracted many at Hull House and at the University of Chicago. The two, essential manifestations of Progressive Era Chicago, harbored adherents of what Boris described as the two segments of "art" and "craft" as the ideas of Ruskin and Morris were established in America. "[O]ne segment of the movement focused on transforming labor and the other on transforming taste," Boris wrote. The movement "articulated a vision of art related to labor that promised an alternative—perhaps even an oppositional—model of society."[63] Though the movement in the United States was not closely tied to labor or socialist movements as it was in Great Britain, it was represented on the western shore of the Atlantic in at least two forms—one that of Boston, which Boris described as "Brahmin" and having more to do with taste and exalting craftsmanship than with social reform, and that of Chicago. The city was, she claimed, still young and brash; Morris enthusiasts such as Oscar Triggs regarded arts and crafts as a means of transforming society; the social scientists and reformers affiliated with Hull House and the university found it "an appropriate aesthetic for their new order rather than a means in itself to achieve industrial democracy and social betterment."[64] The great success of the World's Columbian Exhibition of 1893—symbolized not only by the "Great White City" of neoclassical architecture on the shore of Lake Michigan but by George Washington Gale Ferris's famed wheel on the Midway—confirmed the city's sense of its own possibilities.

The Chicago Arts and Crafts Society grew out of an exhibition at Hull House in the spring of 1897. Early members, in addition to Addams and Starr, were the reform-minded writer (and friend of Charles Ham) Henry Demarest Lloyd, architects such as Wright and others associated with the developing Prairie School style, artists and professors, plus wealthy supporters with famous names like Buckingham and McCormick. Mainly given to sponsoring exhibitions, lectures, and classes, the group's constitution "embodied the crusading zeal of the social settlement," according to Boris. Its membership grew quickly; its projects included the social surveys and housing reform programs associated with Hull House, some in connection with the Chicago Architectural Club.[65]

More closely related to the new industrialism was an organization that shared both concerns and members with the Arts and Crafts Society. Organized in 1899, the Industrial Art League was a particular project of Oscar Lovell Triggs, a popular young lecturer in the University of Chicago's extension program. A Minnesota native, he had acquired a doctorate at Oxford University before coming to Chicago.[66] A compelling and complex man, Triggs was a Morris enthusiast and tireless promoter of associating art and labor, to which cause the league was dedicated. In addition to teaching, Triggs wrote numerous articles, compiled a history of the Arts and Crafts Movement, and attempted to build an experimental center for industrial arts under the auspices of the league. Given his known socialist inclinations, it is interesting that Triggs was able to find supporters of the league in Chicago's elite. Among them were lawyer and gentleman farmer Frank Lowden, son-in-law of the Manual Training School trustee George Pullman; later (1917–1921), he was governor of Illinois. Others included real estate magnate Potter Palmer, whose wife Bertha Honoré Palmer was responsible for the Women's Building at the Columbian Exposition and would later be known for her discerning collection of Impressionist art. University of Chicago president William Rainey Harper was on the board, as were progressive rabbi Emil Hirsch and Gabriel Bamberger of Chicago's Jewish Manual Training School. Architects Wright and Louis Sullivan and others, plus booksellers and publishers, also lent their names if not their time to the organization. The league sponsored lectures and exhibitions, plus, in 1902, a national conference on industrial art and education.[67]

Also on the board was Margaret Warren Springer, president of the Illinois chapter of a then-new organization called the Daughters of the American Revolution (DAR), which sponsored *The New Industrialism* and a series of lectures, of which those by Triggs, Jackman, and Wright were only three. Other speakers in the series, given between October 1901 and April 1902, included Wright's uncle Jenkin Lloyd Jones on Ibsen, Jane Addams on the "newer ideals of peace," and sociologist Albion Small on the coming society. The talks were given in the Fine Arts Building, an elegant remnant of the era that still stands on Michigan Avenue two blocks south of Symphony Hall. Triggs's talk "Industrial Art," the second in the series, followed another on the U.S. Constitution. His talk addressed three questions: what industrial art is, what it means, and where it is headed.[68] Delivered a dozen years after the two contrasting talks on the manual training movement—those by Nicholas Murray Butler and William Torrey Harris—Triggs's comments relate manual training to industrial art and suggest where the latter might be leading the former.[69]

Declaring that the "question of art is a social question," Triggs began with an extensive passage from Thomas Carlyle, father to the ideas that led Ruskin and Morris to establish arts and crafts as a significant social as well as aesthetic movement. A British historian and essayist a generation older than Ruskin, Carlyle held views on serfdom and democracy that today sound abhorrent, but he also romanticized the ideas about the work one is to do in the world that led Addams to establish Hull House.[70] The son of a cleric, Carlyle, unlike Ruskin and Morris, actually did have to work for his living, which he was able to do though his pen and ability to coin memorable phrases—such as the one about man's reliance on tools that appealed to Charles Ham. Other Carlyle comments with which Triggs spiked his own include "Know thy work and do it," "man perfects himself by working," and "blessed is he who had found his work" for "he has a life-purpose" [46–48].[71]

These references to Carlyle were essential to Triggs's argument because they led to Ruskin's contribution to industrial art (and to its elder sibling, manual training). If Carlyle "set the world to work" but cared not what kind of work, Ruskin developed the doctrine into an "economical system" [50] that distinguished between a mercantile and a political economy—the first serves the welfare of business and the other the "welfare of the people at large." Rather than asking "what the product required," Ruskin "asked what man required." Thus far, Triggs argued, the "gospel of work" had "two main truths": one that of Carlyle who claimed for work a nobility; the other that of Ruskin, who claimed that "work is made for man and not man for work" [52]. And that brought Triggs to his description of industrial art: Carlyle announced the doctrine, Ruskin elaborated the system, and "Morris gave the first practical example" [54].

To relay the meaning of "industrial art," Triggs contrasted the work of the artist, whose reward is in the process, and that of the laborer, whose reward is in his wages. Industrial art seeks to combine them: "The modern problem of art is to make art social, that is useful. The modern problem of labor is to make labor artistic" [56]. These principles were at the time revealing themselves in education: "We are introducing into our schools to-day something that is called manual training. We have brought a workshop into the schools that have hitherto been devoted to intellectual development." For Triggs, a transformation was underway: "The school and the studio will become workshops, and the workshop in its turn will become a studio and a school." In industrial art, "art and education will tend more and more to be industrial; industry will tend to be artistic and educative" [57].

Triggs's goal was not only to explicate a theory; it was to describe the new "industrial commonwealth" he saw underway, one that he called a "copartnership of men." This would be a workshop that, per Ruskin, would "place the man before the work" [58]. And in the person of Morris, there was an actual example of such a master craftsman and educator: according to Boris, he "learned to dye, weave, embroider, and print in order to design for the peculiarities of each craft."[72]

If "Industrial Art" laid out a set of new relationships among art, labor, and education, Wright's "Art and Craft of the Machine" conceptualizes a reinterpretation of the history and status of all three. Further, in the version appearing in *The New Industrialism*, he does so in a more coherent way than in the more widely known version given at Hull House in March of 1901.[73] That talk, before the Chicago Arts and Crafts Society, took its members to task for being disdainful of the machine out of too great a reverence for William Morris. In both, Wright began by juxtaposing architecture to printing—the first had from antiquity to the Renaissance subsumed all arts under itself. Gutenberg's invention of printing brought in the age of the machine. Architecture since then had declined until, in 1900, it largely "bangled" its former glory through imitations of Greek and Roman temples. And, as he pointed out, these had been produced by "chattel slavery"; the machine, on the other hand, liberated the laborer from drudgery and made possible the democratization of art through its ability produce multiple items inexpensively.[74]

The 1902 version, given a year later, makes the same points, but Wright's bombast was delivered with a bit of grace: architecture, once "the chief register of humanity," had become "a corpse from which the spirit has flown" [83, 85].[75] In both versions, he chastises the Art Institute (without naming it) and its school for failing to connect "science" (the machine) and "art." But in 1902, he wrote that in its galleries "we find the same reverence for the past at a cost to the present and of doubtful value to the future" [89]. Both talks discuss materials and the machine's ability to "simplify" a host of crafts because it respects materials: "Simplicity teaches us that the beauty of wood lies in its qualities as wood" [93]. It is a fault of both the machine and the user when materials are worked to seem to be other than what they are. His advice to both audiences: artists and students alike should be educated in the possibilities of the machine; they needed classes before hosting more exhibitions.

The relative brevity of Wright's arguments in 1902 provided room for points that remain salient and, indirectly, complement Triggs's talk—they both learned something from the other. While in 1901 Wright expressed limited concern for the efforts of either artist or laborer, by 1902 his views had changed. Toward the talk's end, he made claims for the machine that might have revitalized the manual training school as Ham and Woodward had conceptualized it two decades before. He advised more training in tool use: "Not one artist in one hundred has taken pains to educate himself by contact in the field with the technical conditions which he must master before he can express himself." And, the "machine must be studied in its own sphere at the factories, in process, and in economics with the men who invent, organize, and direct its enormous activities" [103]. It should be studied sympathetically for its possibilities rather than as a means of doing little more than imitating handicrafts. He conceptualized an "experimental station" wherein all the machine tools of lithography, metal work, and ceramics would have their place, where the "best and truest" artist could mingle with the "best young scientific blood"—a machine version of the workshops Morris actually established and those Triggs imagined as the soul of his school of the new industrialism.

Wright's argument becomes utopian as he expands upon it, except that many 1902 arguments barely appear in the 1901 version of "Art and Craft"; the latter reads like a draft of the former. Art, he wrote in 1902, "is a matter of seeing and portraying in any medium the harmony of organic tendencies," and this "organic growth is working irresistibly the will of life through the medium of man" [105, 106]. Rather, he seems to have argued, than having the mind of man drawn into the maw of the machine, might the artist draw us out? Both talks end with a construction in which he declared man's "glory and his menace" to be "the greatest of machines, a great city," which he described as an organism of veins and tissues with the Corliss engine as a "visible brain in action" [106-8]. Both pieces end similarly, if rather more elegantly in 1902: this great machine, the city—and many of Wright's allusions are to Chicago—is a "forerunner of the democracy we hope for." "A magnificent truth" undisguised by "tattered garments long outgrown"; "the outward sign of an inner plan wherein combinations of capital and great industrial tendencies are but symptoms, government's imperfect manifestations, whereof wear and friction are social injustice and waste is war" [110, 111].

If the contributions of Triggs and Wright to *The New Industrialism* ascended to new sets of relationships among art, labor, and education, the address by educator Wilbur Jackman returned the discussion to ground level. Noted as an originator of nature study in schools, he had been brought by Parker to establish such a program at the Cook County Normal School. At the time of his 1902 address, Jackman was struggling to find a place for himself in the merger of the schools headed by Parker and by Dewey; it was not going well.[76] His "The Future School" made no reference to this or to the new industrialism, but it did begin with a claim that "educational matters are in the early stages of a revolution."[77] His new schools would prepare students for citizenship while instructing them to live in harmony with nature and with each other. Jackman's article is interesting mainly because of his later conflicts with Dewey; their disagreements and several related issues virtually ensured that the Chicago Manual Training School would gradually disappear. Whether it instead might have evolved into something like the workshops foreseen by Triggs or Wright, particularly had a Charles Ham been on hand to proselytize for such an outcome, is an intriguing what-if, a little-known aspect of the oft-told tale about the demise of Dewey's pedagogical laboratory.

The Brief Life and Early Death of the School of Education

The 1902 catalog for the Chicago Manual Training School carries a statement from William James, then a professor of philosophy and psychology at Harvard; in it, he referred to manual training programs as "the most colossal improvement" recently seen in secondary schools. And not just because they taught practical skills of use in homes and factories but because they "give us citizens with an entirely different intellectual fibre." They aid "insight into nature's complexity" and "confer precision... honesty... and self-reliance," plus they "occupy the pupil in a way most congruous with the spontaneous interest of his age." On the other hand, purely academic preparation with books alone carries pupils through life with a "certain remoteness from reality," the quotation continued.[78] It was likely included at the suggestion of John Dewey. Though he had never studied under James, they were friends and Dewey was a member of *The Metaphysical Club*, the scattered society of pragmatic thinkers emanating from James's office in Cambridge about whom Menand has written.[79]

Though the comment was surely not meant as an epitaph for the school, within a few years, the Chicago Manual Training School would no longer exist in recognizable form. It had, by 1902, become part of a "vast educational empire" under Dewey's leadership, and what was, ultimately, an unrealized dream of William Rainey Harper.[80] For Henry Belfield, these years would be "the most unsatisfactory" of his long professional life.[81] Though the university's 1897 acquisition of the school began with promises from its board of trustees that its intentions were to "maintain the high reputation of the school" in the form established by the Commercial Club,[82] it became increasingly clear as the century turned that what the trustees, and possibly Dewey himself, had in mind was the nucleus of a program in technology.[83] Even E. W. Blatchford, long the school's most ardent supporter at the Commercial Club, said of the school at a 1902 commencement ceremony that it was becoming the "nucleus of a polytechnic."[84]

Until the fall of 1903, when CMTS physically moved to a new building on the Midway campus, it remained on Michigan Avenue, led by Belfield and the faculty he had brought together; in 1901, that numbered thirteen members, many of whom had been there for several years.[85] Though there were some changes in the school's curriculum to accommodate students who wanted preparation for business careers or to attend liberal arts colleges rather than engineering schools (courses in bookkeeping and Latin appeared, for example), its students still spent half their day in drawing and shop classes. Tuition remained higher than at other similar schools in the city, though it was now the same for all three levels of students: $60 per term and $120 per year for juniors, middle, and seniors.[86] About half of CMTS students dropped out or transferred before graduating. Half of the graduates went to work in manufacturing or sales; half continued their education. By 1902, the number of graduates headed for liberal arts colleges equaled those going to engineering schools.[87]

The school continued to hold its well-attended annual exhibitions and its athletic teams continued to compete with those at other schools, but newspaper notices suggest that Belfield's chief concern was enrollment. Though the number of new students jumped up substantially in 1899, perhaps in response to the affiliation with the university, it fell again over the next few years.[88] There were some complaints about deteriorating conditions in the neighborhood and with some aspects of school maintenance, which may have affected enrollment as well. Further, in the fall of 1900, Belfield became ill and was away from the school for a few months; reports of meetings about the future of Dewey's "empire" suggest he was not involved. Nevertheless, Harper at the time wrote of Belfield: that he "had performed a unique service, the benefit of which is felt in every institution in the West," meaning the nation's other manual training schools. And that the school was now about to take up a new, "unique position."[89]

In January 1901, Anita Blaine announced that the $1 million she intended to use to endow the Chicago Institute for Francis Parker would instead go to the University of Chicago for its new School of Education, a conception that was a dream in Harper's head if not that of Dewey. Over the next few months, meetings were held among Harper and Dewey, Jackman and Parker, to discuss which responsibilities each would assume in this new unit. There were not only the several schools and academic departments, but publications produced by each. Neither Parker nor Dewey was willing to cede authority to the other, but Harper carried on, assuming differences would dissolve for the good of the whole.[90] At some point that spring, he told Belfield about the Blaine gift and the new role CMTS would have; Belfield had hoped that some of the money would go directly to his school, which was not to be.[91]

Despite the potential difficulties, Harper ordered a lavish series of events to announce the new School of Education, which coincided with a decennial celebration of the university's founding. Held in mid-June 1901, it included conferences and concerts, talks by several university presidents, and a commencement address by John D. Rockefeller, its initial funder. Events to honor him and Mrs. Rockefeller also involved their daughter Edith, who was married to Anita Blaine's brother Harold McCormick. Monday, June 17, was designated Educational Day to mark the university's acquisition of the Chicago Institute; ground was broken for its new home, to be called Blaine Hall. Nicholas Murray Butler, soon to become president of Columbia University, spoke, as did Francis Parker. Neither Dewey nor Belfield, however, were among the scheduled speakers.[92] Perhaps as a sign of their limited enthusiasm, members of the CMTS faculty resisted donning academic garb in order to participate in the gala events.[93] As the new school got underway, it had two heads—Dewey and Parker. The former would continue to head the academic departments, his laboratory school, CMTS, and another university-affiliated secondary school called the South Side Academy; Parker would remain in charge of the model school and the teacher-training program, which would still be known as the Chicago Institute. Until the opening of Blaine Hall—still two years off—these various components would continue to operate in their own buildings.[94]

Figures 12 & 13. Circulated in 1901, this announcement may have represented William Rainey Harper's intention for the role CMTS would play in the university's new School of Education, but there is limited indication that either Henry Belfield or John Dewey dedicated their talents to the plan.

CIRCULAR

To the Alumni, Patrons, and Other Friends of the Chicago Manual Training School:

THE Chicago Manual Training School, founded by the Commercial Club in 1882, became a part of the University of Chicago in 1897. The building erected in 1883, at the corner of Michigan avenue and Twelfth street, will be vacated in June, 1902, when the school will be moved to its new building on the Midway Plaisance, between Monroe and Kimbark avenues.

It is intended by the University authorities that this change shall inaugurate a wider sphere of usefulness for the school. It will be in the immediate neighborhood of the University; and in the same block with the Chicago Institute of Education and the South Side Academy, which institutions are ultimately to be united under the name of the University of Chicago School of Education.

Notwithstanding this union, the identity of the Chicago Manual Training School will be preserved. Its course of study will be strengthened rather than weakened. Its students will enjoy, as fully as heretofore, the benefits of the combination of purely intellectual and manual work, as expressed in the motto of the school: "Mente atque manu ad virtutem." All of the work of the school—recitations, shopwork, drawing—will be conducted in the school building. It will have its own corps of permanent teachers. The diploma of the school will be granted as hitherto, and will mean all that it has meant in past time. The school will continue its three years' and four years' courses; preparing for business and for technological schools in three years, and for scientific and classical schools in four years. There will be no just reason why the certificate of the Director of the school will not admit to many eastern and western colleges, as heretofore.

The new building will be far superior to the present building, which was erected when manual training was only an experiment. The equipment will be improved, and enlarged sufficiently to meet the new demands upon it. The Colliau Cupola, which the school has owned for ten years, but for lack of a suitable place has not used, will be erected in a first-class foundry. New forges will be procured, and the forge room will be high, light, and well ventilated. Everything possible will be done in building, equipment, and teaching force to have the school hold its position in the very front rank of similar schools.

It is hoped that the many friends of this school, which has done so much for the betterment of secondary education, and which is favorably known even beyond the limits of the United States, will believe that it is the intention of its Board of Trustees to maintain the high reputation of the school, and to fulfill to the letter and in the spirit the agreement made with the representatives of the Commercial Club, when the school was transferred to the University of Chicago.

WILLIAM R. HARPER,
President of the University of Chicago.

JOHN DEWEY,
Head of the Department of Education.

HENRY H. BELFIELD,
Director of the Chicago Manual Training School.

JULY, 1901.

A circular for CMTS patrons and friends, issued in July 1901, announced that the school would soon be relocated to the Midway, where it would be housed with the institute and the academy. Signed by Harper, Dewey, and Belfield, it promised that the school's unique program would be maintained, but in a new building with new equipment. The school's Latin motto—in English, through mind and hand to manhood—would remain, as would the current faculty, enabling it to "hold its position in the very front rank of such schools."[95] Although the inauguration of the School of Education meant that Belfield officially reported to Dewey, the former never acknowledged that and continued to go directly to Harper with his concerns.[96]

Though Dewey had once acknowledged Parker as the "father" of progressive education and had helped support him in struggles with the city's board of education, differences between their goals and personalities quickly surfaced. Robert McCaul, in his classic study of the demise of Dewey's experimental school, described them as Parker focusing on the child as a part of nature; Dewey as the child living in a world of humans. Parker's course of study centered on science, aiming at helping the child understand rocks and trees and the laws of the universe; Dewey's centered on social studies and acquainting the child with the structure and materials of the human community. Further, the two were not involved in the same kind of work—Parker headed a practice school for the training of teachers; Dewey headed a laboratory to test educational principles and hypotheses.[97]

In the mind of Ella Flagg Young, a colleague and contemporary of both, the differences were both subtle and substantial. A forty-year veteran teacher and administrator in the Chicago Public Schools—which employed graduates of Parker's normal—Young had joined Dewey at the university in 1899. After receiving a doctorate in 1900, she taught in Dewey's department and served his Laboratory School—it is said that she named it such—as supervisor of instruction.[98] In 1901, she wrote essays about Parker and Dewey in a brief book on educational theory. While she admired Parker, her comments suggest that she was troubled by a lack of consistency in logic and tone in Parker's writings; though she respected his instincts and dedication, she felt his curriculum was too dependent upon his presence and charisma. Dewey's theory, on the other hand, was more exportable; approaching education as a scientist, he sought hypotheses and then tested them in the real world of school. Dewey's goal was to provide teachers with intellectual tools they could employ in their work of encouraging students' growth and ability to function in a complex society; Parker's aim was providing teachers with a spiritual methodology through which they could guide students to an understanding of man and nature.[99] These different purposes clashed, intensified by the cultish devotion Parker's teachers felt toward him and his methods. Teachers at the Dewey's school were equally dedicated, but more to his ideas than to his person.

The complexities of the relationship between the Parker and the Dewey schools only got more complicated in March of 1902 when Parker suddenly died, leaving his half of the unconsummated union without a head. Wilbur Jackman, Parker's second in command, tried to maneuver himself into a position to replace his late boss as head of the Chicago Institute, but the job went instead to Dewey, which added substantially to his administrative burdens.[100] Harper had assumed that Dewey might at this point focus on secondary education, and that the Parker and Dewey elementary schools could merge, an unrealistic assumption at best given the differences between them.

In this clash of personalities and principles, Belfield and CMTS were largely ignored, as was the South Side Academy—Harper's plan was that both would merge into a University High School, an idea that did not please Belfield. As he would later write, CMTS students "despised" the South Side Academy, thinking it a "school of low grade." According to them, "if you can't do the work at CMTS, you go to Armour, and if you fail at Armour, you go to the South Side Academy. Anybody can stay in it."[101] Nevertheless, Harper persuaded Belfield to agree to a joint graduation ceremony in 1902, the one at which Blatchford noted the coming "polytechnic"—but that would be the extent of their cooperation for the year.[102]

That fall, both the academy and the manual training school remained in their different buildings. Belfield, in an effort to inform incoming students about the school's expectations, addressed them in a September 1902 "My Dear Young Friend" letter. In it, he stressed the importance of self-reliance, "moral character," "rectitude," and good health. The curriculum would probably demand "more study than has ever before been required of you," and that "idleness," "mischief," and "disregard of school regulations" would not be tolerated.[103] The wording suggests Belfield's influence rather than that of Dewey, who over the summer wrote an article describing the amalgamation of these several separate institutions and programs. It stated that the aim of the School of Education was the "training of teachers—teachers thoroughly interested in educational progress" competent in the classroom, and the "general spread of whatever is best in elementary training." CMTS received a brief mention: it was described as a "classic example of the claims and functions of manual training and technological work." The South Side Academy merited only brief mention as well.[104] In December, CMTS faculty voted not to attend a function at the School of Education; budget cuts and difficulties about allocation of space in the new Blaine Hall had led to friction between Belfield's faculty and their new bosses.[105]

A year earlier, in the fall of 1901, Dewey had engaged a graduate student to develop plans for uniting teacher-training with the laboratory method, an idea that resulted in controversy with Parker's loyal faculty.[106] Dewey's intention to use CMTS in part as a means of preparing manual training teachers may have been part of the study as well. His three-part program for college-level students in the School of Education announced in 1902 included one called Arts and Technology, a two-year course that did not lead to a degree but would make use of "technological courses" at CMTS. The two other parts of the program would prepare teachers for teaching in kindergartens to normal schools.[107]

The university's *Annual Register* for 1902–1903 indicated CMTS's status in the administration of the School of Education. Its officers included Dewey as director, Jackman as dean, Belfield as "Dean of the Technological Course of the University High School," and Wilbur Owen, head of the South Side Academy, as "Dean of the Academic Course" for the high school. Alice Chipman Dewey was listed as principal of the University Elementary School; the merger of Parker's model school and Dewey's pedagogical laboratory had taken the name given his experimental school seven years before.[108] In the fall of 1903, the various institutions composing the School of Education all moved together into Blaine Hall; however, the mechanical and technological equipment so important to CMTS did not move with it until January of 1904.[109] Of the thirteen faculty members listed in the CMTS catalog for 1901, only seven remained in 1903.[110] Though Dewey did appoint Belfield to a few committees that fall, there is no evidence that he attended their meetings.[111]

That fall, 1903, Dewey spoke to a group of parents on "The Significance of the School of Education." He began by romanticizing its various components, starting with the arrival of Parker at the Cook County Normal and the founding of CMTS in 1883. Both were "pioneering efforts" to overcome the "bookishness" of traditional schools at the time. He went on to describe the origins of the South Side Academy and then, his own school for the "scientific investigation and research into the problems connected with the psychology and sociology of education." With the gift of Mrs. Blaine in 1900, the school would "develop a body of thought regarding what teachers do that would be dependent upon more than a set of abstract and general theories." These could be tested in a real classroom with real students. Further, this union of varied elements could "bring to bear the intellectual methods of which the modern university is the appropriate home." Ending with a plea for cooperation from parents and an "espirit do corps," it was all quite brave.[112] But it was not to be.[113]

In 1901, John Dewey had appointed his indispensable wife and partner Alice Chipman Dewey to be principal of the Laboratory School, and when it was merged with the Chicago Institute's model school in Blaine Hall in the fall of 1903, he named her principal of the conjoined schools. Though widely respected for her intellectual vitality and contributions to her husband's ventures, Alice Dewey was not a good "mixer" and seems to have antagonized teachers loyal to Parker's method and memory.[114] Further, President Harper and others at the university were uncomfortable with having a husband and wife working together in the same unit. So, in late March 1904, as he was preparing for hospitalization—soon he would learn that he was suffering from the stomach cancer that would take his life in January 1906—Harper and Mrs. Dewey met to discuss her future at the school. The meeting did not go well. At the time, Dewey was on a two-week lecture tour in New York City, and upon learning that Harper had asked for Mrs. Dewey's resignation, both resigned from their positions at the School of Education. Within a week or two, Dewey also resigned from his position as head of the Department of Philosophy. Hoping not to lose one of his most prominent faculty members, Harper enlisted some of Dewey's colleagues in an effort to persuade Dewey to reconsider.[115] It was not to happen; by May 3, an announcement of his resignation and appointment to a rapidly endowed chair in Columbia University's Department of Philosophy appeared in a Chicago newspaper.[116]

Ten days later, the university celebrated the dedication of Blaine Hall with two days of conferences, speeches, luncheons, and receptions.[117] Sessions on Friday, May 13, included one on teacher training chaired by John Dewey, a talk on aesthetic development given by sociologist Charles Zueblin, and others on manual training and the household arts. The general conference on Friday afternoon, chaired by Henry Belfield, included an address on the manual training movement delivered by Thomas Balliet, a leader in the movement from Massachusetts, and one by A. C. Bartlett, founder of a major hardware wholesaling firm and strong supporter of both CMTS and the Laboratory School. His remarks, according to a newspaper story, focused on how manual training programs would result in more harmonious relations between capital and labor.[118] The Saturday sessions began with one on the various curriculum areas given by faculty at both the Parker and Dewey schools; chaired by Ella Flagg Young, it included remarks by Wilbur Jackman. During the afternoon, Harper led the formal dedication of Blaine Hall; featured was an "oration" by Nicholas Murray Butler, who was introduced by John Dewey, soon to make the switch from the former's university to that of the latter. Butler's message, according to a reporter, was that great teachers make great universities.[119]

In the weeks after the ceremony, the Deweys packed up their lives in Chicago and prepared to spend several months in Europe prior to their move to New York; among recurrent differences between Dewey and Harper

Figure 14. Named for the family of philanthropist Anita McCormick Blaine, this building represented Harper's ambition for a merger of Dewey's school with one founded by Francis Parker, with CMTS and several other programs. The elaborate dedication ceremonies for it in May 1904 were held a week after Dewey announced his resignation from the university. The building, located on the Midway, is now home to the Laboratory School.

was not only financial support for his pedagogical laboratory but income sufficient to support the Deweys' comfortable lifestyle, which included a large apartment, several servants, a summer home in the Adirondacks, and frequent trips to Europe.[120] One of Dewey's biographers has commented that Harper's attitude toward one's career demanded sacrifice; he arguably overloaded Dewey with a burden of responsibilities that no one person could handle. Dewey's colleagues in the Department of Philosophy continued to do significant work, but their involvement with pedagogy diminished when their friend moved on.

After the Deweys' departure, Jackman became principal of the merged Dewey and Parker schools, which eventually became officially known as the Laboratory School and loosened its connections to the university. Anita Blaine shortly transferred her loyalty to a school named after Parker and located on the city's north side. In 1905, Harper named Nathaniel Butler, a member of Dewey's academic department, dean for the School of Education; Butler nominally headed a four-man team that took over Dewey's administrative responsibilities.[121] Harper's great School of Education, which he foresaw as leading a major reformation of American education, would founder for a while, until in 1908 when Charles Judd, another psychologist, was named its head; he would put his own imprint on the field, but take it in a different direction than Dewey would have.[122]

Belfield remained as one of two deans at the University High School; the other was William B. Owen, formerly principal of the South Side Academy. As the latter school was co-educational, the merged programs were as well; however, a 1907 circular signed by both men suggests that the program in technology—one of four offered by the school—welcomed boys alone. The other programs, in classical and modern languages, plus science, seem to have been intended mainly for college-bound students.[123] Belfield wrote in his autobiography that combining the two schools was an awkward venture, due to the university's "red tape," and "its ignorance of the history, character, and aims of the Manual Training part of the High School, and the seeming contempt of it on the part of University officials." He complained that he was looked upon as an intruder, plus it was frustrating that he had "no undivided authority." He had no argument with Owen; their relations were cordial, but they had different ideas about conducting a school. When things were going in a way Belfield disapproved of, he let it go, feeling that university authorities would "sustain" Owen rather than himself.[124]

Owen, for his part, was generous to Belfield; he later claimed that the Chicago Manual Training School was a highly successful experiment. In 1909, after a few years at the University High School, Owen became principal of the Chicago Normal School, the school made famous by Francis Parker. In taking that job, he followed Ella Flagg Young, who had become principal of the normal school after departing the university in 1904. She served in that role between 1905 and 1909, when she was named superintendent of the Chicago Public Schools.

In June of that year, Belfield attended the fiftieth anniversary of his graduation from Iowa College, by then renamed Grinnell; it was a school that had set him on his way and eventually awarded him an honorary doctorate. That fall, at age sixty-eight, Belfield retired from the university, ending what he called an "unpleasant condition" while acknowledging that the university continued to pay him 60 percent of his salary. Though he felt that Harper had not sympathized with his educational ideas, Henry Pratt Judson, who became president in 1906 after Harper's death, "had real sympathy with my ideas" and always approved Belfield's suggestions regarding the school. Belfield's comments suggest that the retirement may not have been wholly voluntary; he says it was "done with great tact" as Judson "wanted to soften the blow as much as possible," but it was a blow.[125]

Belfield's epitaph for the school, written in 1909, was that "as the history of CMTS recedes into the past," and he has "the opportunity to compare its work with that of other schools," he was "more and more convinced of the excellent character of its instruction, its discipline, and its influence on students." He commended the loyalty of the school's graduates, but he had to admit "the old school is dead." The "manual training department of the University High School is an entirely different and inferior school."[126] On the differences, he was right. The 1911 catalog for the University High School relegated manual courses to a department, along with languages and public speaking, mathematics and math, plus home economics and household arts. Among its courses were those in woodworking, pottery, clay modeling, and general technology; in these courses, students gained practical experience in "handling material rather than skill in manipulating tools."

The Soul of a School for Uniting Art and Labor

In the 1870s, Calvin Woodward had complained that his students had too little knowledge of basic tools; in 1902, Frank Lloyd Wright complained that handcrafters a generation later had too little knowledge of the machine. Woodward's solution was the manual training program; that of Wright was an "experimental station" where the machine could be studied "in its own sphere at the factories"—a Morrisonian vision of the ancient guild wherein the master craftsman could model the use of tools and machines while being true to the materials at hand: wood, ceramics, fabrics. In 1901, Oscar Lovell Triggs had proposed that schools become experimental centers for industrial art—yet another laboratory-based approach to education. Might there have been parallels among the laboratories advocated by Woodward, Dewey, and Wright? Could an Industrial Art League have persuaded corporate leaders, some of whom were members of the league, to implement John Ruskin's ideas about making work for man rather than man for work? Unlikely, but it is all rather dizzying to contemplate. The machine, Wright argued, democratized art. Thus, it extended Ham's curriculum for making instruction in tool use parallel to the study of machines and technological progress. Could labor, freed from its connection with servility, actually realize Ruskin's imperative? When hardware magnate A. C. Bartlett, noted earlier as a supporter of the CMTS and the Laboratory School, proposed that manual training programs could ease the antipathy between labor and management, might he have had Triggs's ideas about labor working for art rather than for wages alone in mind? Likely not, but there was William

James proclaiming that manual training programs were yielding citizens of "an entirely different intellectual fibre."

Writing early in 1904 about Dewey's work at the University of Chicago, James announced that "Chicago has a School of Thought," which could "figure in literature as the school of Chicago for twenty-five years to come." It was characterized by "a great sense of concrete reality" and makes "value and fact inseparable." Dewey saw ideas as real things; James recognized that the Chicago school of thought stood for "continuities and purposes in things." James predicted for it a "great future" and certainly "something of which America may be proud."[127]

Dewey's school of thought combined education and philosophy to "make concrete" ideas about schooling in his pedagogical laboratory; the ideas experimented with in Chicago came to define an American system of education.[128] Wright, in his Chicago experiments with staying true to the nature of materials used in his buildings and furniture, defined an American style of architecture and design.[129] In their distinctive ways, both men were utopians; neither was content with the contemporary relationship between men and machines: Dewey wanted workers to have greater insight into the work they did so as to humanize their jobs; Wright saw machines as both freeing laborers from the drudgery of industrial work and "democratizing" art so it would be accessible to more people. In a talk given in 1905, Dewey said, "let us begin asking ourselves what industry, conceived in the spirit of art, may do for the school."[130] Despite some striking parallels in their thinking and their host of mutual acquaintances, Dewey and Wright appear never to have met, but had they, a compelling exchange might well have taken place.[131]

Thus, it is tempting to consider whether William Rainey Harper, the great educational entrepreneur, might have been able to get Wright and Dewey into a room and, with guidance from William James, have them combine the pedagogical laboratory of one with the experimental stations of the other into an institution that might have persuaded Dewey to remain in Chicago. It did not happen, but as Wright's buildings influenced architecture worldwide, representations of Dewey's ideas influenced schools throughout the nation and the world over the rest of the century and beyond.[132] One of these was a unique institution initially established in 1886 in central New Jersey, a school that would eventually attract positive attention from James's student W. E. B. Du Bois. By uniting Theodore Weld's ideas about manual labor in literary institutions with Booker T. Washington's version of progressive education and Calvin Woodward's manual training program, it became a school that manifested Du Bois's priorities for schooling, one that enabled its students to be both African and American. To that school's story our attention now turns.

CHAPTER 4

A "Star of Hope" Defines Industrial Education

> Resolved that the New Jersey Council of Education defines "manual training" as "training in thought expression by other means than gesture and verbal language, in such a carefully graded course of study as shall also provide adequate training for the judgement and the executive faculty." The training will necessarily include drawing and constructive work, but experience alone can determine by what special means this instruction may best be given.
> —"An Authoritative Definition of Manual Training," *Science* 13, no. 309 (January 4, 1889)

When, sometime in 1886, the Rev. Walter Allan Rice and his wife Ella acquired two small wooden buildings near the center of Bordentown, New Jersey, and gathered together a group of eight young people who seemed in need of solid schooling and a stable homelife, they might not have anticipated that their humble venture would over the next several decades evolve into an institution serving hundreds of students and attracting the attention of some of the most notable intellects of the day, along with talented musicians, athletes, and politicians, plus a host of other people of accomplishment nationwide. But that is what they did.

The story of the school they established has been infrequently told, in part because its distinctions and accomplishments got caught up in ideological disputes of a later day. Too often ignored in recountings of manual and industrial training, whether for Black students or white, is the sort of work or careers such schooling enabled students to pursue. But as the story of the Rices' school demonstrates, the education it provided gave graduates a sense of agency; through their education, they acquired some degree of mastery over their fate—an idea that was particularly important to John

Dewey and emphasized in his writings during the first two decades of the twentieth century. The school offered a democratic opportunity denied to so many of their fellows.

Though the Rices likely had in mind Hampton Institute in Virginia as a model for the school they wanted to establish, and in its heyday during the 1930s it was often called a "Tuskegee of the North," such a comparison suggests limited understanding of what all three schools set out to accomplish. An origin story for the Rices' school also has to include ideas promoted by Calvin Woodward: its curriculum was a balanced half-trade and half-academic. After 1915, its growth and development were nurtured by a new principal who had applied some of Dewey's ideas at a school for Black students in Indianapolis; and during the 1920s, its program merited positive attention from W. E. B. Du Bois.

Named the Manual Training and Industrial School for Colored Youth (MTIS) in 1894 when it was acquired by the state of New Jersey, its story is complex. From its origin until its closure in 1955, "Bordentown" was a place at which winds of conflict swirled above and around its campus. But its competent faculty and adroit leadership kept the school on course despite pressures to offer something inferior to "the sort of education the Afro-American most needs" to quote an early supporter.

The Rices' choice of Bordentown as a site for their school was auspicious but not surprising. A shipping port on the Delaware River and a major connection point between Philadelphia and New York City, the town had been home to several men and women prominent in the American Revolution. Located just ten miles south of Trenton, the state's capital and a growing industrial city, Bordentown remained largely residential; it also had an active Black community. Although it is often lauded as the site of the state's first free public school, that of Clara Barton established in 1852, it was also the site of a far less noted small, private school for Black students, which had been established a decade earlier.

Rev. Rice, born enslaved in South Carolina, arrived in New Jersey after service in the Union army during the Civil War and teaching briefly at a Freedmen's Bureau school in his home county. Ordained a minister in the African Methodist Episcopal (AME) church after attending Lincoln University in Pennsylvania, Rice served several New Jersey congregations during the 1870s and 1880s as a presiding bishop. One of them was in Bordentown, and while there he married Ella Mount, organist at the town's Mt. Zion AME Church.[1] Around 1880, Rev. Rice and other AME pastors formed what became known as both the Technical Industrial Educational Association and the Colored Industrial Education Association of New Jersey."[2] By whatever name, the group's goal was twofold: "to disseminate information upon industrial education in all its branches... to stimulate public opinion in its favor" and to train students of both sexes in "such industries as shall enable them to be self-supporting."[3]

Whatever the exact year, it is clear that Rev. Rice and his fellows were pioneers; Tuskegee itself was not founded until 1881. As the school's early records disappeared in a 1906 fire, the founders' intentions cannot be known for certain, but the founding organization's name suggests that its members were aware of efforts around the nation to incorporate manual work and industrial training into schools. Hampton Institute, established in 1868, is thought to have been a model for the group; it, however, focused on preparing teachers, as did Tuskegee. Further, Hampton's roots were in the Society for Promoting Manual Labor in Literary Institutions and similar initiatives of the 1830s, such as the Negro Convention Movement with which Frederick Douglass was associated prior to the Civil War.[4] By the mid-1870s, there were scattered across the South a half-dozen schools offering secondary-level manual or industrial training to Negro students, often in conjunction with teacher training.[5] These were also likely models for Rice and his fellows, as would have been the Institute for Colored Youth, which had been established in Philadelphia in the late 1860s and was led by Fanny Jackson Coppin. An Oberlin graduate, she too believed that manual work in schools should complement academic work.[6] Given that he was already active in New Jersey at the time, it is even possible that Rice himself may have attended the Philadelphia Centennial of 1876, the event most often associated with the start of the movement for manual training in the United States.

Though that movement traces its origins to Boston and St. Louis in the late 1870s, New Jersey was not far behind. The state assembly in 1881 passed an Industrial Education Act, through which the state promised to match local funds on a fifty-fifty basis.[7] By the following year, Montclair had established manual training courses at both its elementary and secondary schools.[8] Over the next decade, a dozen more New Jersey cities did. Although the state assembly had, in 1881, also passed legislation that disallowed public schools from excluding students on the basis of religion, nationality, or race, the act was largely ignored.[9] Thus, the school in Bordentown established for Black students in 1842 remained essential. Located just a few blocks from the school associated with Clara Barton—which is now a state landmark—it would continue to grow over the following decades. The historical record is incomplete, but it suggests that the AME church at which Mrs. Rice played the organ also housed the school for several years. At some point, it became known as School No. 2, and in 1880 Bordentown actually erected a building to house it. A contemporary newspaper article states that it was a substantial structure with desks for one hundred students. Located barely a block away from the AME church, it too was close to the Barton school.[10]

Establishing a Distinctive Legacy

Though this historical detail may seem peripheral to the origins of the Manual Training and Industrial School, it augments what little is known about the school's beginnings. School No. 2 offered only an elementary education—few students, white or Black, in New Jersey or elsewhere, had much more at the time. But Walter and Ella Rice wanted to provide something more substantial. Further, they actively recruited homeless and abandoned girls and boys in the area and decided from the start that theirs was to be a boarding school. The two frame buildings they had acquired to house it were also near the church and School No. 2.

Because the school's early records were lost in a fire, its first years have to be reconstructed from various sources; the most thorough is a 1997 application for national landmark status, written by a researcher named Nan Pillsbury (various histories prepared by the school include some conflicting information).[11] These sources suggest that for eight years, Rice struggled to keep his school afloat, relying on contributions from "local businessmen" by one report. By 1895, the school had forty-two students, both boys and girls, roughly ages twelve to twenty, and had grown to occupy several buildings in Bordentown. Of the school's curriculum, Rice wrote in an 1897 report that it aimed to train students for "particular and useful industries falling to their race" such as dressmaking and housekeeping, cookery and carpentry, agriculture and horticulture "together with free-hand drawing, typewriting, and a good English education."[12] In sum, it was similar to programs offered in Chicago and elsewhere at the time; however, as a school established by a pastor and his wife, it emphasized schooling of the heart as well as heads and hands. A study written by a woman who attended there during its closing decade claimed that from the school's start, "religious and moral training" were emphasized along with academics. The school program was designed to protect students from "social dangers" of city streets, thus it "inculcated high standards of citizenship" and "offered a wholesome environment for children who had seen little of either."[13]

In May of 1894, the state of New Jersey acquired the struggling school, and a few years later the state superintendent of education called it a "star of hope" deserving of greater support.[14] The state began by providing an annual appropriation of $3,000, which it may have acquired through federal legislation known as the Second Morrill Act of 1890; these funds were to

Figure 15. Installed in 2019 by the Bordentown Historical Society, this banner is one of many honoring the New Jersey town's significance. This brief recounting of MTIS's origin and attributes suggests that the school deserves wider recognition. Its founder, Rev. Rice, was influenced by the same trends that led to the establishment of both CMTS and Tuskegee Institute.

be directed toward agricultural schools for Black students.[15] A year later, in 1895 and through fortuitous circumstance, it also acquired land on which to build a real campus. Via this transaction, the school earned its nickname "Ironsides," which later became the name of the school newspaper. The land, situated on a high bluff overlooking the Delaware River, had belonged to Commodore Charles Stewart, the naval hero who had captained the USS Constitution, popularly known as "Old Ironsides," during the War of 1812. In 1874, the estate passed to his daughter Delia Stewart Parnell, who had married an Anglo-Irish aristocrat and lived abroad. Again, the historical record is incomplete, but for part of the 1870s and 1880s, she had been living on the Bordentown estate with one or two of her daughters; thus she may have learned of Rev. Rice and the school he had established.[16]

What is well documented is that the Stewart and Parnell families had substantial sympathy with the Irish peasants who farmed, with limited compensation, land that belonged to absentee British landlords. Two of Delia's sons served in the British Parliament and were known as advocates for Irish home rule. One, Charles Stewart Parnell, was the founder, in 1879, of the Irish National Land League.[17] Further, their concern for the less privileged they shared with their grandfather. As Pillsbury wrote, "apparently out of respect for the support her father gave for the cause of educating African-Americans," Delia Parnell agreed to lease the land to the state, so long as it would be used as a site for the school.[18] Another clue to its early intentions is that the school was briefly called Ironsides Normal.[19]

After the state acquired the school, it continued to grow, if slowly. By the end of the 1896–1897 school year, it had fifty-five students, thirty-two boys and twenty-three girls. Plans for a more ambitious school began to take shape; the state hired an architect to design additional buildings.[20] Though no reason is known for the decision, at some point during the 1896–1897 school year, state officials also hired a new principal.[21] Rev. Rice, whose good idea had taken on a life of its own, departed Bordentown; together he and his wife started another school elsewhere in the state. In January of 1899, just two years later, Rice died. He was only fifty-four years old, but his health had not been good.[22]

A Scholar Takes Charge

The new principal was James Monroe Gregory, a man whose prior career lent the school additional distinction. After preparing for higher education at Oberlin Academy, he became one of the first students recruited for Howard University; he was also a member of its first graduating class in 1872. For over two decades, he taught at Howard as a professor of mathematics and later of classics. In 1886, he joined Booker T. Washington and Fanny Jackson Coppin at a panel on higher education for Black students. Long a member of the Washington, DC, board of education, in 1893 Gregory convened the first meeting of the American Association of Educators of Colored Youth and became its president; also that year, his biography of Frederick Douglass, one of his mentors, was published.[23]

Gregory's arrival in Bordentown was concurrent with the school's move to its new campus in the fall of 1897. His son Montgomery reported that the Parnell house was in a shambles, having been unoccupied for some time, and that his family—including a brother who would soon join the faculty—cleaned it up so that it could be used for classes.[24] Though the land had once been an active farm, its fields had long lain untended; a few years would pass before an extensive agricultural program was established. The extent to which the Rices had been able to establish other manual aspects of the curriculum in the school's rented space in Bordentown is not known. Pillsbury reports that Gregory began by building on the Rices' curriculum, with academic courses in the morning and manual work in the afternoon, just as students did at CMTS in Chicago. Boys learned carpentry and farming; girls,

Figure 16. *Ironsides Echo* was the name of the MTIS newspaper and yearbook; the name honors the memory of naval hero Charles Stewart, commodore of the ship called "Ironsides" during the War of 1812. In the late 1890s, the state of New Jersey acquired his former estate for the school's campus. The 1901 Administration Building commands a bluff above the Delaware River; it still stands.

domestic skills. The purpose, Gregory wrote, was to coordinate the manual and literary aspects of the curriculum so as to "secure, as far as practicable, an all-round development for each student." There were soon courses in music as well as drawing, with military training for the boys.[25]

The school admitted students with a great variety of educational backgrounds; it covered grades six through ten, and students were often older than their grade. According to the school's official chronology, its first commencement was in 1898.[26] That year had seen a substantial increase in enrollment—Pillsbury claims 116 students, with many more boys than girls; several came from out of state, a practice that would be curtailed later.[27] A brief piece in the *Ironsides Echo* for May 1898 reported that Delia Parnell had died and that the state was in the process of purchasing the full ninety acres from her estate.[28] In 1901, the state assembly allotted $20,000 for the land and also for construction of what became in 1903 an impressive Administration Building. In 1900, control of the school had moved to the state Department of Education, rather than a separate board of trustees as before. In his 1902–1903 report, Gregory told of the coming dedication ceremonies for the new building; with several state officials expected to attend, "the event will be the most significant occasion in the history of Negro education in the North," he wrote.[29]

In the fall of 1905, the *New York Age*, one of the nation's leading African American newspapers, published a laudatory article about the school, noting its "salubrious site" on an "estate rich and inspiring in its associations"—not only the Parnells but Commodore Stewart and his guests. Titled "School of Great Promise," the article cites the leadership of Gregory and his wife, its "equal stress on industrial and literary branches," support from the governor, and generous appropriations. Claiming that its purpose is "essentially industrial," to give "every graduate a trade to be practically used in the home or as a profession." Industry in this sense meant carpentry and agriculture for boys; sewing and cookery for girls; as part of the program, students received practical experience repairing buildings and serving meals, just as had students in manual labor schools several decades earlier. Among Gregory's innovations was to provide boys with training in military tactics and discipline; throughout the school's history, male students dressed in military uniforms. Girls, too, wore a school uniform of white blouses and dark skirts.

"Literary aspects" were emphasized, too, for "without literary training, pupils would be poorly trained for any line of work," according to the *New York Age* article. The school offered instruction in English language and literature, mathematics and the sciences, with opportunities for advanced work. Developing character, "the basis for all genuine success," was also stressed through encouraging high ideals and those "qualities of heart and mind" that make "good citizens." At the time, the school enrolled around a hundred students, most from New Jersey but others from neighboring states. Its graduates—the school still only went through the tenth grade—became teachers and carpenters and dressmakers and housewives.[30]

Although the article carries no byline, it reads as though it was written by the editor of *The New Age*, T. Thomas Fortune, a brilliant writer and agitator then living across the state in Red Bank. Noted since the mid-1880s as a consultant to and ghostwriter for Booker T. Washington, Fortune had also written in 1884 *Black and White: Land, Labor, and Politics in the South*, a book that one of his biographers has claimed had no peer until W. E. B. Du Bois's *Black Reconstruction* appeared fifty years later.[31] Among Fortune's models for the manner in which Black Americans should do battle with their oppressors was that given by none other than Charles Stewart Parnell, who had toured the American South during the 1870s before returning to Ireland to lead the struggle for land reform.[32] In 1898, Fortune had written a brief article on education for Afro-Americans—a term he tried to popularize—that provides a theoretical background for the piece on the Bordentown school.

Appearing in *The Southern Workman*, a periodical published by Hampton Institute, Fortune's 1898 article claimed that in the three decades since the end of the Civil War, an educational foundation had been laid in the South; it had produced tens of thousands of teachers and ministers, lawyers and doctors. But needed then was "more training of the hand and less training of the head." Though before the war, much of the skilled manual work in the South had been done by enslaved mechanics, the situation changed after the war: "We need educated farmers, mechanics, and tradesmen in the South today more than we need the graduates of higher schools of learning," Fortune wrote. The call then was for more training in the "bread-winning occupations" and for "skilled captains of industry." Encouraging signs at the time included the interest shown by northern philanthropies, which were funding the kind of schools needed, and those southern parents who heeded "the importance of giving their children a practical education."[33]

Whether Fortune had actually penned the "School of Great Promise" article, it did emphasize aspects of the Bordentown curriculum that reflected his thinking. Some state authorities, however, may have had a different vision for the school's future. New Jersey's superintendent of public instruction had made a visit to Tuskegee, and in May of 1907 Booker T. Washington visited the MTIS campus to attend a state board of education meeting being held there. He advised the school to strengthen its manual training courses. The following month, Fortune himself was a commencement speaker, perhaps reiterating Washington's points.[34] However, among the challenges Gregory faced was the expense of acquiring and maintaining the expensive equipment manual training programs required. Further, as a boarding school, it had to have dormitories, and the existing ones were inadequate.[35]

A lengthy issue of the *Ironsides Echo* in 1908 provides insight into the school's funding and operations under Gregory's administration. The state's annual subsidy was increased to $5,000 in 1897, and in 1901, the legislature provided a special appropriation of $35,000 to purchase the land and erect an Administration Building. There was another appropriation of $49,000 in 1907, designated for new dormitories and agriculture equipment. That year, there were 128 students being prepared to become "intelligent citizens skilled in industrial arts and agricultural pursuits."[36] The Gregorys toured the state to acquire needed equipment such as a sewing machine, a typewriter, a piano, and band instruments. The dozen faculty members offered practical instruction in tool use, carpentry, and "domestic economy"; all students contributed to campus maintenance. Students spent three days a week in the "literary department" and another three in trades.[37] Religious services continued; a band and a football team had been organized.

Though the state wanted to encourage agricultural work, the school's graduates, who then numbered sixty-six, had other careers in mind. The *Echoes* published a list of twenty-five who had graduated between 1898 and 1905: nine were schoolteachers and principals (including two music teachers), four were store clerks and managers, three were nurses. One had joined the navy; others had become a journalist, a carpenter, and dining hall supervisor. Three had acquired college degrees, one to become a pharmacist, another a park designer, and a third was still in graduate school.[38] There were no farmers.

A 1909 report by the board of education's Bordentown School Committee focused on the institution's "almost parsimonious economy"; its annual expenses amounted to $20,000, half of which went to pay salaries. (Although tuition was free, students had to pay a modest monthly amount for room and board.) To prepare the school's fields for serious farming—land purchases had expanded it to 225 acres—stumps and weedy undergrowth had to be cleared. Orchards of fruit trees had been planted or brought back into production (a particular project of Mrs. Fannie Gregory) and were producing fruit. That year, the girls had canned two thousand quarts of fruits and vegetables. Boys in the carpentry program not only built furniture for the school but bookcases for a travelling library. The report anticipated that an agricultural program might eventually become self-supporting; although most of the food produced that year was consumed by the 150 people who lived on the campus, $800 worth had been sold.[39]

The report noted that the school had been criticized for shutting down in the summer—the male students might instead be keeping the agricultural program going. In reply, the report noted that most of the students were poor, and that they had to work during the summer to pay their school expenses. "But if the state wants the school, that is the strictly industrial side of it [farming, carpentry, blacksmithing, etc.] to be maintained ten or even twelve months of the year, there will be required a larger appropriation for the purpose."[40] Soon, there would be signs that Gregory the classics scholar felt pressed by the state of New Jersey to focus more on its industrial attributes rather than its academic ones.

Facing Pressure from the State

In 1909, the New Jersey state legislature established a Commission on Industrial Education to undertake an extensive survey of such programs nationwide and then make recommendations that would meet the needs of industries and "best serve the interests of the state." The commission's report is a valuable compilation of programs not only around the country but in Europe as well. It noted the end of apprenticeship programs, the lack of skilled workmen, and the fact that 95 percent of students between fourteen and seventeen left school lacking any idea about their future vocation. More courses in industrial drawing, math, and English were needed. Whereas manual training as then taught was valuable as preparation, it was insufficient as training for a trade—its purpose was "purely cultural" rather than directly vocational. In the section on programs in New Jersey, the report commended schools in Newark, Hoboken, and Trenton, claiming that they returned to society the cost of the schooling they provided.[41] The overall purpose behind all these programs was providing young people with opportunities they might not have had without them.

Founded in the mid-1880s by their municipalities, the schools in Newark and Hoboken both served several hundred students; most were secondary level; adults attended in the evenings. The cities' annual investments of $7,000 were matched by the state. Courses of varied duration were offered in construction, woodworking, electricity, and plumbing; girls studied cooking and sewing. Trenton's School of Industrial Art had been established only a decade earlier; it, too, offered day and evening classes, in bookbinding and mechanical drawing, plus several in ceramics as that was an important local industry. The Manual Training and Industrial School offered somewhat fewer industrial courses than the others, but the latter did not offer academic courses as Bordentown did. It also served far fewer students—enrollment at the time was fifty boys and sixty-eight girls; none, it claimed, were from out of state. Students paid no tuition, but six dollars per month for room and board.[42]

Changes, however, were underway for the Bordentown school. "Until recently," the report noted, "little more was done [there] than to duplicate the opportunities offered in existing public schools, but the school now finds its more useful career along the lines of Hampton or Tuskegee."[43] This suggests that the commission's members may have been more influenced by perceptions than familiarity: the chief function of those famous schools was preparing teachers; their industrial aspect was more in the work required of students to help maintain the facility in the fashion of the earlier manual labor schools. Also, the students were encouraged to acquire practical skills needed in the communities where they would go teach.[44] More significant for

Bordentown's future was an indication that the state was not fully satisfied with Gregory's leadership. He was, according to the Pillsbury report, given high marks for his administration, but the school's board "increasingly felt that the curriculum was becoming unbalanced in favor of academics and too light on manual training."[45] Perhaps in response to pressure from the state, Gregory fell ill in 1909 and took a two-year leave.[46] An interim director, J. Thomas Caruthers, had been appointed, and "the industrial departments were being developed rapidly," the report noted.[47] At the time, Caruthers was the school's sole teacher of agriculture, according to a school catalog.

Also in 1911, the year Gregory resumed his role as principal, the Bordentown school acquired a loyal and influential supporter, a man who would advocate for its interests for over twenty years. D. Stewart Craven, who used the military title "Colonel," acquired as officer of the state national guard, was a member of the state board of education from 1911 until the mid-1930s. At various times, Craven served on the board's committees on normal schools and vocational education; most significantly, beginning in 1915 or so, he chaired its committee on the Manual Training and Industrial School. A resident of Salem in the state's southwestern corner, Craven was an executive in a family-owned glass company there.[48] Salem County had, between the 1870s and the 1930s, the state's highest concentration of African American residents, which could explain his concern about the manual training school's well-being.[49]

Another person who would have a major impact on MTIS was Calvin Kendall. A nationally noted educator, he was selected as New Jersey's commissioner of education by Woodrow Wilson, who became governor in 1912; Kendall's task was to "stimulate and reorganize" the state's schools.[50] Soon after his arrival, Kendall invited Booker T. Washington to make another visit; it took place in August 1913 as part of a fundraising tour of the state. The school, Washington wrote in his report, should focus its efforts on the "prevailing occupations" among the state's "colored people"; these, he assumed, were in farming, gardening, the building trades and related mechanics, plus domestic science and dressmaking for girls. However, "academic work ought not to be neglected"; "dovetailed into these practical industries, [this integration] gives a more severe mental training than... old-form abstract book education," he wrote.[51] "Dovetailing" was a practice Washington often advised.[52]

Although likely back on campus by the time of Washington's visit, James Gregory may not have welcomed such suggestions. The *New York Age* reported in February 1915 that the state board had determined that the Bordentown school was to be "made primarily an industrial school instead of a school for the academic training of pupils" and that the Gregorys had resigned in response—Mrs. Gregory was the school's "matron," a common role for the principal's wife. "The principal and the matron admitted that they did not feel equipped to care for the needs of a purely agricultural and mechanical arts school," the article stated.[53] Gregory's health problems had also reoccurred, and he died in December that year at his daughter's home in Baltimore. He was only sixty-five years old. A month earlier, Booker T. Washington, had died in Tuskegee; he had not yet reached his sixtieth birthday.

The extensive celebrations of Gregory's life indicate the esteem in which he was held. There were three: in Washington, Boston, and another in Bordentown, all attended by some of the most prominent African Americans of the day. Eulogies noted not only Gregory's accomplishments but suggested the conflicts and accommodations with which he and his peers were grappling. The funeral itself, held at the Plymouth Congregational Church in Washington, was "among the most impressive ever held in Washington," according to a newspaper report.[54] It was presided over by a family friend, Francis Grimké, an eminent cleric and frequent visitor to the Gregory home in Bordentown. The article quoted Grimké as saying that James Gregory "had always battled for the equality of his race in education and politics." Further remarks were delivered by Stephen Newman, then president of Howard University, who commended Gregory for leaving well-established Oberlin for unknown Howard, for his long career at the university, and for demonstrating as Bordentown principal "the dependence of industrial education upon the broader cultural training of the higher institutions of learning." Pallbearers included Kelly Miller and Alain Locke, both prominent members of the Howard faculty; honorary pallbearers were T. Thomas Fortune and several other noted writers and educators.[55] Three days later, the Gregory family gathered at Mount Auburn cemetery in Cambridge, Massachusetts, near Harvard University. They were joined by a few friends, including William Monroe Trotter, editor of the *Boston Guardian*, which had carried the article about Gregory's funeral. Known for its staunch opposition to Booker T. Washington, the paper's account of the eulogies suggests that point of view.

The April 1916 memorial service for Gregory held on the Bordentown campus was a testament to his leadership there. The major address was given by Alain Locke, then as prominent an intellectual as W. E. B. Du Bois; other remarks were made by state officials Stewart Craven and Joseph Frelinghuysen. In addition to several educators who had worked with Gregory, a Bishop Coppin spoke; likely this was Levi, the husband of Fanny Jackson Coppin, former principal of Philadelphia's Institute for Colored Youth.[56] In sum, attendees at all three gatherings represented the era's varied strains of thought regarding education for African Americans.

Nearly a year earlier, in May of 1915, a new principal had arrived to take Gregory's place at Bordentown. If the school's first principal was a pastor and the second a scholar, the third was an educator. The choice had been urged by Calvin Kendall, the state's education commissioner, and the new principal was William R. Valentine, whom he had known in Indiana. A graduate of Montclair High School, in New Jersey, and of Harvard College, class of 1904, Valentine had for a decade been principal at a school in Indianapolis known as PS 26. The school, not incidentally, had been lauded in *Schools of Tomorrow*, a 1915 book by John Dewey and his daughter Evelyn. Located in a poor, crowded, and under-resourced "colored" district, the school had lessons for any school serving children from homes with "meager surroundings," the Deweys wrote.[57] Though the community had been hostile to the school, Valentine turned that around by making of the school a "plant" that met residents' needs. Aspects of Dewey's Laboratory School and Hull House in Chicago, plus manual training courses, were apparent in the program Valentine had devised. Students learned carpentry, shoe cobbling, and dressmaking; they managed a bank and a soup kitchen; they gardened and designed a model apartment. All aroused a "spirit of cooperation" where there had been distrust.

If the state had felt that the Manual Training and Industrial School was in need of revitalization and redirection, Valentine seemed the man for the job. He likely knew that Tuskegee was the model he was expected to follow, and he may have had some experience working there as a college student,[58] but he likely also noted that the Deweys had compared an aspect of PS 26 to a school in the well-to-do town of Riverside, Illinois. It and other schools were aiming at an idea associated with Tuskegee—that of better equipping "pupils for their life in the community with the hope of improving the community itself."[59] With the varied experiences that had influenced him—schooling in a prosperous suburban community, a Harvard education, working in Indianapolis, and his own developing ideas about the school as a social settlement, Valentine was well suited to his new post.[60] In addition, he brought with him his wife Grace Valentine, who was also an experienced educator, and their two young children.

An Ascendance and a Nadir

The nearly two decades during which James Gregory headed the Manual Training and Industrial School were momentous and sadly disappointing for the nation's African American citizens. By 1895, Jim Crow practices were firmly entrenched in the South; the opportunities available during Reconstruction—education and enfranchisement—had diminished there and

Figure 17. James Monroe Gregory, in a photo published in 1908, had arrived at MTIS a decade earlier after a distinguished career at Howard University. His presence brought the school to the attention of leading Black intellectuals of the day; his administration was complicated by contrasting notions about the most appropriate education for African American young people.

then largely disappeared.⁶¹ A reign of terror settled over the South, and the situation was met with indifference in the North, where aspects of Jim Crow surfaced in schools and seaside resorts, workshops and stores. Considered by some a "Mississippi of the North" because of its southern sympathies, New Jersey—which was the last northern state to eliminate slavery, and it neglected the Fourteenth and Fifteenth Amendments on citizenship and male suffrage—it may not seem an obvious site for working out in an actual institution the tensions over the "kind of education the Afro-American most needs," to quote T. Thomas Fortune's 1898 article on the topic.⁶² But it was, and Gregory needed to maneuver the Manual Training and Industrial School through pressures that influenced its course both directly and indirectly.

As a noted scholar, Gregory was inclined to insist on the importance of a "literary" education; as an administrator of an industrial school dependent upon state support, he had to heed its prerogatives. And he had to do this while an increasingly vigorous debate on academic versus industrial education was taking place nationally. Recounted as a difference between the Hampton-Tuskegee model that emphasized self-reliance and practical skills and an opposing model that insisted upon full citizenship and academic opportunities, the conflict is most often characterized as one between Tuskegee head Booker T. Washington and W. E. B. Du Bois, a man of equal talent but a contrasting set of experiences. The first was the accommodating self-made man; the other an erudite essayist. Though chronicles of the lives of both men and of "Negro thought" in the era emphasize that their differences were more a matter of means and degree than of long-term direction and goals, it has been convenient to pose them as adversaries.[63] Two years before Gregory became MTIS principal, Washington gave what is remembered as his "Atlanta Compromise" speech. In it, he pledged to encourage his fellows to work hard and build a solid economic foundation for their communities while delaying a quest for social equality with white society. Initially, in the mid-1890s, Du Bois did not take issue with this approach, and an amicable relationship existed between them for the next few years, a time during which Gregory endeavored to develop a school that in name seemed to be hewing to the Washington model despite the fact that, going only through the tenth grade, it could not be a normal school like Tuskegee.

That period between 1895 to 1915—years that nearly matched those of the Gregory administration—have been labelled those of Washington's ascendancy by August Meier in his classic 1963 study *Negro Thought in America, 1880 to 1915*. Frederick Douglass had died in February 1895; after his speech in Atlanta the following September, Washington "rose to become the principal negotiator between the two races," a role that Douglass had long held.[64] Washington quickly became a power broker, advising presidents on policy and appointments, raising money in the North and distributing it in the South to projects that were in accord with his priorities.[65] His growing ability to do this rankled Du Bois, who felt Washington gave up on the quest for political rights in return for philanthropists' support for Tuskegee.[66]

Du Bois, in his famed study of Philadelphia conducted in 1896, concluded that it was necessary to look beyond schooling alone as a source of problems facing Negro communities.[67] The following year, 1897, he began an article called "A Rational System for Negro Education," in which he endeavored to reconcile the divergent tendencies between making a living and making a life. Though his system recognized the "vogue" for industrial education, Du Bois argued that the isolation of Negro communities demanded an "indigenous leadership" of college-trained industrialists and scholars.[68] In 1897, Du Bois moved on to Atlanta University; during a dozen years of working there, he produced a series of studies about the conditions of Negro life and culture based on conferences and thorough questionnaires.

Washington, ever respectful of how tenuous his position and that of Tuskegee were—dependent upon both Southern goodwill and Northern money—continued to stress that questions about full equality should await a firm economic base. The Negro, he wrote, should "deport himself modestly in regard to political claims"; their "full exercise" would be "a matter of slow, natural growth."[69] Du Bois countered that voting was essential to protecting any property acquired and that submitting to injustice undermined self-respect.[70] For Washington, political rights would follow economic accomplishment; for Du Bois, there would be little of the latter without the former.

In 1901, Washington's *Up from Slavery* appeared to considerable positive notice, at least initially, in both the North and the South. An exception was a review written by Du Bois, which was, according to a biographer, "calmly unfavorable" to its "educational and economic outlook."[71] Despite this, the two men remained friends, visiting and vacationing with each other. But soon after the turn of the century, when it became clear that Washington's approach was not going to usher in a Negro nirvana, the sharp division between what were known as "Bookerites" and "anti-Bookerites" became clear.[72] Washington's position was such that he could dine at the White House—a 1901 invitation from Theodore Roosevelt aroused considerable controversy from many quarters[73]—but he could not stop lynching in the South nor, in either the North or the South, a practice known as whitecapping, which employed violence to harass Black people using tactics for which the Ku Klux Klan would later be noted.

In 1902, the first of Du Bois's two studies of the Negro artisan appeared; it was based on a conference in Atlanta at which Washington and others had spoken.[74] Among its valuable points is that prior to the Civil War, "there were a large number of Negro mechanics in the Southern States; many of them were expert blacksmiths, wheelwrights, wagon-makers," and masters of construction trades. But these skills were neglected after the war because, while a white man with property would hire an enslaved mechanic, he was less inclined to hire a free one. So, these skills were not maintained—and other white men, those formerly kept out of such trades, began competing for the jobs.[75] Several mutual friends had encouraged Washington to invite Du Bois onto the Tuskegee faculty, an invitation that was proffered more than once. Several others encouraged him to accept, but it was said that Du Bois wanted to leave the South after a dozen years in Atlanta.[76]

In 1903, an intrepid publisher in Chicago brought out Du Bois's collection *The Souls of Black Folk*, essays that sang of the inner spirit of his subjects while offering two distinctive concepts destined to long outlive the book's initial publication. One is that the color line would be the problem of the twentieth century, the other, the idea of the "veil," or double consciousness:

can one be both a Negro and an American? he asked.[77] *Souls* also included "Of Mr. Booker T. Washington and Others," an essay that made its subject's 1895 speech more famous than it had been when delivered. At this point, "the gloves were off" between the Bookerites and the anti-Bookerites, which Washington's camp referred to as "the opposition."[78]

Several events at around the same time served to push the two sides further apart. Northern activists and intellectuals such as Chicago's Ida B. Wells greeted *The Souls of Black Folk* with considerable enthusiasm. The publisher, with her husband Ferdinand Barnett, of an influential paper in Chicago called *The Conservator*, Wells-Barnett wrote to Du Bois that "We are still reading your book with the same delighted appreciation."[79] In January 1904, a gathering of many opinions was held at Carnegie Hall in New York; an effort to affect a compromise, it resulted in a series of resolutions to which supporters of both sides agreed to subscribe. But Du Bois's partisans began to suspect that Washington was dictating terms of the agreements.[80] At the same time, the Afro-American Council, the chief national organization for the previous dozen years, foundered as Washington's influence declined, particularly among the educated elite in the North. His steady hand was losing its grip, and by 1906 the council was essentially moribund, but not yet replaced by another.[81]

Events that year, particularly a bloody riot in Atlanta, which took the masks off of seemingly cordial relations between Black and white in that southern capital, indicated that new leadership was needed. In 1905, a group of twenty-nine men led by Du Bois met on the Canadian side of Niagara Falls to discuss "principles, not men."[82] Though it led to a movement rather than an organization, it prepared the way for a National Negro Conference, held in New York City on Abraham Lincoln's one hundredth birthday in 1909. Speakers included Du Bois and John Dewey, who argued that members of all "races" should have the same opportunities; it was society's responsibility to provide the environment that "will utilize all of the individual capital being born into it."[83] It was the first time the two, who were natural intellectual allies given their education and political priorities, had ever met; the second time would be twenty years later.[84]

The following year, 1910, the National Association for the Advancement of Colored People was established as an outgrowth of the Niagara Movement. Among its distinctions was that Blacks and whites joined together to lead it; initial board members included white progressives such as Oswald Garrison Villard, Jane Addams, anthropologist Franz Boaz, and radical Chicago attorney Clarence Darrow. Washington was not among its founders, and it was designed to take legal action rather than to take sides. The organization grew quickly; its periodical *Crisis*, edited by Du Bois, had a circulation of over thirty thousand copies within a few years.[85]

Though white philanthropists from the North had since the Civil War underwritten and led numerous efforts to establish educational institutions throughout the South, both elementary and college level, leadership of such groups was seldom integrated. For example, there were the two Mohonk conferences on Negro education held in 1900 and 1901; though they attracted a distinguished roster of white men (Hampton's Armstrong, Cornell president Andrew D. White, U.S. Commissioner of Education William T. Harris, among several others), no Black people—not even Washington—were invited.[86] White paternalism prevailed, and it surely aggravated Du Bois, whose erudition was on par with men like Dewey and other members of the university-educated elite but who could not be considered for even a visiting appointment at any American college other than those established for Black students.

A still-influential version of these events and decisions is Henry Allan Bullock's 1967 *History of Negro Education in the South*, in which he argued that after Reconstruction ended in 1878, attitudes toward schooling for the millions whose minds and bodies had been held in bondage took a "Grand Detour." It moved away from the humanitarian vision of the New England schoolmarms who had gone to the South after the Civil War to lay foundations for a school system there; it headed instead toward a "special education," one that limited the aspirations of Black students and communities. The special education Bullock disparaged was the version of manual and industrial training that he saw being imposed upon Blacks in the South.[87] This imposition was funded by Northern philanthropists and, it has been assumed, led by Washington and his minions.

In 1915, Du Bois delivered his version of this history in testimony before a congressional commission. In it he argued that the question of education for Negroes sat on the horns of a dilemma: an industrious and law-abiding people cannot be kept in ignorance, yet much of the South feared the power that would be the inevitable result of remediating that ignorance. He urged honesty by those in power: either provide decent public schooling for Negroes, including normal schools and useful industrial education, or face the consequences.[88] The school that Gregory led through this tumultuous period, in the most "southern" of northern states, was able to strike a working balance between his inclinations as a scholar and the need to satisfy the sources of the school's funding, some of whom were not yet convinced about the value of a solid education for the state's Black citizens.

In *Black New Jersey*, Graham Hodges described the environment in which Gregory worked on a more local level. New Jersey had long had a Black population, scattered throughout the state until after the Civil War when first emancipation and then Jim Crow brought southerners to the state in greater numbers. Initially, these new residents settled in the state's southern counties, first as agricultural workers and then as service staff for Cape May resorts and, around 1900, those in Atlantic City. Black and white communities were largely integrated until more Black residents arrived; whites responded by throwing up barricades.[89] Schools, according to Marion Thompson Wright's 1940 *Education of Negroes in New Jersey*, tended to be integrated in northern counties and segregated in southern ones, though as the century moved along, funding and dividing lines between the two began to diverge—facilities for white children were far superior to those for Black children, even if they were nominally integrated. In 1881, the state legislature disallowed segregation in schools and other public facilities, but the law had been largely ignored.[90] Recall that in 1880 the board of education in Bordentown had erected a new building for its Black students, a new School No. 2, rather than welcome them into the schools that white children attended.

Hodges refers to the years that Meier described as Washington's ascendency—1895 to 1915—as ones in which the situation for Blacks in New Jersey fell to its nadir. While there were some gains, as with a growing middle class, segregation and racial antagonism increased.[91] Meier described the same pattern as existing on a national level: deteriorating race relations plus actions that increasingly hampered aspirations of the mass of Black people, while the entrepreneurial and professional classes prospered.[92] Those participating in the observations of James Gregory's life and accomplishments represented the good and ill of these developments—they were among the Black people who most benefited from the positive aspects of this era, by virtue of their education and national perspective, but they were also most acutely aware of the potential long-term damage—and they used their platforms, in pulpits and papers, to rail against what they saw happening.

Gregory's Memorials in Historical Context

One of the most intriguing of those who celebrated the life of James Gregory was Francis Grimké; he had visited the Gregorys in Bordentown and was pastor at a prominent Presbyterian Church in Washington, DC. With his brother Archibald, an attorney and widely published civil rights advocate living in Boston, Francis exemplified in his own personal history the ambiguities of being Black in his era—Du Bois's concept of double consciousness surely applied to both. Born on a South Carolina plantation to the son of a prominent family and an enslaved woman, they had both the privileges of their father and the restrictions to which their mother was subject. This was particularly so after their father died on the eve of the Civil War and the family became the property of an uncle, who was ill-disposed to treat them kindly. After some horrendous experiences during the war, the boys escaped, having caught the attention of people who noted their talents and funded their enrollment at Lincoln University, the earliest college for Black students, established in 1854 outside Philadelphia. Once there, they caught the attention of their aunts, fierce abolitionists and feminists Sarah Grimké and Angelina Grimké Weld, who had not known of their existence—the two had fled their large family in Charleston nearly forty years before. Along with Angelina's husband, Theodore Weld, the sisters had moved from New Jersey to Boston, and they took their newly discovered nephews under their wing. Archibald attended law school at Harvard; Francis, the Princeton Theological Seminary.[93]

In the account of Gregory's funeral given by his son Montgomery are quotations about the event that appeared in the *Boston Guardian*. Generous though they were to Gregory—"among the most impressive" held in the church—they can also be interpreted as a sally in the struggle between the Bookerites and the anti-Bookerites. The *Guardian* had been established by William Monroe Trotter in 1901 as an unapologetic advocate of the latter. The article's comment that Gregory had "always battled for" equality in education and politics reiterated Trotter's point of view. As the ideological struggle between the two forces had developed in the early 1900s, Trotter made clear which side he was on—and may even have pushed Du Bois to a more extreme position than he might have otherwise held.[94] Any institution with the words "manual training" or "industrial" in its name was suspect, whatever the merits of such a school; however, there is some evidence that savvy Black educators may have appended the words to make their schools more inviting to potential white funders.[95]

Trotter had joined the Gregory family at the late December 1915 graveside ceremony in Cambridge, possibly—though this is totally speculation—as a means of claiming that in the ideological struggle between Washington and Du Bois, the latter had won. Thousands may have honored Washington in Tuskegee after his death a month before (and in New Jersey as well, according to Hodges's history), but the cognoscenti were honoring Gregory and his insistence upon the necessity of an academic education.

Also honoring Gregory at the funeral in Washington as an honorary pall bearer was T. Thomas Fortune, who was then a struggling writer in New Jersey and Philadelphia, as he had lost control of his *New York Age*. Since the mid-1880s, Fortune had been both hired pen and bullhorn for Washington. In one of the most remarkable alliances of the era, Fortune provided sharp phrasing the stolid Washington could not muster, and both served each other's purposes for over twenty years. Fortune's brilliance, however, could not assuage his demons—alcohol and financial instability would ever limit his long-term effectiveness, despite his near-unparalleled ability to speak truth to power.⁹⁶ Fortune's laudatory comments about the Bordentown school published in 1905 can been read not only for their own merit but as an effort to shore up his waning relationship with Washington, who was then offering financial support to Fortune's *New York Age*. As the record indicates, Tuskegee's "wizard" did the same for other publications that took his side in the ideological struggle with Trotter's *Boston Guardian*, the Wells-Barnett's *Conservator* in Chicago, and several other papers.

Trotter, who frequently had the support of Archibald Grimké, may not have been aware of the role the latter's family played in the development of the manual training programs he was wont to disparage. Grimké's uncle (by marriage) Theodore Weld, who had died in 1895, or six years prior to Trotter's starting the *Guardian*, had during the 1820s and 1830s been a forceful advocate for the virtues of manual labor in a literary education, as noted in chapter 2. His 1833 report on the topic had claimed among other things that "bodily exercise" and honest labor were indispensable to man's intellectual and moral well-being, as well as his "individual happiness and social usefulness." It should be incorporated into seminaries and other forms of education, as it had been at the Oneida Institute that Weld had helped lead.⁹⁷ Further, the consensus of such opinion had sent missionaries of this particular gospel not only to the Mississippi Valley where it inspired two of the men behind the establishment of the Chicago Manual Training School—Eliphalet Blatchford and Henry Belfield—it had also sent them further afield to the Sandwich Islands, soon to be known as Hawaii. There, in 1833, a young man named David Lyman with his wife Sarah had found themselves in a small settlement on the island of Hawaii where they soon established a school eventually known as the Hilo Boys Boarding School, an institution that shared its inspiration with that of the schools Blatchford and Belfield had attended. The idea was that students would do manual labor not only because it helped pay for their education, but also because it inculcated New England virtues such as hard work, diligence, accuracy, thrift, and a morality characterized by self-restraint.⁹⁸

Among visitors to the Lymans' school was Richard Armstrong, another missionary who had arrived in the islands prior to the Lymans and had become the Hawaiian monarchy's superintendent of public instruction. On occasion he would bring with him his young son Samuel. According to accounts of the Hilo school, it not only prepared young Hawaiian boys to participate in the beginnings of a bureaucracy that could prevent the islands from being overwhelmed by the rapacious instincts of the more acquisitive societies in the East and West that were invading the islands, it also served as a model for similar institutions throughout the Pacific.⁹⁹ Samuel Chapman Armstrong, after returning to the mainland, obtaining an education at the same schools that had inspired the missionary impulse of the 1830s, became a Union officer in charge of a regiment of Black troops, men he came to respect for their eagerness to serve. After the war, he worked with the Freedmen's Bureau and agonized over a possible future for the hordes of homeless former bondsmen and women under his supervision near Hampton, Virginia. The example that had sent Theodore Weld's fellows to Illinois, Indiana, and Hawaii became a model for him to follow. As he wrote in a letter to a family member, "There may be a place for me in the struggle for right and wrong in this country."[100]

Arguably the history of Armstrong's motivations and accomplishments has become entwined in the ideological conflicts of later times.[101] The Hampton Normal and Agricultural School that he established in 1868 served not to send Black students back to work in the fields, but to use their labor to support the school following Weld's ideas so that they could go out into the countryside to impart the basics of an elementary education to their fellows.[102] While Armstrong was paternalistic toward his students and believed that they needed schooling in practical skills accompanied by the basics of a secondary education, he was not intent upon their pauperization as some have claimed.[103] Booker T. Washington arrived at Hampton in 1872 and, as he told the story, used his instinct for thoroughness to sweep a floor so well that a New England schoolmarm admitted him to Hampton. He then went on to Tuskegee where he learned to make bricks so that he could teach his students the same, and so that together they could construct the buildings necessary to establish a school.[104] The product of a middle-class home and education, Trotter may have ignored the significance of those experiences to a less-privileged young Booker Taliaferro.[105]

Whether James Gregory and Francis Grimké discussed the century-old origin of manual labor schools during afternoon conversations in the garden Fannie Gregory had created on the Bordentown campus, we will not know. But the presence of Gregory's Howard colleague Kelly Miller at his funeral suggests the regard in which he was held by those who endeavored to steer a middle course between Trotter and the Bookerites. The son of a Carolina "cash-rent" cotton farmer, Miller attended Howard and later Johns Hopkins to become a mathematician of recognized brilliance. Known outside the university for perceptive and influential essays on the condition of his fellows, he promoted compromise, pragmatism, and harmony. Though he remained friendly with Washington, Miller gradually migrated to Du Bois's camp after 1900, but later he pictured the latter as a "frenzied dreamer who had turned from scholarship to agitation."[106]

Alain Locke, another honorary pallbearer, represents an even more complex history. After a childhood in Philadelphia and Camden, he had attended the University of Pennsylvania and gone on to be the first African American Rhodes Scholar. His relationship with the Gregory family was more personal than political. A noted esthete—an admirer of John Ruskin who had inspired the contemporary Arts and Crafts Movement which shared principles and priorities with manual training schools—Locke worked with James Gregory's son Montgomery in establishing the Howard Players, the nation's first Black theater company. Slight of build and prone to various ailments, he would not have joined Washington in his brick-making endeavors. Nor did he join his fellow Harvard-educated intellectual Du Bois—both had also spent time at German universities—in a public role or become involved with organizations such as the NAACP. His contribution was to lead the Harlem Renaissance and define the "new Negro" in the process, but in 1915 that was still in the future.[107]

Locke was not only a pallbearer at Gregory's Washington funeral, he was also the chief speaker at the memorial service held in Bordentown the following April. Whether Locke or Miller or Grimké were aware of the pressure on Gregory to adhere more closely to a Tuskegee model as New Jersey officials understood it would be speculation, but two of the other speakers likely were. One was Stewart Craven, head of the board of education's Manual Training and Industrial School Committee, and Joseph Frelinghuysen, a member of the famed New Jersey family and known not only for supporting the Bordentown school but for advocating for an antilynching bill as a senator.[108] The two may have been Gregory's defenders in the state government when he needed them—reading between the lines of two reports on the school in 1909 suggests that Gregory was being pressured to turn the school into a training ground for agricultural workers on the state's increasingly mechanized farms. It was in that year that Gregory began a two-year leave from the school to restore his health.

Setting comments in the state's 1909 Industrial Education Commission report in the context of the national debate about the value of industrial education suggests why Gregory needed defenders. The state's Black population was growing, as was school enrollment—from 50 or so students when Gregory arrived to somewhere between 120 and 130. Some reports claim all were from New Jersey; others that they came from various states. The commission report stated that "until recently, little more was done . . . than to duplicate opportunities in existing schools, but it now finds its more useful career along the lines of Hampton or Tuskegee." This statement is misleading: both the *New York Age* article of 1905 and the 1908 *Echoes* report cited the kinds of "industrial" instruction going on. For boys, there was practical work in carpentry and agriculture; there was a well-equipped shop for the former and 225 acres for the latter. For girls, there was practical work in sewing and cookery; they took responsibility for preparing many meals as well as making curtains and the like for campus buildings. Further, as noted earlier, the Gregorys traveled the state gathering needed donations such as sewing machines and typewriters, pianos and musical instruments.

The report seems to ignore the fact that the Bordentown school served students in sixth though tenth grade—whereas Hampton and Tuskegee were both nominally post-secondary schools and largely teacher-training institutions. This suggests that writers of the report knew little about either institution, and perhaps not much about MTIS either. In December of 1909—presumably after the Industrial Education Commission report was published—the Bordentown School Committee of the State Board of Education issued a report of its own, one that can be seen as a rebuttal to that of the commission. It stressed not only all the practical work going on at the school, but also that some of the programs were remunerative and that the school used the state's money well. Further, the committee responded directly to critics who complained that the school should be open ten or twelve months of the year in order to maximize potential income from its fields.[109]

One implication of the 1909 commission report is that some members of the legislature wanted the school to produce students trained to do manual work in the state's agricultural industries. But the school's defenders on the board of education said, in effect, "Hey, wait a minute. If that's what you want, you legislators are going to have to appropriate a lot more money to equip the school with the equipment needed in mechanized agriculture." Further, the students by their choice of vocation were resisting any effort to send them back to the fields—as noted above, those who had graduated during the first ten years of the Gregory administration became teachers and nurses and store managers, a journalist and a carpenter; a few had gone on to college.

Just What Is an Industrial Education?

When members of the New Jersey Council of Education in 1889 declared that an "Authoritative Definition of Manual Training" meant "thought expression" by means other than "verbal language" that would provide "training for judgment and the executive faculty," it was a definition that would have pleased Calvin Woodward, manual training's most widely known advocate at the time.[110] Further, by a decade later, over two dozen public grammar and high schools in the state offered several thousand students some form of manual training; however, in keeping with national trends, these programs were increasingly less purist in their understanding of what manual training meant.[111] By 1909, when the state's Commission on Industrial Education issued its report, the programs that received extensive descriptions—those in Newark and Hoboken—were unapologetically aimed at preparing students, who ranged in age from youths to adults, for jobs. Manual training at the pre-secondary level received less attention in the report, except for the comment that fifty school districts in the state received some state aid for their programs. Courses prepared boys for jobs in construction, electrical work, and plumbing, and for girls in sewing. The "state homes," which served students in need of such structure and discipline, offered similar courses, plus others in dairying, gardening, and laundry.[112] The point of these programs was not to limit student aspirations, but to provide a means for young people to take their place in a healthy democratic society.

The report lists with similar thoroughness the kinds of industrial courses offered elsewhere in the nation. Such specificity, though, is missing in works like Meier's *Negro Thought*; it makes numerous mentions of "industrial" programs without describing what it means by the term. The same is true in Bullock's *History of Negro Education in the South*; it tends to equate "industrial education" with condescending ideas like "uplift," claiming that the chief purpose of such schooling was to limit the aspirations of Negro children. Other than vague references to agricultural work, it offers few specifics about the kind of schooling or jobs implied by the term "industrial"; instead, it discusses at great length the work of philanthropists in encouraging such preparation at the expense of higher education.[113]

In neither book are there references to contemporaneous national movements in support of industrial education, efforts that also aimed to build character and respect for the dignity of labor—ideas that abounded in the writings of Theodore Weld, Calvin Woodward, and even Nicholas Murray Butler.[114] Bullock looked askance at the idea that students should be expected to perform manual labor in return for their education—an idea that was essential to both Hampton and Tuskegee, as well as to many colleges for white students, particularly those established by missionaries.[115] Washington wrote that he had to fight against this anti-labor attitude: parents of some Tuskegee students wanted their children to engage in "book learning" rather than to do manual labor—an objection, by the way, that Woodward met at his manual training school in St. Louis.[116] Further, Bullock expressed dismay at the idea that girls in their math classes would be required to figure, for example, the amount of fabric needed to make dresses of various sizes.[117] In his more recent history of education for Blacks, James Anderson took issue with this idea as practiced at Tuskegee, wherein normal school students studied composition through writing about blacksmithing and carpentry—a practice that Washington called "dovetailing."[118] Neither Bullock nor Anderson, noted historians both (though Bullock died in 1973), acknowledge how very Deweyan such lessons were—the basic idea of the Laboratory School was that students would learn academic skills through studying the occupations common in their community. Making math and science and English relevant to the work of the world was also a significant aspect of industrial education programs promoted for white students during the 1920s.[119]

Although Derrick Alridge, in his 2008 study of Du Bois's educational thought, does not place the industrial vs. liberal arts discussion in the context of Weld and Woodward and the manual training movement, he recognizes the very substantial connections between Dewey and Du Bois. They were "kindred spirits," he wrote, who believed that children should have "both experiential education and education in the humanities."[120] Connections between Dewey and Washington are made even more explicit in a book that claims the latter was actually an "architect of progressive education." Written by a community college official named Donald Generals, the book asserts that Washington applied the Pestalozzian idea that schools can regenerate the social order and that the Tuskegee curriculum encouraged students to be engaged in activities that were meaningful to their lives.[121] Though Alridge does not discuss Dewey to the extent that Generals does, he claims that Du Bois deserves recognition as a significant education theorist, a claim that Generals makes for Washington as well.

Generals further claims that the industrial education offered at schools like Tuskegee enhanced rather than hampered students' economic mobility: a follow-up of Tuskegee graduates "revealed that more than half had later entered the professions of teaching, school administration, nursing and medicine, or were in graduate school." He also noted that graduates in agriculture and business both were well equipped to enter fields otherwise closed to them.[122] The Tuskegee model adhered neither to the purposefully nonvocational model of early manual training schools nor to an idealized "occupations" model as developed in Chicago by Dewey fifteen years after the Alabama school opened. Instead, it started where its students were and, like the Bordentown school would later do, took what was useful from progressive ideas of its day. With its combination—or dovetailing—of academic and "industrial" subjects, Tuskegee anticipated by two decades the sort of program for a comprehensive high school that Dewey would advocate beginning in 1910.[123]

In ending *Up from Slavery,* Washington wrote that Tuskegee offered the kind of education its students needed at the time and at the place where he found them: the rural South where schooling for Black students was limited at best and economic opportunities even more restricted. He wanted every student to graduate "with enough skill, coupled with intelligence and moral character, to enable him to make a living for himself and others." The young men did receive training in agriculture and carpentry; the girls in "gardening, fruit-growing, dairying, bee-culture, and poultry-raising."[124] But how was this different from the schooling offered white students, North and South, in a time when only 10 percent even attended high school?

The 1912 edition of *The Negro American Artisan*, coedited by Du Bois, provides a detailed analysis of the kinds of industrial training offered in secondary and postsecondary schools (at the time, there was limited distinction between the two) for Black students.[125] Most were in carpentry, blacksmithing, printing, and domestic skills. The report concluded that much of the training was for increasingly outdated skills and done on makeshift equipment, though it notes that Hampton, Tuskegee, and a few others operated along more "modern" lines. It also quoted from a Tuskegee publication that surveyed nearly four hundred recent graduates and former students. Substantially over half of them were (in descending numbers) brick masons, blacksmiths, nurses and carpenters, tailors and dressmakers; another one hundred were "carrying on business in connection with trades."[126] Few if any were engaged in any form of agriculture.

In his 1915 testimony before the U.S. Commission on Industrial Relations, Du Bois painted a somewhat different picture. While Hampton and Tuskegee and similar institutions were arguably preparing their graduates for middle-class jobs—as suggested by his 1912 report—and were doing so with money raised largely in the North, he in 1915 claimed that prominent philanthropies such as the Rockefeller-funded General Education Board were being disingenuous. These philanthropists were giving far more money to industrial schools than to colleges and were often too eager to surrender to southern prejudice. Instead, he argued, southern Negroes needed a decent public school system, one that would make normal and industrial education an integral part of the schools, and that both should be supported by public money equitably distributed between Black students and white.[127]

Though he does not mention this testimony, Alridge appears to suggest that what Du Bois took issue with was the tendency for white philanthropists to assume that they knew what was best—and that they placed too much reliance on Washington's leadership and priorities. Perhaps, had they consulted Du Bois, their philanthropy may have taken a more balanced approach. Du Bois realized that industrial training was necessary, but that did not mean that Black students should be denied exposure to the broader democratic culture of which they were a part. This was a very Deweyan argument as well.[128]

At the time Du Bois gave this testimony—early in 1915—James Monroe Gregory had decided to retire from the Bordentown school, given we might assume the sort of pressure that Du Bois claimed northern philanthropists were putting on secondary and beyond schools for Black students in the South. In his history of New Jersey, Hodges claimed that leadership tended to follow southern attitudes toward the state's Black residents, particularly as their numbers grew after 1870. If agricultural work predominated while the Black population was concentrated in the state's southern counties, this changed as other kinds of work became available. While Black workers flocked to jobs in resort industries, they were kept out of those in manufacturing, except in the lowest-paying positions. Hodges quotes a 1903 wage survey that referred to this practice and union hostility: as he concluded, the "combination of white worker antagonism and employer fears restricted black workers' mobility."[129] A later survey of Bordentown graduates, some of whom would have been students around 1915, indicates that the school had prepared them to do skilled work as auto mechanics and machinists, printers and carpenters, dressmakers and homemakers. Some had become teachers and social workers, and many had continued in school.[130]

In 1914, Washington made another tour of the state, where he remained popular despite his dwindling reputation among northern opinion leaders. Hodges writes that "the wizard" was greeted with local choirs singing spirituals, and that he found a middle class of barbers and hairdressers, druggists and physicians, coal dealers and contractors, dressmakers and a silversmith; ministers predominated among professional men.[131] Interestingly, this conflicts somewhat with the advice Washington had given Calvin Kendall, the state education commissioner, when he had visited the Bordentown campus a year earlier. His advice then was that the school should note that most of the state's Black residents were engaged in agriculture, and that the school ought to focus on preparing students for such work.[132] Bordentown graduates had little interest in doing so, however.

Much of the antipathy toward manual training and industrial schools among later historians comes from a review Du Bois wrote in 1918 of a recently published major study of secondary and higher education for Black Americans. The review, published in the *Crisis*, referred to the study as "dangerous and unfortunate" despite its "many praiseworthy features."[133] His review repeats many of the claims Du Bois had made in his 1915 testimony—that philanthropists too often acceded to southern prejudice, that they prioritized industrial education over higher education, and that often the industrial education taught outmoded skills. While it is difficult to deny that Black students needed public schools as much as white students did, much of Du Bois's criticism suggests a lack of familiarity with the manual training movement of the previous four decades. He wrote that manual training schools "deliberately shut the door of opportunity in the face of bright Negro students."[134] For one, the experience of students at Tuskegee

> # Weekly Letter
> ## OF
> ## The Manual Training and Industrial School
>
> | Number 2 | Bordentown, N. J. | December 28, 1920 |
> |---|---|---|
>
> ### DR. BOOKER T. WASHINGTON'S REPORT ON BORDENTOWN
>
> ABOUT seven years ago Dr. C. N. Kendall, Commissioner of Education and the State Board of Education of New Jersey, invited the late Dr. Booker T. Washington, founder of the Tuskegee Institute, to visit the Bordentown School. Following is a letter to Commissioner Kendall from Dr. Washington under date of August 1913, in which he outlines briefly the results of his observations and suggestions for making of the school a strong and useful institution:
>
> "The location of the Bordentown School is one of the best and most attractive of any school in the country and from that point of view I think presents a good opportunity for the building up of a good, strong, useful institution.
>
> "I find that there are in the State of New Jersey not far from 90,000 colored people. In order to make this school of the greatest assistance to these people I would suggest that a rough inexpensive survey be made with the view of finding out just what the prevailing occupations are among the colored people. After getting this information I think the occupations in which the majority of them are now employed would serve as a pretty safe basis as to the kind of instruction that ought to be most emphasized at Bordentown.
>
> "My own feeling is that the school can be of high service to our people in that State. Just now, by getting hold of the farming classes, I think an examination would show that there are

Figure 18. This newsletter suggests the balancing act essential to MTIS survival. That the school's leaders in 1920 felt it necessary to publish comments from Washington's 1913 visit suggests pressure from some state officials to focus on agricultural labor. In 1922, Du Bois would visit the school to talk on "A Choice of Vocation," which more closely complemented the school's purpose and curriculum.

and at Bordentown suggest that this was not necessarily so; further, it also echoes a criticism John Dewey made at the time of industrial education for white students.[135]

The survey that so aroused Du Bois's ire had been published by the U.S. Bureau of Education, funded by the Phelps-Stokes Fund of New York, and produced under the supervision of Thomas Jesse Jones, who had been on the faculty at Hampton Institute. In two volumes and at over 1,500 pages in length, it was a massive survey of institutions North and South. A dispassionate analysis of its opening "General Survey" suggests the study's sympathy for the Negro population and the impoverished condition in which they were forced to live, an awareness of the "wide divergence in per capita expenditures" for white and Black students, and the paucity of opportunities for the latter. Citing the efforts of Armstrong and Washington, it noted that education, "whether literary or industrial," needed to be adapted to the "needs of the pupil and the community." It pointed to inadequate accounting at many institutions, but it was more concerned about the pressing need for more schools. While some comments can be viewed as patronizing, its mention of character and morality were long-stated goals of manual training programs for white students as well.[136] As with Du Bois's review, these introductory comments make no reference to industrial education programs nationwide. Dewey's name does not appear in the book's index, nor do those of others with whom Dewey was actively disagreeing at the time.[137]

The second volume of the study includes descriptions of the hundreds of schools studied. One is the Manual Training and Industrial School for Colored Youth in Bordentown. The survey staff's visit was made in May of 1915, which coincided with the arrival of William Valentine as principal. It notes a total of ninety-five students, all but fourteen from New Jersey, and a staff of eighteen, including three non-teaching staff members, all "colored"; the teachers were roughly balanced between trade and academic subjects. Students' days were half the latter and half the former; the description claimed that, with the exception of carpentry, the industrial courses were of "slight educational value." It recommended that the reorganization then underway be encouraged, without noting that the school had been without a leader for several months.[138]

A contemporary view of Jones's work and that of the Phelps-Stokes Fund deserves mention here. A lengthy review published in 2004 refers to Jones's efforts in the South and later in Africa as "the (White) search for (Black) order" and characterizes it as emerging from a "civilizationist ideology" that prioritized values associated with European-American societies.[139] An oft-quoted line from Jones's report states that "The concern of the North is the maintenance of such school activities as will produce manhood and womanhood of good physique, discerning minds, and sound morals."[140] Seen through a Du Boisian lens, this sounds condescending; however, strong minds, muscles, and morals had been the goal of manual labor programs beginning at least with Theodore Weld if not the log colleges and earlier.

The need for such "uplifting" of African Americans in the half-century after the Civil War, the goal of Jones's efforts, has been a controversial idea since then. Ever the iconoclast, T. Thomas Fortune wrote in 1904 of his impatience with the idea. While attending a Hampton graduation ceremony, he noted that its students were being sent out to "lift up" their whole race and neglecting to first lift up themselves. This was, he claimed, something asked only of the "Negro and Indian" students, and he called it a "false theory of education."[141] Other American students were urged upon graduation to develop their own talents first, for only by lifting up themselves would they be able to benefit others and society as well. Acknowledging that this manifestation of the social gospel sprang from the Puritan heritage, Fortune felt it in need of reconsideration by educators of African American citizens of his day.

That said, the educational needs of Black communities, particularly in the South, were immense at the time. Centuries of slavery had enforced illiteracy upon the men and women in bondage, and the white leadership of southern states was slow to provide even basic schools in the age of Jim Crow. The most substantial effort to counter this reality was among the last undertakings of Booker T. Washington's life. With the financial assistance of Chicago philanthropist—and long-time head of Sears, Roebuck—Julius Rosenwald, an effort began to eradicate illiteracy in the South. The outcome was over five thousand elementary schools built throughout the South between 1915 and the mid-1930s. Communities wanting a school had to raise half of the necessary funds for a building and persuade local officials to help maintain it; the Rosenwald fund would supply plans for a building and the other half of its cost. Though forgotten by many historians, some of these school buildings still exist; made obsolete by the end of legal segregation, some are cherished and maintained by people who recognize their importance to their ancestors' ability to uplift both themselves and their communities.[142]

Perhaps because of controversies about Jones's *Negro Education*, it would be sixty years before another history of vocational and industrial education for Black students would appear. Begun as a doctoral dissertation at Bradley University in Peoria, Illinois, it was compiled by Clyde W. Hall, who noted in his introductory remarks that he had "taken several courses in the history of industrial training at different institutions and found that the subject of the history of industrial training for blacks has not been adequately covered."[143] Bradley, which had been founded in the 1890s under the auspices of William Rainey Harper, was for decades home to the Manual Arts Press; the latter had been established in the 1920s by Charles A. Bennett, author of the two books on manual and industrial training that remain the most extensive histories yet done and publisher of the periodical *Manual Training*. Hall, since deceased, went on to head the division of technical services at Savannah State College in Georgia.

Hall, whose book has rarely been cited in other studies, said of the school in Bordentown that it "witnessed many needed improvements" under

Professor Gregory and "really moved forward" after [Calvin] Kendall got more state aid for it and Valentine arrived as principal. He wrote that such schools were "imbued with the philosophy of Hampton and Tuskegee and flourished between 1890 and 1910," but they began to degenerate after the passing of Booker T. Washington and when the approach of World War I limited the amount of philanthropic aid available. Further, "Another thing which hastened the demise of these institutions was the hardening of the opposition of blacks toward industrial education based on a suspicion that whites were urging a caste educational system which would confine them to industrial pursuits."[144]

At the closing of his book on Washington as a progressive educator, Generals wrote that the "distortions related to Washington and to the concept of industrial education" have been unfortunate and have prevented blacks from pursuing opportunities through technical-vocational education.[145] As the occupations chosen by graduates of both Tuskegee and Bordentown suggest, such education led not only to stable careers but for many a chance to pursue a professional education as well.

Industrial Education in Black and White

If the years of Gregory's administration can be bracketed by Washington's rise to national prominence and his early death, they can also be bracketed by the establishment in 1896 of Dewey's experimental school in Chicago and the publication in 1915 of *Schools of Tomorrow*, which featured a chapter on the school Gregory's successor had headed in Indianapolis. The following year, Dewey's *Democracy and Education*—with its highly relevant chapter "The Vocational Aspects of Education"—appeared. At the time, both Dewey and Du Bois were working and living in Manhattan, perhaps within walking distance of each other, but despite their common interests, their professional paths never crossed, arguably to the detriment of Du Bois's understanding of industrial education and of Dewey's value to a community most in need of an enlightened education.[146]

Dewey's understanding of "vocation" and "occupation" were complex; he had begun to work them out with the occupations-oriented curriculum at the Laboratory School, and at the time he was engaged in a well-publicized dispute with those who would employ "vocation" as a means of limiting schooling for students assumed to be heading for "industrial" jobs. For Dewey, the two terms were also interchangeable: occupation is "a continuous activity having a purpose" [309] that leaves open the possibility of change. Life itself, or growth, is "the dominant vocation of all human beings" [310]. To avoid the class stratification of past societies, "school materials and methods" must be gradually reconstructed to "utilize various forms of occupations . . . to bring out their intellectual and moral content" [315]. Further, he argued, any scheme for education based on current divisions within society would only perpetuate them" [318].[147]

With one exception, none of Dewey's writings on vocation or industrial education considered how they might apply to African Americans. That exception was "The School as Social Settlement" in *Schools of Tomorrow*—the chapter that described the program in Indianapolis headed by William Valentine, which had been written by Evelyn Dewey. Given the proximity of the time in which both books were published, it is curious that beyond this one chapter Dewey did not commit to writing any thoughts he might have had about how his conceptions applied on both sides of the color line.

In his study of "vocation" as a means of liberalizing education, the late Arthur Wirth—long a professor at Washington University, the school where Calvin Woodward had established his manual training program—offered context for the chapter on the Indianapolis school and for considering what "industrial education" meant at the time Dewey was writing about it. The term had many meanings and manifestations, Wirth wrote, from kindergartens to land-grant universities. Such schooling was in part an attack on the classics, which after the Civil War were no longer an adequate response to the demands of industrialization. Thus, it led to schools for the study of engineering and agriculture, to manual training schools, and to Dewey's Laboratory School.[148]

Valentine's school in Indianapolis was another outgrowth of these developments, Wirth argued. Its education program was designed to improve the life of the community. Through Valentine's initiative, it became a place where local cobblers and carpenters could share their skills and tools with neighborhood children and their parents. The idea behind this and similar schools elsewhere in the country was, according to the Deweys, not to train workers for a trade, but to motivate students to take an interest in their environment and the meaning of the work they did in school.[149] As with Dewey's neglect of Black students other than in this brief chapter, Du Bois's apparent neglect of Dewey's conception of "vocational aspects of education" is curious—though it does surely provide significant evidence of Du Bois's color line. Thus, the first three decades of the Manual Training and Industrial School become even more valuable as a means for understanding industrial education in the historical context swirling around it—a context that existed in both black and white.

However, the Bordentown school's heyday was yet to come. Under Valentine's leadership, it grew to house and educate hundreds of students each year, taught by a cadre of sixty teachers, all Black and all graduates of notable colleges and universities. It was a self-contained community that offered culturally rich extracurricular activities to its students and a summer home to African American organizations not welcome elsewhere. MTIS was an iconic institution that honored priorities not only of Washington and Dewey, but of Du Bois as well. During the 1920s, Du Bois made more than one visit to the campus and wrote fondly of the experience. Though Dewey also made a visit in 1928, no record of his impressions has been found.[150]

Highlights of Bordentown's illustrious future are even more compelling when considered in the context of later writings by Dewey and Du Bois; both took up the social significance of education and work in books, articles, and speeches. Though Dewey had largely ignored it, the manual training school in Chicago had spawned several others that were also indebted to Charles Ham and Calvin Woodward; one was the state industrial school founded in 1899 on the Dakota prairie 1500 miles to the west. To it, this story now turns.

CHAPTER 5

The People's School on the Prairie and How It Grew

> The NI is a school which has fostered the idea that work of any kind is honorable—that there is dignity in labor be it that of the mechanic, the artisan, the farmer, the housewife, or the teacher. This outstanding feature has tended to break down class distinction and instilled among the students a democratic spirit which fulfills one of the principal objects for which schools were created.
> —Ina Randall Graham, 1924

On June 4, 1897, Calvin Woodward spoke at a meeting of the Dickey County Teachers Association in the recently settled town of Ellendale, North Dakota. The talk had been arranged by the local superintendent of schools, Warren Hicks; in notices announcing the event, he referred to Woodward as an "eminent authority . . . rarely if ever heard in this part of the west." A follow-up article on the talk itself appeared in the same paper, the *Dickey County Leader*, a week after it was held. The article noted that "the lecture gave our people a new interest in the state manual training school," which was scheduled to be built there; it added that the school's trustees met with Woodward after his talk and "got some valuable suggestions as to the building."[1] Two years later, a school for manual training and industrial education, free to all and supported by the state, would be established in Ellendale; provision for it was part of North Dakota's constitution, which had been written in 1889, eight years earlier.

Though Ellendale's little school on the prairie developed into a unique institution, it shared certain characteristics with both the schools in Chicago and Bordentown as well as other manual training programs around the country. However, it was distinctive in several ways. One was its eventual name: by 1907, it had become a "normal and industrial school," a term more often associated with schools for African American students. Further, it did not grow into a multi-program state college as did many such schools, whether founded for Black students or white; and it continued to offer individual courses for local students who wanted to improve the skills they needed to earn a living, whether on a farm, in a store, or in an office. Also unique was the school's close connection with the community in which it had been established: Ellendale remained a small town, smaller than others that hosted such institutions, but both the NI, as it was fondly known for most of its seventy years, and Dickey County had a mutually reinforcing relationship. Though it was nominally a postsecondary institution, and did eventually become a college, its initial distinction stemmed from the sophisticated faculty it attracted during its first decade; they offered a rich variety of secondary-level courses au courant with aspects of the "new education" promulgated in the larger colleges and cities from which they had come.

Ellendale's NI was similar to Bordentown's MTIS in that its programs aimed at enhancing students' ability to make a living while also offering a solid academic education for students wanting to pursue a postsecondary degree. It was similar to Chicago's CMTS in that it attracted students from the community's "leading" families and prepared its graduates to maintain solid middle-class status; as a tuition-free school, it also attracted students from less-privileged backgrounds, as did MTIS. As at both schools, NI students developed a sense of agency about their lives—that they could do work of their own choosing, requirements stressed by both W. E. B. Du Bois and John Dewey. In its normal and industrial aspects, the NI was rather like both Hampton and Tuskegee, in that it prepared teachers trained in the practical skills needed by rural residents. But it also met one of Calvin Woodward's priorities—that of preparing teachers for manual training programs, which many (mainly male) NI graduates did, taking jobs nationwide. Many of its female graduates remained in the area, initially teaching in rural schools prior to marrying, managing homes, and playing active roles in their communities.

Warren Hicks, host for Woodward's appearance, had been born and educated in Michigan, where he was exposed both to Woodward and to John Dewey. Hicks had arrived in the Dakotas while it was still a territory; he taught in another nearby town and edited a newspaper—its motto was "Liberal in Everything, Neutral in Nothing"—before being called to teach in Ellendale in 1892. He soon became principal of the high school and, in 1898, county superintendent. Hicks took an active interest in Ellendale's manual training school and became its first president. Later noted as a national leader in industrial education, Hicks became in 1905 assistant superintendent in Cleveland, Ohio, and then, in 1912, moved to Wisconsin where he oversaw its extensive system of vocational and technical schools.[2]

In 1901, when Ellendale's rapidly growing Manual Training School had its first graduation ceremony, a young woman named Ida Randall—whose 1924 statement about it appears above—delivered an oration titled "Industrial Training in the Schools." Her remarks, preserved in an elegantly printed pamphlet, include phrases associated with Woodward—"skilled hands and cultivated minds" for one—but its references to Newton, Cicero, and John Ruskin, and her lyrical expression of their ideas, suggest that she had a copy of Charles Ham's books and articles on hand as she wrote. "Education is the harmonious development of all the powers of man," she began, "and a system of education that fails to accomplish this end is one-sided, incomplete, and unscientific." Hands, she wrote, should execute what the brain, informed by books, directs. The arts "stimulate a feeling of love for the good, the true, and the beautiful," she continued.[3] In sum, it is quite a piece of writing for a 19-year-old graduating from a school established two years before in a town that barely existed the year she was born.

The Site for a "Living Symbol of Democracy"

Though this little Manual Training School on the prairie may seem obscure, and it closed in 1970 in its last manifestation as a branch of the University of North Dakota, the motivation for its establishment and its complementary relationship with the town of Ellendale tell a significant story about how manual and industrial education was implemented during the Progressive Era.[4] The school's origins were covered in a 1930 history of Dickey County, which claimed that the school, founded "for the people," became a "living symbol of democracy."[5] Two decades later, in 1947, a brief history of the school said of the people it served that they had "developed a very keen insight into the needs of their fellowmen and how to cope with problems that must be met."[6] More recently, the relationship between the school and the town have become the topic of works by Ken Smith, editor of the *Dickey County Leader*, former professor at the college that now occupies the campus of the original school, and head of the local historical society. His prospectus for a dissertation called "'Mind and Hand': Formative Years of a Prairie Town" focuses on the people who brought both into being; among them were Warren Hicks, Ina Randall Graham, and the town's two delegates to North Dakota's 1889 constitutional convention, Alexander Flemington and Lorenzo Bartlett.[7] That convention, whose delegates had heard praises for the "new education," wrote into the constitution that the state would establish a half-dozen schools of "higher learning," all to be funded by 40,000-acre federal land grants assigned to each. The school designated for manual training Flemington and Bartlett snagged for Ellendale, which then had a population of fewer than a thousand people.[8]

In the two decades prior to the school's opening, the town and the county, both initially unnamed, had developed out of little more than surveyors' stone markers on an unbroken short-grass prairie that extended, nearly flat and treeless, in all directions. In the geographical middle of the North American continent, this land was one of the last to be settled by people of European descent. Between the late 1870s and 1890, the Dakotas, then still a territory, experienced what has been called the "Great Dakota Boom." Though explorers had regarded the land as too arid for cultivation, railroad promoters and other boosters attracted tens of thousands of people there in little more than a decade.[9] As few Native Americans inhabited the area that was to be Dickey County, Indigenous inhabitants were not dislodged by the arrival, in 1881, of a railroad running north and south or another a few years later that ran east and west.[10] Ellendale, like many other prairie towns, was a product of these railroads, which brought people and their goods in and took their produce out. The men and women who founded these towns brought with them the host of institutions and organizations—schools and churches, newspapers, literary and fraternal societies—they were familiar with in the towns and countries from which they had come.[11]

Geographic historian John Hudson has provided a context for understanding these small towns in the central Dakotas created by the railroads in the 1880s; there were hundreds, most of which no longer exist. He argues that their success depended on three sets of variables: their *people* (the settlers who remained for a while), their *activities* (their social and economic behavior), and the *structures* (a site's natural advantages and the physical forms built on it). Those towns that succeeded did so because, according to Hudson, of the "influential *people* who organized the same mix of structures and activities found elsewhere, only more successfully."[12] Ellendale historian Ken Smith uses Hudson's hypothesis to explain how and why it thrived while so many other towns did not:

> [it was] "a common devotion to an ideal way of life in which citizens are masters over their own labor, and that by obtaining the requisite skill and perseverance, they can use basic elements to bring into existence both material and cultural goods that represent and are recognized as constituting prosperity and success."[13]

Surviving—or prevailing over the droughts and blizzards, the relentless sun and wind, the mosquitos and gophers of the fertile if arid prairie—meant that one had to perform "through independent thought and action" the labor essential to providing for themselves and their families. Ellendale, Smith argues, was unusually blessed by strong personalities that embodied these characteristics; further, the "core ethos that underlay the town's early development" was the manual training school that served "as a focal point for the town's identity and mission."[14]

The work of labor historian Roseanne Currarino has provided Smith with another basis for understanding how Ellendale developed; this is the concept of "producerism," a model of citizenship that combines individual virtue with productive labor. Such citizens produced what they earned through their own effort and thus were less dependent on the whims and will of others. Currarino contrasts this model of citizenship with a contemporary one in which citizens are more dependent upon corporations, labor unions, and government agencies than on their own efforts to survive.[15] As both Smith and Currarino acknowledge, these models overlap, and the former presupposes a male-dominated society of individuals free from the bonds of slavery, servitude, and great poverty. Nevertheless, the conviction that individual virtue and productive labor are two sides of a coin was a birthright of early Dakotans.[16] This independence and self-sufficiency, and resistance to control by corporations, were to become issues during the rise of the Nonpartisan League in which Ellendale played a role between 1915 and 1925.

The Great Dakota Boom that helped bring Ellendale into being was equally a product of newspapers that aided the boom's promoters—the newspaper men and the railroad men were a mutually reinforcing pair. In Ellendale, one of the latter was Ed Leiby, a master telegrapher for the town's railroad. Later Leiby became county auditor, mayor, board member for both the public and the manual training schools, and proprietor of its leading drug store. The newspapermen Smith profiles include the founding editors of the *Dickey County Leader*, men who were also writers, whose works illustrate the "producerist" marriage of head and hand; the *Leader*, established in 1882 by two of them and later run by the widow of another, became a three-generation family business.[17]

The two men credited with getting the state's manual training school located in Ellendale had arrived with the railroad. One, Alexander Flemington, had come in 1882 with a law degree from the University of Wisconsin and brief experience as a schoolteacher. Raised on a farm and the son of Scottish immigrants, he espoused the "democratic, homely virtues of that country," according to his daughter. He felt that the classical education of his day was insufficient; these new states needed "keen minds in useful, healthful bodies," "respect for honest labor," and citizens with a well-developed "sense of the values of living."[18] Flemington quickly became prominent as an attorney; later he became a circuit court judge who was known for his "scrupulous honesty."[19]

Lorenzo Dow Bartlett, Ellendale's other delegate to the constitutional convention, had followed a distinctive path to arrive there. Named after an early-nineteenth century evangelist, he later became a follower of Robert Ingersoll, a noted agnostic. Bartlett had been a steamship captain on the Mississippi and later a land agent for a river town. Recently widowed, he became a Dickey County homesteader at age fifty-four, arriving in 1883 with his daughter Caroline. A journalist in Minneapolis, "Carrie" periodically returned to the area to conceive new undertakings, which would include becoming a Unitarian preacher and noted feminist.[20] Called "Doc" by his neighbors because of his wide reading, Bartlett was respected because he "always [fought] for the common man."[21] Despite some of his daughter's ideas and his experience on a riverboat, he was opposed to feminism; he also opposed the use of alcohol and gambling, and he endeavored to get prohibitions against both of the latter into the constitution.[22]

The convention that led to the constitution had opened on the Fourth of July in 1889; it was held in Bismarck, established in 1872, where the Minneapolis-based Northern Pacific Railroad crossed the Missouri River, and that was named to attract German immigrants to the area. On the western side of the river was a settlement of the Mandan tribe, who in the fall of 1804 had welcomed the Lewis and Clark Expedition and introduced them to Sacajawea, the young woman who would guide the explorers toward the Pacific in 1805. At that time, thirty to forty thousand, perhaps more, lived in what became, in 1861, the Dakota Territory. Composed of several tribes that spoke numerous languages, they were largely nomadic peoples, though some would summer in temporary villages to raise corn and squash.[23] During the 1800s, French and English trappers, aided by Indigenous hunters, decimated much of the buffalo herds. After the Civil War, what had been largely friendly relations between the Native Americans and the newcomers became increasingly hostile as settlers of European origin took over land they thought had been made available to them through the Homestead Act of 1862.[24] An account of these interactions, largely sympathetic to the Indigenous peoples, was given in a 1925 textbook history of the state coauthored by R. M. Black. He would in 1914 become president of the school in Ellendale; the balanced history given in this and in his later book about Dickey County suggests something of the man's temperament and the values he wanted to instill in the school's students.[25]

Flemington and Bartlett were among the seventy-five delegates who gathered that July in 1889 to write the new state's constitution; all but thirteen had been born in the United States or Canada and all but a few were under forty years old.²⁶ Most, like Bartlett, were farmers; others, like Flemington, were lawyers. Though the convention was to take one month, it took two. Major issues, in addition to prohibition, were locations for the several state institutions, which included the university and the land-grant school for agriculture, established in Grand Forks and Fargo (two towns on the Red River along the state's eastern border), plus two normal schools, a trade school, and five others for dependent people unable to support themselves.

As a history of the school written in 1947 tells it, questions about where these institutions would be located almost derailed the signing of the constitution. Considerable federal beneficence was involved: land grants of forty thousand acres were available to support each of the schools. Thus, a great deal of vote trading, as well as chicanery and finagling, went on as delegates advocated for the towns that had sent them. Eventually, the controversies were settled for the benefit of the whole and the schools were awarded to towns accessible to the railroads.²⁷ Slightly over 35,000 citizens of the new state voted on the issue of adopting the constitution, all but 8,100 voting yes. In the 1890 census, the state had a population of 182,719 people; by 1900, the population would grow to 310,146.²⁸

Flemington and Bartlett, along with a third delegate from Dickey County, were apparently persuasive, as it must have been no little feat to have this manual training school located just a few miles north of the South Dakota border. Dickey County was formed in March of 1881—after whom it was named is disputed—and at the same time, the Chicago, Milwaukee, and St. Paul railroad was building tracks into the county, heading north from Aberdeen, another new settlement about forty miles away. In that fall of 1881, a few enterprising men filed claims on the land that was to become the town of Ellendale, and a few remained over the winter. This was according to terms of the Homestead Act, by means of which Dakota land moved from transient occupation by Native Americans to ownership by Americans of European descent. The land had been divided into mile-square sections and subdivided into quarters of 160 acres each; through filing a "claim" with a land agent and paying a small fee, a homesteader could call a quarter or more his or her own by building a structure on it and farming it for five years. However imperfect or controversial this system was, through it much of the land beyond the Mississippi River came to become some of the world's most productive farmland.²⁹ Further, because of a provision in the land ordinances of the 1780s, the income from the sale of section 16 (and later section 36 as well) was to be used to support a system of local public schools.³⁰

That winter of 1881–1882, the railroad stopped near where Ellendale would be established, and potential settlers, hearing of the Great Dakota Boom, began arriving by the hundreds in the spring, filling dozens of hastily constructed structures, shops, and saloons. In July 1882, the territorial governor came to christen the town and designate it the county's seat. Its name was derived from that of Mary Ellen Merrill, wife of a railroad executive, a woman who reportedly took an interest in the town for many years. It was served not only by the railroad, but by several stagecoach lines and other hastily devised means of transportation.[31] Often the men came first, located and claimed a likely quarter, constructed some sort of a shack, then returned to Wisconsin or Michigan or other states to bring their families. Most came through Aberdeen and Minneapolis, three hundred miles southeast, by way of "immigrant cars" that carried them, their household goods, farm supplies, and sometimes their livestock. Other towns were founded in the area as well. The largest was Oakes. Located twenty-five miles away along the James River on the county's eastern side, it also developed rapidly.

Early in 1882, the town had been platted on a grid system; soon, a post office and a school opened, and the *Dickey County Leader* began publishing a weekly issue. These were followed by a lumber yard, hardware store, a bank, and a blacksmith. A Methodist minister arrived in the spring of 1883 and held services in the railroad depot, thus far the largest building. The first school was soon outgrown, and in 1884 a two-story structure was built to replace it.[32] Staffed by a principal and two teachers paid six dollars weekly, it had a 38-week school year beginning the first Monday in September.[33] In 1885, the county built a courthouse. Four years later, residents in the town and county had organized themselves sufficiently well that local leaders had begun to emerge; from them were chosen the delegates to the 1889 constitutional convention.

The weather both helped and hindered development. There was a great blizzard in January 1888, after which trains did not run for a few months; though it created numerous hardships and some loss of life, it helped Dickey County's homesteaders produce a bumper crop of wheat the following year. Thus, it was not as catastrophic as the series of blizzards that hit the central Dakotas during the winter of 1880–1881, a tale poignantly told in Laura Ingalls Wilder's *The Long Winter*. The storms left her town of DeSmet without train service for several months; its hundred or so residents barely survived. Caroline Fraser's *Prairie Fires*, a retelling of the history that made Wilder famous, portrays the challenges of settling these communities far more grimly than did Wilder herself. Black's *History of Dickey County*, Hudson's *Country Towns*, Smith's "Mind and Hand," and a host of other books focus more on the heroism and fortitude of those who survived and then prevailed than on those who did not. Fraser questions decisions made by Wilder's parents and perhaps the ethos of the town in which they lived.[34] Early DeSmet, it seems, lacked some of the advantages Ellendale had.

"To Guide the Hand"

As with blizzards, Dickey County was subject to events outside its rapidly filling perimeter. One was the national depression that began in 1893, an economic downturn that hampered private donations to the Chicago Manual Training School and to the Rices' struggling Ironsides in New Jersey. These financial challenges led both of these earlier schools to find shelter under larger institutions, the University of Chicago for the former and the state for the latter. A drought in the early 1890s left the new state of North Dakota with limited funds to underwrite the development of the colleges and other state schools envisioned in its constitution. Despite this, in 1893 its legislature authorized the governor to appoint trustees for the Ellendale school, and a March 30 article in the *Dickey County Leader* indicates that the town wasted no time in doing so. At a Saturday afternoon meeting, Alexander Flemington reported that a likely piece of land had been chosen; he and other attendees selected the trustees. The article, titled "To Guide the Hand," instructed readers in the school's mission: students would be taught "not so much from books as from the practical work in all the branches by the most skilled and scientific workmen." And having such an institution there would "bring many families" to the town, where they would make homes, purchase groceries, and educate their children.[35]

Warren Hicks, then principal of Ellendale's high school, later wrote of the manual training school's origin: his teachers at Ypsilanti—a Michigan normal school of distinction—had "made a profound impression on me that education was a full development of the life of children." And to his mind, the ordinary school program of the time "left little for the bringing out of the individual talents and bent of youth." Schools should instead "give a fair and equal chance to all."[36] In 1897, Hicks and Ben Crabtree, a young man who would become the town's leading banker, traveled to schools in St. Louis, St. Paul, and Wisconsin, gathering ideas.[37] Also that year, the legislature passed a new law that set out the new institution's mission:

> [It was to be] instruction in a comprehensive way in wood and iron work and the various other branches of manual training; and in cooking, sewing, modeling, artwork and the various other branches of domestic economy as a co-ordinate branch of education together with mathematics, drawing and other necessary common school studies.[38]

Another blizzard the preceding winter had also stopped train service for a month or more, but it left sufficient moisture in the soil to produce another good harvest. Dickey County's residents—over six thousand in the 1900 census—were increasingly motivated to have the school open; at some point,

Ellendale residents themselves raised $600 to move the project along. Also in 1897, the state empowered the school's board to sell bonds and construct a building that would accommodate "not less than 100 nor more than 500 students" and allocated $15,000 for its construction.[39]

In 1898, land along the town's eastern edge was settled on as the site for the campus. Then, in June of 1899, a ceremony was held to lay a cornerstone for the first building. An event of "dignity and formality" organized by Ellendale's Masonic Order, it drew a crowd of hundreds; the local militia was on hand with an honor guard of two dozen young women who wore matching dresses made for the occasion. They heard several addresses, one of which was by Oakes resident and state senator Thomas Marshall. He said that the school was destined to be successful because it was in "direct line with the thought and progress of the age." The school would welcome all, rich and poor, boys and girls; they would learn how to "make the best uses" of themselves.[40] It was a matter of pride, future NI president Black later wrote, "that when this school opened its doors in September 1899, North Dakota had founded the only free manual training school in the United States, and it was the first and only one of the state's higher institutions of learning to open in its own building."[41]

In the beginning of August, the *Dickey County Leader* published a lengthy report on the building's construction. E. W. Van Meter, its architect, was a local man with a practice in Aberdeen, a growing city across the border in South Dakota; he had also been engaged in building the normal school there. A construction crew was brought in from St. Paul, and in less than two months they erected a three-story structure of red brick with brownstone trim—its contents and organization were similar to that of the Chicago school constructed over four months in 1883, seventeen years earlier. In the basement were an engine room, as well as machine and blacksmith shops; on the first floor, a darkroom for photography, offices, and closets. A circular stairway of oak led to carpentry and mechanical drawing shops, plus classrooms for dressmaking, on the second floor. The third floor held an assembly hall with "100 seats for recitations," plus the art department and classrooms for cooking. Large windows let in natural light; it would be another decade before the building had electricity. It had cost $10,500 to construct.[42] The remaining part of the state's allocation would pay for the school's initial programs.

The *Leader* article went on to describe the "competent and trustworthy corps of teachers" who had been selected; parents, it said, "need have no fear of bad influences surrounding their children at the school." Warren Hicks, still superintendent of Dickey County's schools, later wrote that he had expected the new school would enroll 140 students that first fall—far more than either the Chicago or the Bordentown school began with—but a near majority of Ellendale's young people signed up, many to take just a few classes. Several dozen more actually enrolled that first year.[43]

"A Howling Success" Refines Its Purpose

Among the students who enrolled when classes began on September 4, 1899, was one who recorded his or her impressions for another local newspaper. The account began: "The State Manual Training School... is, in the eloquent language of the West, a 'howling success,'" and it continued with praise for Prof. Dunphy, in charge of manual training and the school's acting principal. Lillian Tingle, who taught languages as well as sewing and cooking, was lauded for doing the latter on a "strictly scientific basis"; she also taught physiology in connection with cooking, so that students could understand basic nutrition. Painting and drawing, along with other branches, were taught by Ellen Anderson, who had "the true artist's spirit of imparting the love of the beautiful to her pupils" and "quickening their imaginations." The account ended with a request to the people of the state that they encourage "this glorious institution." It should be a "strong tower towards the uplifting of industrious, honest, intellectual manhood and womanhood."[44]

Hyperbole aside, the school was off to a solid start, but just what sort of school was it? Delegates to the constitutional convention who had authorized the six institutions for "higher learning" anticipated that they would be at the postsecondary level: the two normal schools, the trade school, and the colleges at Fargo and Grand Forks. But, except for the latter two, slotting such schools at one level or another presents a challenge. Two nationwide compilations done a century apart suggest that the distinction between secondary and collegiate was far less clear than it would become by 1920 and later. The 1900 edition of Charles Ham's *Mind and Hand* categorizes several hundred schools by level (grammar, high school, or collegiate), by ownership (public, private, charitable), by function (manual training, technical, normal), and by race; most schools fell into multiple categories, moved from one to another, or both, in the three decades (1870s to 1900) covered by his compilation.[45] In her *The American State Normal School*, published in 2005, Christine Ogren includes a list of over two hundred such schools, several of which provided industrial courses as well as teacher training.[46] Some students at these schools had completed a secondary education; some had not; some were in their late teens, others in their late twenties.

The Ellendale school, according to Warren Hicks, "went where the crowd pushed."[47] Though it would in its first decade begin to focus on teacher training and by the mid-1920s begin granting bachelor's degrees, when its doors opened in September of 1899, it offered a three-year academic curriculum along with courses in manual training and fine art, plus domestic arts and sciences. The school's founders wanted it to offer "more and better opportunities" for young people in the area; its enthusiastic reception and its first catalog indicate that it did indeed do so, but at a secondary level.[48]

Forty boys and girls "registered for training" on the school's opening day, and after the "harvesting and threshing" were completed, enrollment more than exceeded Hicks's earlier estimate of 140 students. A list of students shows that they were overwhelmingly from Ellendale and other Dickey County towns, not the state as a whole.[49] In the first official report on the school, offered in October of 1900, Hicks noted that eighty-seven of these students enrolled for the three-year combined academic and industrial program; another seventy-three signed up only for some of the domestic science and industrial courses.[50] Over the next several years, the Manual Training School would attract far more students than did Ellendale's high school, even though the latter was in 1900 considered one of the state's better ones; with an enrollment of 51 students, it was also one of the largest—only Grand Forks, with 120 students, had appreciably more, and it was home to the state's university.[51] Thus, Ellendale's new school attracted far more high school age students than those other secondary institutions.

The appeal of the new Manual Training School is evident in its *First Annual Catalog*, published in 1900. The school's object—instruction in wood and iron work, domestic economy, and "other necessary studies"—had been determined by the state two years before. Albert E. Dunphy, in describing the manual training curriculum, noted the school's advantages to students arriving with various kinds of preparation: those who had already attended secondary school could acquire a manual training diploma with just a year's additional work. Others would find, as Ham and Woodward had argued, that time spent in shop work would enhance their academic performance. Graduates would be well prepared for either college or for joining the workforce. In his note to parents, Dunphy asked for their cooperation in the school's effort "to elevate ... your boys and girls to high standards of quality" and noted that this would mean work at home and refraining from "entertainments" other than on weekends.[52]

More elegance than admonishment characterized the purpose of the Fine Arts Department as described by instructor Ellen Anderson. "Enrichment of the life of the pupil" through exposure to "order, unity, and harmony" in works of art and of nature was the program's aim. Students' mode of expression would come "from within and not from without." Though Ogren's book on normal schools suggests that intellectual sophistication was often wanting in both faculty and students around the century's turn, the Ellendale school seems an exception to that rule.[53] The students sketched from nature, from illustrations, and from casts in charcoal and watercolor; illustrations show the girls at desks and easels—suggesting that the school was well-equipped despite its newness and distance from cities and suppliers.[54]

The description for the Domestic Arts and Sciences Department begins with a quotation from Ellen Swallow Richards, the Boston-based sanitary engineer regarded as the founder of home economics: "The prosperity of a nation depends upon the health and morals of its citizens, and the health and morals of people depend mainly upon the food they eat, and the homes they live in," it read.[55] The department's instructor, Lillian Tingle, had been chosen from dozens of applicants for the job; British born, she came from a family of academics and had studied abroad before arriving in Ellendale. She remained there for four years, then moved on to Oregon where she became a noted food journalist and taught at the university in Eugene.[56]

Tingle's program description continues by claiming that one can learn household management by trial and error or by instruction in the fundamentals: "Domestic Science," she wrote, "is the application of scientific principles and methods of work to the problems of homelife." The program she devised would not only supply training for the homemaker but lay a "solid foundation for the technical work involved" in preparation for a professional career in the field.[57]

Courses included work in physiology and nutrition, hygiene and keeping household accounts; information was imparted to students by both reading standard works and practical experience. Domestic Art began with training the eye and hand through needlework, then moved on through the selection of good material and lessons in workmanship to dressmaking; students would be expected to make their own graduation dresses. Tingle's description ended with a quotation from John Ruskin: "It is only by labor that thought can be made healthy, and only by thought that labor can be made happy."

Among the students in Miss Tingle's classes was Ina Randall, the daughter of a pioneer merchant who had attended college and taught school before bringing his growing family to Ellendale; there he served on the school board and as a state senator.[58] Ina was born in 1882, the year her family arrived in a covered wagon. It was a lively group, one of her daughters reported. As an adult, Ina wrote not of an "obscure country town," but of a "wonderful kaleidoscopic world which never ceased to enthrall her."[59] What is most impressive, however, is the "oration" Ina delivered upon being a member of the Manual Training School's first graduating class in 1901.

Titled "Industrial Training in the Schools," young Ina Randall's remarks read like a talk by an erudite principal, wise and persuasive, not as one by a teenager in a small town a day away by train from the nearest major

Figure 19. The NI's first graduating class in 1901. Ina Randall, whose commencement oration attracted considerable notice far beyond her hometown, is at the left; manual training instructor Albert Dunphy is at the right.

university. The type of school her talk lauded was one that "elevates labor," that "not only instructs but educates," that meets the "growing demand for a complete man." It teaches not to produce "a polished piece of furniture" but "how to play the game of life successfully." After quoting John Ruskin on art—"a medium through which a mind may receive and give impressions"—Randall extolled the "language of drawing" and claimed that art can be as well represented by "the blacksmith with his hammer and anvil . . . as by the painter with his brush." And she continued: "So it is that the useful arts are as fine as the fine arts."[60]

Parts of Randall's talk appear prompted by Charles Ham's writings, but its actual progenitor is likely closer to home. Ellen Anderson, the instructor of fine arts whose eloquent program description suggests she had spent some time with the writings of John Ruskin, contributed more than a reading list. A graduate of New York City's Pratt Institute, Anderson's background may well have enabled her to coach this most promising pupil or otherwise aid the writing of her oration. Another key to the origin of Randall's talk is her reference to Raphael's Sistine Madonna, a painting that hangs in Dresden; its museum was on the Grand Tour that teachers of the time took if they could afford it.⁶¹ Lillian Tingle had traveled to Germany prior to her arrival in Ellendale; given her future career as a noted writer and teacher, she could have extolled the impressionable Ina with the painting's glory as recalled from an earlier trip.

Another key to the oration's genesis is the quotation from Ellen Richards in Tingle's description of the Domestic Arts and Science program. In the second half of her talk, Randall became quite the ardent feminist: "Industrial training demands that male and female education be placed side by side" and "no land will be what it ought to be until woman is given opportunity for a thorough education with man." The reference to Ellen Richards suggests that Tingle was as well read in her field as was Anderson in hers; Richards's advocacy for domestic science was as fervid as was Woodward's for manual training. Instructed by Richards via Tingle, young Ina told her audience: "If women are to be barred from trades and professions, let her at least be trained in what she alone can idealize and perfect—domestic science." She ended her talk with the proclamation that "the age of ornamental learning is passing away, the age of science and art has come"; "industrial training will point to the machinery that harnesses the torrents, . . . the statues that breath[e] life, . . . and the homes that ensure happiness." Ina's talk, thus, was not just that of an eloquent young woman, but a creative collaboration between herself and two of her instructors.

After the *Dickey County Leader* printed an elegant copy of Ina Randall's oration and then distributed it widely, it was reprinted in newspapers throughout the area; the editor of one called it a "masterpiece," which it was. Excerpts from it hang in Ellendale's museum, but according to Ken Smith, numerous other young people in the town were also doing highly sophisticated writing on a wide variety of subjects. Their pieces were printed in local newspapers, which also ran excerpts from books and speeches that indicate these prairie towns may have been far from major cities, but they were hardly isolated from main currents of contemporary thought.⁶²

Another indication of Ellendale's intellectual vitality is a *Dickey County Leader* editorial that ran when the school was just three years old; the piece pointed to the young school's popularity by putting it in a national context. MIT's John Runkle, an early advocate for manual training, had died in August 1902, the editorial noted, before listing his "educational principles" as set forth in 1884: "hand instruction . . . if adapted to the age of the pupil . . . [can be] a valuable adjunct to the purely literary studies . . . because the social and industrial conditions have so changed as to make such teaching necessary." The editorial also cited the work of Francis Parker and a "score of other leaders" whose promotion of the new, industrial education had persuaded North Dakota's constitutional convention to establish

> "When manual training asks for admission in the regular school course, it does not say, 'Discard your books and use my tools,' but it does say, 'Book learning is not enough, let me add tool learning; let the hand execute with my tools what the brain informed by your books, directs.' To neglect the education of the hand is to lower respect for manual labor, and contempt for manual labor makes a nation recede from civilization. Manual labor is the foundation of a nation's prosperity and the labor class stands in the foreground as the substantial element of its population, for it is labor, not territory, that is its source of wealth."
>
> --Ina Randall, 1st graduating class of the M.T.S. (1901), from her graduation address.

Figure 20. Ina Randall's widely circulated commencement oration was called a "masterpiece" by the editor of another newspaper that reprinted part of it. Its contents suggest that some of her talented instructors aided her research and writing. It remains a vibrant piece of work a dozen decades after it first appeared. This excerpt hangs in Ellendale's Coleman Memorial Museum.

Ellendale's MTS. Though the state's "financial condition" had initially stalled the school's opening, the popularity of the "new education" had encouraged universities and normal schools nationwide to establish mechanic arts departments.[63] And Ellendale would not be left behind.

Going "Where the Crowd Pushed"

Commenting on the school's situation in 1902, the year he officially became the school's head, Warren Hicks later wrote that "the president went where the crowd pushed . . . pupils and parents spoke out and prompted some new courses."[64] Some of the students were not quite prepared for the lofty ideals Anderson and Tingle aimed to impart; Hicks's response was twofold: one, a short-term teachers' institute begun in the summer of 1903 to provide better training for teachers in the county's rural schools; the other, a preparatory course for students established in the fall of 1903. Where "the crowd pushed" had earlier meant, in 1901, adding commercial courses in bookkeeping and stenography.[65]

The school's growing enrollment meant it needed more space. For this, Hicks called on his ally in the neighboring town of Oakes, Thomas Marshall, who had arrived in the Dakotas as a surveyor and settled in Dickey County. Hicks had earlier persuaded him of the value of industrial education, and as a member of the state legislature Marshall had been instrumental in securing for the school a needed $7,500 appropriation in 1900.[66] But Marshall's greatest service to the school was in 1902. After his election to Congress, he had become acquainted with Andrew Carnegie, who at the time was endowing libraries nationwide. The Manual Training School needed a new building, and the state was unable to fund it. Though Carnegie was not in the habit of loaning money, or so the lore goes, Marshall persuaded him to make $35,000 available; it was secured by the school's land grant and was fully repaid two decades later. With the loan, an imposing four-story structure rose on the campus, opening in the spring of 1903 with classrooms and dormitory space.[67]

The school's bulletin for 1905–1906 suggests that the crowd of parents and pupils was pushing in multiple directions, one of which was the secondary program: a four-year course of study, including one for preparation, in standard academic areas along with those in mechanic and domestic arts.[68] The number of graduates—fourteen in 1905 and eleven in 1906—indicates a full-time student body of fewer than a hundred, but enrollment was at least twice that. So, another way the crowd pushed was, as Schultz described it, for students who came "with the idea of learning something practical, something they could make use of immediately."[69] They were there to master office skills or enhance their ability as music teachers. In 1906, a three-month short course in dressmaking began; two years later, there was another in farm engineering.[70]

Reflecting its broadened role, the school got a new name in 1907: it was no longer the State Manual Training School but the State Normal and Industrial School (commonly, the NI). The state's department of education also redefined the school's mission; it was to "provide instruction in . . . the various branches of manual training . . . and domestic economy" plus other liberal courses to prepare teachers in the science and art of teaching "with special reference to manual training."[71] Pedagogy and psychology were added as electives to the secondary curriculum; in addition to standard academic ones, students could choose among courses in carpentry and forging; hand and machine sewing, printing and the fine arts, as well as cooking and home nursing.[72] All students were expected to take a class in music; physical education was required each term and boys participated in a militia unit. An armory with a gymnasium had been built in 1905. A girls' dormitory was added in 1907, as the school's reach began to extend beyond Dickey County and students had to board there. As R. M. Black, who was then teaching at another state school but would come to head the NI in 1914, explained the new role in a letter written many years later: high schools nationwide wanted to introduce industrial subjects, but there were too few people prepared to teach them; however, "graduates of the Ellendale school proved efficient teachers in such positions."[73]

In an intriguing bit of irony, education officials overseeing the school's changing role noted that, as Black recalled, "the training given at the manual training school helped the country teacher to a better understanding of home and farm life." Thus, Ellendale's Normal and Industrial School was distinguished among others in the country for a reason the broad-minded Black might have appreciated. According to Ogren's compilation of state normal schools, the name "normal and industrial" applied to fifteen or so schools: two (in Texas and South Carolina) were for women. All the others were for African American students, with two exceptions—the Normal and Industrial School in Ellendale and the other across the border in Aberdeen, South Dakota.[74] Further, as the normal and agricultural institutes established in Hampton and Tuskegee were designed to familiarize students with skills necessary to prevail over the challenges of rural life, so, too, was the Ellendale school designed to accomplish the same. The NI had a further connection with institutions for African Americans: though its founders touted it as the nation's first free, state-supported manual training school, that distinction actually belongs to Bordentown's Manual Training and Industrial School, which the state of New Jersey assumed responsibility for in 1894. Its students paid no tuition either.[75]

A New Administration Further Refines the School's Mission

In 1905, the Manual Training School's ardent supporter Warren Hicks moved to Cleveland, and he was replaced by W. M. Kern, an Indiana native with a master's degree from its state university. Schultz described him as "a man possessed of a great deal of foresight [and] initiative."[76] Though as Kern surely noted, given the contents of the catalog for the year he arrived, the school he headed had found its mission not in the vision Calvin Woodward had come to Ellendale to advocate a decade earlier, but in a smorgasbord of Latin, psychology, and physiology, as well as short courses in farming and stenography.[77] Nevertheless, an address he gave late in 1906 to the North Dakota State Teachers Association indicates that Kern had the sophisticated awareness of national trends that were so evident in the course descriptions by Tingle and Anderson. He warned his audience that the enthusiasm for manual training had spread so rapidly that "quality has fallen short of quantity." To promote the proper principles of schooling hands and heads, he employed arguments from psychology (quoting Nicholas Murray Butler) and pedagogy (William James, among others). Further, manual training "is in harmony with the American spirit" because here we "leave the individual free to select his own vocation," rather than assuming he will follow that of his father.[78] After a reference to a comment by Henry Belfield—that manual work enhances the quality of academic work—Kern repeated the quotation from William James that had appeared in the 1902 catalog for the Chicago school: manual training schools are "the most colossal improvement" in secondary education in recent years, not only because they make people more handy in domestic life and "better skilled in trade," but because "they will give us citizens of an entirely different intellectual fibre."[79]

Kern's address was published in the school's quarterly bulletin; it was followed by manual training instructor A. E. Dunphy's report on how a school, situated as the NI was, could provide its students with the needed equipment at reasonable expense. Well-illustrated with photographs, drawings, and numerous lists, Dunphy's article, along with that of Kern, suggests the bulletin had a wide audience in mind. It ends with a brief bibliography that includes Dewey's *School and Society* as well as *Manual Training Magazine,* which by 1906 had moved from its initial home at the University of Chicago to Bradley University in Peoria, Illinois.

When a new catalog appeared in July of 1910, it noted the state's urgent need for well-educated teachers; the Normal Department would meet it by offering three sets of courses:

1. Academic: because "accurate scholarship is the teacher's most fundamental weapon."
2. Industrial: "in which the student's powers of expression are trained jointly with his receptive faculties."
3. Professional: because a "clear comprehension of the theories that underlie practice" is as essential as scholarship.

Thus, it offered an "elementary course for rural teachers," a one-year course for high school graduates, and both four- and five-year courses for eighth-grade graduates, either in regular or in manual training and domestic science programs.[80]

By mid-1910, its faculty had grown from three to nearly twenty, including a president and a librarian; a dozen of them were women. All but two had at least one college degree, mainly from state universities in the Midwest;

three of the women had graduated from Carleton. They were young, but not without experience; all but a few had two or three years of teaching prior to arriving in Ellendale. Together these faculty members were responsible for ninety-five courses, ranging from grammar to dressmaking, quantitative analysis to blacksmithing. These were organized in various departments of liberal arts, domestic arts and sciences, manual training and music, commercial arts and steam engineering. Tuition was still free, but students who boarded paid $3.50 per week for the privilege. Students of "good moral character" who had completed a "common school" course were admitted without examination. In order to graduate, students had to accumulate a standard number of credits in required courses; 10 percent were electives.[81]

Of the faculty in 1910, three would remain for decades; another three moved on after only two years. Of the original trio in 1899, Tingle had remained for four years, Anderson for nine. Dunphy would teach there for sixteen years; afterward, he established a hardware store in town. In 1909, he married Jessie Howell, a music teacher who had studied in Germany.[82] Ellen Anderson, the original art teacher, was replaced by another who would go on to further distinction. Marie Louise Pinkney, an Iowa native and graduate of Teachers College, Columbia, spent only two years in Ellendale, but the description of her art department suggests she did it with verve and influence. As Louise Pinkney-Sooy, she would later serve for four decades as a popular teacher at UCLA and author of *Plan Your Own Home*, published by Stanford University in 1946.[83] Pinkney's sure hand likely guided production of the *Snitcher,* the school's handsome yearbook that made its first appearance in 1912. Its artwork and typography indicate talented, well-trained students with affection for and a sense of humor about their fellows.

The July 1910 *Catalog* noted that the demand for teachers of manual training and domestic sciences "greatly exceeds the supply" and thus results in higher wages; further, "no other school in the northwest is better equipped to train teachers in these special subjects."[84] Reconstructing who the NI's students were then and why they were there requires some extrapolation, but through combining student rosters and lists of graduates compiled after the school's first decade, some generalizations are possible. First, enrollment for the 1909–1910 academic year was 297; as the senior class for that year had 32 students, it is safe to assume that less than half that number were of regular high school age and full-time students. This suggests that another 150 or more were taking only a course or two at a time and not matriculating; this had also been the case in 1905. An additional 74 attended the year's summer session; most of them were practicing teachers.[85] The students were still predominantly from Ellendale and other nearby towns, but once graduated,

Figure 21. A young photographer named Elmer Thompson took dozens of remarkable photos of students in and out of class for the NI's first yearbook, published in 1912. For this picture, he later reported, he asked that the only light be from the windows. Art teacher Louise Pinkney's hand appears to have directed the yearbook's design. Thompson later became a noted inventor of consumer electronics; Pinkney would teach and write books about interior design.

at least a third moved on, mainly out of state—to Texas and Washington as well as Nebraska.[86]

The class of 1912—those who produced the first *Snitcher*—included thirty-one young women and fifteen young men, serious-minded youth as pictured in the yearbook's oval-shaped portraits. All were active in activities such as choral groups, literary clubs, and athletics; the girls' basketball team was particularly popular. Of the forty-six graduates, six were headed to college; most of the others became teachers—half the girls graduated from the normal program, several with a domestic science focus. Ten of the boys focused on manual training; most intending to teach it as well. The yearbook includes group pictures of thirty short-course students, half male and half female; some were in mechanics and agriculture; others in domestic arts and sciences. At over 120 pages in length, the last twenty-four in this first *Snitcher* include advertisements from dozens of businesses, one as distant as Rochester, New York (which pictured its wood-working machines for manual training courses); most, though, were local. Together, they suggest the school's widespread support; further, the *Snitcher* had paid for itself.[87]

Figure 22 & 23. All full-time NI students were required to participate in physical activities: boys were in a militia; girls attended gym class. Basketball was particularly popular with girls. Students also had to take some kind of music course; the school's orchestra made events such as this Valentine's Day dance possible.

The extensive advertisements likely made possible not only the appealing design, but the profusion of photographs illustrating campus activities. These are not only a valuable record of school life at the time, but the first published collection of Elmer O. Thompson, a 1912 graduate who would go on to considerable accomplishment as musician, cinematographer, and particularly an inventor of consumer electronics. During a long career at firms such as AT and T, he was awarded thirty patents and devised progenitors for devices such as the "remote" that became ubiquitous in the decades after his death in 1983.[88]

New Presidents and New Oversight

In 1912, the State Normal and Industrial got a new president; Kern had left in 1911 to study in Europe for a year along with his wife, Caroline Evans Kern. A Carleton graduate who had studied at the University of Chicago while Dewey was there, Mrs. Kern also taught Latin at the NI. A. E. Dunphy became acting president for a year; he was followed by two other brief presidencies. The first was not successful; the second far better. Willis Johnson became president in the fall of 1913 but served only a year before being called to the presidency of the Normal and Industrial school in Aberdeen, South Dakota, where he had previously been on the faculty; he, too, had studied at the University of Chicago. A report he gave to the trustees shortly before his departure summarized the school's accomplishments over the previous two years: attendance had grown to 348, with roughly the same number of male and female students; 81 were there for a short course; a smaller percentage than before were from Ellendale and surrounding towns, some were from out of state. The 1914 six-week summer school program conducted with four other counties drew 248 teachers; these were in addition to the 348 registered for the academic year. Accomplishments included an improved agriculture lab, a "reel"—or moving picture—about the school's activities, lectures and a "chautauqua" (which had become a generic term), and a School Peace League done with the militia group.[89]

The school's expanded programs and usefulness to the state necessitated more funds: for construction and maintenance, for a greenhouse, and better heating and lighting, Johnson stated. Electricity had come to the campus, and the town, in August 1909, but not until the fall did the buildings have "incandescent lights throwing their light in all directions," according to an enthusiastic reporter.[90] Despite this advantage, teachers' salaries were still "woefully inadequate," Johnson wrote, and more land was needed to expand the agricultural program—in part so that it could begin producing vegetables, dairy products, and meat for the school's dining rooms.[91]

A surprising aspect of the school's curriculum in those early years was the strength of its music programs. All full-time students had to include it in their course work for at least three years; for normal students, its purpose was to prepare them to teach music rather than to perform. In 1911, the NI had lured a Professor Jacob Schutz to its faculty. Educated at the conservatory and university in Christiana, Norway, he had taught there and in Alabama before arriving in Ellendale. The catalog description of the music program under his leadership indicates the elevated intentions Anderson, Tingle, and others had when the school opened. Through instruction in piano and voice, harmony and music history, students were to understand that "music, like all art, must touch the soul of man" and "be an expression of character, personality, and individuality."[92] There is no record of the extent to which this was accomplished, but during and after Schutz's tenure there were several choral groups along with an orchestra composed of students and staff. All continued for several years after his departure in 1914. However elevated the music program may seem, it was perhaps typical for the time. Ogren claimed that most normal schools included courses in drawing and vocal music in the elementary curriculum.[93]

Ryland M. Black took over as president in 1914 and remained as the school's head for the next twenty-two years. Well known to students as coauthor of the *Brief History of North Dakota*, he had previously taught at the state's School of Science at Wahpeton, a town east of Ellendale on the Minnesota border; he, too, had studied at the University of Chicago. It was Black who claimed, in the history of Dickey County he edited, that the school had become "a living symbol of democracy." As it encouraged long service from its faculty, an "excellent school spirit as well as high efficiency in instruction and attainment" had built up.[94] In the first decade of his tenure, the school grew from one operating largely as a secondary school with many part-time offerings to one granting college degrees, though it continued to enroll non-matriculating students.[95] The road between the two was not always smooth; catalogs for the years 1913 to 1918 indicate that students were divided into five levels—first through third, and then juniors and seniors. Most students continued to come directly from a "common school," but the NI also welcomed students who had attended, even graduated from, high schools.[96]

A major administrative change the year after Black's arrival was greater supervision by the state. In July 1915, a statewide board of regents took control of all North Dakota public institutions of higher learning; one of its first actions was to initiate a survey conducted by the U.S. Commissioner of Education's office. The resulting report aroused some criticism in Ellendale—supporters of the school's industrial programs worried that state education officials would discontinue courses the former felt were essential

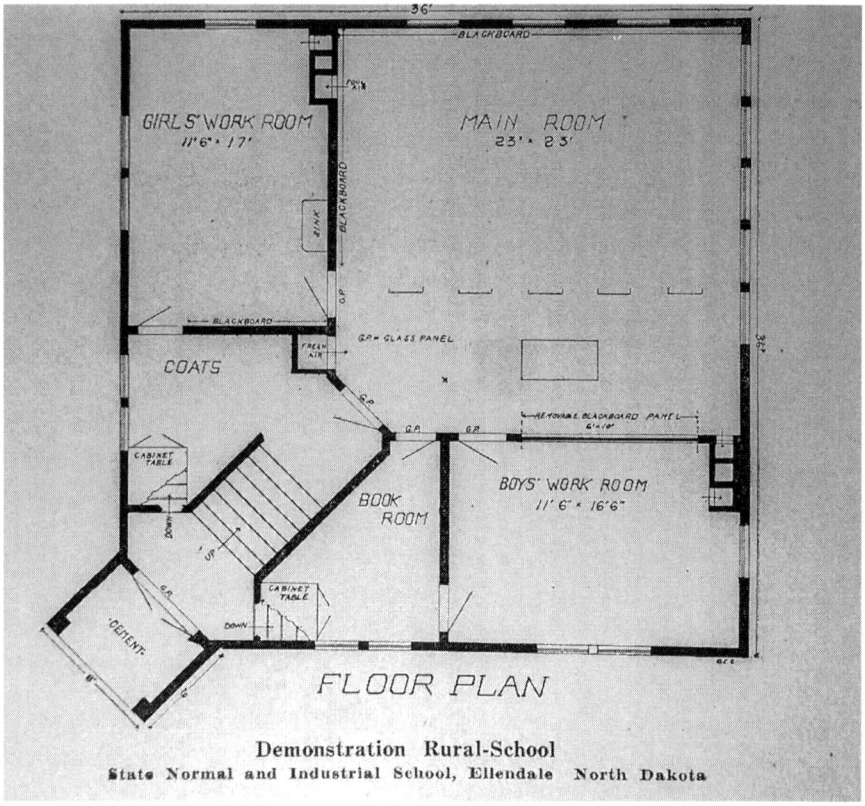

Figure 24. As a Normal and Industrial School, one of the NI's functions was to prepare teachers for manual training and domestic science programs. Aspects of these topics were taught in some of the state's five thousand one-room schools. In 1917, the NI constructed a model rural school that incorporated numerous innovations remarkably sensitive to its purpose, but its expense and school consolidation limited its impact. This floor plan appeared in a special issue of the NI *Bulletin* for January 1919.

to their community, such as those in mechanical and domestic skills taken one at a time. That did not happen; the report noted the valuable "equipment for work of this kind" that the school had accumulated and advised that courses making use of it be continued for the time being. The report's strongest recommendation was that the NI should "cease at once to function as the local high school" for Ellendale. It should also "immediately make some arrangements for practice teaching" and drop classes with low enrollment—average attendance in NI classes was 12.7, considerably lower than that at the state's other normal schools.[97]

The 1916 report also criticized the geographical distribution of the NI's students. The percentage residing in the home county of the state's three other normal schools ranged from a third to a half; for Ellendale, it was 72 percent, a percentage that would never fall below half for most of the school's existence.[98] In meeting with the recommendation that it immediately improve its "arrangements for practice teaching," the NI responded with a model for one-room schools across the state.

Designing a Model Rural School

For the previous decade, Ellendale's public school had been providing practice teaching experience for NI students, but inadequately. Among the limitations of a "city" school—for that is how it was regarded—was that many graduates of the NI's teacher preparation programs would begin their careers teaching in rural, one-room schoolhouses. Ellendale's elementary school, highly regarded around the state, could accommodate too few teachers in training; further, it had separate classrooms for all the grades—and NI graduates needed to be prepared to handle eight grades in one room, oftentimes one that was "wretched" and ill equipped. Practice schools, or classrooms, had become a standard aspect of normal schools nationwide since the 1870s, but with some possible exceptions, most were confined to a few rooms in an education department building or classrooms in a local school system made available for that purpose.[99] Actual laboratory schools were established by several state normal schools; those affiliated with an African American institution may have been most prominent in great part because their normal school students were not welcome in schools for white children.[100]

The NI responded to the commission's recommendation in a distinctive way: it built a Demonstration Rural School on the campus. This not only provided practice teaching experiences for NI students, it served as a model building after which school districts around the state could improve their own one-room schoolhouses. This was indeed a great service: when the Demonstration School opened in December of 1917, North Dakota had 5,273 "common" schools and 90 percent of them—approximately 4,700—were one-room buildings in each of the state's townships; Dickey County alone had 31 townships and 98 schools.[101] In a commentary lauding the Demonstration School's dedication, the editor of the *Dickey County Leader* wrote: "it is a curious fact that we often live next to greatness without knowing it."[102] While "greatness" is subjective, singular is not—and NI's model Demonstration Rural School may have been one of the country's few designed with white students in mind. Two years earlier, the Rosenwald Fund had begun its philanthropic effort to help rural Black communities throughout the

South build decent schoolhouses, and it provided them with architectural plans along with partial financial assistance. Around five thousand schools for Black students resulted.[103] Whether such plans for schools serving white students were common is not clear; some state normal schools had one-room schoolhouses on campus, but their focus was on curriculum and instruction, not on architecture.[104]

That aside, the dedication ceremony held on a snowy December day attracted considerable attention, much of it pointing to the NI's origin in manual training and the need to equalize opportunity for both rural and "city" children.[105] Mattie Crabtree, Dickey County's superintendent of schools (and niece of the town's banker who had worked with Warren Hicks to design the Ellendale school), noted that 30 percent of the county's schoolteachers were (like her) NI graduates and 70 percent had taken additional training there. The president of another normal school praised work with the hands as essential to learning; one of his comments echoed John Dewey in claiming that "the standard of the best home must be the standard of the school." Florence Marsh, an experienced rural teacher brought from Wisconsin to head the demonstration school, emphasized connections between the home and the school and the obligation both had to teach social responsibility and "respect for the rights of others." For students in the demonstration school, Marsh had recruited twenty-one children in grades two to eight from rural districts in Ellendale township.

According to the *Leader* article, other speakers articulated two major concerns: one was providing rural students the same advantages city students—i.e., those in Ellendale—enjoyed; the other, encouraging sympathy for rural life in the NI's "city"-trained teachers. Olin Combellick, head of the NI's normal department and the person most responsible for the new building, spoke about the need to "enrich and enlarge the life of rural people." The state superintendent of public instruction, Neil C. Macdonald, noted that the NI prepared more of the state's teachers than did any of North Dakota's other normal schools. He claimed that "Progress" meant keeping rural schools in tune with scientific and mechanical inventions and in "pace with city schools." As a community center, the school would impress upon children the "joy of service": "noble character" would be formed there. Children must learn that they cannot "live by the sweat of others' brows," Macdonald claimed.

A year after the demonstration school opened, the NI published a 24-page booklet describing its distinctive features, its cost, and how rural communities could adapt the plans to meet their own needs.[106] Combellick's overview suggests he had a broad audience in mind: the nation's towns and cities, he wrote, could only thrive by cooperating with rural districts, yet educational advantages were not equally distributed. These attributes suggest that little escaped Combellick's attention: its square shape maximized space with minimal material; its high ceilings enabled an efficient ventilation system. Sited to avoid prevailing winds, the small entrance porch was at ground level, avoiding steps that would ice over in the winter; the stairs leading up and down were actually inside the building. The large windows maximized natural light; the toilets were designed for districts without running water.

Further, the teacher, standing at the front of the classroom, could not only supervise students there but see into both the girls' and the boys' workrooms off to the side; the door to the boys' workroom could be closed to avoid distracting students in the main room. As Combellick explained: focusing student attention on the "study of texts when others are doing industrial work in the same room ... works against a fundamental psychic law of child mind." The school could be a social center as well: desks could be moved aside so the classroom could become a stage. The basement playroom not only offered space for calisthenics and dancing but could also serve as a separate classroom. Church functions could be held in the building; kitchen facilities in the girls' workroom eased the preparation of refreshments.

Combellick's instructions suggested how students could help in preparing lunches and cleaning up on a rotating basis; how teachers could move from one subject and grade level to another. He and Marsh responded to criticisms that "newer activities"—manual training, cooking, and "handwork"—took up too much of the school day; the booklet ended with the claim that times for these subjects "were taken from different terms," so the "fewest number of regular subjects" were omitted at any one time.

In planning and execution, the demonstration school aimed for ideal conditions—a highly skilled teacher, supportive parents, and self-disciplined children. In this ideal, it suggests a rural adaptation of the manual training program Charles Ham had outlined for Chicago three decades earlier in his 1886 *Manual Training*. Combellick, in his plans for the school, might have been influenced by the contemporaneous interest in model schools emanating from Teachers College; as he had spent part of 1915 studying at the University of Chicago, he was likely aware of them. One, the 1902 Speyer School located near the Teachers College campus, was designed to serve as both school and community center; it accommodated manual training and domestic science courses with its workshops, kitchens, and laboratories. Another is the attention garnered by Abraham Flexner's 1915 promotion of a "Model School." Though noted mainly for the reforms he initiated in medical education, Flexner's goals for elementary students resulted initially in the 1917 opening of the Lincoln School in New York City. Its founder's hope was, according to historian Lawrence Cremin, that it would serve as a "leavening agent in the nation's educational dough."[107]

Combellick may have hoped that his plans for the Demonstration Rural School would have a similar leavening effect on North Dakota's schools. As with Ham's curriculum and the Lincoln School's grand intentions, Combellick's plan did not materialize as he had hoped.[108] Whether many rural districts in the Dakotas or elsewhere actually adopted the ideas behind the NI's plans is unknown. Though they were uniquely well suited for farm communities on windswept prairies and could accommodate more than one teacher, district consolidation over the next decade would have diminished the model school's long-term impact. The building remained on the campus and still stands over a century later. But, per Black's history, after a few years as a model for rural schools, it first housed Ellendale's public kindergarten and later became another school in the Ellendale system. Still, it offered practice work in the grades for NI students.[109]

The People's School Midst Populist Politics

The 1916 Commissioner of Education report and the building of the Demonstration Rural School were two steps in moving the Normal and Industrial School toward the role it would serve for the next fifty years: more normal and mixed industrial. As Black described the school during its early years: NI students could "take a course in carpentry, blacksmithing, agriculture, home economics, music, painting, drawing or in some phase of business or industrial work" for which they showed a "special aptitude or ability."[110] This service the NI would continue to perform for area residents at least until it was redefined as a branch of the University of North Dakota in 1965. But as that later acquisition indicated, the school's function as a "normal"—a term that fell out of use after 1920—increasingly exceeded that of its being an industrial school. Several steps in that new direction were taken under Black's leadership: as he noted in the 1930 history of Dickey County that he edited, the school became a member of the American Association of Teachers Colleges in 1920, and in 1926, a member of the North Central Association of Colleges and Secondary Schools. In 1925, the state legislature authorized the NI to extend its curricula to four years and the following year gave the school approval to grant a bachelor of science degree in industrial education. In 1927, the graduates included a half-dozen young people holding such degrees.

The first of these steps took place in the midst of momentous times in the state and nation; one was the rise of a populist movement in North

Dakota known as the Nonpartisan League, which began in 1915; another was World War I. Several students served in it, and a few faculty members took leave to do so as well. The League (commonly, the NPL) contributed to a reformist movement that influenced political developments in the Dakotas, Minnesota, and Wisconsin for several decades. Ellendale residents played leading roles in both support for and opposition to the NPL during the years the NI was evolving from secondary school to college. Among them were prominent attorney Frederick Graham, the local newspaper editor Herbert Goddard, and Hector Perry, an Ellendale publisher turned well-connected investor in land.

Though the NPL had no direct impact on the NI, both the school and the political movement were unique products of North Dakota. In the four decades since the start of the Great Dakota Boom in the late 1870s, North Dakota's population had grown to almost 650,000 people; most were migrants from other midwestern states, both native and foreign born; this was particularly true of Dickey County.[111] The egalitarian self-sufficiency that had characterized Ellendale's early settlers did not necessarily characterize all Dakotans, though; opportunists and dealers in dubious propositions of varied kinds—those inclined to live off the sweat of others' brows—arrived there as well. The NPL's grassroots membership grew because farmers felt that men who exploited their labor had come to dominate the state legislature, according to a history of the movement written by political scientist Lloyd Omdahl.[112]

More dependent on agriculture than any other state, North Dakota was also highly dependent on wheat, a crop that had little value unless it could get to the mills that turned it into flour and bread. And for that, farmers were dependent on the railroads that shipped their wheat, mainly to Minneapolis. And the railroads, the major millers, the bankers, and the grain dealers based there could collude to determine shipping rates and prices per bushel. Despite their self-sufficient impulses—the "producerist" mentality described earlier—Dakota farmers began to see themselves as pawns in a great exchange: their labor was essential to growing the wheat, but they had limited influence over the price at which it could be sold. In 1915, anger against a system that seemed rigged against them drove farmers to join the NPL. In the election of 1916, league members were elected to the state's lower house in sufficient numbers to pass legislation intended to limit rapacious rate-setting and encourage cooperative ownership of elevators and mills. But the state senate declined to pass the legislation, so the NPL's ambitious agenda remained a set of goals, not a reality.[113]

Disagreements about what the NPL represented were a major issue in the 1920 election, which marked the end of the Progressive Era in the nation as a whole. In North Dakota, the contest for an open seat in the U.S. Senate pitted wealthy Ellendale resident Hector Perry against Edwin Ladd, a renowned agronomist who had served as the state's commissioner in charge of food safety and was at the time president of the land-grant school in Fargo. Perry was nominally a Democrat and Ladd a Republican, but that affiliation was less significant than the latter's NPL membership and his well-known advocacy of consumer issues. To *Dickey County Leader* publisher Herbert Goddard, the issue between the two was clear: "On the one side, are the forces that want to carry into full operation a system of expensive and experimental socialism... and the other side is contending that too many of our resources are being put at stake to try out idealistic theories."[114] For Goddard, Perry was the obvious choice. Ladd was the candidate associated with "socialist" ventures such as state ownership of essential businesses and banks. The manner in which Dickey County voters—which for the first time included women—decided the issue indicates both the complexity of the issues and the independence of its voters. Candidates from the top of the ticket on down to county officials who were identified with the NPL got a "severe drubbing" at the polls statewide in 1920. The one exception was Edwin Ladd; though he took Dickey County with only a slight lead over hometown candidate Perry, he won overwhelmingly in the state.[115] Ladd's well-known campaigns for protecting ordinary North Dakotans from predatory businesses held more sway with voters than did the editorialists who labelled him a socialist.

In 1926, what can be viewed as two versions of populism—the jingoist version associated with orators who captured voters' attention and the arguably more authentic version represented by the Farmer-Labor Party into which the NPL evolved—were at issue. Edwin Ladd, as admired as a member of the U.S. Senate as he had been in North Dakota, died suddenly in 1925; in a memorial to his service, a colleague claimed that Ladd was always "in deep sympathy with the struggles of the people who had sent him there."[116] Following Ladd's death, the governor called a meeting of two dozen men prominent in the state to advise him on choosing a replacement; the leading candidates were Ellendale attorney Fred Graham and Gerald Nye, an energetic young newspaperman from the center of the state. An opinionated writer whose "spirited editorials" spouted radical ideas, Nye had gained a broad following.[117] Graham stood for the coherent set of populist ideas that Ladd represented. The governor's decision, as described by Ellendale historian Ken Smith, surprised many members of the governor's advisory committee; discussion among them had suggested support for Graham, but the governor chose Nye. However, as a senator, Nye was not the credit to the state Ladd had been; prone to advocating conspiratorialist theories, he eventually became an isolationist.[118]

Though neither Smith nor Graham's admiring descendants can say what kind of senator he might have been, his career in Ellendale indicates a principled devotion to the ideals upon which both the town and the college were founded. Born in Michigan in 1881, Graham arrived in Dickey County with his parents, via covered wagon, in 1884. Raised on a farm northwest of Ellendale, he learned something of diversified agriculture from his father, and went on to graduate from the NI and the University of North Dakota law school. In 1906, he opened a law practice in Ellendale and, in 1912, married Ina Randall, who had given the noted oration at her 1901 graduation from the NI; together the couple had four children, one of whom has written of her parents' accomplishments. Graham's political career began in 1915 when he was elected state's attorney for the county; he later became a judge and served on the Republican National Committee. He represented Dickey County in the state legislature during the 1940s and was always an "ardent champion" of the NI. The campus library for which he had secured an appropriation in 1930 was named for him after his death in 1951. Later, an Ina Graham Memorial Room was dedicated.[119]

An Education "To *Live* and to *Do* the Work of One's Choice"

Whether Ellendale's combination of people, activities, and structures—the trio of attributes as described by geographic historian John Hudson—was indeed unique and led this little town and its college on North Dakota's southern border to nurture people like the Grahams awaits perusal of numerous other informal histories of counties and colleges, publications that were abundant as such places celebrated silver, gold, or diamond jubilees over the past century. The only question that can be addressed here is what the NI actually accomplished and how. The long-term loyalty of its faculty is one measure of this, as are the lives and careers of NI's graduates. For the 1918 school year, the faculty had grown to twenty-six members, the largest it would ever be.[120] One member, hired to teach chemistry that fall, later stated that the NI's science courses when he arrived were definitely at the secondary level, due mainly to the students' lack of preparation. A decade later, when the NI was no longer functioning mainly as a high school, the course level was more that of a college.[121] A few of the early members of the faculty remained for five to ten or more years.[122] While brief biographies of early faculty members suggest their youth; pictures of the faculty in later yearbooks suggest a certain maturity.

As for the students, an "Alumni Directory" published in the 1917 *Snitcher* gives hometowns for 220 of those who had graduated between 1901 and

1915. Half or more of the men had gone to the West Coast; a large majority of the women remained in North Dakota. Places of employment were given for most of them; surprisingly few were farmers, and several had continued their education. More than half were teachers; many of the men were heading manual training programs.[123]

The 1924–1925 *Snitcher*—the twenty-fifth anniversary edition—included a list of nearly a hundred graduates, giving their hometowns and their careers. Most of those who responded lived out of state; a half-dozen lived abroad, and twenty of the men lived in California, Washington, or Oregon. Over two dozen men had careers in fields related to manual training, many as teachers. The one farmer on the list claimed to be an aviator as well. Several were merchants; a few were bankers, dentists, or attorneys. Of the women, whether married or not, most were teachers, many of them school principals. One woman was a physician; another had studied music in Germany. Two, though by 1925 teaching in Minnesota, claimed to "have had the privilege of sowing NI ideals in West Africa." As President Black wrote at the top of this list of alumni: "The NI—a school for everyone—educates a person to *live* and to *do* the work of his choice."[124]

Over the following half century—until what had been the NI closed for good in 1970—the school somewhat joined the mainstream, following the course described by Christine Ogren in *The State Normal School*. It differed from most in that it continued to offer the industrial courses that remained one of its chief virtues for the community it served, and it never grew into a state college or university as did many of the schools described by Ogren.[125] But with a growing state university located forty miles away in South Dakota and other North Dakota colleges within a few hours' drive to the north or east, that was not necessary. Declining enrollment and other challenges led to a loss of vitality; then, in January 1970, a disastrous fire consumed both the original Manual Training Building and the Carnegie Building, taking many of the school's records as well as furnishings and equipment. Trinity Bible College rose in its wake.[126]

During the years the NI was developing its distinctive program, the idea of industrial education evolved into vocational education, stirring controversies as it went. An overview of those is the topic of the next chapter—and the NI's Warren Hicks played a role in them.

CHAPTER 6

Agency and Efficiency

Manual Training Becomes Vocational Education

> In this government, the young cannot be trained for any particular station, for no one can foretell what that will be.
> —Ella Flagg Young, 1900

> For the pupils are not taking the course to become carpenters, or electricians, or dressmakers, but to find out how the work of the world is done.
> —Evelyn Dewey, 1915

The years during which Warren Hicks was involved with industrial education were pivotal in determining the direction the field would take over the next several decades, so following aspects of his career illustrate some of the highlights. In 1897, Hicks had brought prominent advocate Calvin Woodward out to a new community in the Dakotas to discuss manual training; he then guided a rural manual training school through its first few years. In 1906, he became assistant superintendent in Cleveland with responsibility for the city's new technical high school, and in 1912 he went to Wisconsin to oversee the development of its "continuation" skill-training programs for young people who had dropped out prior to entering high school. These years were also a momentous period for developments in industry and agriculture, transportation and communications, developments that had major impacts on educational institutions. In sum, Hicks was on the ground level during a period in which educators and others struggled to devise programs and policies that would meet the needs of individual students, their communities, and the state governments that would fund much of it—all in response to pressures, from industry and agriculture, over which the schools had no control.

These years, the first two decades of the twentieth century, would see major changes in the kinds of work available, particularly that for young people: industries and manufacturing firms grew and consolidated; technology eliminated many of the skilled (and unskilled) jobs that had been prepared for through apprenticeships; telephones and pneumatic tubes replaced messenger jobs; mechanized agriculture sent rural youth to cities where they competed with rising numbers of immigrants. By the century's turn, the nation's workforce had completed the transition from artisans and yeomen to employees of factories.

Some educators such as William Torrey Harris, who served as U.S. commissioner of education from 1889 to 1906, continued to espouse the value of a traditional education that emphasized literature, mathematics, and natural philosophy—teaching self-reliance along the way. Others, led initially by Harris's sparring partner in St. Louis, Calvin Woodward, shifted their espousal of manual training from its value as a cultural asset for urban youth to its necessity for keeping young people in school until they were at least modestly equipped to assume responsibility for self-support and citizenship.[1]

Educators on the ground such as Warren Hicks went, as he once said, "where the crowd pushed," endeavoring to offer programs that their communities asked for. Others, such as Chicago's Henry Belfield, bemoaned the changes imposed upon manual training programs they had earlier guided into existence: parents and students pushed Belfield toward offering something other than what he wanted to provide, and as a result he was pushed aside. In New Jersey, James Monroe Gregory had not only had to devise programs that would attract and retain a "crowd" denied an education for generations but to do so in an environment that had conflicting visions of how best to accomplish that—and at the same time satisfy state officials responsible for funding his endeavors.

Beyond Belfield, Gregory, and Hicks, and hundreds of others in positions like theirs, were national figures like Harris and Woodward who endeavored to influence the direction industrial educators would take. As the century turned, the national figures became both more numerous and more prominent, including Nicholas Murray Butler at Columbia University in New York and John Dewey. With assistance from people like Ella Flagg Young, Dewey could not only influence the work of teachers but extrapolate from his mastery of psychology and philosophy implications both had for the nation's future as a democracy. Too often confined to discussions of industrial education for African Americans were two other nationally prominent sources of influence: Booker T. Washington and W. E. B. Du Bois, whose prodigious talents as philosophers of education deserve greater recognition.[2]

Others who were to play a major role in the course industrial education would take from 1900 to 1920 include David Snedden, commissioner of education for Massachusetts and later professor at Teachers College, and his one-time deputy Charles Prosser. The latter would run the National Society for the Promotion of Industrial Education (NSPIE) founded in 1906 and write the major piece of federal legislation enacted in 1917 that would influence the course vocational education—as it was by then called—for the next several decades. In 1915, Snedden and Dewey engaged in a published and oft-quoted exchange in a new publication known as *The New Republic*.[3] Their arguments turned on ideas about efficiency and agency: for Snedden, the issue was whether a program made "efficient" use of human capital and public resources; those that did so would be most democratic. For Dewey, the question was whether a program helped students have some mastery over their industrial fate, an idea known today as student agency; for Dewey, that was more appropriate to a democracy.

Earlier that year, in February of 1915, Du Bois had provided testimony to a Congressional committee in which he spoke eloquently about misguided ways in which industrial education was being imposed upon Black students in the South.[4] By that year's end, Washington, more earnest than eloquent in his advocacy of industrial education, had died at the relatively young age of fifty-nine. Though not often construed as a form of the efficiency versus agency argument, the one between Washington and Du Bois turned on economics: the former prioritized economic power, claiming that political power could come later; the latter argued that economic power was impossible without political power. Dewey, whose principles and priorities stood rather midway between those of Washington and Du Bois, never really engaged with either.

The following chapter considers arguments pro and con, beginning with a section on how historians over the past five decades have told the process by which manual training became vocational education. It then covers the origin of the National Society for the Promotion of Industrial Education. Next, it reviews how Chicago and a few other cities responded to calls for schools to provide preparation for work as well as for citizenship, discusses how these changes were perceived by the public, and analyzes conflicts over the control of industrial education once there was widespread agreement that it was a good thing.

While historians have tended to offer a top-down version of these developments, relaying their history through analyzing stands taken by leaders of various national organizations, this chapter offers a ground-level version:

it focuses on local initiatives undertaken by leaders of civic organizations, businesses, labor unions, and educational institutions. Both versions—the policy and the implementation level—were a response to the ever-more apparent reality that the nineteenth century common school could not meet the demands of the twentieth century. But the two vantage points evaluate the responses differently. While the policy-level histories have concluded that the movement for industrial education was either a failure or an elitist imposition, an implementation-level view suggests otherwise. The experiences of teachers and students and administrators, plus their community supporters, and their interaction with state officials, indicate that the movement had more successful outcomes. By devising programs that responded to local needs and were managed by local officials, many industrial education programs persuaded young people to stay longer in school and enabled them to embark upon adult employment better prepared than they would have been otherwise.

One of the textbook histories refers to "obscure education professionals" who shepherded their versions of an industrial education into programs that they felt met the needs of the communities they served. One of those might be Warren Hicks, who when an old man was recalled as the "father of vocational education" in Wisconsin.[5] Though the written record of why he might deserve such recognition is at best limited, the professional positions that he held between 1906 and 1917 placed him at the center of two major controversies: whether high schools should be comprehensive—that is, offer both a traditional academic education and some trade-training in one institution—or should instead track students into either an academic or a trade school. This dispute is often referred to as the "unit" versus the "dual" system. The other controversy was about how communities could respond constructively to the needs of young people who dropped out before they started high school. In Ellendale, Hicks witnessed how a manual training school had far more appeal than even a good, though small, high school had. In Cleveland, he saw how a high school that called itself "technical," though it was part of a unit system, actually turned out to be rather comprehensive.

Less obscure but essential to the story is Ella Flagg Young, Chicago's brilliant and decisive "educational stateswoman," a title she was given for her deft mastery of classroom teaching and political astuteness as superintendent of the city's schools.[6] Though Young is given considerable credit for her contributions to Dewey's efforts in Chicago and often mentioned for her opposition to a dual system of schools, her leadership as an initiator of vocational education programs has not received as much attention as her other accomplishments. During her superintendency from 1909 to 1915, the number of vocational education programs in the city and the number of students participating in them grew substantially. As a theorist, Young offered an alternate version of "scientific education," one that placed more importance on student initiative, or "agency," than did psychologists of the time who thought they had explicated an "efficient" science of education.[7]

Using Agency and Efficiency to Frame Opinions about Industrial Education

There is a truism among educators that one teaches as one was taught; the same might apply to writers about education: one's recounting of its history relays aspects of the writer's biography. As noted in the preface, historian Herbert Kliebard recalled his two years of teaching at a vocational school during the 1950s as a disquieting experience, especially when contrasted with his years at a suburban high school. The "opportunity gap" between the two schools was all too obvious, he wrote, as was the "split between vocational and general education."[8] It led to the skepticism about the former evident in his 1999 classic *Schooled to Work*, a bias illustrated by the book's chapter titles. One includes an 1885 quotation that describes a forging shop at Calvin Woodward's Manual Training School in St. Louis; there a *score of young Vulcans*, according to a chapter title, learn how metals are wrought through heat and anvil. The chapter then describes early manual training programs with a sharp, questioning tone.[9] However, another reading of the passage could regard the "young Vulcans" as privileged youth attending a private polytechnical school. They were learning to use a forge along with several more basic tools; their lessons were complemented by a history of technology in a curriculum later idealized by Chicago's Charles Ham.[10] Students spent half their day in the school's well-equipped workshops and the other half in its classrooms, mastering the academic subjects that would prepare them for Washington University or a similar future.

Kliebard, though, may never have read Ham; the latter's rhapsodizing about manual training in its early years influenced schools far beyond those of Chicago and St. Louis, but it disappeared from later accounts of industrial education. Woodward's young vulcans were not the progenitors of the less-privileged students at Bronx Vocational two generations down the road; reading Kliebard's book though could lead one to think so—and to share his skepticism. *Schooled to Work* is full of such passages; wary readers can ignore them and value instead the otherwise useful history the book provides.

That said, no one book can cover all the arguments about what industrial education should be or about what organizations could best offer it. Kliebard wrote that manual training fundamentally altered the purpose of schooling, a claim that historian Lawrence Cremin had made nearly forty years earlier in *The Transformation of the School,* his telling of the progressive movement of which manual training was a part.[11] Appearing a decade after the latter was Edward Krug's still seminal *The Shaping of the American High School;* he argued that the two most significant accomplishments of the movement for industrial education between 1900 and 1920 were the continuation school and vocational guidance.[12] The latter, in one form or another, lasted long after disputes about industrial education were history; the former, which appeared in various guises in the two decades under study, arguably did have the impact Krug assigned to it. But continuation schools are ignored in much of the literature. A somewhat neglected history of industrial education, that of the distinguished labor economist Paul H. Douglas first published in 1921, devotes useful chapters not only to continuation schools, but to other significant aspects of the movement between 1900 and 1920.[13]

Efforts to summarize developments over these years inevitably leave out important aspects; omissions suggest the writer's priorities. Douglas, for example, wrote with a quantifier's focus on numbers. More widely known is a compact volume titled *American Vocationalism,* edited by historians Marvin Lazerson and W. Norton Grubb. Published in 1974, its introductory essay focuses on policies; its excerpts from significant documents make it particularly useful. Another essential book is *Work, Youth, and Schooling,* edited by Harvey Kantor and David Tyack; published in 1982, its nine essays by noted historians each take up a different aspect of the subject.[14] One topic these books tend to ignore is interweaving the history of schooling for workforce participation with a substantial history of how work changed during the nineteenth century. Of the latter, Daniel Rodgers's *The Work Ethic in Industrial America* is an exception, but he also contributed a chapter to the Kantor and Tyack book.[15]

Kliebard's chapter on the "young Vulcans" ends in 1905, a year that Krug claimed marked the end of an era.[16] Among reasons for this turning point were the establishment that year of the Massachusetts Commission on Industrial and Technical Education and the 1906 retirement of William Torrey Harris as U.S. commissioner of education; with his departure went a devotion to the idea that promoting intellectual effort was the school's chief purpose. For Kliebard, manual training could at the time look both "backward and forward" simultaneously—back to the era of the independent artisan and ahead to the new industrialism.[17] Schools, prodded somewhat by Dewey's *School and Society,* published in 1900, were accepting the social function that Charles Ham among others had urged upon them. What had begun as manual training—hand work supplementing head work—in the 1880s would, by 1920, be vocational education. However, several steps were involved in getting there.

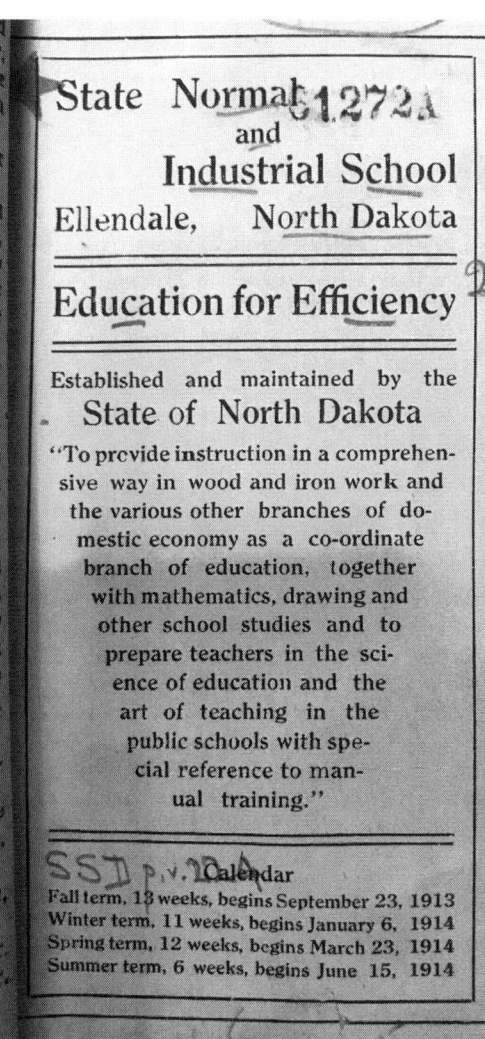

Figure 25. This cover for an NI flyer created in 1913 succinctly states the ideals that led to the establishment and maintenance of the school. The flyer, which appeared just as a new president was installed, likely expresses the way many educators nationwide regarded the idea of "education for efficiency" at the time.

One of the first steps, Krug suggested, was that schools were increasingly seen as social centers, which was the title of a talk Dewey gave in 1902.[18] In it, Dewey argued that the increasing diversity of urban communities and the industrial division of labor necessitated the assumption by schools of new responsibilities; among them were to encourage the commingling of peoples and to provide instruction that helped students better grasp the meaning of their work. If Dewey would construe this *social service* function as benefitting students' ability to develop a sense of their value and an ability to have some control over their future—or agency, as it is being used here—others construed it as a form of *social control*, a term popularized in 1901. And that became the somewhat less benign idea of *social efficiency*, which can be understood as restraining an individual's freedom of action so as to benefit some larger whole.[19]

Like industrial education, the word "efficiency" has also been met with disfavor by later historians, an attitude encapsulated in the title of a 1961 book, *Education and the Cult of Efficiency*. Though the title simplifies the arguments the book makes, it encouraged the revisionist historians of the 1960s and 1970s to view "efficiency" with some suspicion.[20] More recently, intellectual historian Michael Knoll has done some revising of his own. A chapter in his 2022 *Beyond Rhetoric*, a book that offers refreshing insights into the work of John Dewey, takes up "the origin and meaning of 'social efficiency'" and follows the term's passage from the 1890s through the 1960s.[21] Its stop at the NI in North Dakota in 1914 likely expresses how many educators nationwide used the term at the time.

Ella Flagg Young, as both practical educator and theorist, may have best grasped the complexities behind the meanings of all these words. Despite Knoll's nuanced explication, *efficiency* has often been associated with those who view the school's role from the top down and through the eyes of policy makers. On the other hand, *agency* might best be associated with those who view schools from the position of those affected by policies. Young's long career in education began decades before she joined Dewey in 1899 at the University of Chicago. Departing in 1904, she undertook a year-long tour of schools in Europe. In 1905, she was chosen to head the Chicago Normal School. In all these positions she argued, as she had written in 1900, that in America one's role was not wholly predetermined by that of one's parents.[22] But she also recognized the necessity of social cohesion. How, she once asked, "can the school fuse all these diverse elements so as to produce the unity essential to a democracy?" Her answer was that such an end can only be attained by "spreading intelligence and a sense of responsibility for the control of the social whole."[23]

Young's notion of the school was that it should provide sufficient "intelligence"—or academic and practical education—so that members of a social group would voluntarily assume responsibility for their role in the group. "Unity" was volitional; it expressed agency. "Uniformity" was imposed, arguably by proponents of social efficiency.[24] Coming out of the years she worked with Dewey, it is not surprising that her statement of the schools' function bares considerable similarity to that of Dewey's conception of the school as social center. Further, this distinction provides a useful lens through which to view developments in industrial education over the fifteen years that followed 1905.

A Report from Massachusetts Focuses the Discussion

Massachusetts, from the time of the Puritans on through Horace Mann's promotion of a school "common" to all social groups in a community, has long led the determination of policy and priorities regarding education. And so it was in the spring of 1906: the state's Commission on Industrial and Technical Education released a report that received a great deal of attention.[25] Popularly known as the Douglas Commission for the governor who had appointed its members, the group's report was thorough in its data gathering and became a "precipitating event" in the national demand for an industrial education.[26] It construed such education as a means for "grappling with the variety of problems . . . to which city life gives rise" and encouraging "greater efficiency," more "self-reliance," and "steadier habits of industry and frugality" on the part of wage earners. Such an education would serve the needs of many—both workers and employers—and would encourage "industrial intelligence" on the part of the former. A term often associated with Dewey, such intelligence was defined in the report as "mental power to see beyond the task which occupies the hands for the moment to the operations which have preceded and to those that will follow." It also considers materials, their cost, and a "conscience which recognizes obligations."[27] More practically, the report noted that existing programs failed to meet "modern . . . conditions" and that labor unions tended to be suspicious of the trade schools the commission concluded were necessary.[28]

Calling the report a "summation" of the issues, Berenice Fisher wrote that it added little new material but "picked up many of the diverse themes" of the discussion. It did, however, offer a "new interpretation of work in social terms" and recommended that high school math and science courses be related to local industries. Fisher also referred to the companion report issued the following year; it was, she wrote, a "fairly direct appeal for trade training." This 1907 report proposed a state commission to oversee such schools, relating them to the existing public school system but to actually be separate.[29] This became one of the report's more controversial aspects; it either launched or contributed to a discussion that would become heated over the next decade: should high schools offer both academic and vocational education in one building or should the courses and the students taking them be separated into a dual system?

Another significant aspect of the 1906 Massachusetts report was an appendix compiled under the direction of sociologist Susan Kingsbury. Assigned to study the relation of children to industries, she and her committee wrote a report that garnered considerable attention. It calculated that there were 25,000 children in Massachusetts between fourteen and seventeen years of age who were not in school; fully half of them had not gone beyond the seventh grade. Though they may have been employed, some in the textile firms prominent in Massachusetts at the time, they were in jobs without a future.[30] In what became a famous phrase, the report claimed that these were "wasted years"; the future of these children was "the most important question which faces the educational world today." No longer subject to compulsory schooling, these youngsters languished. Further, helping to support their families did not drive such children from school; it was their own lack of interest in being there.[31]

Though Kingsbury's report reflects concern for these children, and its findings were broadly influential, some other reports suggest that Kingsbury and her committee had come to some arguable conclusions. Fifteen years later, economist Paul Douglas offered considerable evidence that poverty was indeed a reason why so many young people left school in their early teens. Citing several studies conducted around 1910, Douglas demonstrated that children's wages were often essential. His report, like that of Kingsbury, faulted schools for students' lack of interest: "The teaching is so dull, scholastic discipline so severe, and above all the curriculum has so little connection with life, that the child is discouraged." That said, their employment prospects were bleak, their jobs unsteady, and possibilities for on-job training unlikely. Another memorable phrase came from his report as well: of the youth he studied, Douglas wrote, "He had nothing to sell but his youth; he sold it and received nothing in return."[32]

In a different take on youth employment, historian David Hogan undertook a complex study of the relationship between school attendance and immigrant status in Chicago during the decades around 1900. His study provided substantial reasons for family dependence on children's wages and how it changed over time. As he concluded, many immigrant parents were skeptical about the value of schooling; quickly establishing a firm financial foundation was more important. "The high levels of home ownership were associated with high rates of child labor and low rates of school attendance," Hogan claimed.[33] Over time, as families acquired that financial foothold, their children were far more likely to remain in school.

National Organizations Coalesce around a Widespread Concern

Whether their initiative was spurred by the release of the report from Massachusetts or just parallel to it is incidental, but in June 1906 a meeting of a dozen men concerned about issues raised by the report was held at the

Engineers' Club in New York City. Organized by Charles Richards, head of the manual training program at Teachers College, and Paul Haney, director of manual training for New York City's schools, it heralded a decade-long period of initiatives on both national and local levels that led to the Smith-Hughes Bill in 1917.[34]

Attendees at that first meeting agreed that the nation's schools were failing many and not keeping pace with changes in technology or the economy. They called for a far larger meeting during the following January. It was to be held at Cooper Union in lower Manhattan, a significant choice given the group's agenda. Established in 1859 as a private school, Cooper Union's initial mission was to provide courses in technology for working adults, and it was free and open to all, women and men, regardless of race or class or previous education. Charles Richards would assume its presidency in 1908.

Among the 250 attendees at the January 1907 meeting were a host of social reformers along with representatives from major organizations; among them were the fifty-year-old National Education Association (NEA), the National Association of Manufacturers (NAM) founded in 1895, and the American Federation of Labor (AFL), which had been organized in 1886. Attendees included Jane Addams, Jacob Riis, and Andrew Carnegie; even President Theodore Roosevelt made an appearance.[35] Chosen to chair the gathering was Nicholas Murray Butler, an early supporter of manual training who had been named president of Columbia University in 1902. As a dominant member of the NEA's board of trustees, Butler was fully acquainted with its members' anxieties about the "fundamental shift in the school's center of gravity": moving from preparing citizens to preparing workers. "Butler was giving voice to the increasingly widespread opinion that a broad range of interests all had something to gain from a system of industrial education," Kliebard wrote.[36]

Established as the National Society for the Promotion of Industrial Education (NSPIE), this diverse coalition influenced the direction industrial education would take for the next dozen years. Its objectives were: "to bring to public attention the importance of industrial education" through study and discussion and "to promote the establishment of institutions for industrial training."[37] Exactly what those institutions would be was left unstated, but agreement as to the need for new forms of schooling was broad based. Initially an uneasy alliance of contending forces, through focusing on shared concerns the group accomplished several objectives.[38]

Among those who cautiously endorsed NSPIE's objectives was Samuel Gompers, the brilliantly decisive force behind the formation of the AFL twenty years earlier. A born organizer and son of immigrants, Gompers was self-educated—in part through attending lectures at Cooper Union—and has been credited with moving the labor movement from its earlier concerns about social reform to the "bread and butter" issues attainable only through economic power.[39] Under his leadership, the AFL voiced a shared concern about the youngsters of fourteen to sixteen who drifted from one marginal job to another. However, unions in general worried that widespread industrial education would flood the workplace with marginally prepared workers; these would compete with union members, function as strikebreakers, or both. Though wary of working with the NAM, Gompers determined that by being part of the movement, unions could influence its direction.

In 1909, the AFL established a Committee on Industrial Education, often known as the Mitchell Committee as it was led by miners union leader John Mitchell. The stated priorities of its first report, which came out in 1910, were keeping youngsters in school and retaining public control over public schools.[40] Eventually the AFL endorsed the idea that schools could teach the "higher technique of our various industries."[41] Schools, the argument became, should be more closely connected with places of work so as to produce both better workers and better citizens.

One of NSPIE's first projects was to initiate a survey of "influential leaders," an undertaking that went on between 1907 and 1910 and resulted in a series of bulletins. The society's chief challenge was reconciling the interests of labor and of business. Unions pushed for a strong voice in setting national policy, but the NAM at the time was hostile to organized labor and reluctant to make concessions. The two groups agreed that industrial education should be done at public expense, but they differed on the question of dual systems. Both groups did, however, agree that "industrial education" meant "learning the skills of a trade" rather than the more expansive "industrial intelligence" as defined by the Massachusetts report and pushed by reformers such as Dewey and Jane Addams.[42]

Both Krug and Kliebard note the significance of NSPIE's second meeting, held in Chicago in the summer of 1908. Its opening address was given by Charles W. Eliot who had just retired after forty years as president of Harvard University. Though closely allied with the priorities of William Torrey Harris and chair of the NEA's 1892 Committee of Ten that outlined the essential academic components of a secondary education, Eliot was also aware of the focus on school dropouts detailed by the 1906 report from his home state of Massachusetts. In his address, he proposed a dual system of trade schools separate from regular public schools. In answer to a question about which students would attend one and which the other, Eliot arrived at an unfortunate construct, one that has however acquired a place in the lexicon of talk about schooling: the teachers in elementary schools, he said, ought to sort pupils "by their evident and probable destinies."[43]

Though, according to Krug, Eliot later attempted to modify his statement, the term "probable destinies" aroused considerable attention; some felt that Eliot had been misunderstood. His address also called for guiding each child "into that path in which he can be most successful and happy" and that providing for all young people the "happiness of achievement" would be consistent with "the best definition of democracy."[44]

Whether or not Eliot was misunderstood, his comment did bring out a challenge facing promoters of industrial education: who would most benefit from it? Employers, who would get a steady supply of trained workers? Or the students themselves? These questions were complex and would dominate discussions of industrial education, for the decade to come and beyond.

In sum, NSPIE's initial report restated many familiar arguments; the nation needed to remain competitive internationally, to provide greater economic returns and occupational mobility for working classes, to reduce social unrest, and to democratize education. Plus, it added a new one: young people were geographically mobile; thus, one state could not be expected to pay for the training of workers who would be employed in another state. In short, as Kantor argued in the introduction to his 1982 compilation, "training for a national labor market required federal support."[45]

Manual Training Leads High Schools to Define Themselves

While these discussions were going on at the policy level, administrators like Ella Flagg Young were overseeing how school systems could adapt to the demands of a changing economy. The pressure was particularly strong on secondary schools, which saw their function change from largely academic to a mix of practical and traditional courses between 1900 and 1910. Even the word used to describe them was redefined: whereas "secondary" school had implied college preparation, "high" school meant the height of the public system. In a collection of articles Young wrote between 1907 and 1910 she noted the implication of these changes. A lengthy report she wrote for the NEA in 1907 commented on progress in schools over the preceding two years: the departure of William Harris, the work of the Douglas Commission, the growth of vocational training, and NSPIE's efforts to provide a "broader and deeper" understanding of industrial education. At the same NEA meeting, Young delivered compelling thoughts on the amount of scientific knowledge—of chemistry, electricity, and physics—with which all sixteen-year-olds had a right to be at least somewhat familiar.[46]

Young's words are relevant for several reasons, not the least of which is her long and substantial role as an administrator in the nation's second

Figure 26. The fifty-year career of "educational stateswoman" Ella Flagg Young culminated in her years as Chicago's superintendent of schools (1909 to 1915) and her year (1910–1911) as NEA president. As head of the city's schools, she fostered the development of vocational education programs that were markedly successful in encouraging young people to remain in school until sixteen years old.

largest school system. Chicago, and the state of Illinois, had industrialized more rapidly than other cities of comparable size. Its workforce had moved from one of independent workers before the Civil War, when Young began teaching, to factory employees a half-century later. Her incisive, disciplined intelligence and ability to "see things squarely" (an attribute for which she credited her mother) enabled her to communicate on par with the leading intellects of the day as well as hold the respect of the city's teachers and parents.

Three other articles she wrote at the time articulated high schools' responsibilities and how they should be met. For one, there is a reciprocal relationship among subjects and these connections should be reinforced through practical experience (such as manual work). For another, the curriculum needed to achieve a balance between scope (on one hand) and accuracy (on the other), a particular challenge for the new industrial curriculum being developed around the country; the components of a classical curriculum, she claimed, had been worked out earlier. Further, she argued, the high school's loyalty had to be to its students and to encouraging them to remain in school; this she set in opposition to the secondary school's loyalty in times past to the colleges.[47]

In addition, increases in enrollment put as much pressure on these schools as did their changes in function. High school enrollment began to grow substantially after 1890, and it accelerated after 1910, in response both to immigration and to demand. Whereas in 1870, only 2 percent of the nation's seventeen-year-olds had a secondary school diploma, by 1910, 9 percent did. This growth, though, was not quite so dramatic as what would happen next: in 1900, 10 percent of the nation's youth fourteen to seventeen years of age were enrolled in high schools; by 1920, this number would grow to 25 percent.[48] In numbers of students, this meant 519,000 in 1900; 915,000 in 1910; and 2,200,000 in 1920, a doubling in every decade. There was a gender differential as well: in 1900, 60 percent of high school students were girls. Though only 12 percent of those enrolled actually graduated, this imbalance led to a national concern about too many female teachers and an insufficiently practical curriculum.[49] The proportion of boys attending high school would increase as more schools incorporated vocational programs.

In Chicago, spurred in part by the Chicago Manual Training School, various forms of industrial education had become part of both public and private institutions prior to the turn of the century. The first public program was offered by the English High and Manual Training School in 1890, but it was limited in scope and enrollment until 1902 when it was moved into a new building further west of the city's downtown. In 1903, it was renamed for Richard T. Crane, the head of a major plumbing and heating supply firm. An original member of the CMTS board, Crane was a noted advocate for technical training in the city's schools. In its new facility, enrollment at the school grew from 575 boys in 1900 to 1,865 in 1920.[50] Apparently, young men would remain in school if programs were appropriate.

In 1908, two other specialized schools opened. One, Lane Technical High School, located northwest of the city's center, was named after a former superintendent who had fought vigorously for technical education. Beginning with only one hundred students, Lane had four thousand by 1925. The third, which had begun in 1905 as a small manual training school located near the Loop, moved to the city's South Side in 1908; renamed Tilden Technical High School in 1915, it initially offered programs for both boys and girls. Further, between 1900 and 1905, shop work was added to the curriculum in some of the academic high schools.[51]

Beyond national interest, there were several explanations for this flurry of openings in Chicago. For one, the city's business community supported the idea; for another, Edwin Cooley, the superintendent at the time, was known as an advocate of specialized high schools and several were established during his administration.[52] Another was the election in 1905 of a reform-minded mayor; among his first moves was to appoint other progressives—a labor leader, a journalist, a philanthropist, and others, including Jane Addams—to the board of education.[53] The following year, Addams would also join the NSPIE board. Her concern, like that of her fellow reformers, was to steer the system toward how best to meet the needs of the city's diverse and growing population. Yes, the city's commercial interests were important, but children should be encouraged to find their own role in it.[54]

Another of the 1905 reformist board's first actions was to name Ella Flagg Young as principal of the Chicago Normal School. Both in that position and in her next, as superintendent of schools, Young would put a definite stamp on the city's industrial education programs. Like Addams, her priority was schools that met the needs of the city's students and families. Somewhat like Warren Hicks in Ellendale—who had claimed that its manual training school "went where the crowd pushed"—Young insisted that the schools belonged to the public, and they should supply the needs of the people rather than holding to schemes proposed by others.[55] As head of the normal school, Young insisted that it was *not* a trade school; its purpose instead was "to give professional training" along with the "artistic, scientific, and literary knowledge and attainments that give the young teacher a comprehensive idea of education and make for an appreciation of the worth of life."[56] This was not instruction by rote in specific how-tos outside of their intellectual context. Instead, it was a version of the "industrial intelligence" described in the 1906 Massachusetts report.

In 1909, Young was named superintendent of schools in Chicago; thus, a woman headed the nation's second largest school system; her salary of $10,000 per year made her one of the highest paid educators in the country. Newspaper reports on her ascension focused on her support for vocational education.[57] One article claimed that she believed it should be extended further throughout the schools; another that its "proper place" was to complement academic subjects. Having children work with their hands did not mean turning schools into factories; instead, schools should aim for the unity of art and industry that Young had tried to establish at the normal school.

Soon after taking office, Young issued a circular to hundreds of businesses in the city that listed commercial and technical courses for young workers available in public evening schools; it urged them to encourage their employees to take advantage of these opportunities.[58] In the following year, the *Chicago Tribune* ran a lengthy article on Young's first year that quoted her extensively. She said that young people who had dropped out of school should have an opportunity later to learn what they had missed; important topics included the "Scientific knowledge requisite for advancement," plus "citizenship, economics, and history."[59] In her 1910 report to the board of education, Young wrote that, since the technical high schools had opened, "high school attendance, especially of boys, has increased about 40 percent."[60]

Young's biographers, beginning with John McManis, a member of the Normal School faculty while Young was principal, state that the vocational programs and the resulting increase in enrollment were the accomplishments of which she was most proud.[61] Figures support this claim: whereas enrollment at all three levels—primary, grammar, and high school—increased substantially between Young's taking office in 1909 and her departure in 1915, it was far greater at the secondary level.[62] During that six years, primary enrollment increased by 8 percent and grammar enrollment by 17 percent—but that at the high schools increased 61 percent. It grew from 14,920 in 1910 to 26,500 in 1914, or an increase of nearly 12,000 students.[63] Of these high school enrollments, over half were in one or another of the city's vocational programs. Young's goal was to "keep the children going on into the higher grades," McManis claimed; the vocational programs apparently accomplished that.[64]

Young, both in articles and interviews, not only stressed the importance of industrial education, but claimed that it should begin early.[65] Some kinds of handwork should begin even in primary grades, and applications to the workplace should be incorporated into, for example, arithmetic classes. English classes in which the modern language was tied too closely to ancient Latin was a sure way to drive boys from school. Life, she said, was mostly labor, so children should be guided into activities that would aid them in finding the work for which they are most suited.[66] Students, doing work that interests them, need not be prodded to do it.[67]

Despite the cost of these programs, Young was able to get the board to agree to them: when she arrived in 1909, there were 159 manual training rooms and 61 cooking rooms; by 1915, this had increased to 231 of the former and 199 of the latter.[68] Her aim was to provide some manual training for all boys in elementary school and some form of household arts for all girls.[69] As finding an adequate teaching staff was also a challenge, Young instituted a program in which skilled workers "from the trades" could begin teaching with a year of special preparation; for all, spreading intelligence and intellectual independence were guiding principles.

The most innovative program established during Young's administration was the two-year vocational program in the city's high schools. Begun in the fall of 1910, these were designed to keep young people in school longer. They were apparently successful: of the 27,000 or so students in the city's high schools in 1915, nearly a third were enrolled in the two-year program. It offered courses in accounting, stenography, mechanical drawing and design, carpentry, electricity, and household arts; required academic courses included business English, history, science and math, plus modern languages.[70] The high schools also offered both academic and vocational four-year programs, plus another for teacher preparation.

During Young's third year as superintendent, the city's schools offered another innovation—a high school for girls. Named after a woman known for her work on the juvenile court system and as a technical education advocate, the Lucy Flower High School opened in 1911; it was Chicago's sole all-girls school and only the second such in the nation. "We've been doing a great deal in this city for the boys," Young had argued, two years before its opening, "and I want to do something for the girls."[71] To head the school, Young choose Dora Wells, a forthright educator with whom she had worked at the Chicago Normal School. In keeping with priorities of both women, the school was more "technical" than "vocational"; while both recognized that many women had to support themselves, they wanted the school to expand students' ideas about what constituted "women's work." Though it offered a four-year course, its two-year vocational one was initially more popular.[72]

Conceptually, the school was ahead of its time.[73] Not only did Young and Wells recognize that many women would spend several years in the work force, they also took a sophisticated approach to its home economics program. Following the focus on sanitation, nutrition, household management, and accounting advocated by the field's founder Ellen Swallow Richards (ideas that were also behind the domestic arts program established earlier in Ellendale), Wells aimed to educate a girl so well that her life would benefit not only her family but her community as well.[74]

Chicago was not the only city that moved rapidly to establish industrial or technical high schools. In St. Louis, Calvin Woodward, who had initiated the establishment of the private Manual Training School there in 1878, was between 1897 and 1911 director of the city's public schools. In 1904, he oversaw the establishment of two "cosmopolitan" high schools. Built at the cost of one-half million dollars each, these two new schools, both co-educational, included shops and laboratories as well as regular classrooms. Their emphasis on manual work reflected the system's intention of graduating "intelligent and industrious" students able to "adjust quickly and efficiently to the vocation which [s]he will enter." Enrollment figures reflect the new schools' popularity: in 1900, St. Louis high schools enrolled 2,349 students; by 1910, this figure had grown to 6,255 and by 1920, to 11,393. As a proportion of high school–age youth in St. Louis, the growth was from near 3 percent in 1900 to almost 11 percent in 1920.[75]

In 1906, Warren Hicks was called to Cleveland, where he joined an administration charged with expanding vocational programs.[76] Initially, this manifested itself as the Technical High School of Cleveland, which opened in the fall of 1908. Designed to prepare students either for the workplace or for entrance into a technical college, it offered boys standard courses in mechanical drawing, cabinet-making, and blacksmithing. Girls had instruction in art and design and what were called the "household arts"; the latter included dressmaking, nutrition, hygiene, decorating, and managing family accounts. Courses were designed with a view to their "ultimate utility" rather than mere "general culture," the system's superintendent argued.[77] As such, math problems were those likely to be found in a shop; English courses considered problems of labor, manufacturing, and product distribution. By their third year, boys would be encouraged to consider "the particular branch along which his abilities" lay and to focus on those; girls would study industrial art and domestic science with a view toward fitting themselves "for the intelligent direction of a household."

Two chapters of Kliebard's *Schooled to Work*, both written with his former graduate student Carol Kean, focus on how Milwaukee developed programs that were responsive to the needs of a rapidly increasing and diverse population; some had been underway prior to the century's turn.[78] Controversies remained, though: cost was one issue; the curriculum another. Some objected that the programs prepared students neither for the workplace nor for further education. But as Kean wrote, "By 1905, no school manager in Milwaukee could afford to challenge the educational and practical value of manual training or be dilatory in incorporating it into the curriculum."

Over the next decade, trade schools for boys and for girls were established; the thought was that courses should complement Milwaukee's industrial strengths, which at the time were the making of iron and steel and the manufacture of products made from them. Plumbing, woodworking, and basic electrical work were added, along with various kinds of drafting. While in some cities, unions opposed such training, a socialist flavor to Milwaukee's politics dampened such opposition. In sum, an alternate form of secondary schooling was underway; like those offered in Cleveland, academic courses tended toward applying math to problems found in industrial work. The programs for girls, supported by women activists, were designed to prepare them for homemaking, but organizers knew that many girls would need some preparation for the workforce as well and should be given opportunities to become skilled for appropriate jobs.[79]

Similar programs were established in other cities throughout the Midwest, so much so that one writer has called the region the "cradle of vocational education." Others may argue with that assertion, but the abundance of industrial enterprises established in the Midwest, its central location and access to raw materials, plus extensive transportation networks, make it a plausible argument. Its egalitarian traditions suggest that an elitist system of industrial education would not have been welcome.[80]

Cooley Controversy in Chicago: Contemporaneous Views

One historian of the movement has pointed out that the nation's newspapers focused public attention on industrial education around 1912. A survey of papers published in Chicago at that time supports the assertion.[81] In 1909 when Young became superintendent, two of the city's most widely read papers—the *Chicago Tribune* and the *Inter Ocean*—ran 51 articles on the subject. Three years later, in 1912, there were 157—a tripling of coverage. The following year, the number fell to 144; by 1915, there were only 60 articles. This rapid increase and then fall reflects a nationwide controversy over how industrial education should be delivered, a controversy that was particularly potent in Chicago, in part because of legislation proposed by Edwin Cooley, the city's former superintendent of schools.[82] Especially valuable for students of industrial education is a December 1912 series published in the *Tribune*; written mainly by educators in the city, they reflect statewide concerns that, in sum, are more edifying than the controversy that inspired them.[83]

The overwhelming sentiment expressed in Chicago papers going back to 1909 was that the nation's public schools were no longer sufficiently democratic to meet the nation's needs. Articles repeatedly pointed out the high dropout rates of seventh and eighth graders: if only 10 percent of the nation's youth were attending high school, that meant that schools were ignoring the other ninety percent, which was broadly construed as undemocratic.[84] The figure alarmed a wide range of educators, reformers, union and business leaders, plus some politicians—the same group that had coalesced around NSPIE a few years earlier. There was considerable agreement that industrial education would address the problem, along with considerable disagreement as to how. In Illinois, by 1912, three different groups had organized to write reports and propose legislation. During that fall, both the *Tribune* and the *Inter Ocean* ran a host of articles by and about the supporters of these various plans, culminating in the former's useful series; excerpts from several follow.[85]

The statewide effort to address the problem began in 1910. Chicago's prestigious Commercial Club, which had funded the Chicago Manual Training School thirty years earlier, sent Edwin Cooley on a fact-finding tour of Europe that fall to learn how schools there were preparing young people for adult responsibilities. He returned a year later to write several articles and oversee what became known as the Cooley Bill. His proposal involved a system of compulsory schools, separate from the existing system and administered by "practical men" from the vocations, because only they knew the workplace sufficiently well, Cooley argued.[86]

Whatever the validity of that claim, Cooley's proposals met with immediate opposition. Margaret Haley, the forceful head of the Chicago Teachers Federation, asserted that schooling was for the whole development of the child, not just preparation for a job.[87] The bill also met with opposition from the Chicago Federation of Labor (CFL), which claimed that it "was intended to turn the public schools into a supply house for docile workers" while middle-class children would receive the benefits of an academic education.[88] The Illinois Federation of Labor echoed the CFL's objections, if with a bit of hyperbole: the bill was "the most vicious thing introduced" to the legislature in recent memory and would place the education of workers' children "under the complete control of corporations."[89] In stating her opposition, Ella Flagg Young told a group of school principals in the fall of 1912 that she didn't care whether she was superintendent or not, "but there ought not be two superintendents of schools."[90]

A second proposal was said to "avoid extremes"; it suggested that Illinois communities could establish either voluntary or compulsory programs organized to meet local needs.[91] Sponsored by the reformist-minded Chicago City Club and identified with George Herbert Mead, a sociologist at the University of Chicago, it was funded by Anita McCormick Blaine; her earlier gifts to the university had supported other educational enterprises. The club's specific priorities are somewhat buried in its extensive compilation of industrial education programs in the United States and abroad, and it may never have resulted in an actual piece of legislation.[92] An article Mead wrote noted that the plan's emphasis was on local control, well-prepared teachers, and opposition to a separate board of education.[93]

A third group has received the least attention, but it may have raised the most significant issues, in part because it also considered rural areas. Called the Bankers Bill due to its affiliation with the Illinois Bankers Association, its board represented a refreshingly wide swath of interest groups. Chaired by Edmund James, president of the University of Illinois, its members included heads of state farm and labor organizations, the superintendent of public instruction, two other education officials, a banker, Cooley, and Julius Rosenwald.[94] In August 1912, the group had sponsored a conference on the need for schools that would better prepare boys and girls for their life work. The group's proposed bill would require the state to pay half the cost of both industrial and agricultural programs in high schools; there was some debate as to whether elementary schools should be included, but local control was emphasized. A committee member claimed that, as a result of this bill, the state would have a model system for industrial education.

The *Tribune*'s series ran between Wednesday, December 18, and Sunday, December 22. The first two articles were by Francis Blair, the state's superintendent of public instruction, and B. F. Harris, head of the bankers association's vocational education committee and a large landowner and resident of Champaign. Blair noted the needs of rural schools and suggested that traveling teams of industrial and agricultural educators could make up for the lack of these programs there. Harris reiterated that point (at the time, Illinois still had several thousand one-room schools; they served over half of the state's elementary students).[95]

The following day, two more articles appeared; one was written by Walter Sumner, a former member of Chicago's board of education and dean of the city's Catholic schools. He opposed a dual system as needless duplication and asked for more cooperation from merchants and manufacturers. For him, vocational training should not only help children choose their "life work" but lead them to enjoy the "fruits of their labor." The other article was by Theodore Robinson, who wrote on behalf of the Commercial Club. He pointed out the club's decades of work for the public welfare, reiterated its concern for the 90 percent of youth who never attended high school, and stated that the club's plan would rely on local boards of educators and employers.[96]

Chicago Public School officials were responsible for the next two articles. William Roberts, an assistant superintendent, noted the system's existing programs, many of which had been organized in conjunction with labor unions and associations of employers. He claimed that these courses were particularly "relevant" because they connected math and English to work in the trades. The commentary by Robert Hitch, a district superintendent, noted that the nation's transition from an economy of independent workers to one of wage earners was particularly rapid in Illinois and that the state's institutions of higher education had long emphasized the importance of practical work. He claimed that existing school laws already gave local boards sufficient authority to offer "courses deemed valuable for the community." A duplicate system, he wrote, would lead to "disastrous competition" for resources.[97]

In his contribution to the series, Charles Judd, dean of education at the University of Chicago, stated his opposition to a dual system by explaining why he felt the American common school was superior to its German equivalent. Rather than establishing a vocational system, U.S. schools should instead continue their focus on basic knowledge of science and efforts to retain youth in the seventh and eighth grades. Schools, he wrote, are to produce citizens, not workers; they need to give children a "chance at a broader life."[98]

Frank Leavitt, who headed the industrial education program at the University of Chicago, wrote from a broad perspective; he'd also worked on both the City Club and Bankers association plans. His focus was on what all sides to the controversy could agree to: enhancing the "character, intelligence, and economic efficiency" of our young people. And he offered a "statement of principles" as a starting point; one noted that over the previous decade high schools had been adding vocational programs and that their enrollment had doubled as a result. He also noted that a plan appropriate for Chicago would not work as well for smaller cities; thus, there might be "separate measures" for those whose population exceeded fifty thousand and those that were smaller.[99]

The Continuation School Saga

Another preamble to the controversies of 1912 was a visit from Georg Kerschensteiner, head of a widely noted continuation school program in Munich. In the fall of 1910, around the time that Edwin Cooley sailed for Europe to survey industrial education programs there, Kerschensteiner began a two-month tour of the United States. His trip, like that of Cooley, was reportedly paid for by Chicago's Commercial Club; Kerschensteiner's was also sponsored by NSPIE. The significance of these trips is less in what either accomplished than in how widely they have been misunderstood. Though Paul Douglas in 1921 and Edward Krug in 1964 stated that continuation schools were an effective means of addressing a necessity apparent to many—keeping young people in some form of formal education until age sixteen—they have been largely ignored by other writers.

But the name Kerschensteiner came to arouse as much enmity as that of Cooley—even John Dewey, not given to ill-informed rants, at one point claimed that adopting the continuation school model would be akin to "Prussianizing" American schools.[100] Other critics claimed that continuation schools were a ploy by businesses and manufacturers to install a permanent class system in the United States.[101] Such accusations reflected real concerns about how schools should best serve American democracy in a

Figure 27. This plaque honors Charles McCarthy, who played a substantial role in conceptualizing and implementing the "Wisconsin Idea," a set of progressive principles emanating from the university in Madison. Among them were the locally managed continuation schools established in Wisconsin and elsewhere after 1912. This plaque hangs in the legislative chamber of the state capitol; it was installed in 1923, two years after McCarthy's death.

time of rapid industrial change, but they also tell a story relatively untethered from historical reality.

According to Michael Knoll's reconstruction of differences between Dewey and Kerschensteiner over continuation schools, the idea behind them had been known before 1910. Though she seldom used the term in describing programs in Chicago, Ella Flagg Young may have visited one during her 1904–1905 trip to Europe; its purpose was to review educational innovations there. One American advocate of the model, Charles McCarthy of Wisconsin, is known to have studied them on his own fact-finding trip to Europe in either 1909 or 1910. Continuation schools in the United States were one outcome of this trip, and if there was a father of the idea in this country, McCarthy would be it.

The son of an immigrant cobbler in Massachusetts, McCarthy had traveled around the country before settling in Madison; there he studied with Frederick Jackson Turner and others. With a doctorate in hand, in 1901 he established one of the nation's first legislative reference libraries, an innovation that provided lawmakers with expertise that could lead to more effective legislation.[102] Recalled as well for articulating the "Wisconsin Idea"—the notion that state-supported colleges were obliged to be of benefit to every household in the state—he helped the university's president, Charles Van Hise, put his progressive inclinations into actions.[103] Among McCarthy's concerns at this time was the number of young people, particularly boys, who had dropped out of school in the seventh or eighth grade and were languishing in the streets of Wisconsin's cities. The "Wisconsin Idea," he argued, ought to include a means for more constructive use of their time and talents.[104] Feeling that the continuation schools he had seen in Germany were a means to do so, he helped the state legislature write enabling legislation. In 1911, it was passed and implemented.[105]

The law required cities of five thousand residents or more—Wisconsin had about thirty such cities at the time—to establish a board for vocational education to be composed mainly of local educators and employers. Their function was to organize programs that would keep young people under the age of sixteen attending school for at least five hours per week; employers were obligated to give their young employees time off to attend these programs; the curriculum for each was to complement local industries. The state was to award each participating city $3,000 per year; the cities were to match or exceed that.[106]

In the summer of 1912, Warren Hicks was called from Cleveland to oversee these continuation school programs, and data his office gathered about them indicates that even initially reluctant educators cooperated with the idea. In the law's first year, thirty schools were established; over half of

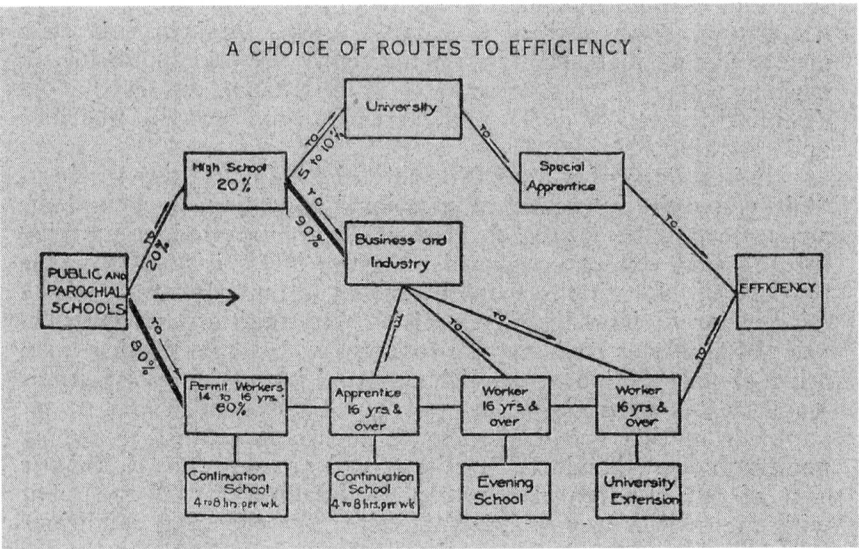

Figure 28. This chart first appeared around 1912 in a pamphlet created by Wisconsin's Committee on Industrial Education. It represents Charles McCarthy's comprehensive plan for the state's continuing education programs, which, like the extension programs McCarthy also revitalized, were an effort to unite the state's schools and businesses in an educational system that would implement the ideals of "humanitarian" efficiency.

the superintendents reported that their initial skepticism had proved to be unfounded—the separate boards were "unhampered by tradition" and gave the programs new "impetus." Students, too, had responded favorably: for the 1912–1913 school year, total enrollment was 11,721 boys and girls—about 85 percent of those eligible. Those fourteen to sixteen, most of whom were employed, were required to receive five hours of general instruction each week; further, their employers were not to dock their pay for these hours in school.[107] Thus, Wisconsin's system extended compulsory schooling beyond age fourteen, a standard nationwide at the time, to sixteen, which was favored by many educators.

Whether Wisconsin was on Kerschensteiner's itinerary is not known, but his U.S. tour included a visit to Chicago; while there, he toured schools, met with Ella Flagg Young, and gave talks at the University of Chicago and the city's Union League Club.[108] Apparently, he was well received; the Commercial Club was his host and published his lectures after his departure.[109] Two weeks after his Chicago visit, Kerschensteiner was in New York City, where he lunched with John Dewey at the Columbia Faculty Club. Though their meeting was cordial, Dewey felt Kerschensteiner's program put too much emphasis on the students' responsibility as citizens and too little on a broader conception of their individual potential.[110]

In his 1921 book, Paul Douglas wrote that the continuation school helped to "break down class stratification" and thus was the "best single system of industrial education that there is." He also claimed that the best systems of continuation schools were in Wisconsin and Pennsylvania.[111] Despite this endorsement, later historians have either ignored continuation schools or questioned their efficacy.[112] Aspects of the idea were incorporated into the 1917 Smith-Hughes bill, and one historian has suggested that the Civilian Conservation Corps of the 1930s, which provided young men with an opportunity to work for pay and receive an education at the same time, was a stepchild.

The "Hot-Air Engine": Unit versus Dual System

During the years when school systems in Illinois, Wisconsin, and elsewhere began establishing vocational or technical programs that responded to local needs, national campaigns were underway to determine what these programs ought to be. In October of 1913, the two approaches met at a NSPIE conference in Grand Rapids, particularly at a session called to discuss whether the state of Michigan should continue with its "unit" state board of education or supplement it with a board of vocational education, creating a "dual" system of schools. Because speakers at the session included two major figures associated with conflicting positions on this question—John Dewey and David Snedden—it offers insight into what has come down as the heated controversy between advocates for both systems of schools.[113] At one point in his presentation, Dewey—not often noted as an adroit wordsmith—referred to this discussion as a "hot-air engine."

With theatrics over the Cooley Bill providing a backdrop, NSPIE's October 1913 meeting in Michigan focused on the unit versus the dual system.[114] The session's chief topic was the administrative structure for Wisconsin's continuation schools; though the state had only one superintendent of education, he had two deputies: one headed the traditional schools in the system; the other, Warren Hicks, had responsibility for the vocational schools, basically the continuation program.

Leading the NSPIE session off was Louis Reber, dean of the university's active extension division, which was another product of the "Wisconsin Idea." He began by stating that there was a definite lack of clarity about what either "dual" or "unit" actually meant.[115] The Cooley plan, he said, addressed a new problem in education, one that demanded a different type of school to meet the needs of those who left at fourteen. After describing the Wisconsin law's provisions, Reber said that one of the law's first hurdles was overcoming initial opposition from "schoolmen," some of whom were still opposed to vocational training in the public school. However, a 1912 questionnaire had polled the superintendents; they reported that the "duplex system" had worked out to be "advantageous" for "both lines of school work"—the general and the special.

Cooperation rather than separation governed aspects of program administration, Reber claimed. Many of the teachers were "practical" men, most of whom had never taught before—but quickly acquired respect for the teacher's work. Though there were difficulties, they were not insurmountable; many of the industrial board members had worked together previously as members of other boards. Reber summed his comments up by saying that Wisconsin's dual system was serving both its students and a "democracy that dignifies labor," a "democracy that opens a new world to those who have not the taste nor the capacity for academic education."[116]

Over the summer of 1913, Hicks, as part of his oversight responsibility, had compiled a separate set of reports from superintendents across the state; they offered additional confirmation of the program's success. That written by the school superintendent in the manufacturing city of Chippewa Falls was particularly positive: "almost perfect" attendance, the "cooperation of prominent businessmen," and a focus on local applications of academic subjects, such as reading about the "industrial and commercial activities of the city" were among its attributes.[117]

Comments from John Dewey followed those of Reber, and he began by expressing modest chagrin about his stalwart opposition to dual systems given the efficacy of Wisconsin's program.[118] All agree, he said, that industrial education programs should "pay more attention than does the current system to the education of wage earners"; further, the Wisconsin system had "fundamental features of unit control" and was "distinguished by the amount of cooperation between educators and employers." Schools, he stated—echoing claims by Hicks and Young—"are what the people demand"; groups that move "public opinion" toward the need for supplemental functions are a good thing as well.[119] But states that are "distinctly industrial and manufacturing" have to be careful that they not segregate these programs from other important aspects of the industrial education movement," such as "prevocational programs" in the elementary schools. Here, Dewey was—either intentionally or not—commending efforts of the Young administration in Chicago.

Following Dewey, Warren Hicks addressed the question by asking whether Michigan should immediately adopt a compulsory part-time program or allow local communities to work toward it gradually.[120] But unlike his experience in North Dakota a dozen years earlier, where community pressure dictated the manual training school's initial programs, at this point he felt that the public needed some pushing. Humanity's "natural immobility" might mean that a community would resist the pleas of pulpit, press, and politicians to keep their children in school longer; a state wanting to "budge" this tendency might have to employ "efficient part-time schools, state aid, and compulsory attendance laws" in order to do so. In Wisconsin, cities that failed to enforce the compulsory aspect of the 1911 law were refused state aid.

Among other reasons why the Wisconsin law worked, Hicks continued, is that it respected the "desires" of the youth involved—they wanted to "learn something new," something related to their "new life problem," that is, that they needed to learn how to support themselves in a rapidly changing economy. The compulsory part-time schools had to offer something new; students needed to know that they were getting something concrete that was "related to their social and economic life." The high participation rate in Wisconsin indicated that the programs instituted there had "drawing power"—but Wisconsin's system might not work for all. Small cities and "country districts" would have to move more slowly, waiting until experience pointed "more clearly" to what programs would be effective.[121]

The following speaker, the head of vocational schools for the state of New York, was, like Dewey, somewhat taken aback by the success of Wisconsin's program: "I had intended to state dogmatically and even assertively . . . that there were many difficulties in the way of establishing and maintaining compulsory continuation schools," he began, but "Mr. Hicks' paper" left him in the "embarrassing position" of having to modify his arguments.[122] Read a century later, his academic generalizations suggest the "hot air" Dewey referred to: the loudest voices had too little experience implementing programs at the school level; they had instead spent time in discussions at the policy level.

These talks, combined with reports of the programs in Chicago and Wisconsin, suggest a significant aspect of industrial education at the time: those programs devised and implemented at a local level, by educators and employers working together, were most likely to be successful. They had the advantage of taking local industries into consideration—both as potential employers and as examples that could be worked into academic materials: the history of the logging industry could be of particular interest to a student of carpentry, for example. Of primary importance, though, was that student needs and interests were a prime motivation for the programs' designs. Their goal was to provide democratic opportunities for students they would not otherwise have had.[123]

"Theory Run Mad": Applying Utilitarian Efficiency to Vocational Education

Another of Dewey's apt phrases—"theory run mad"—was used a century later in the title of an article by the cultural historian Joseph Kett; in it, he adroitly skewered proponents of something called "real vocational education."[124] Among the latter's staunchest advocates was David Snedden, commissioner of education in Massachusetts. In his summary to the 1913 NSPIE meeting on Michigan, he ignored the remarks by previous speakers, spoke in general terms about issues regarding vocational education, and then asserted that educators were too impractical to conceptualize or implement such programs. His "forecast of probable developments" looked toward federal legislation that would make his version of "real vocational education" compulsory nationwide.[125] Though his remarks did not define what he meant by this, his colleague Charles Prosser was in the process of doing so; Prosser's vision was that all jobs could be reduced to a set of specific skills and each of these could be taught in a series of "short-unit" courses such as the several steps to pruning a tree or to setting a table.[126] Industrial training centers nationwide would, in this conception, impart these skills to compliant students. But the idea had many critics. According to Arthur Wirth, the U.S. commissioner of education (Philander Claxton at the time) reacted strongly against the "brutal efficiency" of their scheme.[127]

This Prosser plan and aspects of a bill passed that year by the Indiana legislature were what Dewey termed "theory run mad" in an article that set off his noted 1915 exchange with Snedden published as "Two Communications."[128] Though a member of the Indiana commission on industrial education had also attended the 1913 NSPIE meeting and praised his state's new law as one of the nation's best, Dewey did not agree. In an article titled "Industrial Education—the Wrong Kind," he wrote that his chief objection was that the law "put a fence around industrial education" by strictly separating such programs from general education. What made it "mad" was the limits it placed on the use of state funds; they could only be applied to courses related to the job a worker currently held: a farmer, for example, would not be able to take a class in plumbing, nor a plumber one in market gardening.[129] Thus, state money could not be used to help students find a more amenable kind of work.

Snedden's response, as published in "Two Communications," failed to address Dewey's concerns. Instead, he summarized vocational education from above by discussing schools for lawyers and theologians as well as courses established by railroads and textile manufacturers. He claimed that if the children of the working class—the "rank and file"—wanted a general education they could get it by remaining in a regular high school. Efficiency and productivity were his aims, and only "practical men" were prepared to provide it. "School men" could not do so.[130]

Dewey's reply disputed Snedden's intentions: vocational education needed to expand rather than contract the student's or the worker's ability to live in a wider world. His comments also contributed another memorable term to the lexicon of industrial education: it should aim to make workers, as much as possible, "masters of their own industrial fate." He asked: how could the separation of vocational from traditional education make either aspect broader, richer, or more effective? And then he suggested that Snedden might engage in some ground-level discussion: how did he regard either the Gary system or the Cooley Bill in Chicago, for example?[131] There are many ways in which their differences could be summarized: one of the simplest might be that for Snedden, schooling was training *for* an occupation; for Dewey, it was training *through* an occupation.

Understood this way, these "Two Communications" set the stage for further clarification of their differences, indicated in part by the work they took up later in 1915. Snedden left his post in Massachusetts and returned to Teachers College, where he continued working in the fields of educational administration and educational sociology, writing several books on the topics.[132] As Dewey suggested, Snedden did study the "Gary system," and reported on it at the NEA's national meeting in 1915.[133] But the two men took different lessons from this study.

The system established in Gary, Indiana, a few years earlier has aroused substantial interest both then and since. Of note here is the contrast between how proponents of "utilitarian efficiency," as defined by Michael Knoll, viewed the system and how proponents of "humanitarian efficiency" did.[134] John Franklin Bobbitt, a young psychologist teaching at the University of Chicago (who would later be known for his studies of school curriculum) was in the former category.[135] Evelyn Dewey was in the latter. For Bobbitt and Snedden, Gary's schools offered a valuable model for "maximizing" a system's resources. For Dewey, they put into practice her father's theories about using "occupations" as a basis for constructing a curriculum.

Devised beginning in 1908 by an energetic and charismatic young superintendent named William Wirt, the Gary plan was called a "work-study-play" system; through it, students moved from one room or activity to another in "platoons."[136] The system was Deweyan in that students sampled the skills essential to common occupations, acquiring essential academic knowledge along the way; it was also highly efficient in that, by moving children around from classroom to gymnasium to auditorium to workshop to playroom, maximum use was made of all school facilities.

Among Bobbitt's concerns was eliminating "waste" in education—and to him the Gary system did that extremely well. In a 1912 article, he commended Wirt's system for using "all the available plant all the available time," and he employed numerous charts to illustrate that it used people as efficiently as premises.[137]

Three years later, in *Schools of Tomorrow*, the book on innovative schools she wrote with her father, Evelyn Dewey was equally fulsome in her praise. Gary's schools were a well-orchestrated demonstration of how an occupations-oriented curriculum could teach subject matter and self-expression, all at minimal cost. The "pupils are not taking courses to become carpenters or electricians or dressmakers, but to find out how the work of the world is done," Evelyn Dewey wrote.[138]

The following year, John Dewey's *Democracy and Education* was published. For some, it offered the theory behind the educational adventures praised in *Schools of Tomorrow*. For all who attend to its well-outlined contents, it dissects each subset it takes up: education as direction, as growth, as both conservative and progressive. Its constructs are equally self-evident and incisive: occupation is a "continuous activity having a purpose"; "education is that reorganization and reconstruction of experience which adds to the meaning of experience and which increases the ability to direct the course of subsequent experience."[139] Soon after it appeared, Ella Flagg Young reviewed it, commenting that it should appeal to a large audience and had appeared at an appropriate time. It untangled the muddled notions of work and schooling: "Vocational education, not vocational training, is from the nature of Professor Dewey's democratic attitude of mind treated as an integral part of education, not as a separate and independent thing." Its aim is to "make America the land of opportunity for every child within its confines."[140]

In 1915, Charles Prosser left his NSPIE post and became the head of the Dunwoody Institute, a vocational education school in Minneapolis. There he continued his efforts at turning all skill training into small pieces that could be easily taught and repeatedly performed by a compliant workforce. Kett, Kliebard, and others claim that the Snedden-Prosser system owed much to the ongoing efforts associated with Frederick Taylor's *Principles of Scientific Management*, which would maximize factory efficiency by reducing all jobs to the smallest possible components. Whatever the case, "real vocational education" never gained a substantial foothold; in Kett's recounting, "theory run mad" increasingly dominated the thinking of Prosser and Snedden, then became largely irrelevant during the 1920s.[141]

At one point, while the debate about what kind of vocational education was "real" raged on, Ella Flagg Young expressed some disdain for it, but she also had other concerns. Early in 1913, she visited Tuskegee Institute on a tour sponsored by Chicago philanthropist Julius Rosenwald. While there, she referred to the school as "the world's greatest university for vocational training," according to a newspaper report.[142] Back in Chicago, Young had her own battles to fight. Opponents on the board of education had attempted to restrict her authority, and she resigned late in 1913, but public outcry was so great that the city's mayor was forced to reconstitute the board in order to reinstate her. Among demonstrations on her behalf was a gathering of four thousand supporters at the cavernous but elegant Auditorium Theatre.[143] When Young did finally resign in the fall of 1915, there were tributes aplenty, including telegrams from superintendents nationwide, newspaper articles in Chicago and elsewhere, and a banquet attended by former colleagues, admirers, and members of the general public.[144] She relocated to Los Angeles, but continued writing and appearing at NEA meetings; it was not in her nature to retire.

Vocational Education Gets a Federal Law

In February 1917, just over a year after Young's departure from Chicago, Congress passed the Smith-Hughes Act, the first piece of federal legislation that offered direct aid to states to establish certain kinds of schooling.[145] Though it was promoted by NSPIE, largely written by Charles Prosser, and became the basis for federal vocational education legislation for several decades, Smith-Hughes did not lead to the dual school systems nationwide that he and Snedden had proposed. High school enrollments did keep growing and vocational education remained an important aspect of it, but secondary education in the U.S. was provided in the comprehensive schools Dewey had advocated.[146]

Getting a grasp on the ultimate impact of a dozen years of national agitation about vocational education—from 1905 when the Douglas Commission in Massachusetts was established until the passage of Smith-Hughes—is complicated by ideological presumptions, then and now, along with historians' tendency to rely on policy pronouncements from national or state commissions rather than on what was actually happening in schools and communities around the country.[147] A reading of the Smith-Hughes Act a century after it was written suggests that it had noble aims.[148] The two men whose names it bears were senators from Georgia, at the time an agricultural state; their backing and the bill's inclusion of agricultural education were essential to its passage.[149] In his 1982 summary of the act, Larry Cuban, a historian and educator of broad experience, wrote that Smith-Hughes provided for education in agriculture, trade and industry, and home economics and that it was intended to fit students of fourteen and older for "useful employment." Federal funds could be used for paying the salaries of vocational teachers and for their preparation.[150]

Paul Douglas, in his 1921 study, provided an evenhanded evaluation of both the intent and initial implementation of the act, one suggesting that extremist interpretations of its purpose and impact are not justified. All schools receiving funds from the act were to be publicly controlled and of "less than college grade." One-third of the monies were to go to continuation schools or classes for workers fourteen to eighteen; roughly five hours of instruction per week were to be in subjects that would (quoting from the act) "enlarge the civic and vocational intelligence" of the worker. Douglas had, in the same book, commended "state-wide compulsory continuation schools" as "the only effective means of educating the juvenile worker"; he also claimed that such schools gave "a greater opportunity for the abler members of the lower economic classes to rise in industry."[151]

Smith-Hughes established the "general principle" that teachers in these vocational programs were to have relevant work experience supplemented by some instruction in teaching rather than be teachers with limited exposure to a trade, Douglas wrote. Despite some opposition, the act placed its administration under the federal Bureau of Education; thus, the unit system had prevailed, and fears that "large industrial interests" would dictate policy proved unfounded. Another result of the act's early years was that more money overall went to vocational education; state and local governments increased their support in addition to accepting the federal money. "Perhaps the most important issue in vocational education," Douglas wrote, was whether the training given should be "solely" in the "trade at which the student works" or "prepare him for other trades." On this, implementation of the act veered toward the narrow rather than the broad, he said disapprovingly: "it was manifestly improper to train boys and girls only for the occupations at which they are engaged." He, too, had expressed disapproval of the Indiana bill.[152]

John Dewey, speaking a week or so after passage of the Smith-Hughes Act, was less sanguine about its provisions than was Douglas. In an address to the Public Education Association in New York, he noted the numbers of young people who dropped out prior to entering high school and then reviewed his priorities for vocational education. Among them: the unit system, assurance that workers of the future be "aware of their rightful claims as citizens," and that education yield a "respect for useful work" and an ability to enjoy leisure time. To his mind, though the act was largely fair to both employers and employees, it was "scandalously inadequate" as a "representation of educational ideals."[153]

Dewey's objections were overwrought, but they were consistent with his belief that the American industrial system as a whole needed an overhaul. The figures Douglas gave as to initial participation in vocational education programs suggest that the American public had more enthusiasm for the act's outcomes than did Dewey. By July 1920, nearly 200,000 students were enrolled in vocational programs, presumably those funded in part by Smith-Hughes. Roughly two-thirds were male—a goal of industrial education programs—and the rest female. Of these, 73,000 were attending continuation schools; others were in all-day or evening programs of various kinds; thus, the chief target group of fourteen- to sixteen-year-olds were being compelled to remain in school.[154] Despite this success, the act did not immediately impact any large percentage of the nation's youth. According to the 1920 census, the population of fourteen- to seventeen-year-olds was 7,870,000.[155] If 25 percent of these young people were enrolled in secondary education—roughly the figure at the time—this suggests that only one out of ten was enrolled in some form of vocational education.

Agency and Efficiency after Smith Hughes

Available catalogs and other publications from both Ellendale and Bordentown do not mention the Smith-Hughes Act, but aspects of how the two schools developed in the decade after its passage suggest that its impact was positive. Thus, might it be that historians' criticism of the act have either misunderstood or misinterpreted its intentions and implementation?[156] Such criticisms are a topic of Larry Cuban's 1982 review of federal vocational education legislation, of which Smith-Hughes was the first; he argued that though the act's origins are widely agreed upon, much less is known about its implementation.[157] Whether Charles Prosser's aim in his enthusiastic backing of the act before and after its passage—his version of "efficient" vocational education—actually did prevail is subject to debate. This study of two schools presumably affected by the law suggests that student "agency" prevailed instead.[158]

In Bordentown, William Valentine was surely aware of the Smith-Hughes Act. It is also likely that he knew of the exchange between Dewey and Snedden about the legislation in Indiana that discouraged farmers from becoming plumbers and vice versa: Valentine had been brought to Bordentown by Calvin Kendall, the man who had been superintendent of schools in Indianapolis around the time of the bill's 1913 passage. And in 1914, Valentine had been visited by Evelyn Dewey while she prepared the chapter that would appear in *Schools of Tomorrow* on the school he headed in Indianapolis.[159] Given Valentine's background and what he accomplished in Bordentown, it is fair to assume that he and members of the MTIS faculty were aware of the act, whether or not it had any impact on their programs.[160]

The NI from 1912 or so had been producing teachers of manual training and home economics, and their numbers grew both before and after 1917. R. M. Black, who became president in 1914, claimed that the school was widely respected for its ability to graduate well-prepared industrial arts teachers.[161] The *Dickey County Leader*, published in Ellendale, mentioned Smith-Hughes a half-dozen times between 1917 and 1927. In December of the year it was passed, a brief article noted that the state's agricultural college in Fargo wanted Smith-Hughes programs to be held there; that plan was surely scrapped when officials recognized that the funds were intended only for "schools of less than college grade." Occasional articles during the next decade indicate that over two dozen high schools in the state received Smith-Hughes funds; the NI may have been among them in 1922 but it was not in 1925. A 1927 article about a high school competition in Fargo attracted six hundred students from thirty-nine "Smith-Hughes and non-Smith-Hughes" schools, which would indicate that the term was known among the paper's readers. By that time, the NI was more a normal school than a high school, so it would not be surprising that it did not participate.[162]

Both schools belie a common assumption many historians have made about Smith-Hughes and other vocational education programs—that their chief purpose was "social control": directing lower-class students, whether white or Black, into low-skill, menial occupations.[163] The New Jersey legislature and Bordentown School Committee may have used Smith-Hughes funds to help make it possible for the school to triple its enrollment in the first decade after the act's passage—from a hundred students when Valentine arrived in 1915 to over three times that by 1927—but they did not regard the act as dictating the school's curriculum. Though Black residents of New Jersey, a population that continued to grow during that period, may not have had the political power to influence the size of state appropriations, they did have the social power to refuse to send their children to the school. Except for a few students who were wards of the state, no one was forced to attend MTIS, but they did attend in great numbers and regarded it as a privilege. Whether or not this was a direct outcome of the Smith-Hughes Act, were they not expressing a form of agency?

The political situation in Ellendale was different; Dickey County residents did have some political power, but it was their social power as well that determined the NI's success. Whether students came to take a short course in the repair of farm machinery, to enhance their skill as a dressmaker or a music teacher, or to sign up for a five-year normal degree, they did so of their own volition. Was that not a form of agency as well?

In his 1982 article, Cuban made many valuable observations about the act's impact in the sixty-five years between its enactment and his writing. One of his comments quoted another study in saying that laws can have a largely symbolic purpose—that they are a form of "political theater."[164] Smith-Hughes, thus, may have codified national agreement that schooling had become primarily a form of preparation for the labor market rather than its earlier chief purpose of instructing students in the basics of "culture" and the responsibilities of citizenship.

But at least as significant as symbolism in Cuban's mind were the questions remaining, such as why Congress continued its generous funding of vocational education though critics claimed such schooling had limited positive impact—either in mandating certain kinds of programs or in increasing enrollment in them. While writers have agreed on the act's provisions, they have disagreed on its effects.[165] Cuban wrote that though vocational education did respond to educational, social, and economic pressures of its times, criticism continued; further, state and local practices often resisted congressional intentions. Nevertheless, Congress continued its appropriations. What, he asked, were the reasons for this resilience?[166] Aside from the arguments about social control, some critics claimed that Smith-Hughes was too rigid in the kind of schooling it would fund, others that its provisions were embedded in pre–World War I assumptions about work, and yet others that it was so flexible that states could devise their own means of meeting those provisions.

One answer might be that the funds were distributed to the states which then had to match them with their own contributions. The resulting programs themselves were determined on a state or a local level, and the public on the whole seems not to have objected to how this money has been used. Might this be a form of agency as well? Vocational education programs may not have turned out as David Snedden and Charles Prosser intended, but were those ground-level participants—students, parents, teachers, and administrators—satisfied with the results?

Cuban ended his essay by writing that the absence of detailed descriptions of what happened in local school districts retards any serious interpretation of the effectiveness of vocational schooling, and the "lack of serious histories of vocational schools and descriptions of teacher and student behavior also prevents the reaching of conclusions that go beyond mere speculation."[167] Though this book has been an effort to describe and analyze just three schools, only two of which might well have benefitted from the Smith-Hughes Act, it has been an effort to accomplish Cuban's objective. That its observations run counter to conventional wisdom among historians about industrial or vocational education may be due in part to where we all have started our studies. This one began with Comenius in the seventeenth century, Pestalozzi in the eighteenth, and Von Fellenberg, Froebel, and Weld in the nineteenth century. It views the rigidity of Snedden's and Prosser's prescriptions as aberrations, not as standards to be followed. One's conclusions are often a product of one's questions.

In closing—some historical anomalies. In 1917, after the United States entered what we remember as the First World War, Warren Hicks took a job as director of training at an army camp outside Des Moines, Iowa. Early in 1917, Montgomery Gregory, the son of Bordentown's second principal, a Harvard graduate and then a professor at Howard University, organized a group of similarly educated Black men; their goal—being able to train as officers to aid the war effort. Eventually their efforts paid off, and in May of 1917, a training program for Black officer candidates was established at Fort Des Moines.[168] Whether Hicks and Gregory had any contact there can never be more than a question, but it is intriguing to speculate.

In 1960, shortly before his death, Hicks received a commendation from the Governor's Commission on Human Rights in Wisconsin. It noted not only Hicks's contributions to vocational education but also in "matters pertaining to the aspiration of the human spirit." And "he practiced what he preached about the worth and potential of each individual in a democracy," the proclamation stated.[169] Montgomery's career was equally distinguished; after serving in the army, he went back to teach at Howard where he helped establish the Howard Players, the nation's first Black theatre corps; later he became superintendent of schools for Atlantic City. Both men not only had a sense of their own agency, but apparently passed it on to others.

As for efficiency, in considering the long-term outcome of Charles Prosser's doctrine of "efficiency," it is worthy of note that two high schools have been named after him: one in his hometown of New Albany, Indiana; the other in Chicago. On their websites, neither school refers to the efficiency of their programs. That of the Prosser Career Academy in Chicago refers instead to students' potential, regardless of "race, income, gender and learning differences." Innovation, collaboration, a safe and supportive environment are what it promises instead of prescriptions about what any student's future might be. Further, for the last thirty years of his career, Prosser headed the Dunwoody Institute in Minneapolis. Under his leadership, the school apparently offered an early form of rigidly programmed instruction; students punched in on time clocks.[170] A century later, the school's website claims that it welcomes students with a passion to "learn, create, make, and refine," which sounds more like Dewey than Prosser.

In addition to numerous schools named after John Dewey, there is a society dedicated to his memory and his vision for the nation's schools. There are no such societies honoring either Snedden or Prosser. Thus, one might ask, what won? Agency or a "utilitarian" view of efficiency?

Epilogue
Lessons on Education and Work from Bordentown and Ellendale

> Founded as a school for the people, [the NI] has been a living symbol of democracy.
> —Ryland M. Black, 1927
> President, North Dakota Normal and Industrial School, 1914–1936

> The object of education is not to make men carpenters but to make carpenters men.
> —W. E. B. Du Bois, 1930
> Graduation Address at Howard University

What is clear from the group of sources upon which several chapters in this book rely are certain gaps in conventional understandings about industrial education; most significant is that between work-related schooling for Black students and that for white students. But there are other substantial gaps as well. One is the connection between Progressive Era industrial education and democratic opportunity; by focusing on policy-level studies, historians of the former neglect how local programs fostered the latter.[1] Another is that between histories of labor and histories of industrial education: though Madison, Wisconsin, between 1905 and 1915 was home to significant developments in both, that connection gets little or no mention.[2] One early labor leader, George MacNeill, who began working as a teen at a textile mill in Connecticut, summarized in 1887 one of this book's major themes: "The problem of today, as of yesterday and tomorrow, is how to establish equality between men."[3] MacNeill's concern was the worker's relationship with his employer, but it can apply as well to the purpose of work-related schooling. As the NI's graduate Ina Randall Graham wrote in 1924: the school's function was to "break down class distinctions" and to instill among students "a democratic spirit which fulfills one of the principal objects for which schools were created."

An aspect of the latter, an issue with which American society is still grappling, is the many gaps between Black citizens and others. While there were numerous similarities between the curricula at Ellendale's NI and MTIS in Bordentown, coverage of industrial education both contemporaneously and historically suggests the two existed in separate spheres. A thorough examination of this contention and its implications would require another research project; what follows are a few observations from this one. Papers delivered at the 1913 NSPIE conference, for example, include no mention of African Americans; the following year, however, when the group met in Richmond, Virginia, the program did include a visit to Hampton Institute.[4] The two chapters in Kliebard's *Schooled to Work* that focus on Milwaukee include no mention of Black students, though as with Chicago, Cleveland, and St. Louis, the city's Black population was substantial at the time, and it would increase as a result of the Great Migration.

Racism and inequities abounded, as the story of the furor in Cleveland and nationwide that resulted when a Black girl won the NEA's spelling bee there in 1908 demonstrates.[5] Studies of the vocational education programs in Chicago's high schools, or at least those referred to in the foregoing, make no reference to the impact of African American migration to the city on the kind of programs offered. There is one exception, though, and it is a 2001 article about Lucy Flower High School; it noted that the school was particularly popular with African American girls.[6] And Ella Flagg Young, in her 1901 *Isolation in the School*, did write about a group of Black women who came to her while she was a deputy superintendent during the 1890s to voice their objection to the sympathetic coverage of slavery in a school textbook.[7]

In Paul Douglas's otherwise laudable history of industrial education published in 1921, the index contains no reference to Negroes and a close reading of the book found none.[8] Four decades later, when Edward Krug's book on the American high school appeared, the word Negro does appear in the index, as do two references to the subject: one notes William Torrey Harris's 1895 defense of higher education for Negroes; another refers briefly to conflicts over the two-volume *Negro Education*, edited by Thomas Jesse Jones and published in 1917.[9] W. E. B. Du Bois was harshly critical of it in a 1918 article in the *Crisis*, but his comments indicate his dedication to the idea of higher education for Negroes rather than familiarity with the industrial education movement as a whole.[10]

However, in a speech titled "Education and Work" that Du Bois gave in 1930, he took a different approach and brought considerable balance

Figure 29. William Valentine served as principal of MTIS in Bordentown from 1915 until 1950. During his years there, the school grew from a modest institution unsure of its role into a selective one that enrolled four hundred students, provided an innovative education that mixed academic with practical work, and greeted a variety of Black individuals and organizations unwelcome elsewhere.

to his discussion of the relationship between schooling and working. The occasion was Howard University's commencement that June, and the talk was published two years later in the inaugural issue of the *Journal of Negro Education*.[11] To begin, Du Bois summarized the "Two Schools of Thought" that had governed Negro education at century's turn: a college education or some industrial training. He argued that the "object of education was not to make men carpenters, but to make carpenters men." Much had been accomplished over those three decades, Du Bois wrote; there were many more Black students in both high schools and colleges and illiteracy had been vastly reduced. But the controversy had not been settled. While colleges had prepared many Black people for positions of leadership, it had also "turned our attention from any disposition to study or to solve our economic problems." The industrial school had also accomplished a great deal, but it could not keep up with changes in technology. Nor could it convince labor unions to admit Black men as members. While "the world must eat before it can think," Black workers had still found themselves "hired last and fired first."[12]

Echoing an argument that Charles Ham might have made, Du Bois claimed that "wealth despises work and the object of wealth is to escape work." Further, Du Bois's solution to the problem was one Ham, along with

Dewey and Ella Flagg Young, would have signed on to: "Our educational institutions must graduate to the world men fitted to take their place in real life by their knowledge, spirit, and ability to do what the world wants done." Some of Du Bois's subsequent arguments also read like an endorsement of what the Bordentown school was doing: the teacher "has got to be able to impart his knowledge to human beings whose place in the world today is precarious." Learning how to live and to earn a living is of just as much importance as "the content of the knowledge taught."[13]

Further indication of Du Bois's changed attitude toward industrial education is a story Zoë Burkholder related in her 2017 article about the Bordentown school. Du Bois had visited the campus several times during the 1920s, and in December of 1930, six months after his Howard University speech, he wrote to *The Nation*, proposing an article on Valentine's work at the school, commending its combination of academic instruction and vocational training. The magazine's editors declined the article, but Du Bois's correspondence, which Burkholder quotes from, expressed his admiration for the school and its principal.[14]

Dewey, as noted in chapter 4, had visited the Bordentown campus in May of 1928, having been urged to do so by Albert Barnes, the Philadelphia entrepreneur and founder of the Barnes art collection in Philadelphia.[15] Though no record exists of his reaction, Dewey's oft-expressed ideas on the necessity of combining academic education along with industrial training suggests that it would have been positive.

In 1931, according to Derrick Alridge, Du Bois wrote to Dewey three times, asking him to contribute an essay on Black education to *The Crisis*. At the time, per Alridge, Du Bois was rethinking his ideas on the virtues of integration versus segregation, and he welcomed Dewey's thoughts. That Dewey apparently declined is evident in Du Bois's side of the communication.[16] Given the two men's similar views on education and on the "necessity of both experiential education and education in the humanities," as Alridge wrote, this seems surprising. A century later, it also seems unfortunate. The two men had much to teach each other; we will never know how industrial education, for Black students and for white, might have benefited had the two come to some agreement as to how it might be offered.

Though *The Nation* declined an article about MTIS, other articles about the school did appear elsewhere. One, published in late 1930 by the *New York Evening Post*, called it "Jersey's 'Tuskegee of the North,'" a comment meant as a compliment. It noted that the "amenities of life as well as the trades" were taught at the school and that it had a "perpetual waiting list" of those who wanted to join its 400-member student body.[17] Another article, which appeared in the *Southern Workman* a year later, noted that the

Figure 30. In 1998, MTIS graduate John Medley commissioned the late Ladybird Strickland to paint this idealized image of the campus as it appeared around 1930. Note the Delaware River in the background, the parade ground in front of the Administration Building, the fields and barns, dormitories and work sheds, that enabled the school to be a self-contained community.

school was "properly equipped" and preparing students for "something more than domestic service and unskilled labor." Among faculty members singled out for praise was a Radcliffe graduate named Frances Grant; she not only taught English and Latin but "made herself one of the strongest forces at the school."[18]

The school's heyday was during the 1930s, when MTIS was increasingly regarded as an elite and selective institution, even though it was obligated to accept students in need of a structured environment.[19] This period is the focus of the 2009 documentary about the school. Called *A Place Out of Time*, it features filmed footage from the annual Decoration Day events that attracted thousands of people.[20] According to the film's narrator, Ruby Dee, the school was a "unique education utopia... an incubator for intellectual and life skills." Interspersed with the school's history are interviews with people who were MTIS students in the early 1950s; they praised the education they had received there. One, noting the maintenance and agricultural work required of all students, claimed that he had learned more math in auto mechanics than in a math class; another said that "we had no self-esteem problem... the faculty always built us up." She graduated with a beautician's certification; later, she acquired a doctorate and became a college dean.

In the summer, the Bordentown campus played host to gatherings of Black organizations not welcomed elsewhere.[21] During the school year, students were offered a rich variety of cultural programming: lectures, concerts, and extracurricular activities. *Ironside Echoes*, the student newspaper, won several awards, as did some of the school's livestock. The school attracted visits from leading intellectuals, musicians, and athletes, including Mary McLeod Bethune and her friend Eleanor Roosevelt; Duke Ellington and Albert Einstein, Althea Gibson and Paul Robeson were also among them. Distinguished members of the faculty included William H. Hastie, who taught history at the school during the 1930s; later he became a federal judge and a U.S. ambassador. Samuel A. Haley, father of *Roots* author Alex Haley, taught agriculture at MTIS before being hired by the Farm Security Administration in 1943.[22]

In her 1940 study, conducted while a doctoral student at Teachers College, Marion Thompson Wright wrote that, through the "intelligent application of certain vocational principles," the school had been more successful placing its graduates in skilled and semiskilled occupations than any other such institution in the state.[23] But after World War II, MTIS began to attract criticism, especially from some middle-class Black New Jerseyans who complained that it was an anomaly once integrated schools became available for their children.[24] This put Valentine somewhat on the defensive, as indicated in an article published in 1948.[25] Saying that many students needed the structure and discipline the Bordentown school provided—and that it attracted 1,500 applicants per year—he claimed that the school's role was to set students' "minds on wholesome ideas." Exposing students to a trade was not to make laborers of them but to point out the kinds of work people do to earn a living—a point with which both Dewey and Du Bois would agree.

In 1950, Valentine retired after thirty-five years as the school's head; though he was quickly replaced, some students recall feeling that their "education utopia" was about to disappear. After the *Brown v. Board of*

Education decision in 1954, New Jersey's governor, a progressive-minded Democrat named Robert Meyner, and the state board of education decided that the school had to close; the reason given was that it had failed to attract white students.[26] As the decision was challenged by a Republican-led state assembly, a public hearing was held in May 1955.[27] Though only seven of the twenty-seven people who testified supported the closure—and faculty members claimed that no efforts had been made to integrate the school—the die had been cast. The school's four hundred acres on a bluff above the Delaware River, and thirty-plus buildings, were coveted by another worthy cause—a needed home and research center for developmentally challenged children—and Gov. Meyner had made up his mind. At a press conference announcing his decision, he claimed that "there is nothing to justify the existence of this school. I think any educator would tell you that Bordentown is not much of an educational institution. It isn't very high grade."[28] Readers of this book might contest that assertion.

Despite the school's imminent closure, a final commencement was held on June 12, 1955. Choirs sang, speakers inspired, and fifty-nine graduates were awarded diplomas. Those who attended included Montgomery Gregory, son of the second principal, and both of William Valentine's children; their father had died a year earlier.[29] Over the next half century, the campus served various functions, including being a correctional facility, but it also became a state and national landmark. In 2002, a large piece of black granite from Zimbabwe was placed at its former entrance to mark its distinguished legacy.[30] In sum, the Manual Training and Industrial School's faculty and principals had employed their considerable talents to maintain its mission—equipping students with the skills needed to determine their own course through life.

The life span of Ellendale's NI was, like that of Bordentown's MTIS, the proverbial three score and ten. Another similarity was their curricula and the attributes they imparted to students; in addition, they were distinctive examples of institutions that existed to serve the particular needs of their time. MTIS may have been markedly successful in doing so, but it was only one of a hundred or more somewhat similar schools, a few of which also boarded their students.[31] The NI may have been even more distinctive; with one exception: the only other co-educational normal and industrial school serving white students (the others were for Black students) was just across the border in Aberdeen, South Dakota, and it quickly dropped "industrial" from its name.[32] Christine Ogren's thorough study of state normal schools has been helpful in writing about the Ellendale school, but it refers to manual and industrial training programs only in passing, and the NI rather backed into becoming a normal school. North Dakota's 1889 drive to establish a manual training and industrial school was a product, in part, of the national movement for such education.[33]

But it was a product as well of a tradition perhaps unique to the Dakotas: the last part of the continental United States to fill with non-Indigenous people who came from more established parts of the country, its settlers arrived in great numbers and with unprecedented speed during the Great Dakota Boom of the early 1880s. Along with their livestock and literary societies, they brought with them a respect for education and some sophistication about organizing school systems that had developed over the previous century.[34] Those midwestern migrants who gathered in Bismarck in the summer of 1889 to write the new state's constitution knew that schools were essential to the kind of society they wanted their new state to become. They were aware of the "new education," at least in its broad outlines; that they voted to establish several state-supported schools of higher learning suggests that they had acquired some of it themselves in their states of origin. Ogren writes that many state legislatures at the time were reluctant to support higher education, and the normal schools frequently had to struggle for funds; that a new state like North Dakota voluntarily established several, albeit backed by federal land grants, suggests a certain enlightenment on their part.

The NI shared several characteristics with the normal schools Ogren wrote about, but it differed in significant ways as well. While a normal school education was seen as a means of entry into the middle class, most of the students who populate the NI's early yearbooks seem to have felt they were already there: as Ina Randall Graham noted in her 1924 memory of the school, it "tended to break down class distinction and instilled among the students a democratic spirit." For the NI, the relationship between town and school may have been distinctive as well—during its first five decades, most students were drawn from Ellendale and surrounding Dickey County towns and farms. Ogren writes that most normal schools were located in cities of moderate size for their time—places with populations of ten thousand or more.[35] Ellendale's population was only 750 when the school was established; it was 1,300 in 1920; that of Dickey County grew from 6,000 to just over 10,000 during the same period.[36] Ethnic origins may have played a role, too—migrants to Dickey County came mainly from other midwestern states; family surnames suggest largely British stock. School rosters are also sprinkled with names of Finnish or Norwegian origin, and there was a large Russian-German community in the western part of the county; some of its young people began attending the school after 1920.

The industrial courses contributed not only to the school's initial attraction; they contributed to its democratic nature as well. At least half of the students during its first two or three decades were there to take only a course or two; they had not the luxury of joining the literary societies or sports teams, but they attended mechanical and domestic courses along

Figure 31. The NI campus in 1912, as seen from its entrance. The large building to the left is the 1903 Carnegie Hall; the original 1899 Manual Training Building is in the center. To the right is the 1905 Armory, which also housed the gym and some of the metalworking classrooms. Other buildings included a three-story dormitory and a power plant with classroom space. Fields for athletics and agricultural use were behind the main buildings.

with other students. Further, there seems to have been no sense in which the NI community felt isolated from either the countryside or the wider world, nor did they regard themselves as "provincials."

But at twenty-five, the NI had lost some of its youthful exuberance. Program descriptions were no longer sprinkled with quotations from John Ruskin, as was that of Ellen Anderson in 1900; the 1925 "Home Economics" program description was more a prosaic list of those who taught in it than the tribute to the field's founder that Lillian Tingle had contributed in 1900. In a 1924 "History and Scope of the N.I.," its writer proudly proclaimed that the school was where one could learn how to "operate and repair farm machinery, construct buildings properly," maintain soil fertility, eliminate disease and safeguard health, and manage a home efficiently; in sum: "how to train the hands as well as the head."[37] This list suggests that the industrial and home economics programs were emphasized, but at the time the faculty was equally split between standard academic subjects and those more directly career or job related.

In the epilogue to her book, Ogren discusses the "mission creep" beyond teacher preparation that afflicted state normal schools in the 1920s. Though they had always been more than teacher-training institutions, these schools did become colleges offering increasingly varied programs to an ever-growing number of students after World War I. That did not happen to the NI, which never grew beyond an enrollment of four hundred or so, many of them part-time students. In another sense, though, the NI did join the mainstream as Ogren described it: activities and athletics became increasingly important. Lists of students at the NI from 1912 on no longer stated the career on which each was focusing, but the clubs to which they belonged. The NI's lists of graduates between 1925 and 1937 did give the degree or diploma each received, but it also listed the activities in which they had participated.

For the seventy-one years of its life, the NI remained a small school serving a limited geographic area, offering individual courses and programs students wanted, whether to begin a career—usually that of a teacher—or to enhance their ability as farmer, music teacher, or bookkeeper. It continued to attract faculty with degrees from noted colleges and universities, and it never lost its close connection to the town and the people it served. Not until 1945 did the NI become a normal and industrial *college* rather than school; fifteen years later, its name was changed to the State Teachers College at Ellendale. In 1965, it became the University of North Dakota, Ellendale Center, offering a two-year program but neither degree nor diploma. It might have continued as such for a few more years, but in January 1970, a disastrous fire destroyed two of its main buildings. Seeing that devastation, and knowing the drop in enrollment, state officials determined that the NI had served its purpose and it would not be wise to rebuild. The school closed, and its campus was sold to Trinity Bible College, which remains there at the town's eastern end but reaches far beyond through many online programs. Ellendale itself may never have much expanded beyond its 1900 borders, but the NI's influence had extended to California, to West Africa, and to numerous points in between.

Despite similarities in longevity, mission, faculty competence, and graduates' loyalty, there were significant differences between the Ellendale and Bordentown schools, in addition to the racial background of students and staff. For one, MTIS has been the subject of three dissertations, one book, at least three academic papers, plus newspaper articles and a documentary; the NI cannot compete in that category. But as significant is the kind of attention it has received. In an interview broadcast when *A Place Out of Time* appeared on PBS in 2010, the video's producer said that when he first heard the story, he asked why no one had told it before. It had "all the elements" he said: the centuries-long struggle for education plus people who were still alive to tell the story. But discussing industrial education for Black students could be "uncomfortable," he said.[38] A newspaper review put the quandary more bluntly: "Sure, it's great to educate blacks, so long as they are educated to be chauffeurs and laundresses."[39] The comment says far more about the writer's preconceptions than about the school or the documentary—some chauffeurs may have been among the school's early graduates and later students worked in its laundry as part of their maintenance responsibilities, but it wasn't something for which anyone received certification.

Despite some recent attention, there is a general unawareness of the Bordentown school's accomplishments. For example: an informal survey of encyclopedias about African American history found no mention of William Valentine or the school.[40] Equally surprising is that the editor of a 2015 book about other progressive schools for Black students had never heard of it; further, the authors of a significant study of such schools conducted in the 1940s did not mention it.[41] Might historians have a bias against schools for African Americans that have either "manual training" or "industrial education" in their names? Though MTIS never saw producing upper-class professionals as part of its mission, it did do admirably well in preparing hundreds of members of a Black middle class. In the 1930s, some historians noted an unfortunate tendency for Black Americans to be clustered at either end of the employment spectrum with too few in the middle.[42] Thus, might ignoring the contributions of schools like MTIS have had regrettable consequences?

A 1982 article on Black vocational education by historian James Anderson chronicles the numerous challenges that have faced Black workers, at least since the 1830s. Racism and discrimination, of course, are chief among them. But in many ways, the education provided at MTIS seems an antidote to the barriers Anderson described. Neither MTIS nor the successes chronicled as outcomes of the 1940s study mentioned above are discussed in his article. However, it does offer numerous fields further research might pursue: why was MTIS so successful and might there be lessons from its educational program that could be copied today?[43]

Anderson's article begins in the 1830s, noting that a group of men (including abolitionist William Lloyd Garrison) proposed in 1831 a Negro "Manual Labor College" to be built in New Haven, Connecticut. Among its financial backers was New Yorker Arthur Tappan, who also helped fund the Society for Promoting Manual Labor in Literary Institutions the same year.[44] Though Anderson does not mention the latter group, this connection and similar ones would be another fruitful area of research—and counter the current reality that industrial education for Black students and for white are often treated as though they existed in separate universes.

Equally useful would be a series of books and articles similar to Ogren's study of normal schools, studies that would include institutions that served

Black students as well as white. All manual training and industrial education programs emphasized their contributions to molding character, inculcating good work habits, and schooling of the hands and the head. As Henry Belfield recalled of his own education at an Iowa college established in the spirit that motivated Arthur Tappan, the physical labor and skills required to maintain the school provided lessons that he incorporated into the curriculum at the Chicago Manual Training School.

Were such a compilation of industrial education schools to be done, it might look forward as well as backward, forward to the ways in which work is changing and will continue to change at a pace that exceeds that of the Industrial Revolution which brought about manual training in the first place. The end of chapter 3 in this book asks whether the school as communal laboratory conceived by John Dewey might have merged with the workshop as experimental station articulated by Frank Lloyd Wright: might such a merger have invigorated and made relevant the new industrialism proposed by some of their contemporaries in Chicago circa 1900? Recent works by the pragmatist philosopher Richard Sennett suggest, indirectly, that there could be value in considering the two together.[45] His 2006 *Culture of the New Capitalism* analyzes how rapid changes in communications and in technology have and will continue to alter the workplaces of the global economy. His *The Craftsman*, published two years later, offers a history of craft and comments on how innovative craftsmen have altered industry since humankind first began making things; as such, it complements Charles Ham's history of technology, published a century earlier. Though Sennett did not conceive his history as a curriculum in the same manner that Ham did, both books offer a spine that could support new educational programs intended to meet the needs of both the work and the worker of today. Sennett maintains that both manual and mental labor are involved in mastering any craft, that even the transient workplaces of the foreseeable future must leave room for craft, which he defines as the skill of doing work well for its own sake. The dignity of work is in the value and use of the products it creates.[46]

Following Richard Sennett's contention that both manual and mental effort are involved in all work, might learning and labor be seen as complementary, as Jonathan Baldwin Turner claimed they were in the 1850s? Might William James's observation of 1899—that manual training in schools give us "citizens of an entirely different intellectual fibre"—deserve renewed recognition? Learning to do and doing to learn may still be most closely associated with John Dewey, but the idea predated him by three hundred years. It worked as well in Chicago as it did in Bordentown and Ellendale. Nor has it lost its potency in the decades since.

Notes

Chapter 1. Through Mind and Hand to Manhood

1. Belfield, "Inaugural Address." For motto, see the cover of CMTS "Fourth Annual Catalogue, 1886–1887," in CMTS Records, Bound Catalogs; the translation is given in Gustafson, "The Origin and Establishment of the University High School," 12.
2. Belfield, "Inaugural Address," 1.
3. Ibid., 6–7.
4. "Manual Training School," CIO, June 20, 1884, 8.
5. Belfield, "Inaugural Address," 8–9.
6. Ibid.
7. Ibid., 11–13.
8. "Miscellaneous," CIO, April 4, 1884, 8.
9. Belfield, "Inaugural Address," 13–14.
10. "John Eaton, Jr.," Britannica.com, accessed October 17, 2023, https://www.britannica.com/biography/John-Eaton-Jr.
11. "Manual Training School," CIO, June 20, 1884, 8. The *Chicago Tribune* also ran an extensive story about the event: "Manual Training: Anniversary Exercises of the Chicago School," CDT, June 20, 1884, 9.
12. "Manual Training School," CIO, February 5, 1884, 8.
13. "Chicago Manual Training School: Cornerstone Impressively Laid," CIO, September 25, 1883, 8.
14. Miller, *City of the Century*, 303–5.
15. "Solon Spencer Beman," Wikipedia entry; see also Grossman, Keating, and Reiff, *Encyclopedia of Chicago History*, numerous entries.
16. The student drawing of the building in Figure 5 also appears as frontispiece in Ham, *Manual Training*.

17. A family history of William Gold Hibbard relays this story. Hibbard, along with CMTS supporter A. C. Bartlett and Franklin Spencer, established the major hardware wholesaling firm of Hibbard, Spencer, and Bartlett in the 1860s. The trio was followed, according to this story, by a carriage, should weather or other antagonists impede their progress.

18. Gustafson, "University High School," 8.

19. "Manual Training: A School for the Education of Youth in the Mechanical Arts," CDT, March 27, 1882, 7. This issue carried an extensive story about the meeting of the Commercial Club; it includes verbatim accounts of Charles Ham's remarks and those of his colleague Augustus Jacobson.

20. The comments that follow are all taken from "Manual Training," CDT, March 27, 1882.

21. Ibid.

22. Woodward, "Complimentary Nature of Manual Training," in Woodward, *Manual Training School.*

23. In the *Tribune's* March 27 article, Ham claimed $65,000 was raised that first night, but in *Manual Training* (page 340) he claimed $100,000.

24. Ham, *Manual Training*, 340. Biographical information on the founders from Grossman, Keating, and Reiff, *Encyclopedia of Chicago History* and Miller, *City of the Century.*

25. "Dictionary of Leading Chicago Businesses, 1820–2000," in Grossman, Keating, and Reiff, *Encyclopedia of Chicago History,* 909–53. Information on number of employees for the other firms is not given in this appendix to the *Encyclopedia.*

26. For population figures, see "U.S. Census Bureau History: 1893 Chicago World's Fair" on the United States Census Bureau's website at https://www.census.gov/history/www/homepage_archive/2018/may_2018.html (accessed December 12, 2023). The pertinent information is in the bulleted list following the introductory text. For numbers of foreign-born residents, see Grossman, Keating, and Reiff, *Encyclopedia of Chicago History,* 1011.

27. "Annexations and Additions to the City of Chicago," Grossman, Keating, and Reiff, *Encyclopedia of Chicago History,* 22.

28. Herrick, *Chicago Schools,* Appendix C, 403.

29. Schneirov, "Strikes," in Grossman, Keating, and Reiff, *Encyclopedia of Chicago History,* 794–95.

30. Ham, *Manual Training,* 293–94.

31. Ibid. Parts of Ham's argument also appeared in "Co-education of Mind and Hand." A later edition of *Manual Training* appeared as *Mind and Hand,* published in 1900.

32. Campbell, *Colonel Francis W. Parker.*

33. Sandra F. Branch, "Elizabeth Harrison," in Schultz and Hast, *Women Building Chicago,* 356–59; and Harrison, *Sketches along Life's Road.*

34. Knight, *Citizen: Jane Addams;* and Victoria Bissell Brown, "Jane Addams," in Schultz and Hast, *Women Building Chicago,* 14–22.

35. It is thought that some of Burnham's admirers attributed this comment to him; others say it was constructed after his death by some of those same admirers. Still another source credits the following: "Stirred by Burnham, Democracy's Champion," *Chicago Record-Herald*, October 15, 1910.

36. Belfield's biography is compiled from his own "Autobiographical Writings, 1891–1903," found in the Belfield Papers. Additional biographical information is from Rathnau, "The Contributions of Henry Holmes Belfield."

37. Rathnau, "Henry Holmes Belfield," 23.

38. See chapter 2 and its discussion of the colonial-era log colleges and early nineteenth-century efforts at "promoting manual labor in literary institutions."

39. Belfield also noted that some went to aid his father in starting a business; perhaps this was a good investment because Belfield also reported that at the time of his marriage in 1867, he had $7,000 in the bank.

40. Rathnau, "Henry Holmes Belfield," 25–27.

41. Ibid., 9.

42. Dodge, *Reminiscences of a School Master*, 57–59. Dodge also noted that Elbridge Keith, brother of CMTS trustee Edson Keith, was among Howland's friends.

43. Belfield, "Autobiographical Writings."

44. For Ham's major works, see note 31, above.

45. "C. H. Ham Dead," *Morning Call*, Paterson, NJ, October 17, 1902, 2; and "Board of General Appraisers: Ham, Charles H.," accessed October 18, 2023, https://www.fjc.gov/history/courts/board-general-appraisers-ham-charles-h.

46. Both editions of Ham's book, along with his 1890 article, are available in Google Books; although the 1900 edition is listed as a third, there is no second edition in the Google collection.

47. Ham, "Preface to the Third Edition," *Mind and Hand*, iii–v.

48. Ibid., "Preface," v.

49. Parker, "Introduction to the Third Edition," in Ham, *Mind and Hand*, xi–xiii.

50. Ibid., xiii.

51. Edward Beecher, the founding president of Illinois College, was not only a member of the famous Beecher family; he was also among the founders of the Society for Promoting Manual Labor in Literary Institutions, which figures in chapter 2. See also Schreiner, *Passionate Beechers*, 71.

52. "Finding Aid," Blatchford Family Papers.

53. Recounted in Rathnau, "Henry Holmes Belfield," 32–34.

54. Reports from the *Chicago Tribune* and the *Chicago Inter Ocean* in November and December 1883.

55. Ham, *Manual Training*, 340.

56. Ibid., 341–42.

57. Frontispiece, "First Annual Catalog, 1884," CMTS Records, Bound Catalogs.

58. According to Gustafson, "University High School," 60.

59. Rathnau, "Henry Holmes Belfield," 3.

60. Gustafson, "University High School," 31.
61. Ham, quoted in Rathnau, "Henry Holmes Belfield," 6.
62. "First Annual Catalogue, 1884," 13–15, CMTS Records, Bound Catalogs.
63. "Fifth Annual Catalogue, 1887–88," 10, CMTS Records, Bound Catalogs.
64. "Chicago Manual Training School," *Scientific American*; subsequent references, title abbreviated to "CMTS."
65. "First Annual Catalogue, 1884," 8, CMTS Records, Bound Catalogs.
66. "Fifth Annual Catalogue, 1887–88," 22, CMTS Records, Bound Catalogs.
67. Gustafson, "University High School," 31.
68. "Second Annual Catalogue, 1884–85," CMTS Records, Bound Catalogs.
69. "Third Annual Catalogue, 1885–86," CMTS Records, Bound Catalogs.
70. "Hand and Brain," May 1885, CMTS Records, Series I, Box 3, Folder 2. The papers contain only two issues of this newsletter: those for February and for May. It is not known whether there were others.
71. "First Annual Catalogue, 1884." Note that in his "Autobiographical Writings," Belfield claimed that his initial salary was $3,000 per year.
72. "Fifth Annual Catalogue, 1887–88," 11, CMTS Records, Bound Catalogs.
73. "CMTS," *Scientific American*.
74. Gustafson, "University High School," 39.
75. "First Annual Catalogue, 1884," 5, CMTS Records, Bound Catalogs.
76. "Manual Training School," CIO, June 6, 1885, 6.
77. "Other News Items," CDT, September 18, 1887, 4.
78. "Hand and Brain," May 1885, CMTS Records, Series I, Box 3, Folder 2.
79. Quoted in Rathnau, "Henry Holmes Belfield," 65.
80. "Manual Training," CDT, January 30, 1886, 3.
81. "CMTS," *Scientific American*.
82. "First Annual Catalogue, 1884," 3, CMTS Records, Bound Catalogs.
83. "A Long-Felt Want," CST, April 4, 1886, 27.
84. "CMTS," *Scientific American*.
85. "Class of 1889," closing pages of CMTS Records, Bound Catalogs.
86. "Circular to Parents and Guardians," CMTS Records, Series I, Box 1, Folder 8; the "Finding Guide" dates this as 1888.
87. "Third Annual Catalogue, 1885–86," 11, CMTS Records, Bound Catalogs. The *Scientific American* article also noted this, as did Belfield in his "Autobiographical Writings."
88. "Fourth Annual Catalogue, 1886–1887," 16, CMTS Records, Bound Catalogs; also printed in "Graduating Class of the Chicago Manual Training School," CDT, June 25, 1886, 2.
89. "Fifth Annual Catalogue, 1887–1888," 24, CMTS Records, Bound Catalogs.
90. CIO, June 21, 1888, 10.
91. "Summary of Occupations of Graduates," "Twelfth Annual Catalog, 1894–1895" 31, CMTS Records, Bound Catalogs.
92. "Fifth Annual Catalogue, 1887–1888," 10–11, CMTS Records, Bound Catalogs.

93. E. W. Blatchford, "Annual Report," delivered June 1886 to the Chicago Manual Training School Association; the report is in CMTS Records, Bound Catalogs.

94. An illustration of the gate appears in the "Fifth Annual Catalogue, 1887–1888"; a story about the gate appeared in "Chicago Manual Training School," CDT, June 18, 1890, 5.

95. "Political Race Horses at the Illinois State Fair," CIO, October 6, 1890, 5.

96. "Manual Training Alumni," CIO, June 29, 1888, 7.

97. "Chicago Manual Training School," CDT, June 18, 1890, 5.

98. "In Honor of the New Education," CDT, June 24, 1890, 3; the *Inter Ocean* carried a similar article, CIO, June 24, 1890, 1.

99. Gustafson, "University High School," 69.

100. "Hand and Brain," May 1885, CMTS Records, Series I, Box 3, Folder 2; and "Hand Culture," CIO, December 2, 1885, 4.

101. "Ham Urged for School Inspector," CIO, July 31, 1887, 15; "Open Letter to Mayor Roche," CST, July 31, 1887, 8.

102. Letter to the Editor from A. R. Sprague, CDT, September 2, 1887.

103. "Let Choctaw Have Their Language," CDT, September 17, 1887, 15.

104. Gilman, "Plea for the Training of the Hand," 3–15.

105. Belfield, "Manual Training in the Public School," 16–24.

106. Shine, "Development of Technical Education in the Chicago High Schools," 25–26.

107. Gustafson, "University High School," 40.

108. Ibid., 25.

109. "Don't Copy the English," CDT, January 22, 1890, 6.

110. Wells, *The Reason Why the Colored American Is Not in the Columbian Exposition*; Wells wrote this and persuaded Frederick Douglass to write an introduction. She then raised money for its printing and distribution.

111. Miller, *City of the Century*, 542–46.

Chapter 2. Learning and Doing Arrives in Chicago

1. Cremin, *American Education: The National Experience*, 34–39, 408, 487. The great enthusiast for the "mission to the wilderness" was Lyman Beecher (1775–1863), who described this in two works published in 1835: *A Plea for the West* and *A Plea for the Colleges*. He was the father of educator Catherine Beecher, author Harriet Beecher Stowe, Illinois College president Edward Beecher, and numerous other notable figures. See also Schreiner, *Passionate Beechers*.

2. Blatchford Papers, "Finding Aid."

3. A valuable treatment of this idea is Fletcher, *History of Oberlin College*; see also Weld, *First Annual Report of the Society for Promoting Manual Labor in Literary Institutions*.

4. Belfield, "Autobiographical Writings."

5. Though this point is seldom, if ever, made in studies of industrial education for African American students, many of the early abolitionists were also advocates of manual labor in schools and colleges; see Goodman, "Manual Labor Movement and the Origins of Abolitionism."

6. This connection is made by Wirth, *Vocational-Liberal Studies Controversy Between John Dewey and Others*, 65. As a member of the faculty at Washington University in St. Louis, site of the first widely recognized American manual training school, Wirth wrote this valuable study; while sympathetic to the need for practical work in schools, the study endeavored to be even-handed in covering the controversies that roiled its development.

7. The most comprehensive treatment of all these developments is still Cremin's *National Experience*.

8. Ham, *Manual Training*; "Co-education of Mind and Hand"; and *Mind and Hand*.

9. Bennett, *A History of Manual and Industrial Education to 1870*, and *A History of Manual and Industrial Education, 1870 to 1917*.

10. See Gilpin, "Charles A. Bennett," for biographical information.

11. Anderson, *History of Manual and Industrial School Education*.

12. Ibid., 13–16.

13. Ham, *Manual Training*, 13; Anderson and Bennett both give Comenius similar credit.

14. Ham, *Manual Training*, 2.

15. Ibid., 126–29.

16. These comments appear in Ham's lengthy list of contents; both the 1886 and 1900 editions include a thorough list in which he outlines the points on which he will elaborate in each chapter. These, combined with an even more thorough index, make it relatively easy to track his convictions on a range of related topics.

17. On Franklin, see Cremin, *American Education: The Colonial Experience*, 402–5; and Anderson, *Manual and Industrial*, 32.

18. Rush, "Samuel Finley," 166.

19. Anderson, *Manual and Industrial*, 31. Theodore Weld and others stressed this idea, too.

20. Anderson, *Manual and Industrial*, 60, 85.

21. See Bennett, *Manual and Industrial Education to 1870*, 128–209.

22. "Philipp Emanuel von Fellenberg," Britannica.com, accessed October 18, 2023, https://www.britannica.com/biography/Philipp-Emanuel-von-Fellenberg.

23. Anderson, *Manual and Industrial*, 91–95.

24. Owen, "My Student Life at Hofwyl." For a brief, contemporary report on related educational programs in Switzerland, see Hoffman and Schwartz, "Swiss Vocational Education."

25. Both Anderson and Bennett mention Griscom; see also Griscom, *A Year in Europe Comprising a Journal of Observations*.

26. See the Slave Dwelling Project, https://slavedwellingproject.org. Members and participants of the Slave Dwelling Project travel throughout the South to stay in former slave quarters. The site does not say how well the Dents treated their enslaved servants.

27. Bennett, *Manual and Industrial Education to 1870*, 172–86.

28. See Griffith, *In Her Own Right: The Life of Elizabeth Cady Stanton*, 25–28.

29. Fletcher, *Oberlin College*; Goodman, "Manual Labor Movement."

30. Abzug, *Passionate Liberator: Theodore Dwight Weld*.

31. Both Abzug and Fletcher, in *Oberlin College*, tell a similar story about Weld; see Fletcher, 35–43.

32. "Manual Labor Institutions," *Hartford Courant*, April 16, 1833. Material in quotation marks came from the article, which does not make clear whether or not they are direct quotes from Weld's report.

33. Weld, *Society for Promoting Manual Labor*.

34. Fletcher, *Oberlin College*, 43; some complexities of this story are also told in Schreiner, *Passionate Beechers*, especially in chapter 5, 73–114.

35. This story is told in both Fletcher, *Oberlin College*, and Abzug, *Theodore Dwight Weld*.

36. This was published as Weld, *American Slavery as It Is*. Of interest is that Weld's wife Angelina Grimké Weld and her sister Sarah Grimké participated in the writing of this; the Grimké family would also play a role in the history of the manual training school in Bordentown, New Jersey, a story that is told in chapter 4.

37. See Green, *Mary Lyon and Mount Holyoke*.

38. Ham, *Manual Training*, 123–29.

39. Meier, *Negro Thought in America*, mentions their impact on Frederick Douglass and the Negro Convention Movement in the decades before the Civil War, 85–87. See also Levy, "Forging African-American Minds: Black Pragmatism, 'Intelligent Labor,' and a New Look at Industrial Education."

40. Griscom, *A Year in Europe*.

41. Bennett, *Manual and Industrial Education to 1870*, 216–28.

42. Ibid., 246–59.

43. Schreiner, *Passionate Beechers*.

44. Stowe, *Report on the Elementary Education in Europe*.

45. Bennett, *Manual and Industrial Education to 1870*, 241.

46. Fisher, *Industrial Education*, covers this mid-nineteenth century history as well, but in a manner that seems skeptical about the intentions of those involved.

47. Bennett, *Manual and Industrial Education to 1870*, 317–28; 349.

48. See "Institute History," Rensselaer, accessed October 18, 2023, rpi.edu/about/history.html.

49. Bennett, *Manual and Industrial Education to 1870*, 251.

50. Wirth, *Vocational-Liberal Studies*, 8–10.

51. Ibid., 12–14. For an overview of labor history, see Sklansky, "The Work of Class in American History."
52. Wirth, *Vocational-Liberal Studies*, 10.
53. Laurie, *Artisans into Workers*, 101–11.
54. Rodgers, *Work Ethic in Industrial America*, 7.
55. Montgomery, *Fall of the House of Labor*, 2.
56. Laurie, *Artisans into Workers*, 3.
57. Laurie, 218–20; Montgomery, *House of Labor*, 5.
58. Rodgers, *Work Ethic*, 71–72.
59. Bennett, in *Manual and Industrial Education 1870–1917*, did note both Gompers's and the AFL's attitude toward vocational education.
60. Cremin, *American Education: The Metropolitan Experience*, 472, 481.
61. For an overview of these conflicts in Chicago, see Schneirov, *Labor and Urban Politics*.
62. Cremin, *Transformation of the School*; 29n.
63. Ham, *Manual Training*. See, especially, the two chapters on "Automatic Contrasted with Scientific Education," 191–248.
64. Bennett, *Manual and Industrial Education 1870–1917*, 369.
65. Ham, *Manual Training*, "Preface," iii–vi.
66. Ibid., 331–32, quoting a May 22, 1884, letter from Runkle.
67. Ham, *Manual Training*, 328.
68. The two are Woodward, *Manual Training School* and *Manual Training in Education*; the latter was intended largely for an international market.
69. Speech before St. Louis Schools Association in 1878, quoted in Woodward, *Manual Training School*.
70. Troen, *The Public and the Schools: Shaping the St. Louis System*, 157, 167–68.
71. Woodward, "Origins, Aims, Methods, and Dignity of Polytechnic Training," in *Manual Training School*, 240–60.
72. Woodward, *Manual Training School*, 2–3.
73. Woodward, "Extracts from the Prospectus of 1879," in *Manual Training School*, 290–94. Note: the numbers in brackets are the actual pages on which Woodward's comments appear.
74. Woodward, *Manual Training School*, 9–10.
75. Quoted in Ham, *Mind and Hand*, 202.
76. Woodward, *Manual Training School*, 194, note 1.
77. Woodward, "Fruits of Manual Training," in *Manual Training School*, 203–13.
78. From *Biography of the Golden Anniversary of the 1902 Class*, St. Louis Manual Training School Alumni Association, 1952; reprinted in Troen, *St. Louis System*.
79. Ham, *Manual Training*, 336–38.
80. Albert Marble, quoted in Cremin, *Transformation*, 30; Marble was superintendent of schools in Worcester, Massachusetts.
81. Bennett, *Manual and Industrial Education 1870–1917*, 362–64. Though Bennett did not mention this, another person who attended that NEA meeting

was Booker T. Washington; in *Up from Slavery*, he recounts his appearance in a chapter titled "Two Thousand Miles for a Five-Minute Speech."

82. Anderson, *Manual and Industrial*, 186.

83. MacAlister, "Manual Training in the Philadelphia Public Schools," 5–11. Note that the numbers in brackets refer to the page numbers on which the quotes appear.

84. Ham, *Mind and Hand*, 387 and 402. Though Ham did not include the source for his compilations, the general quality of his writings suggest that he endeavored to be accurate.

85. Cremin, *Transformation*, 32–33. A report published by the National Center for Educational Statistics indicates that, in 1890, there were 6,558,000 children ages 14 to 17 in the nation as a whole and that fewer than 10 percent attended high school; see Snyder, *120 Years of American Education: A Statistical Portrait*, Table 1, page 11, and Figure 7, page 27.

86. Cremin, *Transformation*, 29.

87. Cremin, Shannon, and Townsend, *History of Teachers College*, 10–20.

88. Troen, *St. Louis System*, 170.

89. Cremin, *Transformation*, 13–14.

90. Butler, *Argument for Manual Training*, 371–95. This address was delivered to the American Institute for Instruction on July 12, 1888, and initially published by the institute later that year; the numbers in brackets are those of this version. Earlier, in November 1887, the talk had appeared as a leaflet published by the Industrial Education Association, which Butler headed at the time.

91. Harris, "Psychology of Manual Training"; this was read before the NEA's Department of Superintendence, Washington, DC, March 7, 1889; the version appearing in Google Books claims that it was published in a journal called *Education* in May 1889. The numbers in brackets refer to pages of the version published by the NEA.

92. Troen, *St. Louis System*, 157–59.

93. Woodward, *Manual Training in Education*, chapter 2, "The Remedies Proposed," 38–51; the numbers in brackets refer to pages in this chapter.

94. Cremin, *Transformation*, 15.

95. Ham, "Co-education of Hand and Mind," 116–38; the numbers in brackets indicate the page on which the comment appears.

96. "Manual Training: Schools in Which the Value of Knowledge Receives Immediate Practical Demonstration," CIO, March 22, 1891, 9.

97. "Armour to Chicago: Gives a Manual Training School and Endowment," CDT, December 13, 1892, 3.

98. Gustafson, "The Origin and Establishment of the University High School," 38.

99. Rathnau, "Contributions of Henry Holmes Belfield," 238; Rathnau cited $1.6 million as the size of the Armour institute's endowment. He also noted that William Rainey Harper, who was at the time courting the Chicago Manual Training School, was on the new institute's board of trustees.

100. "Lewis Institute Teachers Named," CDT, March 11, 1896, 4. Additional information is from a talk by Catherine Bruck, given on December 9, 2004, at Illinois Institute of Technology; at the time, she was the school's archivist. In the 1930s, Armour Institute became Illinois Institute of Technology, which in 1940 incorporated Lewis Institute as well.

101. "What Chicago's Manual Training Schools Are Doing," CIO, May 23, 1897, 40.

102. Albert Lane, quoted in "The Workshop," CIO, June 20, 1897, 35; the comments from Bamberger and Parker that follow are from the same article.

103. Cremin, *Transformation*, 32–33.

104. Ham, *Manual Training*, 371–72.

105. Ibid., 387–89.

106. Snyder, *Statistical Portrait*, see note 85 for the proportion of youth in secondary schools.

107. Ham, *Manual Training*, 372.

108. "Manual Training Schools," CIO, March 22, 1891, 9.

109. Gustafson, "University High School," Tables 9 and 13.

110. Ibid., 25.

111. "Manual Training," CIO, March 22, 1891, 9; Gustafson made a similar claim.

112. "CMTS Completed 10th Year," CDT, February 3, 1894, 10.

113. Gustafson, "University High School," Table 13, 65.

114. "Work in Manual Training Shown," CDT, June 20, 1894, 3; "Evidence of Skill on View: Commencement Exhibit at CMTS," CIO, June 20, 1894, 8.

115. "Manual Training School Products," CDT, December 13, 1894, 7; "Homemade Tower Clock," CIO, May 24, 1895, 6.

116. "Crerar Will Report," CDT, July 14, 1894, 14.

117. "All Praise the Boys' Work," CDT, June 19, 1895, 8.

118. Gustafson, "University High School," Table 13, 65.

119. Rathnau, "Henry Holmes Belfield," 244; his source was a letter Belfield wrote to E. W. Blatchford. Belfield recounts the same deliberation in his "Autobiographical Writings."

120. Storr, *Harper's University*, 85–86.

121. Rathnau, "Henry Holmes Belfield," 243–46.

122. Storr recounted that the University's trustees were concerned that they would be obligated to maintain the school just as it was.

123. "Harper Has a New Gift," CDT, June 18, 1896, 6.

Chapter 3. Joining Hands and Heads on the Midway

1. Miller, *City of the Century*; and Heise, *Chicagoization of America*.

2. *University and the City*, 4–5.

3. Rice, *Public-School System of the United States*; see also Tyack, *One Best System*.

4. Rice, *Public-School System*, 210–15.
5. That Alice Chipman played a pivotal role in Dewey's interest in education is a point made by Eastman, "John Dewey: Teacher and Friend," in *Great Companions*, and by Mayhew and Edwards, *Dewey School*.
6. Eastman, "John Dewey," 254–72.
7. Storr, *Harper's University*.
8. Ibid., 83–84. There are numerous other recountings of the Harper Report; one that decidedly favored the teachers' opposition is Herrick, *Chicago Schools*; see also Rousmaniere, *Citizen Teacher*.
9. "Their Schools Days End," CDT, June 24, 1897, 8.
10. 10. Rathnau, "Contributions of Henry Holmes Belfield," 256. Though CMTS is occasionally mentioned in books about progressive education, Rathnau's work and McCamant, "Getting to Scale with Moral Education," are the only previous studies of the school.
11. Belfield, "Autobiographical Writings."
12. John Dewey, Letter to the Editor, *Chicago Evening Post*, December 19, 1895.
13. Harrison, *Timeless Affair: The Life of Anita McCormick Blaine*, 87–89.
14. White, "Study of Education at the University of Chicago," 67.
15. Leonard Carmichael, "Introduction," in Dewey, *Child and the Curriculum*, 1956 edition.
16. Harrison, *Anita McCormick Blaine*, 89–92.
17. Storr, *Harper's University*, 296–97.
18. Ibid., 298.
19. An exception to this is Knoll, in *Beyond Rhetoric*; see especially chapter 1, "Deschooling the School: John Dewey's Theory of Curriculum and Instruction," and chapter 4, "The Long Course of History: John Dewey and the Maxim 'Learning by Doing.'"
20. Butler, *Argument for Manual Training*, 380.
21. Ibid., 379.
22. Eastman, "John Dewey," in *Great Companions*, 272, made this comment.
23. Mayhew and Edwards, "Dewey's Principles of Education," in *Dewey School*, 461. For another version of the term's origin, see Knoll, *Beyond Rhetoric*, 161–81; "Dewey and Maxim 'Learning by Doing'."
24. John Dewey, "Introduction," in Mayhew and Edwards, *Dewey School*, xiii–xiv. Knoll, in *Beyond Rhetoric*, offers a less subjective history of the school and the book about it; see chapter 9, "Alice Dewey's Legacy: The Origin and Purpose of Mayhew and Edward's Classic 'The Dewey School.'"
25. Mayhew and Edwards, "General History," in *Dewey School*, 3–19. Note that the numbers in brackets indicate the pages on which comments appeared; as noted, most of these are John Dewey's words.
26. Ham, *Manual Training*; this book is discussed extensively in chapters 1 and 2.
27. Mayhew and Edwards note this seminar in *Dewey School*, 389; the role of the seminar in arriving at the idea of occupations is also given in Tanner, *Dewey's*

Laboratory School, 60. How Dewey arrived at the idea that occupations would be at the center of the school's curriculum has been taken up in DeFalco, "An Analysis of John Dewey's Notion of Occupations," 82–99.

28. Dewey, 1902, *White and Blue*, 317.
29. Mayhew and Edwards, "Evolution of Dewey's Principles of Education," in *Dewey School*, 461–62.
30. Dewey, "The Theory of the Chicago Experiment," in Mayhew and Edwards, *Dewey School*, 465.
31. Dewey, 1896, "Reflex Arc Concept," 357–70; and 1896 (1899), "Interest in Relation to Training of the Will," 209–46. As Dewey's articles in the Bibliography are organized chronologically, the year of publication is given for those cited.
32. Dewey, 1897, "Pedagogic Creed."
33. Dewey, "Theory of the Chicago Experiment," in Mayhew and Edwards, *Dewey School*, 464.
34. Louis Menand makes this point in *The Metaphysical Club*, his study of the psychologists and philosophers who moved in William James's circle in and out of Cambridge.
35. Dewey, 1896, "The Reflex Arc Concept," 97–99.
36. Thanks to Anne Durst; her "Union of Intellectual Freedom and Cooperation," led to this observation.
37. Mayhew and Edwards, "Dewey's Principles of Education," in *Dewey School*, 452.
38. Dewey, *Child and the Curriculum*, 20.
39. Rathnau, "Contributions of Henry Holmes Belfield," 14–17.
40. Belfield, "Autobiographical Writings."
41. In a January 28, 1904, paper read before the School of Education Parents' Association, Dewey made a brief reference to Belfield; see Dewey, 1904, "Significance of the School of Education." In this talk, Dewey also referred briefly to Charles Ham; this appears to be the only time he did so.
42. Dewey, 1897, "University Elementary School," 72–75.
43. Tanner, *Dewey's Laboratory School*, 156–57.
44. Ball, "Manual Training," 177–85.
45. Dewey, 1897, "Plan for Organization of Work."
46. Ibid., 446–47.
47. The Training School for Teachers, to which Dewey referred, had been renamed Teachers College in 1892.
48. Dewey, 1901, "Place of Manual Training."
49. See Richards, "Function of Hand Work in the School."
50. Ham, *Mind and Hand*, Appendices, 397–98.
51. Dewey, 1897, "Ethical Principles Underlying Education," 61–62.
52. "The Workshop," CIO, June 20, 1897, 35.
53. Ibid. The other schools mentioned here are described in chapter 2.
54. Boris, *Art and Labor*, 180–81.
55. Ibid., 89.

56. Freeman-Moir, "William Morris and John Dewey," 21–41.
57. Boris, *Art and Labor*, 46.
58. Floyd, "Cultured Mind and the Skillful Hand."
59. Rodgers, in *The Work Ethic in Industrial America*, in his chapter on "The Mechanicalized Man," explores many of the problems facing workers at the time that concerned those who contributed to *The New Industrialism*; see, especially, 76–84.
60. Boris, *Art and Labor*, 45.
61. Ham, in part quoting Ruskin, *Manual Training*, 152–53.
62. Boris, *Art and Labor*, 7.
63. Ibid., 28.
64. Ibid., 45–46.
65. See Engelbrecht, "Association of Arts and Industries," especially chapter 1, "Those Who Went Before."
66. Information on Triggs (1865–1930) and the league is from a variety of sources: Boris, *Art and Labor*; Engelbrecht, "Association of Arts and Industries"; and Jorgensen, *Thorstein Veblen*. Veblen had been Triggs's neighbor in Hyde Park; a rumored affair between Veblen and Triggs's wife Laura McAdoo led to the departure of both men from the University of Chicago in 1904.
67. Boris, *Art and Labor*, 48–49, and notes on pages 206–7.
68. Springer, *New Industrialism*.
69. Oscar Lovell Triggs, "Industrial Art," 45–60, in Springer, *New Industrialism*. The arguments by Butler and Harris are discussed in chapter 2.
70. Knight, *Citizen: Jane Adams*, 68–69.
71. Triggs, "Industrial Art," in Springer, *New Industrialism*; numbers in brackets refer to the latter.
72. Boris, *Art and Labor*, 8–9.
73. Wright gave several versions of this talk. In March 1901 he delivered it at Hull House and repeated it a week or so later to a group of engineers; this version is widely available online and was in *Brush and Pencil*, a publication of the Chicago Architecture Association. The version that appears in *The New Industrialism* reads as though Wright, or an editor, readied the talk for publication, as it is far more carefully composed. In a published version of a talk with the same title, given to a group of architects at Princeton University in 1930, the introduction refers to a 1900 paper given to the Architectural League of America with the same title; see Frank Lloyd Wright, *Modern Architecture: Being the Kahn Lectures for 1930* (Princeton: Princeton University Press, 1931).
74. Rodgers, in *Work Ethic*, and Laurie, in *Artisans into Workers*, both address this from the laborers' point of view.
75. Frank Lloyd Wright, "Art and Craft," in Springer, *New Industrialism*, 81–111; numbers in brackets refer to the pages in his article.
76. Information on Wilbur Jackman from Harrison, *Anita McCormick Blaine*; James Tufts, "The Significance of Mr. Jackman's Work," *Elementary School Journal* 7, no. 8: 443–46 (1907); and McCaul's articles about Dewey's departure from

the University of Chicago ("Dewey, Harper, and the University of Chicago"), 31–74.

77. Wilbur Jackman, "The Future School," in Springer, *New Industrialism*, 69–75. Jackman's talk was given just two months prior to the death of Francis Parker.

78. This comment came from two sections of James, *Talks to Teachers on Psychology*: the first few lines are in Part V, "The Necessity of Reactions"; the second from Part VII, "What the Native Reactions Are." Originally published in 1899, the full text is available from Project Gutenberg; it has no page numbers. The quotation appears in Chicago Manual Training School, "Catalogue for 1901–1902," 5; CMTS Records, Series I, Box 2, Folder 10.

79. Menand, *Metaphysical Club*.

80. White, "Education at the University of Chicago," 95.

81. Belfield, "Autobiographical Writings."

82. This comment appeared in a "Circular to the Alumni, Parents, and Other Friends of the Chicago Manual Training School"; it was signed by William R. Harper, John Dewey, and Henry H. Belfield, and dated June 1901; Belfield Papers, Series III, Box 3, Folder 1.

83. Storr, in *Harper's University*, 85, claimed that university trustees foresaw that CMTS would become the base for a school of technology.

84. Quoted in Rathnau, "Henry Holmes Belfield," 92.

85. Gustafson, "University High School," Table 7, "Length of Tenure of the Staff."

86. CMTS "Catalogue for 1902–1903," 6, CMTS Records, Series I, Box 2, Folder 10. The catalogs changed in name and appearance after the university took over; they no longer carried ordinal numbers.

87. Gustafson, "University High School," tables 11, 12, 13, 59–65, and Figure 1 on page 67.

88. Gustafson, "University High School," table 11 on page 59.

89. From *University Record*, 1900–1901, 446; quoted in Gustafson, "University High School," 72.

90. Harrison, *Anita McCormick Blaine*, 97.

91. Rathnau, "Henry Holmes Belfield," 264–67.

92. "Day of Worship at University," CDT, June 17, 1901, 9.

93. Rathnau, "Henry Holmes Belfield," 270.

94. In his study of Dewey's years in Chicago, Knoll includes charts of their various responsibilities; see "John Dewey as Administrator: The Inglorious End of the Laboratory School in Chicago," in *Beyond Rhetoric*, 263–316.

95. "Circular to the Alumni, Patrons, and Other Friends of the Chicago Manual Training School," July 1901, CMTS Papers, Series I, Box 3, Folder 7.

96. Rathnau, "Henry Holmes Belfield," 275.

97. McCaul, "Dewey, Harper, and the University of Chicago," 40–42.

98. Goddard, "Ella Flagg Young's Intellectual Legacy."

99. Young, *Some Types of Modern Educational Theory*, 43–67.

100. White, "Education at the University of Chicago," 95. See also Knoll, *Beyond Rhetoric*; in chapter 9, "Dewey as Administrator," he offers considerable evidence of Dewey's shortcomings as an administrator.

101. Belfield, "Autobiographical Writings."

102. Rathnau, "Henry Holmes Belfield," 272.

103. Henry H. Belfield, Letter to "My Dear Young Friend," September 1902, Belfield Papers, Series I, Box 2, Folder 6. For a contemporary view of the "moralizing" that Belfield's letter represents, see McCamant, "Getting to Scale with Moral Education."

104. Dewey, 1902, "The University of Chicago School of Education."

105. Rathnau, "Henry Holmes Belfield," 274–75.

106. White, "Education at the University of Chicago," 105.

107. White, 96; and "The Study of Education," University of Chicago, *Annual Register* for 1902–1903, 133, SCRC. Note that these were published after the end of the academic year.

108. *Annual Register* for 1902–1903, 129.

109. Gustafson, "University High School," 100.

110. These figures were arrived at by comparing faculty lists in the CMTS catalog for 1901–1902 with that in the *Annual Register* for 1902–1903.

111. Rathnau, "Henry Holmes Belfield," 275. The role of CMTS in merging these various entities plays little or no role in the most widely cited studies about the end of Dewey's school; see, especially, Knoll and McCaul.

112. Dewey, 1904, "Significance of the School of Education," 273–83.

113. Another contemporary view of the Laboratory School and its legacy should be noted; its arguments neither support nor dispute the version of the school given here. See Fallace and Fantozzi, "Dewey School as Triumph, Tragedy, and Misunderstood."

114. Knoll, in "Dewey as Administrator" (in *Beyond Rhetoric*), assigns much of the blame for the school's precipitous closure to the difficulty Mrs. Dewey had in working with others—and her husband's reluctance to address the issue.

115. There are numerous sources for the story of the Deweys' departure from Chicago; those already mentioned include Eastman, "John Dewey"; Harrison, *Anita McCormick Blaine*; McCaul's articles in Brickman's *Dewey's Legacy in Chicago*; and White, "Education at the University of Chicago." Others include Jane Dewey, "Biography of John Dewey."

116. "To Leave Midway School," CIO, May 3, 1904.

117. "Dedication of the Buildings of the School of Education," Belfield Papers, Series III, Box 3, Folder 1.

118. "Strike Remedy in the School," CDT, May 14, 1904, 8.

119. "Dr. Butler Speaks at University of Chicago," CDT, May 15, 1904, 8.

120. Eastman, "John Dewey," 278.

121. White, "Education at the University of Chicago," 110–14. Butler (no known relationship with Nicholas Murray Butler) also became active in the industrial education movement.

122. See Lagemann, "Plural Worlds of Education Research."
123. "University High School Circular to Parents," CMTS Records, Series I, Box 2, Folder 11.
124. Belfield, "Autobiographical Writings." Belfield, Jackman, and Owen were, with Nathaniel Butler, members of the four-man team heading the School of Education. Butler described it as a situation of "armed neutrality"; see White, "Education at the University of Chicago," 115.
125. Belfield, "Autobiographical Writings."
126. Ibid.
127. William James, *Psychological Bulletin* I, I (January 15, 1904); quoted in McManis, *Ella Flagg Young and a Half-Century of Chicago Schools*, 101.
128. See Lagemann, "Experimenting with Education"; Dewey credited Young with making his ideas more concrete; Mayhew and Edwards credited her with first using the name Laboratory School for Dewey's venture.
129. Huxtable, *Frank Lloyd Wright*.
130. Dewey, 1906, "Culture and Industry in Education."
131. A century after this article by Dewey appeared, the pragmatist philosopher Richard Sennett wrote two books that pursue aspects of Dewey's concern here; they are *Culture of the New Capitalism* and *The Craftsman*. Both are discussed briefly at the end of the Epilogue.
132. Four decades later, a group of architects and educators with roots in the Prairie Style and the Laboratory School created a distinctive building in Winnetka, Illinois, that represented ideas articulated by Wright and Dewey; known as Crow Island, it became a model for elementary school construction in the post–World War II era.

Chapter 4. A "Star of Hope" Defines Industrial Education

1. Two descendants of Rev. Rice have included biographical information about him in books. One, by his great-granddaughter Susan Rice, is *Tough Love*; Rice was ambassador to the United Nations during the Obama Administration and domestic policy advisor during the first two years of the Biden Administration; her father Emmett J. Rice, an economist, was a governor of the Federal Reserve Board. The other, *Reclaiming African-American Students*, was written by the Rices' granddaughter, Mildred Rice Jordan, a retired college professor in New Jersey. Susan Rice is a descendent of Rev. Rice's first marriage, in South Carolina; Jordan is his granddaughter by his second wife, Ella Mount Rice. There are minor discrepancies in the information provided in the two books, but they do not substantially alter their accounts of Rev. Rice and the school.
2. New Jersey Secretary of State, *Corporations of New Jersey: List of Certificates to 1911* (Trenton: State Printers, 1911; electronic copy available through NJSL).
3. Though the group was initially established in New Brunswick, it later focused its efforts on Bordentown. The quotation is from its articles of

incorporation as given in Pillsbury, "Application for Inclusion for Manual Training and Industrial School," Section 8, page 2. This document is based on several sources, including official reports made by the state, contemporary newspaper articles, and other published materials. Page numbers in it are given as section number/page number in the section.

4. Meier, *Negro Thought in America*, 4–10.
5. Ham, *Mind and Hand*, 396.
6. Levy, "Forging African-American Minds: Black Pragmatism," 43–44.
7. Report of the Commission on Industrial Education, 9 and 106.
8. Ham, *Mind and Hand*, 342 and 389.
9. Wright, *Education of Negroes in New Jersey*, 163–71.
10. In the spring of 2019, the Bordentown Historical Society mounted an exhibition and sponsored several programs about both School No. 2 and the Manual Training and Industrial School. Notes on the history of the former were on display at the society and consist of a few newspaper articles from the *Bordentown Register* in 1880 and 1932, plus other information the group was able to find; this recounting is based on that.
11. Pillsbury, "Application for Inclusion." In addition to the Jordan book noted above, two dissertations have been written about the school (see below). None, however, set the school in the context of manual labor schools or the manual training movement, whether segregated or not.
12. Quoted in Jordan, *Reclaiming African-American Students*, 6. (However, at some point in 1897, Rice was no longer principal.)
13. Adams, "Role and Function of Manual Training and Industrial School at Bordentown as an Alternative School," 10. This is one of two dissertations written about the school; the other is Duck, "Historical Study of a Racially Segregated School in New Jersey."
14. Wright, *Education of Negroes*, 180.
15. This is suggested in a brief history of the school that appears in the *Ironsides Echo*, May 29, 1908, 4, MTIS Records.
16. Information on the Stewarts and Parnells is from various sources, among them a website managed by Shannon Selin, Imagining the Boundaries of History, on which appeared an article about Charles Stewart and his wife Delia Tudor Stewart, "An Ill-Assorted Match" (accessed October 23, 2023, https://shannonselin.com/2014/08/charles-delia-stewart-ill-assorted-match/). Another is "Anna and Fanny Parnell" at the History Ireland website (accessed October 23, 2023, https://www.historyireland.com/anna-fanny-parnell/); the latter two were called "Ireland's Patriot Sisters" for their efforts at land reform in Ireland. After bearing eleven children, Delia Stewart Parnell was widowed in 1859, and left with a title but little money to live on; during the 1880s, she and one or two of her daughters lived on the Bordentown estate. See also "Once Belle of the Ball: Traits and Events in the Life of Delia Tudor Stewart Parnell," *New York Times*, April 29, 1895.

17. Information on the Parnell brothers from Wikipedia and from Fortune, *Black and White*.
18. Pillsbury, "Application for Inclusion," 8/2.
19. "Press Service of the Bordentown School," also "Decade of Progress," MTIS Records.
20. Pillsbury, "Application for Inclusion," 8/3.
21. There is some conflict on exactly when this was. Pillsbury claimed 1894–1895; Gregory family materials say he arrived in 1897. During 1894, Gregory was still on the faculty at Howard University.
22. "Walter Allan Simpson Rice," *Daily Fredonian* 45, no. 307, January 5, 1899 (New Brunswick, NJ), as cited in Pillsbury, "Application for Inclusion," 9/1.
23. Thomas, "James Monroe Gregory," 211–13.
24. Typescript by Montgomery Gregory, made available by his daughter, Sheila Gregory Thomas.
25. Pillsbury, "Application for Inclusion," 8/3.
26. "Through the Years with the Echo," 1955, MTIS Records.
27. Pillsbury, "Application for Inclusion," 8/3.
28. "Mrs. Delia S. T. Parnell," *Ironsides Echo* 1, no. 5. (May 1898), MTIS Records.
29. Quoted in Pillsbury, "Application for Inclusion," 8/4.
30. "School of Great Promise," *New York Age*, September 21, 1905. Though none of the histories of MTIS mention the connection, this description of the school's purpose and curricula suggest that Hampton Institute, which opened in 1868, served as a model. See Peabody, *Education for Life*.
31. Alexander, *T. Thomas Fortune, the Afro-American Agitator*, xvi–xvii.
32. See T. Thomas Fortune, "The Negro in Politics," in Alexander, *Afro-American Agitator*.
33. T. Thomas Fortune, "The Kind of Education the Afro-American Most Needs," in Alexander, *Afro-American Agitator*, 85–91.
34. Pillsbury, "Application for Inclusion," 8/4.
35. Ibid., 8/5.
36. *Ironsides Echo*, May 1908, MTIS Records.
37. Both attributes were aspects of the manual labor idea promoted by Theodore Weld and the half academic, half trade model of the early manual training schools in St. Louis and Chicago; see chapters 1 and 2 in this book.
38. *Ironsides Echo*, May 1908, 12, MTIS Records.
39. Bordentown School Committee, "Report of the Manual Training and Industrial School."
40. Ibid.
41. Report of the Commission on Industrial Education, 1909, 4–11 (NJSL).
42. Ibid., 105–10.
43. Ibid., 11.
44. For information on Hampton and Tuskegee, see Anderson, *Education of Blacks in the South*; Bullock, *History of Negro Education*; Norrell, *Up from History*; Meier, *Negro Thought*; and Talbott, *Samuel Chapman Armstrong*. The latter

is by the founder's daughter; it lauds his accomplishments, as does Peabody in *Education for Life*. A balanced history of Hampton's virtues and limitations has yet to be written.

45. Pillsbury, "Application for Inclusion," 8/4.

46. "Chronology," *The Ironsides Echo*, Historical Edition, June 1955, MTIS.

47. Report of the Commission on Industrial Education, 1909, 109.

48. "Biographies," *Legislative Manual of New Jersey*, 144th Session, 1920, 380–81, NJSL, Digital Jerseyana Collection.

49. For the prevalence of Black residents in Salem County, see "African-Americans" in Lurie and Mappen, *Encyclopedia of New Jersey*, 5–8.

50. "Dr. Kendall and Dr. Thompson," *Journal of the National Education Association* XI, February 1922, 66, available at HathiTrust, https://hdl.handle.net/2027/uiug.30112111456015.

51. "Weekly Letter of the Manual Training and Industrial School," MTIS Records.

52. This was also a form of integrating occupations into the curriculum as advocated by John Dewey. By 1910, it had become a substantial aspect of the academic part of vocational education programs nationwide; see chapters 3 and 6.

53. "J. M. Gregory Out of Bordentown School," *New York Age*, February 11, 1915, 1. (Fortune, by the way, was no longer the paper's editor.)

54. *Boston Guardian*, as quoted in the Montgomery Gregory typescript (see note 24), which gives an account of the funeral. The service was at Plymouth Congregational Church, where Mongomery's brother Frank Gregory was pastor. A notice in the *Washington Post* (December 20, 1915) implied that this was Grimké's church.

55. The Montgomery Gregory typescript is the source for attendees at the funeral and burial services.

56. "Memorial Services in Honor of Professor James M. Gregory," Gregory Papers.

57. Dewey and Dewey, "School as Social Settlement," in *Schools of Tomorrow*, 105–15.

58. Although the Tuskegee Archives have no record of Valentine teaching there, a video about the school claims that he did; see Davidson, *Place Out of Time*. A brief biography of Valentine at the Newark Public Library does state that he had worked at a school in the South as a college student.

59. Dewey and Dewey, *Schools of Tomorrow*, 165. The purpose of the Indianapolis school, also known as PS 26, is subject to debate. Two other accounts of it come to conclusions that differ from that of the Deweys; see Fallace, *Dewey and the Dilemma of Race,* and Margonis, "John Dewey's Racialized Visions of the Students and Classroom Community."

60. "William Robert Valentine," *Harvard Class of 1904: Twenty-fifth Anniversary Report, 1929;* Harvard Archives.

61. Bullock, *Negro Education*. Anderson, *Education of Blacks*.

62. Information on these amendments is from "African-Americans" in Lurie and Mappen, *Encyclopedia of New Jersey*; this is augmented by Hodges, *Black New Jersey*, 108–9.

63. Meier, *Negro Thought*, 190–247. Alridge, in *Educational Thought of W. E. B. Du Bois*, aimed to "move scholars beyond the overly simplified, binary discussions" of differences between the two, 2.

64. Alexander, *W. E. B. Du Bois*, 37.

65. Norrell, *Up from History*, 1–5.

66. Alridge offers a brief, but nuanced, understanding of the differences between Washington and Du Bois, suggesting a need to "move beyond the cliched representations"; see his *Educational Thought*, 54.

67. Alridge, *Educational Thought*, 45.

68. Meier, *Negro Thought*, 195–96.

69. Washington, *Up from Slavery*, 163.

70. Alexander, *Du Bois*, 39.

71. Ibid., 41. The review appeared in the July 1901 *Dial*; the quotations are Alexander's words.

72. Meier, *Negro Thought*, 166–67.

73. Davis, *Guest of Honor*.

74. Du Bois, *Negro Artisan*, 1902; *The Negro American Artisan* appeared in 1912, edited by Du Bois and Augustus Granville Dill.

75. The 1902 study contains numerous testimonies to this effect; see especially *Negro Artisan*, 13–23. The point about enslaved mechanics is mentioned in other sources as well.

76. Meier, *Negro Thought*, 98; Alexander, *Du Bois*, 38.

77. Du Bois, *Souls of Black Folk*; both ideas are introduced in Du Bois's "Forethought," a preface to *Souls of Black Folk*, and discussed in Alexander, *Du Bois*, 44–45.

78. The comment about "gloves off" is from Alexander, *Du Bois*, 48; Meier, in *Negro Thought*, 176, makes a similar point.

79. Quoted in Alexander, *Du Bois*, 43.

80. Meier, *Negro Thought*, 177; Alexander, *Du Bois*, 49.

81. Meier, *Negro Thought*, 172–76.

82. Du Bois, quoted in Alexander, *Du Bois*, 52.

83. John Dewey, 1909, "Address to the National Negro Conference."

84. Similarities between Dewey's and Du Bois's thinking about education, and influences on them, are discussed in Alridge, *Educational Thought*, 39–42.

85. Meier, *Negro Thought*, 183.

86. Barrows, *Mohonk Conferences on the Negro Question*. Initially established to consider education for Indigenous Americans, two of the Mohonk conferences took up the educational needs of southern Negroes; though these reports are seldom mentioned in the literature, the talks do indicate enlightened and experienced opinion for the time although they sound condescending today. See also Fishel, "Negro Question at Mohonk."

87. Bullock, *Negro Education*, 147–67.

88. W. E. B. Du Bois, "Testimony to the Commission on Industrial Relations," February 1915; Du Bois Papers.

89. Hodges, *Black New Jersey,* "The Civil War and Reconstruction," 98–158. For insight into New Jersey's history as a "southern" state, see Geffken, *Stories of Slavery in New Jersey.*

90. Wright, *Education of Negroes,* 163–71.

91. Hodges, *Black New Jersey,* 109–10. The use of "nadir" to describe these years likely originated in an earlier book by Rayford Logan, *Negro in American Life and Thought.*

92. Meier, *Negro Thought,* 165.

93. See Perry, *Lift Up Thy Voice.* A more recent book on the Grimkés paints a rather different portrait of the family; see Greenidge, *The Grimkes.*

94. Alexander, in *Du Bois,* makes this argument. Greenidge, in her biography of Trotter, demonstrates the complexities of his character; see *Black Radical.*

95. A survey of school names catalogued by the Edwin Washington Project in Loudoun County, Virginia, suggests this; see Roeder and Harrelson, *Dirt Don't Burn.*

96. Alexander, *Afro-American Agitator*; Thornbrough, *T. Thomas Fortune.*

97. "Manual Labor Institutions," *Hartford Courant,* April 16, 1833. See also Goodman, "Manual Labor Movement and the Origins of Abolitionism."

98. Beyer, "Manual and Industrial Education for Hawaiians During the 19th Century." Though this account suggests that these schools had a positive influence on students, Beyer wrote a later paper in which he regarded the schools differently; see Beyer, "White Architects of Hawaiian Education." Armstrong's childhood experience with the school in Hilo is covered in Peabody, *Education for Life,* and Talbott, *Samuel Chapman Armstrong.*

99. Moe, "Influence of the Hilo Boarding School on Agricultural Education in the Pacific." (As with Carl Beyer, members of Moe's family had been involved with Hawaiian schools such as the one in Hilo.) See also histories of Hawaii such as Moore, *Paradise of the Pacific.*

100. Talbott, *Armstrong,* 131.

101. See Bullock, *Negro Education;* also Anderson, *Education of Blacks*; Pierson, *Laboratory of Learning*; and Watkins, *White Architects of Black Education.*

102. Talbott, "The Beginnings of Hampton," in *Armstrong,* 155–78. This was also a motivation for the Normal and Industrial School in North Dakota, which is the subject of chapter 5.

103. A somewhat more skeptical version of Armstrong's motivation is given in Norrell, *Up from History,* 31–40. Meier claimed that industrial education was appropriate for "backward" races; Meier's implication was pejorative toward such schooling, but it suggests that he had a limited view of what industrial education actually was.

104. Both stories are recounted in Washington, *Up from Slavery.*

105. Alexander in *Du Bois,* and Meier in *Negro Thought,* both discuss Trotter's background. See also, Greenidge, *Black Radical.*

106. Meier, *Negro Thought,* 216.

107. Stewart, *"New Negro": The Life of Alain Locke*.
108. Information on Frelinghuysen's anti-lynching work is from Hodges, *Black New Jersey*, 130.
109. Bordentown School Committee, "Report of the Manual Training and Industrial School," 1909 (unpaginated).
110. "Authoritative Definition of Manual Training," 9–10 (the full definition appears as the opening quote for this chapter).
111. Ham, *Mind and Hand*, 387–91.
112. Report of the Commission on Industrial Education, 104–12. Hodges, in *Black New Jersey*, noted that such jobs were often at the "lowest grades."
113. Bullock, *Negro Education*, especially 60–166. It is worth noting that at the time, only one or two percent of the nation's college-age youth were enrolled in higher education programs; only 10 percent were attending high school.
114. Writings by all three are discussed in chapter 2.
115. Bullock, *Negro Education*, 82. See also the most extensive histories of manual training: Bennett, *History of Manual and Industrial Education Up to 1870* and *History of Manual and Industrial Education 1870–1917*; plus Anderson, *History of Manual and Industrial School Education*. All three of these books are discussed in chapter 2.
116. Washington, *Up from Slavery*, 108.
117. Bullock, *Negro Education*, 83.
118. Anderson, *Education of Blacks*, 76. As noted earlier, this was a Deweyan practice that was prevalent in industrial education programs at the time.
119. These ideas are discussed in chapters 3 and 6.
120. Alridge, *Educational Thought*, 42. In a footnote, Alridge refers to an interview with Du Bois's noted biographer David Levering Lewis, in which the latter stated that further examination of Dewey's relationship with racial issues of his day merited further study; see note 32, page 145.
121. Generals, *Booker T. Washington*, 1–23. (In 2014, Generals became president of the Community College of Philadelphia.)
122. Ibid., 139.
123. Generals, *Booker T. Washington*, 136. Dewey argued this in several articles, including "Some Dangers in the Present Movement" (1913). Dewey's arguments are covered more fully in chapters 3 and 6.
124. Washington, *Up from Slavery*, 219.
125. Du Bois and Dill, *Negro-American Artisan*.
126. Ibid., 115–27.
127. Du Bois, "Testimony to the Commission," 1915.
128. Alridge, *Educational Thought*, 33–67.
129. Hodges, *Black New Jersey*, 131.
130. "Some Results of Bordentown Training," 1927, MTIS Records.
131. Hodges, *Black New Jersey*, 11.
132. "Weekly Letter of the Manual Training and Industrial School," December 1920, MTIS Records. Du Bois's visit is reported in "Dr. Du Bois Speaks at Bordentown Institute," *The New York Age*, August 19, 1922, p. 5.

133. Du Bois, "Negro Education," in *The Crisis*.

134. Ibid., 175. In Lewis, *W. E. B. Du Bois: Biography of a Race*, the author noted that after Du Bois's mother died, a local white minister suggested that a spirited Black boy such as "young Willie" "would be much improved by learning a trade under lock and key," 34.

135. Dewey, 1913, "Present Movement for Industrial Education" (this is also known as "An Undemocratic Proposal"); and 1915, "Industrial Education-the Wrong Kind."

136. Jones, "General Survey," in *Negro Education*, vol. 1, 1–22.

137. Alridge, in *Educational Thought*, very briefly discusses the Jones report with a few fair-minded comments, 39. Reading those comments, one is tempted to conclude that Jones should have consulted both Dewey and Du Bois in writing his report.

138. Jones, *Negro Education*, vol. 2, 682–83.

139. Yellin, "(White) Search for (Black) Order."

140. Jones, *Negro Education*, vol. 1, 7.

141. Fortune, "False Theory of Education [as a] Cause of Race Demoralization."

142. Deutsch, *You Need a Schoolhouse*. A Rosenwald Park Campaign was established in 2020 by people with ties to Rosenwald schools; enabling legislation to make federal funds available for this effort was signed in January 2021.

143. Hall, *Black Vocational, Technical, and Industrial Arts Education*, 2.

144. Ibid., 156–58.

145. Generals, *Booker T. Washington*, 140.

146. As stated in note 120, in *Educational Thought*, Alridge refers to an interview with David Levering Lewis, in which the latter stated that further examination of Dewey's relationship with racial issues of his day merited further study.

147. Dewey, *Democracy and Education*; numbers in brackets refer to exact pages where the quotations are found.

148. Wirth, *Vocational-Liberal Studies Controversy Between John Dewey and Others*, 9–10.

149. Ibid., 282–83. As noted earlier, the Deweys' evaluation of the school is subject to several interpretations; see Fallace, *Dewey and the Dilemma of Race*; Margonis, "Dewey's Racialized Visions"; and Vaughan, "Progressive Education and Racial Justice."

150. See Goddard, "Bordentown School as Institution and Idea."

Chapter 5. The People's School on the Prairie and How It Grew

1. "Manual Training," DCL, June 10, 1897; the earlier announcements had appeared on April 29 and May 6, 1897.

2. Smith, "Mind and Hand," includes biographical information gathered on Hicks. Though her family moved to Ellendale decades after Hicks had left, my mother and several other relatives attended the NI; my grandparents lived near the campus, and I visited Ellendale often as a child.

3. Randall, "Industrial Training in the Schools."
4. See Goddard, "Howling Success."
5. Black, *History of Dickey County*, 66.
6. Schultz, "A History of the State Normal and Industrial School at Ellendale, ND," 3.
7. Smith, "Mind and Hand."
8. Schultz, "State Normal," 4–6, EHS.
9. Briggs, "Settlement and Economic Development of the Territory of Dakota," and Robinson, "The Great Dakota Boom," in *A History of North Dakota*, 133–56.
10. Though no evidence has been found of Native American communities living in the area when the railroads arrived, recent research into conflicts between the Sioux and U.S. soldiers during the Civil War has altered former narratives. A 1909 monument on Dickey County's western edge marks the 1863 Battle of Whitestone Hill; the battle is now seen as a senseless massacre of a Sioux community; see Barth, "Imagining a Battlefield as a Civil War Mistake."
11. See Goddard, "Unprecedented Yet Unheralded," which is about the rapid development of small towns and schools during the Great Dakota Boom, 1879–1886. My grandmother was born and educated in a central Dakota town shortly after the end of the boom; her parents were homesteaders.
12. Hudson, *Plains Country Towns*, 13.
13. Smith, "Prospectus," 2.
14. My mother, who was actually born in South Dakota, said that the reason her parents bought a farm in Dickey County was because Ellendale was known as a town that valued education.
15. See Currarino, "Introduction," in *Labor Question in America*, 1–10.
16. The noted book by Caroline Fraser, *Prairie Fires*, is a nonfiction account of Laura Ingalls Wilder's work; it tells a very different story of a Dakota community in its early years. According to Fraser, the Ingalls's hometown of DeSmet, 160 miles southeast of Ellendale, was populated by ne'er-do-wells and scavengers who barely survived the elements and failed to build a thriving town; see especially chapter 4, "God Hates a Coward," 93–132.
17. Though the surname of these longtime editors was Goddard, they are not related to me; my mother's family name was Bymers.
18. Mary Flemington Strand, quoted in Schultz, "State Normal," 18.
19. "Historic House," 47.
20. Smith, "1889 Convention Delegate," DCL, July 30, 2020, and "Reform Activist with Ellendale Roots," *DCL*, August 20, 2020.
21. Schultz, "State Normal," 18.
22. Smith, "Mind and Hand," chapter 6, "Shaping Our Tomorrows: The Path to Prohibition," and Black, *Dickey County*, 75–76.
23. Fish and Black, *A Brief History of North Dakota*, 6–9.
24. For recent scholarship on this, see Beck, *Columns of Vengeance*.
25. Fish and Black, *North Dakota*, chapters 1–19, pages 1–117.
26. Ibid., 137–39.

27. Schultz, "State Normal," 6–11.

28. Fish and Black, *North Dakota*, 155.

29. For background on this process, see Clawson, *Man and Land in the United States*, and Gates, *Landlords and Tenants on the Prairie Frontier*. Dahl, *Empire of the People*, offers a contrasting view of this process.

30. See Chittick and Schooler, "The Story of School Lands"; this useful article describes the establishment of school funds in considerable detail. William Henry Harrison Beadle, the Dakota Territory's superintendent of public instruction between 1878 and 1885, was instrumental in insisting that income from the sale of these school lands not be squandered. His distinguished career is told in Dykstra, *Permanent School Fund in South Dakota and the Beadle Club*, a collection that includes the Chittick and Schooler article.

31. This history of early Ellendale and Dickey County is taken largely from Black, *Dickey County*, particularly pages 31–62, 77–96, and 115–23.

32. As noted above, the school systems established in the territory during the Great Dakota Boom set records for the rapidity with which they were established and the organizational structure that provided them with stability. Goddard, "Unprecedented Yet Unheralded," analyzes the development of local schools in another James River community, Huron and Beadle County (named after the early superintendent of public instruction) in what is now South Dakota. For context, see Theobald, *Call School*; one of the advantages Dakota Territory had is that the Midwestern migrants who populated it in the 1880s arrived with shared assumptions about the importance of schools to the society they wanted to establish.

33. *Ellendale 125th Anniversary Book*, "Schools," 122.

34. Fraser, in *Prairie Fires*, wrote that a combination of poor luck and bad judgment made the Ingalls family's life more ordeal than idyll. She referred to Charles Ingalls's decision-making as "equal parts recklessness and passivity," 132.

35. "To Guide the Hand," DCL, March 30, 1893. In the early years of settling the Great Plains, town promoters believed that having a college would promote growth; whether it did so is speculative. In the case of Ellendale, both the town and the school were attractions that reinforced each other.

36. Warren E. Hicks to Otto Schultz, July 2, 1946, quoted in Schultz, "State Normal," 36. In Ogren, *American State Normal School*, the one in Ypsilanti (now Eastern Michigan University) merits frequent mention.

37. *Ellendale 125th Anniversary Book*, "Colleges," 115.

38. School Laws of North Dakota, 1897, quoted in Schultz, "State Normal," 21.

39. This recounting comes largely from Schultz, "State Normal," 25–26, based on reports in the NDR, also published in Ellendale, on May 25, August 24 and 31, 1898.

40. Smith, "Mind and Hand," chapter 1; a lengthy account of the event appeared in DCL, June 20, 1899.

41. Black, *Dickey County*, 65. Though Black was unlikely to know this,

Bordentown's Manual Training and Industrial School shared the first distinction—it charged no tuition. Further, the manual training programs in public schools charged no tuition, nor did many state normal schools. For the latter, see Ogren, *American State Normal*, 77–82. Black, in making his comment, may have had schools such as those in St. Louis and Chicago in mind; they were private institutions and did charge tuition.

42. DCL, August 8, 1899, and Schultz, "State Normal," 28–31.
43. Interview with Warren Hicks, DCL, October 9, 1900, reprinted in Schultz, "State Normal," 38–40.
44. NDR, September 1899, quoted in Schultz, "State Normal," 144.
45. Ham, *Mind and Hand*, Appendices.
46. Ogren, *American State Normal*, 213–35.
47. Warren E. Hicks to E. P. Neibauer, July 8, 1942, quoted in Schultz, "State Normal," 63.
48. Schultz, "State Normal," 32–33.
49. MTS, *First Annual Catalog*, 1900, 29–33 (original is unpaginated; page numbers are added here for convenience), EHS.
50. Interview with Warren Hicks, DCL, October 9, 1900, reprinted in Schultz, "State Normal," 38–40.
51. Schultz, "State Normal," 35.
52. MTS, *First Annual Catalog*, 1900, 14, EHS.
53. Ogren, *American State Normal*, 74–83.
54. MTS, *First Annual Catalog*, 1900, "Fine Art Department," 19, EHS.
55. Ibid., "Domestic Art Department," 23, EHS.
56. Interview with Ken Smith, October 2, 2020. Apparently, Tingle also influenced James Beard, the late and lauded food writer; in a 1979 article Beard noted her influence on him as a child in Portland, Oregon. See Joanne Will, "In the Company of Great Books about Food," CDT, July 26, 1979.
57. MTS, *First Annual Catalog*, 1900, "Domestic Art Department," 23–27, EHS.
58. Smith, "Mind and Hand," chapter 2, "Coming to the Town."
59. *Ellendale 125th Anniversary Book*, Helen Graham Rezzato, "Ina Randall Graham," 400.
60. Randall, "Industrial Training."
61. Ogren, "Teachers Grand Tours of Europe."
62. Smith, "Mind and Hand," chapter 1; Rozum, *Grasslands Grown*, makes a similar point.
63. DCL, November 27, 1902, quoted in Schultz, "State Normal," 62.
64. Warren Hicks to E. P. Neibauer, July 8, 1942, quoted in Schultz, "State Normal," 63.
65. Schultz, "State Normal," 59.
66. *Ellendale 125th Anniversary Book*, "Colleges," 115.
67. Black, *Dickey County*, 65; Schultz, "State Normal," 41–43.
68. MTS, *Bulletin*, July 1905 (unpaginated), EHS.
69. Schultz, "State Normal," 91.
70. Ibid., 75.

71. North Dakota School Laws of 1907, quoted in Schultz, "State Normal," 66.
72. NDR, September 4, 1907, quoted in Schultz, 67–68.
73. R. M. Black to Otto C. Schultz, July 5, 1946, quoted in Schultz, 46.
74. Ogren, *American State Normal*, 235.
75. However, as Ogren notes, tuition charges at all these state-supported schools were either minimal or non-existent; *American State Normal*, 80–82.
76. Schultz, "State Normal," 43.
77. Soon after Kern's arrival, the school produced a brief but gracefully designed two-color booklet called "The School for the People." Its contents suggest that he was trying to make the school's offerings more coherent; see Ellendale MTS, "School for the People," 1905, NYPL.
78. Kern, "Industrial Education."
79. The inclusion of this quotation from William James suggests that Kern may have attended the University of Chicago while Dewey was there; his wife Caroline Evans Kern had done so (see below). In a further connection with Illinois, an O. J. Kern, the superintendent of schools in Winnebago County (Rockford), located in the northern part of the state, gave a series of lectures at the NI in May of 1910 (NDR, May 12, 1910). O. J. Kern had earlier written an article titled "'Learning by Doing' for the Farmer Boy," which was very Deweyan in its inspiration. In 1912, O. J. Kern was a member of a statewide commission considering new industrial education legislation for the state; that story is told in chapter 6. See chapter 3, note 78, for the origin of the James quotation.
80. NI, *Catalog*, July 1910, 11–12 (unlike earlier catalogs, this one was paginated), EHS.
81. Ibid., 3–9; 69–79.
82. Schultz, "State Normal," 119–27; these pages include a list of all faculty members 1899–1944 and their years of service, plus biographical notes on some.
83. Ken Smith, email communication to author, January 20, 2023.
84. NI, *Catalog*, July 1910, 17, EHS.
85. NI, *Bulletin*, January 1909, 80–88, EHS.
86. NI Class of 1912, *Snitcher*, "Alumni Directory," 98–100, EHS.
87. NI, Class of 1912, *Snitcher*. The yearbook was produced under the auspices of the NI's talented art teacher at the time.
88. See "Alumnus Elmer Thompson: Photographer and Inventor," in Goddard, "Howling Success," 27.
89. Willis Johnson, "Annual Report of the President," 1913–1914, NYPL.
90. NDR, August 19, 1909; quoted in Schultz, "State Normal," 143.
91. Johnson, "Annual Report."
92. NI, *Catalog*, June 1912, unpaginated list of faculty (pages 55–56 assigned for convenience), EHS.
93. Ogren, *American State Normal*, 101, n35, 265.
94. Black, *Dickey County*, 66.
95. R. M. Black to Otto C. Schultz, July 5, 1946, reprinted in Schultz, "State Normal," 50–51.
96. NI, *Catalog*, June 1915, 11, EHS.

97. *Higher Educational Institutions of North Dakota*, No. 27, 1916, 90, as given in Schultz, "State Normal," 80–82.

98. Schultz, "State Normal," 84–85.

99. Ogren, *American State Normal*, esp. 40–43 and 136–39.

100. See, especially, Kridel, *Progressive Education in Black High Schools* and Pierson, *Laboratory of Learning*.

101. Educational Directory of the Public Schools of North Dakota, 1918–19, 6, https://hdl.handle.net/2027/mdp.39015076661415.

102. Herbert Goddard, "Model Rural School," DCL, December 20, 1917.

103. Deutsch, *You Need a Schoolhouse*. For a new treatment of the Rosenwald Schools, see Feiler, *A Better Life for Their Children*; for information on architectural plans for them, see Hoffschwelle, *Rosenwald Schools of the American South*.

104. An informal survey of members of the Country Schools Association of America yielded information about one in Athens, Georgia, and another in Cedar Falls, Iowa. Further, an architectural history of country schools in Gillespie County, Texas, has been compiled by Ben Shacklette, a past professor of architecture at Texas Tech in Lubbock. Titled "Sustain and Endure: A Look at the History of German Rural Schools" was published online by *Texas Architect*, March 4, 2021. Though it does not include actual floor plans, as the Ellendale school or the Rosenwald schools did, it does indicate the careful planning that went into many of these buildings. A link to a PDF of the article appears on the website for the Friends of the Gillespie County Schools: https://historicschools.org/press-releases.html. The website also includes a link to a similar article by Shacklette, "Learning from the German Country Schools of Gillespie County, Texas," that has additional information about these buildings and their use.

105. Goddard, "Dedicate Model Rural School at NI," DCL, December 20, 1917.

106. The following description is all taken from Combellick and Marsh, "Demonstration Rural School," in NI, *Bulletin*, January 1919, EHS.

107. Cremin, Shannon, and Townsend, *History of Teachers College*, 87, 109–11.

108. Cost was likely part of the reason the school failed to have a widespread impact. Though Combellick endeavored to keep expenses down, the demonstration school cost $3,700 to construct and $1,700 to equip. This was considerably more than most rural districts could afford.

109. Black, *Dickey County*, 66.

110. Ibid., 68.

111. In Dickey County, the only sizable foreign-born population was German-speaking immigrants from Russia who, after 1890, began acquiring farmland in the county's northwestern corner. Second generation members of the community began to attend the NI, and many became teachers. See Black, *Dickey County*, 309–19.

112. Omdahl, *Insurgents;* a more recent history of the movement is Lansing, *Insurgent Democracy*.

113. Omdahl, *Insurgents*, 11–20.

114. Goddard, "Editorial," DCL, October 14, 1920.
115. Smith, "Election 1920: Ellendale Politician Vied for US Senate amidst Heated Rhetoric," DCL, October 15, 2020.
116. "Edwin F. Ladd Memorial Addresses," May 9, 1926.
117. See Rylance, "A Controversial Career."
118. Smith, "Ellendale Attorney Was Hair's Breadth from the U.S. Senate in 1926," DCL, October 29, 2020.
119. *Ellendale 125th Anniversary Book*, Helen Graham Rezzato, "Fred J. Graham," 399–400.
120. Schultz, "State Normal," 119.
121. J. E. Demmer to Otto C. Schultz, July 20, 1946, quoted in Schultz, "State Normal," 87–88.
122. Schultz, "State Normal," 123–28.
123. NI, *Snitcher*, 1917, "Alumni Directory," 100–103, EHS.
124. NI, *Snitcher*, 1924–1925, 51–52, EHS.
125. Ogren, *American State Normal*, 200–209.
126. *Ellendale 125th Anniversary Book*, "Colleges," 117–18.

Chapter 6. Agency and Efficiency

1. Troen, in *The Public and the Schools: Shaping the St. Louis System*, explains these differences; see chapter 8, "New Directions," 157–83.
2. See Generals, *Booker T. Washington*, and Alridge, *Educational Thought of W. E. B. Du Bois*.
3. "Two Communications," *New Republic*, May 15, 1915, 40–44.
4. Du Bois, "Testimony to the U.S. Commission on Industrial Education."
5. Clark, "W. E. Hicks," EHS.
6. Mead, "Heckling School Board and an Educational Stateswoman," 443–44.
7. McManis, *Ella Flagg Young and a Half-Century of Chicago Schools*, provides details on this aspect of Young's leadership. The most recent article on Young's career focuses on other aspects of it; see Blount, "Individuality, Freedom, and Community." Goddard, "Ella Flagg Young's Intellectual Legacy," analyzes the latter's disagreements with other versions of "scientific" education. See also Young, "Scientific Method in Education," and "Hypothesis in Education."
8. Kliebard, *Schooled to Work*, 15.
9. The chapter's full title is "'Young Vulcans, Bare-Armed, Leather-Aproned . . . Honest Sweat': Manual Training and the American Work Ethic, 1876–1905"; the full quotation is from Calvin Woodward (Kliebard, *Schooled to Work*, 1).
10. Ham, *Manual Training*, 1–14.
11. Cremin, *Transformation of the School*, especially "Education and Industry," 23–57.
12. Krug, *Shaping of the American High School*, especially chapter 10, "The Interlude of Vocationalism," 217–48.

13. See Fisher, *Industrial Education*, and Douglas, *American Apprenticeship and Industrial Education*. The term "continuation school" does not appear in Cremin's *Transformation*, though the book does cover aspects of Wisconsin's innovative ideas about education during this period.

14. Kantor and Tyack, *Work, Youth, and Schooling*, and Lazerson and Grubb, *American Education and Vocationalism*. Also valuable due particularly to its focus on one state is Kantor, *Learning to Earn*, which is about vocational education in California.

15. Daniel Rodgers and David Tyack, "Mapping Critical Research Areas," in Kantor and Tyack, *Work, Youth, and Schooling*.

16. Krug, *American High School*, 214; Wirth, *Vocational-Liberal Studies*, 87, makes the same point. Also of interest is an article Dewey wrote in 1906, "Culture and Industry in Education."

17. Kliebard, *Schooled to Work*, 24.

18. Krug, *American High School*, 256; Dewey, 1902, "School as Social Centre."

19. Krug's discussion of this is useful; see *American High School*, 249–55.

20. Callahan, *Education and the Cult of Efficiency*.

21. Knoll, *Beyond Rhetoric*, 182–214. In "How Dewey Lost," Labaree offers a contrasting analysis of "social efficiency."

22. As suggested by this chapter's opening quotation, Young wrote "In monarchies and aristocracies it may be that the perpetuation of the particular form of government is dependent upon training the young for the station in life for which each is by the social organization destined. In this government the young cannot be trained for any particular station, for no one can foretell what that will be" (*Isolation in the School*, 110).

23. Quoted in McManis, *Ella Flagg Young*, 2.

24. Young developed this idea in the second part of her *Isolation in the School*; there, she discussed "recent constructions" of psychology in its relation to the school; see 44–88.

25. Carroll D. Wright, the noted researcher on manufacturing in Massachusetts and the first U.S. commissioner of labor, was an influential member of the commission; see Rodgers, *Work Ethic in Industrial America*, 71–74.

26. Krug, *American High School*, 216–18; see also Bennett, *A History of Manual and Industrial Education 1870 to 1917*, 513–15, and Wirth, *Vocational-Liberal Studies*, 106–12.

27. Report of the Massachusetts Commission on Industrial and Technical Education, quoted in Lazerson and Grubb, *American Education*, 69–75.

28. Some histories of labor assert that industrialists discouraged education for their workers, contending that such intelligence did not make them better employees.

29. Fisher, *Industrial Education*, 128–29.

30. Krug, *American High School*, 220–21.

31. Kingsbury, "Report of the Sub-Committee," as given in Lazerson and Grubb, *American Education*, 76–80.

32. Douglas, *American Apprenticeship*, 85. For many years a member of the faculty at the University of Chicago, Douglas also served as an advisor to the New Deal and, between 1948 and 1976, a U.S. senator from Illinois. In a poignant version of the statistics gathered by Douglas, Chicago journalist Helen Todd questioned eight hundred boys and girls working in factories nationwide; half of them claimed that their reason for working was the death or illness of their father. See Todd, "Why Children Work."

33. Hogan, "Education and the Making of the Chicago Working Class," 246.

34. Richards, from his position at Teachers College, had already been playing a significant role in defining industrial education; see Richards, "The Function of Hand Work in the School."

35. Bennett, *Manual and Industrial Training 1870 to 1917*, 515–20.

36. Kliebard, *Schooled to Work*, 40–41.

37. Krug, *American High School*, 224, in quoting from a 1907 NSPIE bulletin.

38. See Douglas, *American Apprenticeship*, 315–30; Lazerson and Grubb, "Introduction," in *American Education*, 17–21. The latter also includes excerpts from reports issued by the AFL, NAM, and the NEA.

39. Gompers, *Seventy Years of Life and Labor*; of interest is that this straightforward autobiography fails to mention NSPIE or related issues.

40. Wirth, *Vocational-Liberal Studies*, 75–82; excerpts from both AFL reports are in Lazerson and Grubb, *American Education*.

41. Both Fisher, *Industrial Education*, 120–27, and Kliebard, *Schooled to Work*, 39–44, cover the complexity of labor's response to industrial education particularly well.

42. Kliebard, *Schooled to Work*, 43–44.

43. Quoted in Kliebard, *Schooled to Work*, 43.

44. Krug, *American High School*, 225–27. Krug claimed that Eliot's unfortunate comment did appear in the meeting's official transcript.

45. Harvey Kantor, "Economic and Political Context," in Kantor and Tyack, *Work, Place, and Schooling*, 35. Kantor's source is the Report of the Commission on National Aid to Vocational Education, presented to the House of Representatives in 1914; an excerpt is in Lazerson and Grubb, *American Education*.

46. Young, "Educational Progress of Two Years," and "Proper Articulation of Technical Education within the System of Public Education."

47. Young, "Reciprocal Relations between Subject Matters in Secondary Education," "Public High School," and "New Demands on Schools."

48. Snyder, *120 Years of American Education: A Statistical Portrait*, Table 10, page 40, and table 8, page 34.

49. Krug, *American High School*, 169–93; the source for his figures is surveys conducted by the U.S. Commissioner of Education.

50. Shine, "Development of Technical Education in the Chicago High Schools," 23–24, 34–38.

51. Ibid., 37–38.

52. Cooley's administration was open to differing opinions. Young, in two

editorials, commended him for his advocacy of industrial education; see Young, "Editorial," *Educational Bi-Monthly* 3, no. 1 (October 1908): 93, and no. 4 (April 1909): 326. For a more critical view of Cooley's tenure, see Peterson, *Politics of School Reform*, 160–62; and Wrigley, *Class Politics and Public Schools*. Chapter 3 of the latter, "Conflicts over the Content of Schooling," covers Cooley's efforts in some detail.

53. Herrick, *Chicago Schools*, 105–15.

54. Young, in "Educational Notes," *Catholic Educational Review* 5 (1913): 161–62, made a strong case for the importance of individual initiative in opening doors for young people, but she also expressed patience for those not driven by ambition.

55. McManis, *Ella Flagg Young*, 184–85. Young often spoke forcefully on the importance of thinking for oneself; examples are in some of her "Editorial[s]," in *Educational Bi-Monthly*; see, e.g., vol. 2, no. 1 (October 1907): 88–90, and "The Interpreting of Data," vol. 3, no. 5 (June 1909): 425–26.

56. Young, *Annual Report to the Board of Education*, 1907, 124, quoted in Donatelli, "Contributions of Ella Flagg Young to the Educational Enterprise," 223.

57. See "Mrs. Young for School Head" CDT, July 30, 1909, and "Supt. Ella Young Is Her New Title," CDT, July 31, 1909.

58. See a report on this in "Evening Schools Hold Out Fine Chance," CDT, October 15, 1909, p. 3.

59. "Mrs. Young's First School Report Study of Grave Problems of Age," CDT, September 10, 1910; the title does not reflect the generally positive tone of the article.

60. Young, *Annual Report to the Board of Education*, 1909–1910, quoted in Shine, "Development of Technical Education," 29.

61. McManis, *Ella Flagg Young*, especially chapter 12, "Making Over a City System." Other biographies are Donatelli, "Ella Flagg Young," and Smith, *Ella Flagg Young*; both emphasize the importance she attached to vocational education.

62. Fair, in "History of Public Education in the City of Chicago," claimed total enrollment grew from 296,430 in June 1910 to 377,260 in June 1914; see Table 7, page 129.

63. Ibid., table 7, page 131; Fair's figures were all taken from the Board of Education's Annual Reports.

64. McManis, in *Ella Flagg Young*, 183, also citing Board of Education figures, gives the following: of a total membership of 27,500 (March 1914), 13,063 students were in academic programs and 14,270 in vocational programs.

65. See, for example, Young, "Editorial," *Educational Bi-Monthly* 1, no. 5 (June 1907): 468.

66. Young, "Children Should Have Industrial Education If They Don't Go to College."

67. Young, "Give Them More Vocational Training."

68. McManis, *Ella Flagg Young*, 178–79.

69. Young, *Annual Report to the Board of Education*, 1911, 126, quoted in Donatelli, "Ella Flagg Young," 363.

70. McManis, *Ella Flagg Young*, 178–85, and Donatelli, "Ella Flagg Young," 362–66, summarize the two-year programs.

71. "Urges Schooling for Girl Workers," CDT, September 28, 1909.

72. Green, "Dora Wells," in Schultz and Hast, *Women Building Chicago*, 950–53.

73. A few years after the school opened, Young gave a paper in which she pointed out that whereas women managed most of the nation's kitchens and dressmaking shops, once this work moved out of homes and into restaurants and factories, it was men who handled it, as chefs and tailors, and so on; see Young, "Industrial Training."

74. Richards's work is covered in Dreilinger, *Secret History of Home Economics*. Wells remained principal of Lucy Flower until 1933, shepherding it not only through substantial growth and its move in 1927 to an imposing building on one of the city's boulevards, but she also maintained its reputation as a school that welcomed African American girls and minimized racial tensions. See Green, "Dora Wells."

75. See Troen, *St. Louis System*, 186–88.

76. Hicks served there for six years with the title of deputy superintendent; presumably, overseeing the new high school was among his responsibilities. A distinction while there was to supervise a national spelling bee; it aroused considerable attention when an African American girl won it; see Jamie Stiehm, "A Cleveland Bee Heard Round the World," Creator's Online Syndicate, May 30, 2018. This also led to Hicks producing the popular *Champion Spelling Book*; published in 1909, it remained in print for forty years.

77. Elson, "Technical High School of Cleveland."

78. Kliebard, *Schooled to Work*, chapters 3 and 4, written with Carol Judy Kean.

79. Ibid., 88–103.

80. See Grineski, "The Midwest," and Lauck, *The Good Country*.

81. See Goddard, "Agency and Efficiency," an extensive study of newspaper coverage of industrial and vocational education programs in Chicago during Young's administration. See also Beck, "Public Schools and the Chicago Newspapers."

82. Adding potency to the Cooley controversy was the militance of Chicago's well-organized workers and the fear of them by owners of the city's industrial and manufacturing firms; see Montgomery, *Fall of the House of Labor*, especially chapter 6, "Our Time . . . Believes in Change," 257–329.

83. The paper announced the upcoming series in "Illinois Faces a Vital Problem in Trade Schools," CST, December 15, 1912, p. 1.

84. Two representative articles are "Calls Schools Undemocratic," CDT, August 5, 1910, and "Labor Man Asks Trade Courses," CDT, December 7, 1912.

85. Though the *Chicago Tribune* was widely known as a staunchly conservative

newspaper during the mid-twentieth century, it was notably progressive at the time—in 1912, it endorsed Theodore Roosevelt and his Progressive Party, for example. The *Inter Ocean* was also regarded as Republican; it had a much smaller circulation and tended to run feature articles as much as straight news. See Beck, "Public Schools and the Chicago Newspapers."

86. Cooley, "Need for Vocational Schools," in Lazerson and Grubb, *American Education*, 141–42.

87. See Rousmaniere, *Citizen Teacher*.

88. Wrigley, *Class Politics*, 79.

89. John Walker, quoted in Wrigley, *Class Politics*, 82.

90. "Mrs. Young Attacks Plan for Industrial Education," CDT, October 20, 1912. See also "Mrs. Young Fights Commercial Club School Proposal," CIO, October 20, 1912, p. 3.

91. "City Club Fosters Better School Law," CIO, December 1, 1912, p. 9.

92. Wreidt, Bogan, and Mead, "Industrial Courses and Schools in Chicago" in *Report on Vocational Training in Chicago and Other Cities*.

93. George Herbert Mead, "Gives Plan for Trade Schools," CDT, December 16, 1912. Two weeks earlier, the *Chicago Inter Ocean* ran an article that emphasized the local control aspect of the plan; see above, "City Club Fosters Better School Law."

94. "New System for Schools," CDT, September 5, 1912, p. 3. Rosenwald, the head of Sears, Roebuck & Company, was becoming known for his support of Tuskegee Institute. O. J. Kern, one of the educators on the committee, was the brother of William Kern, president of the Normal and Industrial School in North Dakota from 1905 to 1911. See note 79 in chapter 5 for more about them.

95. "More on Problem of Trade Schools," CDT, December 18, 1912, p. 8.

96. "Sumner Opposes Cooley Measure," CDT, December 19, 1912, p. 8.

97. "Officials Tell of Trade Schools," CDT, December 20, 1912, p. 10; see also Roberts, "Vocational Education."

98. "Urges Against Dual School Plan," CDT, December 21, 1912, p. 6.

99. "Needed Laws for Vocational Plan," CST, December 22, 1912, p. 6. Leavitt was also, during this time, a popular public speaker in Chicago; his name appeared frequently in newspaper articles about industrial education.

100. This claim was based on the fact that the continuation schools in Germany were administered by its minister of commerce rather than of education; see Oscar E. Hewitt, "Says American Schools Prepare Boys for 'White Shirt' Jobs Only," CST, May 19, 1912, p. 16. Hewitt's article may have led several Chicagoans to bring up the charge. Even Dewey made it in an article published in 1916; see Knoll, *Beyond Rhetoric*, 218.

101. See Hogan, *Class and Reform;* its chapter on vocationalism is particularly critical of both Cooley and continuation schools.

102. See Fitzpatrick, *McCarthy of Wisconsin,* for details on his admirable career.

103. McCarthy, *Wisconsin Idea*, 1912.

104. Complementing McCarthy's work, and a sign of the vitality of the state's effort at improving the lives of its citizens, is that of John R. Commons, who

is credited with founding the field of labor history. He arrived in Madison in 1904 and trained the first generation of labor scholars. See Laurie, *Artisans into Workers*, particularly the "Introduction" for his significance to the field.

105. Woerdehoff, "Dr. Charles McCarthy"; Woerdehoff also wrote that this "new scheme of education was founded on the conviction that education was an inherent right and should be accessible to every child ... so that each might be able to receive that education which would best enable him or her to fit and prepare themselves for a better life" (273).

106. Reber, "Industrial and Continuation Schools," 3–18.

107. Reber, "What Laws for Vocational Education Should Michigan Adopt," *NSPIE Proceedings*, 1913, 21–23, hereafter referred to as *NSPIE Proceedings 1913*.

108. "Bring Noted School Expert: Munich Educator Arrives to Be Guest of the Commercial Club," CDT, November 10, 1912, 24; and "Tells German Educational Ideals," CDT, November 12, 1910, 10.

109. Kerschensteiner, *Lectures on Vocational Education*.

110. Knoll refers to the differences between them as "two roads to culture," which is the title of his chapter about the relationship between their ideas; see *Beyond Rhetoric*, chapter 6, 213–43.

111. Douglas, *American Apprenticeship*, 268.

112. See Harvey Kantor, "Economic and Political Context," 36–38, in Kantor and Tyack, *Work, Youth, and Schooling*.

113. The Cooley Bill had been introduced to the Illinois assembly early in 1913; neither of the other bills had made it that far. Transcripts from the meeting are in *Proceedings of the Seventh Annual Meeting*, October 1913 (Peoria, IL: Manual Arts Press, 1914).

114. "Vocational Education in Michigan," *NSPIE Proceedings, 1913*, 15–65.

115. Reber, "Laws for Vocational Education," *NSPIE Proceedings, 1913*, 15–26.

116. Ibid., 26.

117. Hicks, "Annual Report of the Public Continuation Schools of Wisconsin," 14–16.

118. Dewey, "Laws for Vocational Education," *NSPIE Proceedings, 1913*, 27–33.

119. Ibid., 31. Though Dewey did not mention NSPIE by name, this was a clear endorsement of its efforts at drawing public attention to the need for industrial education in schools.

120. Hicks, "What Laws for Vocational Education Should Michigan Adopt?" *NSPIE Proceedings, 1913*, 35–39.

121. Ibid., 38–39.

122. Dean, "Continuation Education," *NSPIE Proceedings 1913*, 40–44.

123. See Roberts, "Development of Part-time Education in a Large City," *NSPIE Proceedings 1913*. Hicks, "Public Continuation Schools of Wisconsin," 10–62, includes actual reports for twenty Wisconsin cities.

124. Kett, "Theory Run Mad."

125. Snedden, "Summation of the Discussion," *NSPIE Proceedings, 1913*, 55–59.

126. Prosser made several efforts to define these beginnings at least in 1913;

some are explained in a government report; see Prosser and O'Leary, "Short-Unit Courses for Wage Earners in Part-Time and Evening Schools," published by the Bureau of Labor Statistics in 1915.

127. Wirth, *Vocational-Liberal Studies*, 223.

128. Dewey, 1915, "Industrial Education-A Wrong Kind," 71–73. This article was followed two weeks later by David Snedden, "Vocational Education," and Dewey's response, "Education vs. Trade-Training—Dr. Dewey's Reply" (1915). The latter two appeared in the *New Republic* as "Two Communications" in that May 15 issue.

129. Dewey, 1915, "Industrial Education—A Wrong Kind."

130. Snedden, "Vocational Education."

131. See "Dr. Dewey's Reply" (1915).

132. Snedden's biographer Walter Drost claimed that the former's effort at streamlining too many aspects of teacher training may have antagonized some state officials; see Drost, "Social Efficiency Reexamined," note 5.

133. Snedden, "Pros and Cons of the Gary System."

134. Knoll, *Beyond Rhetoric*, 181–214.

135. Schubert, Schubert, Thomas, and Carroll, *Curriculum Books*, 40–41.

136. Rury, "Case: Industrialism and Progressive Reform in Gary, Indiana," in *Education and Social Change*, 160–63.

137. Bobbitt, "Elimination of Waste in Education."

138. Evelyn Dewey, "Education and Industry," in Dewey and Dewey, *Schools of Tomorrow*, 126–42.

139. Dewey, *Democracy and Education*, 76.

140. Young, "Review of *Democracy and Education*."

141. Kett, "Theory Run Mad"; Kliebard, *Schooled to Work*, 46–50.

142. "Mrs. Young Opposes Race Consciousness," CIO, February 23, 1913, p. 6.

143. See Blount, "Individuality, Freedom, and Community," 193–98; and Donatelli, "Ella Flagg Young," 317–19.

144. Smith, *Ella Flagg Young*, 183–219, 222–23.

145. In "The Smith-Hughes Act of Vocational Education," *Scientific American*, August 26, 1917, provided a brief, dispassionate commentary on what the act was intended to do, p. 130.

146. See Kett's conclusions in "Theory Run Mad," 509–12.

147. Kantor, in *Learning to Earn*, offers a valuable summary of other historians' evaluations of vocational education programs; see particularly the notes on pages 171–73. The revisionist approach, which became dominant after 1970, assumes that "social control" was the aim of vocational educators; these arguments rely more on policy pronouncements than on the experiences of actual students, on the enrollment increases, or public perception in cities like Chicago.

148. In *American Education*, 28–32, 116–32, Lazerson and Grubb first discussed and then included substantial excerpts from the 1914 Report of the Commission on National Aid to Vocational Education that was presented to Congress that year. They claim that its recommendations were incorporated into the Smith-Hughes Bill with only minor revisions (116).

149. According to Kliebard, Hoke Smith, a "major force in southern politics," had been influenced to support a national version of vocational education by Wisconsin's Charles McCarthy; see *Schooled to Work*, 108.

150. Cuban, "Enduring Resiliency: Enacting and Implementing Federal Vocational Education Legislation," in Kantor and Tyack, *Work, Youth, and Schooling*.

151. Douglas, *American Apprenticeship*, 262–66, 293–306.

152. Ibid., 304.

153. Dewey, 1917, "Learning to Earn."

154. Douglas, *American Apprenticeship*, 305.

155. Snyder, *Statistical Portrait*, 11.

156. Two that are perhaps representative are Werum, "Sectionalism and Racial Politics" and Labaree, "How Dewey Lost." Relying on quantitative data, Werum argued that Smith-Hughes was a product of a southern agrarian elite and was designed to maintain its power; this view contrasts strongly with a chapter in Fisher's *Industrial Education*. The latter's "Geographic Perspective" analyses education and industry in the South before and after Smith-Hughes, 141–94. Labaree, "How Dewey Lost," claims, as its title contends, that "Dewey lost," which is a popular conception. But today's classrooms do not look like either Snedden or Prosser imagined them. See also Lagemann, "Plural Worlds of Education Research."

157. Cuban, "Enduring Resiliency," 45–47. The article also notes that few annotated bibliographies of vocational education had been produced up to that time, but he does review the major ones then available; see 49–53 and n38, p. 308. Little such work has been done since.

158. See Wirth, "Charles A. Prosser and the Smith-Hughes Act."

159. Whether the Indianapolis school offered an education appropriate to the needs of its students—was it "vocational" or "remedial," and was either a "racist" approach to their needs?—has been argued elsewhere, most notably by historians seemingly unfamiliar with the industrial education movement as a whole or of the curriculum at the school in Bordentown; see Margonis, "John Dewey's Racialized Visions of the Students and Classroom Community," and Vaughan, "Progressive Education and Racial Justice."

160. An extensive search through financial records of the state and the school could likely ascertain this, but that is outside the scope of this book.

161. Alumni directories from the NI reported the large number of graduates who became teachers of manual training; many had moved on to the West Coast; see chapter 5.

162. DCL, December 20, 1917; June 22, 1922; September 24, 1925; and May 21, 1927; these have been digitized in the EHS.

163. A recent, highly lauded book about vocational education in Boston makes a similar argument; see Groeger, *Education Trap*. It suggests that some programs offered promise of a future that was later undercut as an elite raised educational requirements for the jobs for which students thought they were being prepared. An article about Progressive Era schools in Chicago claims they were often unresponsive to students' ambitions; see Oram, "Superior Kind of Working Woman."

The implication in both is that the students studied were being subjected to a form of social reproduction and discouraged from pursuing higher education. But could it also be that the students were exercising their own agency in choosing not to further their education? See, for example, the argument in Hogan, "Education and the Making of the Chicago Working Class," which discussed why many young people chose not to attend the city's high schools.

164. Cuban, "Enduring Resiliency," 63–64, in Kantor and Tyack, *Work, Youth, and Schooling*.

165. In Kantor's introduction to the book in which Cuban's essay appears, he claims that the act had limited impact; see Kantor and Tyack, *Work, Youth, and Schooling*, 5–6.

166. Cuban, "Enduring Resiliency," 58–62.

167. Ibid., 78.

168. John Kelly, "When World War I Raged, a D.C. Professor Fought for Black Officers' Participation," *Washington Post*, February 6, 2019.

169. Rebecca Barton, Director, Governor's Commission on Human Rights, *Congressional Record-Appendix*, A790–91, February 1, 1960.

170. Labaree, "How Dewey Lost," n13, 186; it cites Wirth, "Prosser and the Smith-Hughes Act" as the source. Labaree's article also offers useful insights into these and other points of difference between Dewey and the Snedden-Prosser approach to vocational education.

Epilogue

1. Labaree's "How Dewey Lost" is immensely valuable for understanding contrasting points of view on vocational education, but it, too, is based on policy pronouncements from above rather than how these programs were worked out on the ground.

2. An exception is Selig Perlman's review of the biography of Madison's Charles McCarthy; a noted labor historian who taught at the University of Wisconsin, he said of the latter's efforts at encouraging educational innovations circa 1912 that they offered "a new version of the American democracy in action." See Perlman, "Review of *McCarthy of Wisconsin*."

3. Quoted in Laurie, *Artisans into Workers*, 211. Though no source is given for the comment, MacNeill was the author of several studies, among them *The Labor Movement: The Problem of Today*, published in 1892.

4. NSPIE, *Proceedings of the Eighth Annual Meeting*, Richmond, December 9–12, 1914, 12. Published by the Society and available in Google Books.

5. See note 76 in chapter 6; Hicks's remark on that occasion was quoted four decades later in an article about him. He said: "The point is, in our schools every boy and every girl has an equal chance," see Matheson, "City Man, 84, Honored by College He Helped to Found 50 years Ago." Realistically, Hicks's remark suggests good intentions more than the actual situation in schools.

6. Green, "Dora Wells," in Schultz and Hast, *Women Building Chicago*, 950–53.

7. Young, *Isolation in the School,* 101. There is limited record of Young's attitude toward African Americans, but a story told me informally by a historian of Black Chicago indicated that while Young was superintendent, some white students wanted to exclude Black students from the spring prom, Young's response was to say that if all students were not welcome, the dance would not be held.

8. Arthur Wirth, in *Vocational-Liberal Studies,* did mention this anomaly; see 87–89, where he referred to "reluctance to talk about the real problems of black people in the work world."

9. Krug, *American High School,* 209, 322. Jones's *Negro Education,* funded by the Phelps-Stokes Fund, is discussed in chapter 4.

10. Du Bois, "Negro Education." Du Bois's objections are repeated in works such as Watkins, *White Architects of Black Education,* and Pierson, *Laboratory of Learning.*

11. Du Bois, "Education and Work."

12. Ibid., 63–64, 68.

13. Ibid., 70, 72.

14. See Burkholder, "Integrated Out of Existence," 57–58 and n42.

15. From the author's email correspondence with Larry Hickman, October 2020, former head of the Dewey Center at Southern Illinois University, and a brief record kept by John Medley, archivist for MTIS.

16. Alridge, *The Educational Thought of W. E. B. Du Bois,* 41–42.

17. Seinfel, "N.J. Negro School Makes Its Own World."

18. Brawley, "'Ironsides': The Bordentown School."

19. "Princeton University Survey," MTIS Papers.

20. Davidson, *Place Out of Time.*

21. See Hodges, *Black New Jersey.* Though it mentions MTIS only in passing, it provides considerable insight into the varied communities in which African Americans lived and their priorities.

22. Compiled from various sources; most are given in Goddard, "Bordentown School as Institution and Idea."

23. Wright, *Education of Negroes in New Jersey.* After completing her doctorate, Wright joined the faculty at Howard University. In a report written in March 1954, MTIS's then-principal wrote that 30 percent of the school's graduates enrolled in institutions of higher learning; see James E. Seager, typescript, in "Philosophy Folder," MTIS Papers.

24. For an excellent discussion of this, see Burkholder, "'Integrated Out of Existence.'" Further, Douglas in *Jim Crow Moves North,* 240–41, 227, claimed that some advocates of school integration felt Valentine was impeding their efforts.

25. Streator, "Aids Negro Youth," NYT, November 14, 1948.

26. "Jersey to Close All-Negro School," NYT, December 18, 1954, p. 17.

27. "Public Hearing to Investigate Proposed Closing of the Bordentown School," NJSL.

28. "Meyner in Dispute," NYT, June 3, 1955, 11.

29. "Closing Exercises," June 12, 1955, MTIS Papers.
30. Jordan, *Reclaiming African-American Students*, 112–14.
31. For compilations, see Hall, *Black Vocational, Technical, and Industrial Arts Education*, and Roach, "Rich but Disappearing Legacy," 18–24.
32. This is based on the comprehensive list in Ogren, *American State Normal School*; for a history of the Aberdeen school, see *Northern State University: The First Century, 1901–2000* (Aberdeen: Northern State University Press, 2001).
33. The most extensive list is in Charles Ham, *Mind and Hand*, "Appendices."
34. Goddard, "Unprecedented Yet Unheralded," tells this little-known story; it deserves more recognition. See also Theobald, *Call School*, for insight into how schooling evolved in that part of the country now known as the Midwest.
35. Ogren, *American State Normal*, 155–57.
36. See chapter 5, note 111 and accompanying discussion, for details on Dickey County population.
37. *Snitcher*, 1925, 89.
38. CUNY-TV, "African-American Legends: 'The Bordentown School,' with Dave Davidson and Arthur Symes," YouTube video, July 13, 2010, https://youtu.be/gilR9b-iqPs.
39. "How Equal Was This Separate School?" NYT, Monday, May 24, 2010, C2.
40. I conducted this survey when first studying the school's history in 2018.
41. The latter is Brown and Robinson, *Serving Negro Schools*. The 2015 book is a compilation of interviews with graduates of the schools that participated in the 1940s study, compiled by Craig Kridel and titled *Progressive Education in Black High Schools*. In a 2018 email to this author, Kridel wrote that he'd seen no mention of MTIS in any of Brown and Robinson's work.
42. Anderson, "Historical Development of Black Vocational Education," in Kantor and Tyack, *Work, Youth, and Schooling*, 201, 209.
43. See Jordan, *Reclaiming African-American Students*, which suggests this.
44. A Wikipedia article about Tappan also claimed that his summer home in New Haven was burned down as a result of his proposal for the school for Black students.
45. For an introduction to Sennett, I want to acknowledge a paper given by Dewey scholar Kevin Decker at a John Dewey Society Conference in October 2023. The interpretation offered here is my own, but my study of Sennett's work and its implications for industrial education today was stimulated by Decker's paper. As John Ruskin's suggestion that work should be made for man rather than man for work drove the New Industrialism of a century ago, Sennett's pragmatic rather than romantic ideas might drive industrial education today.
46. The last chapter of Sennett's *The Craftsman* focuses on pragmatism and claims that it enables a more fruitful connection between means and ends, between the competence to do the "how" and the ability to ask the "why." A pragmatic attitude encourages the craftsman to pause and reflect on what he (or she) is doing; see pages 294–96.

Bibliography

This Bibliography is divided into three sections: "Books"; "Articles in Periodicals and Chapters in Books"; and "Unpublished Materials"; the latter includes dissertations, conference papers, archival materials, and some government reports. The archives in which these sources can be found are listed in that section.

The endnotes for each of the chapters use short titles to works cited; the only exceptions are those to a work cited only once. In the latter case, a full reference is given in the endnote itself. If a book or article is readily available in an online source, such as Google Books, HathiTrust, or the Internet Archive, that is indicated if known. For some chapters in edited collections that are of significance to the arguments made, a reference to it is in the Articles section, with a full reference in the Books section. Articles from newspapers are, with a few exceptions, given only in the notes. Most are available online, either via Newspapers.com or, in the case of the *Dickey County Leader*, via www.bit.ly./dclarchive.

Abbreviations for newspapers and for archives from which some materials have been taken are in the Articles and the Unpublished Materials sections.

Articles by Ella Flagg Young and John Dewey are listed separately in the Articles section; their books are integrated into the Books section.

Books

Abzug, Robert. *Passionate Liberator: Theodore Dwight Weld and the Dilemma of Reform*. New York: Oxford University Press, 1980.

Alexander, S. L. *T. Thomas Fortune, the Afro-American Agitator: A Collection of Writings, 1880–1928*. Gainesville: University Press of Florida, 2008.

———. *W. E. B. Du Bois: An American Intellectual and Activist*. Lanham, MD: Rowman and Littlefield, 2015.

Alridge, Derrick P. *The Educational Thought of W. E. B. Du Bois: An Intellectual History*. New York: Teachers College Press, 2008.

Anderson, James. *The Education of Blacks in the South, 1860–1935*. Chapel Hill: University of North Carolina Press, 1988.
Anderson, Lewis F. *History of Manual and Industrial School Education*. New York: Appleton, 1926.
Ayers, Leonard. *Laggards in Our Schools*. New York: Charities Publication Committee, 1909.
Barrows, Isabel C., ed. *Mohonk Conferences on the Negro Question*. Reprint. New York: Negro Universities Press, 1969. Also available through the Internet Archive.
Beck, Paul N. *Columns of Vengeance: Soldiers, Sioux, and the Punitive Expeditions, 1863–1864*. Norman: University of Oklahoma Press, 2014.
Beecher, Lyman. *A Plea for the West* and *A Plea for the Colleges*. Cincinnati: Truman and Smith, 1835 and 1836.
Bennett, Charles A. *History of Manual and Industrial Training to 1870*. Peoria, IL: Manual Arts Press, 1926.
———. *History of Manual and Industrial Education, 1870 to 1917*. Peoria, IL: Manual Arts Press, 1937.
Black, R[yland]. M. *The History of Dickey County*. Ellendale, ND: Dickey County Historical Association, 1930. Available online through the Internet Archive.
Boris, Eileen. *Art and Labor: Ruskin, Morris, and the Craftsman Ideal in America*. Philadelphia: Temple University Press, 1986.
Brickman, William W. *Dewey's Legacy in Chicago*. New York: Atherton Press, 1960.
Brown, William H., and William Robinson. *Serving Negro Schools: The Secondary School Study*. Atlanta: Association of Schools and Colleges for Negroes, 1946.
Bullock, Henry Allan. *A History of Negro Education in the South from 1619 to the Present*. Cambridge, MA: Harvard University Press, 1967.
Callahan, Raymond E. *Education and the Cult of Efficiency: A Study of the Social Forces That Have Shaped the Administration of Public Schools*. Chicago: University of Chicago Press, 1962.
Campbell, Jack. *Colonel Francis W. Parker: The Children's Crusader*. New York: Teachers College Press, 1967.
Clawson, Marion, *Man and Land in the United States*. Lincoln: University of Nebraska Press, 1968.
Crawford, Matthew B. *Shop Class as Soulcraft: An Inquiry into the Value of Work*. New York: Penguin Press, 2008.
Cremin, Lawrence. *American Education: The Colonial Experience, 1607–1783*. New York: Harper Torchbooks, 1970.
———. *American Education: The National Experience, 1783–1876*. New York: Harper Torchbooks, 1980.
———. *American Education: The Metropolitan Experience, 1876–1980*. New York: Harper and Row, 1988.
———. *Transformation of the School*. New York: Vintage Books, 1964.
Cremin, Lawrence, David A. Shannon, and Mary Townsend. *A History of Teachers College, Columbia University*. New York: Columbia University Press, 1954.

Currarino, Roseanne. *The Labor Question in America: Economic Democracy in the Gilded Age.* Champaign: University of Illinois Press, 2011.

Dahl, Adam. *Empire of the People: Settler Colonialism and the Foundations of Modern Democratic Thought.* Lawrence: University Press of Kansas, 2018.

Davidson, Dave, dir. *A Place Out of Time: The Bordentown School.* Documentary video. Bethel, CT: Hudson West Productions, 2009.

Davis, Deborah. *Guest of Honor: Booker T. Washington, Theodore Roosevelt, and the White House Dinner that Shocked a Nation.* New York: Atria Books, 2012.

Deutsch, Stephanie. *You Need a Schoolhouse: Booker T. Washington, Julius Rosenwald, and the Building of Schools for a Segregated South.* Evanston, IL: Northwestern University Press, 2011.

Dewey, John. *The Child and the Curriculum and The School and Society.* Reprinted; the individual volumes were originally printed in 1902 and 1900, respectively. Chicago: University of Chicago Press, 1956.

———. *Democracy and Education* (1916). Reprinted. New York: The Free Press, 1966.

Dewey, John and Evelyn. *Schools of Tomorrow* (1915). Reprinted. Grindl Press, 2016. Also available at Google Books, accessed October 11, 2023. https://www.google.com/books/edition/Schools_of_To_morrow/8MUVAAAAIAAJ.

Dodge, Chester. *Reminiscences of a School Master.* Chicago: Ralph Fletcher Seymour, 1941.

Douglas, Davison. *Jim Crow Moves North: The Battle over Northern School Integration, 1896–1954.* New York: Cambridge University Press, 2005.

Douglas, Paul H. *American Apprenticeship and Industrial Education.* New York: Columbia University Press, 1921. Chapter 8 was also published in *Political Science Quarterly*, December 1920.

Dreilinger, Danielle. *The Secret History of Home Economics: How Trailblazing Women Harnessed the Power of Home and Changed the Way We Live.* New York: W. W. Norton, 2021.

Du Bois, W. E. B., ed. *The Negro Artisan.* Atlanta: Atlanta University Press, 1902.

———. *Souls of Black Folk* (1903). New York: Bantam Books, 1989.

Du Bois, W. E. B., and Augustus Granville Dill, eds. *The Negro-American Artisan.* Atlanta University Press, 1912.

Dykstra, Henry, ed. *Permanent School Fund in South Dakota and the Beadle Club.* Aberdeen, SD: North Plains Press, 1976.

Ellendale 125th Anniversary Book, 1882–2007. Ellendale, ND: J and M Printing, 2007. A noncirculating copy is available at the Ellendale Public Library and through EHS.

Fallace, Thomas. *Dewey and the Dilemma of Race: An Intellectual History, 1895–1922.* New York: Teachers College Press, 2011.

Feiler, Andrew. *A Better Life for Their Children: Julius Rosenwald, Booker T. Washington, and the 4,978 Schools That Changed America.* Athens: University of Georgia Press, 2021.

Fish, Herbert Clay, and R. M. Black, *A Brief History of North Dakota.* Chicago: American Book Company, 1925. Available through the Internet Archive.

Fisher, Berenice. *Industrial Education: American Ideals and Institutions*. Madison: University of Wisconsin Press, 1967.
Fitzpatrick, Edward A. *McCarthy of Wisconsin*. New York: Columbia University Press, 1944.
Fletcher, Robert Samuel. *A History of Oberlin College from Its Foundation to the Civil War*. Oberlin: By the College, 1943. Available through the Internet Archive.
Fortune, T. Thomas. *Black and White: Land, Labor, and Politics in the South*. 1884. Reprint. New York: Arno Press, 1968.
Fraser, Caroline. *Prairie Fires: The American Dreams of Laura Ingalls Wilder*. New York: Henry Holt and Company, 2017.
Gamber, Wendy. *The Female Economy: The Millinery and Dressmaking Trades, 1860–1930*. Champaign: University of Illinois Press, 1997.
Gates, Paul W. *Landlords and Tenants on the Prairie Frontier: Studies in American Land Policy*. Ithaca, NY: Cornell University Press, 1973.
Geffken, Rick. *Stories of Slavery in New Jersey*. Charleston, SC: The History Press, 2021.
Generals, Donald, Jr. *Booker T. Washington: Architect of Progressive Education*. Houston: Strategic Book Publishing, 2013.
Gompers, Samuel. *Seventy Years of Life and Labor: An Autobiography*. 1925. Reprint. Ithaca: ILR Press at Cornell University, 1984.
Green, Elizabeth Alden. *Mary Lyon and Mount Holyoke*, 1887. Reprint. Hanover, NH: University Press of New England, 1979.
Greenidge, Kerri K. *Black Radical: The Life and Times of William Monroe Trotter*. New York: Liveright, 2020.
———. *The Grimkes: The Legacy of Slavery in an American Family*. New York: W. W. Norton, 2022. (The author omits the accent over the family name.)
Griffith, Elisabeth. *In Her Own Right: The Life of Elizabeth Cady Stanton*. New York: Oxford University Press, 1984.
Griscom, John. *A Year in Europe Comprising a Journal of Observations*. Two volumes. New York: Collins and Company, 1823 and 1824. Available in Google Books.
Groeger, Cristina. *The Education Trap: Schools and the Meaning of Inequality*. Cambridge, MA: Harvard University Press, 2021.
Grossman, James R., Ann Durkin Keating, and Janice L. Reiff, eds. *Encyclopedia of Chicago History*. Chicago: University of Chicago Press, 2004.
Hall, Clyde. *Black Vocational, Technical, and Industrial Arts Education: Development and History*. Chicago: American Technical Society, 1973. A copy is available in the Schomberg Collection, NYPL.
Ham, Charles H. *Manual Training: The Solution of Social and Industrial Problems*. New York: Harper and Brothers, 1886. Available in Google Books.
———. *Mind and Hand: Manual Training, The Chief Factor in Education*. New York: American Book Company, 1900. Available in Google Books.
Harlan, Louis R. *Booker T. Washington: The Making of a Black Leader, 1856–1901*. New York: Oxford University Press, 1972.

Harrison, Elizabeth. *Sketches along Life's Road*. Boston: Stratford Company, 1930.
Harrison, Gilbert A. *A Timeless Affair: The Life of Anita McCormick Blaine*. Chicago: University of Chicago Press, 1979.
Heise, Kenan. *The Chicagoization of America, 1893–1917*. Evanston, IL: Chicago Historical Bookworks, 1990.
Herrick, Mary L. *The Chicago Schools: A Social and Political History*. Beverly Hills, CA: Sage Publications, 1971.
Hicks, Warren. *Champion Spelling Book*. New York: American Book Company, 1909. Initially published in two parts, this book is widely available from used book dealers.
Hodges, Graham Russell Gao. *Black New Jersey: 1664 to the Present Day*. New Brunswick, NJ: Rutgers University Press, 2019.
Hoffschwelle, Mary. *The Rosenwald Schools of the American South*. Gainesville: University of Florida Press, 2006.
Hogan, David. *Class and Reform: School and Society in Chicago, 1880–1930*. Philadelphia: University of Pennsylvania Press, 1985.
Hudson, John. *Plains Country Towns*. Minneapolis: University of Minnesota Press, 1985.
Huxtable, Ada Louise. *Frank Lloyd Wright: A Life*. New York: Penguin Books, 2004.
James, William. *Talks to Teachers on Psychology*. New York: Henry Holt and Company, 1925.
Jones, Thomas Jesse, ed. *Negro Education*. Two volumes. Washington, DC: Government Printing Office, 1917. Available in Google Books.
Jordan, Mildred L. Rice. *Reclaiming African-American Students: Legacies, Lessons, and Prescriptions, The Bordentown School Model*. Bloomington, IN: iUniverse, 2017.
Jorgensen, Elizabeth and Henry. *Thorstein Veblen: Victorian Firebrand*. Lanham, MD: Routledge, 1999.
Kantor, Harvey. *Learning to Earn: School, Work, and Vocational Reform in California, 1880–1930*. Madison: University of Wisconsin Press, 1988.
Kantor, Harvey, and David Tyack, eds. *Work, Youth, and Schooling: Historical Perspectives on Vocationalism in American Education*. Palo Alto, CA: Stanford University Press, 1982.
Kerschensteiner, Georg M. *Lectures on Vocational Education*. Chicago: Commercial Club, 1911.
Kliebard, Herbert. *Schooled to Work: Vocationalism and the American Curriculum, 1876–1946*. New York: Teachers College Press, 1999.
Knight, Louise W. *Citizen: Jane Addams and the Struggle for Democracy*. Chicago: University of Chicago Press, 2005.
Knoll, Michael. *Beyond Rhetoric: New Perspectives on John Dewey's Pedagogy*. Bern: Peter Lang, 2022.
Kridel, Craig. *Progressive Education in Black High Schools: The Secondary Schools Study, 1940–1946*. Columbia: Museum of Education, University of South Carolina, 2015.

Krug, Edward A. *The Shaping of the American High School*. New York: Harper and Row, 1964.

Lansing, Michael. *Insurgent Democracy: The Nonpartisan League in North American Politics*. Chicago: University of Chicago Press, 2015.

Lauck, Jon. *The Good Country: A History of the American Midwest, 1800–1900*. Norman: University of Oklahoma Press, 2022.

Laurie, Bruce. *Artisans into Workers: Labor in Nineteenth-Century America*. New York: Hill and Wang, 1989.

Lazerson, Marvin, and W. Norton Grubb, eds. *American Education and Vocationalism: A Documentary History, 1870–1970*. New York: Teachers College Press, 1974.

Lewis, David Levering. *W. E. B. Du Bois: Biography of a Race, 1868–1914*. New York: Henry Holt and Co., 1993.

Logan, Rayford, *The Negro in American Life and Thought: The Nadir, 1877–1901*. New York: Dial Press, 1954.

Lurie, Maxine N., and Marc Mappen, eds. *Encyclopedia of New Jersey*. New Brunswick: Rutgers University Press, 2005.

Mayhew, Katherine Camp, and Anna Camp Edwards. *The Dewey School*. New York: Appleton-Century Company, 1936. Reprint. New Brunswick, NJ: Aldine Transaction Publishers, 2007.

McCarthy, Charles. *The Wisconsin Idea*. New York: Macmillan, 1912.

McManis. John. *Ella Flagg Young and a Half-Century of Chicago Schools*. Chicago: A. C. McClurg and Company, 1916.

Meier, August. *Negro Thought in America, 1880–1915*. Ann Arbor: University of Michigan Press, 1966.

Menand, Louis. *The Metaphysical Club: A Story of Ideas in America*. New York: Farrar, Straus, and Giroux, 2001.

Miller, Donald. *The City of the Century: The Epic of Chicago and the Making of America*. New York: Simon and Schuster, 1996.

Montgomery, David. *The Fall of the House of Labor: The Workplace, the State, and American Labor Activism, 1865–1925*. New York: Cambridge University Press, 1987.

Moore, Susanna. *Paradise of the Pacific: Approaching Hawai'i*. New York: Farrar, Straus, and Giroux, 2015.

National Society for the Promotion of Industrial Education. *Proceedings of the Seventh Annual Meeting*. October 1913. Peoria, IL: Manual Arts Press, 1914. Available in Google Books. Papers that were part of this conference are included in the "Articles" section; the title of the collection is abbreviated *NSPIE Proceedings, 1913*.

Newman, Katherine S., and Hella Winston. *Reskilling America: Learning to Labor in the Twenty-First Century*. New York: Metropolitan Books, 2016.

Norrell, Robert J. *Up from History: The Life of Booker T. Washington*. Cambridge, MA: Harvard University Press, 2009.

Ogren, Christine. *The American State Normal School: "An Instrument of Great Good."* New York: Palgrave Macmillan, 2005.

Omdahl, Lloyd B. *Insurgents: The Battle over the Nonpartisan League.* Brainerd, MN: Dakota Territory Centennial Edition, 1961.

Peabody, Francis Greenwood. *Education for Life: The Story Hampton Institute.* Garden City, NY: Doubleday, Page and Company, 1918. Available in Google Books.

Perry, Mark. *Lift Up Thy Voice: The Grimké Family's Journey from Slaveholders to Civil Rights Leaders.* New York: Viking, 2001.

Peterson, Paul E. *The Politics of School Reform, 1870–1940.* Chicago: University of Chicago Press, 1985.

Pierson, Sharon Gay. *Laboratory of Learning: HBCU Laboratory School and Alabama State College Lab High in the Era of Jim Crow.* New York: Peter Lang, 2014.

Rice, Joseph Meyer. *The Public-School System of the United States.* New York: The Century Company, 1893.

Rice, Susan. *Tough Love: My Story of the Things Worth Fighting For.* New York: Simon and Schuster, 2020.

Robinson, Elwyn B. *A History of North Dakota.* Lincoln: University of Nebraska Press, 1966.

Rodgers, Daniel T. *The Work Ethic in Industrial America, 1850–1920.* Chicago: University of Chicago Press, 1974.

Roeder, Larry, and Barry Harrelson. *Dirt Don't Burn: A Black Community's Struggle for Educational Equality under Segregation.* Washington, DC: Georgetown University Press, 2023.

Rousmaniere, Kate. *Citizen Teacher: The Life and Leadership of Margaret Haley.* Albany: State University of New York Press, 2005.

Rozum, Molly P. *Grasslands Grown: Creating Place on the U.S. Northern Plains and Canadian Prairies.* Lincoln: University of Nebraska Press, 2021.

Runkle, John D. *The Manual Element in Education.* Boston: A. J. Wright, 1878.

Rury, John L. *Education and Social Change.* Mahwah, NJ: Lawrence Erlbaum Associates, 2002.

Rury, John L. and Shirley Hill. *The African-American Struggle for Secondary Education, 1940–1980: Closing the Graduation Gap.* New York: Teachers College Press, 2011.

Sennett, Richard. *The Culture of the New Capitalism.* New Haven, CT: Yale University Press, 2006.

——. *The Craftsman.* New Haven, CT: Yale University Press, 2008.

Schubert, William H., Ann Lynn Lopez Schubert, Thomas P. Thomas, and Wayne M. Carroll. *Curriculum Books: The First Hundred Years.* 2nd edition. New York: Peter Lang, 2002.

Schneirov, Richard. *Labor and Urban Politics: Class Conflict and the Origins of Modern Liberalism in Chicago.* Urbana: University of Illinois Press, 1998.

Schreiner, Samuel A., Jr. *The Passionate Beechers: A Family Saga of Sanctity and Scandal That Changed America.* New York: John Wiley and Sons, 2003.

Schultz, Rima Lunin, and Adele Hast, eds. *Women Building Chicago: A Biographical Dictionary.* Bloomington: Indiana University Press, 2001.

Smith, Joan K. *Ella Flagg Young: Portrait of a Leader*. Ames, IA: Educational Studies Press, 1979.

Snyder, Thomas D. *120 Years of American Education: A Statistical Portrait*. Washington, DC: National Center for Educational Statistics, 1993.

Springer, Marguerite Warren, ed. *The New Industrialism*. Chicago: National League of Industrial Art, 1902. Available in Google Books.

Steffes, Tracy L. *School, Society, and State: A New Education to Govern Modern America*. Chicago: University of Chicago Press, 2012.

Stewart, Jeffrey C. *The "New Negro": The Life of Alain Locke*. New York: Oxford University Press, 2018.

Storr, Richard J. *Harper's University: The Beginnings*. Chicago: University of Chicago Press, 1966.

Stowe, Calvin E. *Report on the Elementary Education in Europe*. New York: Harper and Row, 1837. Available online at the New York Public Library.

Syphax, Tracey. *From the Block to the Boardroom*. Trenton, NJ: Privately published, 2012.

Talbott, Edith Armstrong. *Samuel Chapman Armstrong: A Biographical Study*. New York: Doubleday, Page, and Company, 1904. Available in Google Books.

Tanner, Laurel N. *Dewey's Laboratory School: Lessons for Today*. New York: Teachers College Press, 1997.

Taylor, Frederick. *Principles of Scientific Management*. New York: Harper, 1911.

Theobald, Paul. *Call School: Rural Education in the Midwest to 1918*. Carbondale: Southern Illinois University Press, 1995.

Thornbrough, Emma Lou. *T. Thomas Fortune: Militant Journalist*. Chicago: University of Chicago Press, 1972.

Troen, Selwyn K. *The Public and the Schools: Shaping the St. Louis System, 1838–1920*. Columbia: University of Missouri Press, 1973.

Tyack, David B. *The One Best System: A History of American Urban Education*. Cambridge, MA: Harvard University Press, 1974.

University and the City: A Centennial View of the University of Chicago. Chicago: University of Chicago Library, 1992. A catalog was published in a limited edition to accompany a centennial exhibition hosted by the library's Department of Special Collections.

Washington, Booker T. *Up from Slavery* (1902). Reprinted. New York: Signet Classic Edition, 2000.

Watkins, William H. *White Architects of Black Education: Ideology and Power in America, 1865–1954*. New York: Teachers College Press, 2001.

Weld, Theodore. *First Annual Report of the Society for Promoting Manual Labor in Literary Institutions*. New York: S.W. Benedict and Co., 1833. Available online at the Internet Archive.

———. *American Slavery as It Is: Testimony of a Thousand Witnesses*. New York: American Anti-Slavery Society, 1839.

Wirth, Arthur. *The Vocational-Liberal Studies Controversy Between John Dewey and Others*. Washington, DC: U.S. Office of Education, 1970. Available online at ERIC, https://files.eric.ed.gov/fulltext/ED051002.pdf. This is also available as a book, but page numbers refer to the 1970 report. See also Wirth, *Education in a Technological Society: The Vocational-Liberal Studies Controversy in the Early Twentieth Century*. Scranton, PA: Intext Educational Publishers, 1972.

Woodward, Calvin M. *The Manual Training School: Comprising a Full Statement of Its Aims, Methods, and Results*. Boston: D. C. Heath and Co., 1887. Available at the Internet Archive.

———. *Manual Training in Education*. New York: Scribner and Welford, 1890. Available in Google Books.

Wreidt, Ernst A., William J. Bogan, and George Herbert Mead. *A Report on Vocational Training in Chicago and Other Cities*. Chicago: City Club of Chicago, 1912.

Wright, Marion Thompson. *The Education of Negroes in New Jersey*. New York: Bureau of Publications, Teachers College, 1941.

Wrigley, Julia. *Class Politics and Public Schools, Chicago 1900–1950*. New Brunswick, NJ: Rutgers University Press, 1982.

Young, Ella Flagg. *Isolation in the School*. Chicago: University of Chicago Press, 1901.

———. *Some Types of Modern Educational Theory*. Chicago: University of Chicago Press, 1902.

Articles in Periodicals and Chapters in Books

A substantial amount of material in this book has come from historical newspapers; that from the *Chicago Tribune* and the *Inter Ocean* have been accessed via www.newspapers.com. The *Dickey County Leader*, which has been published continually since 1882, has been digitized; past issues are available at www.bit.ly./dclarchive. However, many of the articles and editorials from which information and quotations have been taken are also available in other sources. The 1947 thesis by Otto Schultz, for example, includes many articles and editorials from the *Leader* and from the *North Dakota Record*; the latter was published from 1894 until 1916.

Other newspaper articles are in various archives; those are indicated in the endnote references themselves. Newspaper names are abbreviated in the notes as indicated below. In the notes, these are cited as Writer (if known), Title (if known), Name of paper (abbreviated as below), date of publication, and page number (if known). In those cases where a newspaper is responsible for only one reference, complete information is given in the note itself.

CDT: Chicago Daily Tribune
CIO: Inter Ocean (published in Chicago)
CST: Chicago Sunday Tribune
DCL: Dickey County Leader (in Ellendale, ND)
NYA: New York Age (New York City)
NYT: New York Times
NDR: North Dakota Record (in Ellendale, ND)

As several articles that appear as chapters in books are frequently referred to, these are cited below by the name of the writer and the author or editor of the book in which the article appears. A full reference for the latter is given in the "Books" section above.

Alridge, Derrick P. "Conceptualizing a Du Boisean Philosophy of Education: Toward a Model for African-American Education." *Educational Theory* 49, no. 3 (Summer 1999): 359–79.

Anderson, James D. "The Historical Development of Black Vocational Education," in Kantor and Tyack, *Work, Youth, and Schooling*.

"An Authoritative Definition of Manual Training." *Science* 13, no. 309 (January 4, 1889): 9–10.

Ball, Frank. "Manual Training." *Elementary School Record* 1, no. 7 (1900): 177–85.

Barth, Aaron T. "Imagining a Battlefield as a Civil War Mistake: The Public History of Whitestone Hill, 1863–2013." *Public Historian* 35, no. 3 (August 2013): 72–97.

Beck, John M. "The Public Schools and the Chicago Newspapers, 1890–1920." *School Review* 62, no. 5 (May 1954): 288–95.

Belfield, Henry H. "Manual Training in the Public School." *Educational Monographs* 1, no. 1 (January 1888): 16–24. Available in Google Books.

———. "The New Education." *Hand and Brain* 2 (May 1885): 1–4. Available in CMTS Records.

Beyer, Carl Kalani. "Manual and Industrial Education for Hawaiians During the 19th Century." *Hawaiian Journal of History* 33 (2004): 11–28.

———. "The White Architects of Hawaiian Education." *American Educational History Journal* 442, no. 2 (2017): 1–18.

Blount, Jackie M. "Ella Flagg Young and the Gender Politics of *Democracy and Education*." *Journal of the Gilded Age and Progressive Era* 16 (2017): 409–23.

———. "Individuality, Freedom, and Community: Ella Flagg Young's Quest for Teacher Empowerment." *History of Education Quarterly* 58, no. 2 (May 2018): 175–98.

Bobbitt, John Franklin. "The Elimination of Waste in Education." *Elementary School Teacher* 12 (February 1912): 259–71.

Brawley, Benjamin. "'Ironsides': The Bordentown School." *The Southern Workman* 60 (October 1931): 410–16.

Briggs, Harold E. "Settlement and Economic Development of the Territory of Dakota." *South Dakota Historical Review* Spring/Summer 1936: 151–66.

Burkholder, Zoë. "'Integrated Out of Existence': African American Debates over School Integration versus Separation at the Bordentown School in New Jersey, 1886–1955." *Journal of Social History* 51, no. 1 (Fall 2017): 47–79.

Butler, Nicholas Murray. *The Argument for Manual Training*. Address delivered to the American Institute for Instruction, July 12, 1888. Chicago: E. L. Kellogg & Co., 1888. This talk also appeared as "Educational Leaflet # 1" (November 1, 1887), pages 1–15, Industrial Education Association. The former is available on the Internet Archive.

"Chicago Manual Training School." *Scientific American,* March 19, 1887: 180.
Chittick, Douglas, and James Schooler. "The Story of School Lands." In Dykstra, *Permanent School Fund.*
Clark, Jim. "W. E. Hicks, Vocational Education Pioneer, Still Active at 91." This article was published in a Wisconsin newspaper; copy available in EHS.
Cooley, Edwin. "Need for Vocational Schools." *Educational Review* 64 (1912): 49–54. An excerpt appears in Lazerson and Grubb, *American Education and Vocationalism,* 141–42.
Crawford, Matthew B. "Shop Class as Soulcraft." *The New Atlantis* 13 (Summer 2006): 7–24.
Cuban, Larry. "Enduring Resiliency: Enacting and Implementing Federal Vocational Education Legislation." In Kantor and Tyack, *Work, Youth, and Schooling.*
Dean, Arthur. "State-wide Compulsory Continuation Education." *NSPIE Proceedings, 1913:* 40–53.
DeFalco, Anthony. "An Analysis of John Dewey's Notion of Occupations: Still Pedagogically Valuable?" *Education and Culture* 26, no. 1 (2010): 82–99.
———. "Dewey and Vocational Education: Still Timely?" *The Journal of School and Society* 3, no. 1 (2016): 54–64. This entire issue is dedicated to contemporary vocational education programs.
Dewey, Evelyn. "Education Through Industry" and "The School as Social Settlement." In Dewey and Dewey, *Schools of Tomorrow.*
Dewey, Jane. "Biography of John Dewey." In Paul Arthur Schilpp and Lewis Edward Hahn, eds., *The Philosophy of John Dewey.* LaSalle, IL: Open Court Publishing Company, 1970.
Drost, Walter H. "Social Efficiency Reexamined: The Dewey-Snedden Controversy." *Curriculum Inquiry* 7, no. 1 (Spring 1977): 19–32.
Du Bois, W. E. B. "Education and Work." *Journal of Negro Education* 1, no. 1 (April 1932): 60–74.
———. "Negro Education." *The Crisis* 15, no. 4 (February 1918): 173–78.
Durst, Anne. "The 'Union of Intellectual Freedom and Cooperation': Learning from the University of Chicago's Laboratory School Community, 1896–1904." *Teachers College Record* 107, no. 5 (May 2005): 958–984.
Eastman, George. "John Dewey: Teacher and Friend." In *Great Companions: Critical Memoirs of Some Famous Friends.* New York: Farrar, Straus, and Cudahy, 1959.
Elson, William H. "The Technical High School of Cleveland." *School Review* 16, no. 6 (June 1908): 353–59.
Fallace, Thomas, and Victoria Fantozzi. "The Dewey School as Triumph, Tragedy, and Misunderstood: Exploring the Myths and Historiography of the University of Chicago Laboratory School." *Teachers College Record* 119 (February 2017): 1–32.
"Fellenberg, Philipp Emanuel von." Britannica.com, June 23, 2021. Accessed October 13, 2023. https://www.britannica.com/biography/Philipp-Emanuel-von-Fellenberg.

Fishel, Leslie H. Jr. "The Negro Question at Mohonk: Microcosm, Mirage, and Message," *New York History*, July 1993, 277–85.

Floyd, Barbara. "The Cultured Mind and the Skillful Hand: Manual Training Schools and the Democratization of the Arts and Crafts Movement." *American Educational History Journal* 32, no. 1 (2005): 44–50.

Fortune, T. Thomas. "False Theory of Education [as a] Cause of Race Demoralization." Originally published in *Colored American Magazine* 7, no. 7 (1904): 473–78. Reprinted in Alexander, *Afro-American Agitator*, 171–78.

———. "The Kind of Education the Afro-American Most Needs." Originally published in 1898 by Hampton's *Southern Workman*. Reprinted in Alexander, *Afro-American Agitator*, 85–91.

———. *The Negro in Politics*. New York: Ogilvie and Rowntree, 1886. Reprinted in Alexander, *Afro-American Agitator*, 27–73.

Freeman-Moir, John. "William Morris and John Dewey: Imagining Utopian Education." *Education and Culture* 28, no. 1 (2012): 21–41.

Gilman, Daniel Coit. "A Plea for the Training of the Hand." *Educational Monographs* 1, no. 1 (January 1888): 2–15. Available in Google Books.

Goddard, Connie. "The Bordentown School as Institution and Idea: The Manual Training and Industrial School Honored Educational Priorities of Washington, Du Bois, and Dewey." *New Jersey Studies: An Interdisciplinary Journal* 4, no. 2 (Summer 2018). https://doi.org/10.14713/njs.v4i2.125.

———. "Bordentown: Where Dewey's 'Learning to Earn' Met Du Boisian Educational Priorities." *Education and Culture* 35, no. 1 (2019): 49–70.

———. "A 'Howling Success': Ellendale State Normal and Industrial School, 1899–1929." *North Dakota History* 87, no. 1 (Fall 2022): 18–34.

———. "Unprecedented Yet Unheralded: Schooling in Beadle County during the Great Dakota Boom." *South Dakota History* 53, no. 1 (Spring 2023): 26–56.

Goodman, Paul. "The Manual Labor Movement and the Origins of Abolitionism." *Journal of the Early Republic* 13, no. 3 (Autumn 1993): 355–88.

Green, Nancy Stewart. "Dora Wells." In Schultz and Hast, *Women Building Chicago*, 950–53.

Grineski, Steve. "The Midwest: Cradle of Vocational Education." *Middle West Review* 8, no. 1 (Fall 2011): 455–80.

Ham, Charles H. "The Co-education of Mind and Hand." *Educational Monographs* 3, no. 4 (July 1890). Available in Google Books.

Harris, William T. "The Psychology of Manual Training." *Education*, May 1889, 1–22. Available in Google Books as a paper read before the Department of Superintendence, National Education Association, Washington, DC, March 7, 1889.

Hicks, Warren E. "What Laws for Vocational Education Should Michigan Adopt?" *NSPIE Proceedings, 1913*: 35–39.

"Historic House," *Prairies Magazine* 7, no. 1 (November 1983): 46–51.

Hogan, David. "Education and the Making of the Chicago Working Class, 1880–1930." *History of Education Quarterly*, Fall 1978: 227–70.

"How Equal Was This Separate School?" *New York Times,* May 10, 2010, section C, page 2.

"Jersey to Close All-Negro School Because It Can't Get White Pupils." *New York Times*, December 18, 1954, 17.

Kelly, John. "When World War I Raged, a D.C. Professor Fought for Black Officers' Participation." *Washington Post*, February 6, 2019.

Kern, O. J. "'Learning by Doing' for the Farmer Boy." *American Monthly Review of Reviews* 28 (1903): 456–61.

Kern, William M. "Industrial Education." *Bulletin, North Dakota State Normal and Industrial School,* April 1908: 7–17. Available in EHS.

Kett, Joseph F. "'Theory Run Mad': John Dewey and 'Real' Vocational Education." *Journal of the Gilded Age and Progressive Era* 16 (2017): 500–514.

Labaree, David. "How Dewey Lost: The Victory of David Snedden and Social Efficiency in the Reform of American Education." In Daniel Tröhler, Thomas Schlag, and Fritz Osterwalder, eds., *Pragmatism and Modernities.* Netherlands: Sense Publishers, 2010. This article is reprinted occasionally on the author's blog: *David Labaree on Schooling, History, and Writing.*

Lagemann, Ellen Condliffe. "Experimenting with Education: John Dewey and Ella Flagg Young at the University of Chicago." *American Journal of Education* 104 (May 1996): 171–85.

———. "The Plural Worlds of Education Research." *History of Education Quarterly* 29, no. 2 (1989): 185–214.

Levy, James. "Forging African-American Minds: Black Pragmatism, 'Intelligent Labor,' and a New Look at Industrial Education." *American Nineteenth-Century History* 17, no. 1 (2017): 43–73.

MacAlister, James. "Manual Training in the Philadelphia Public Schools." *Educational Monographs* 3, no. 2 (March 1890: 5–63. Available in Google Books.

"Manual Labor Institutions." *Hartford Courant*, April 16, 1833.

Margonis, Frank. "John Dewey's Racialized Visions of the Students and Classroom Community." *Educational Theory* 59, no. 1 (2009): 17–39.

Matheson, Helen. "City Man, 84, Honored by College He Helped to Found 50 Years Ago." *Wisconsin State Journal*, October 6, 1949.

McCamant, Jane. "Getting to Scale with Moral Education: The Demands of Reproducibility and the Case of the Chicago Manual Training School, 1884–1904." *Teachers College Record* 120, no. 7 (2018): 1–38.

McCaul, Robert L. "Dewey, Harper, and the University of Chicago." In Brickman, *Dewey's Legacy in Chicago.*

Mead, George H. "A Heckling School Board and an Educational Stateswoman." *The Survey* 31, no. 15 (January 10, 1914): 443–44.

"Meyner in Dispute over Negro School." *New York Times,* June 3, 1955, 11.

Oram, Ruby. "'A Superior Kind of Working Woman': The Contested Meaning of Vocational Education for Girls in Progressive Era Chicago." *Journal of the Gilded Age and the Progressive Era* 20 (2021): 392–410.

Owen, Robert Dale. "My Student Life at Hofwyl." *The Atlantic,* May 1865.

Parker, Francis. "Introduction to the Third Edition." In Ham, *Mind and Hand*.
Perlman, Selig. "Review of *McCarthy of Wisconsin*." *Wisconsin Magazine of History* 27, No. 4 (June 1944): 446–48.
Reber, Louis E. "What Laws for Vocational Education Should Michigan Adopt: 'Dual' or 'Unit' Control?" *NSPIE Proceedings, 1913*: 15–26.
Richards, Charles R. "The Function of Hand Work in the School." *Teachers College Record* 1 (1900): 249–59.
Roach, Ronald. "A Rich but Disappearing Legacy." *Black Issues in Higher Education* 20, no. 13 (September 2003): 18–24.
Roberts, William M. "Vocational Education Through the Part-Time School." *NSPIE Proceedings, 1913:* 203–16 (about programs in Chicago operated in cooperation with unions and trade associations).
Rush, Benjamin. "Samuel Finley: New Side Educator." In Douglas Sloan, ed., *The Great Awakening and American Education: A Documentary History*. New York: Teachers College Press, 1970.
Rylance, Daniel, "A Controversial Career: Gerald P. Nye, 1925–1946." *North Dakota Quarterly* 36 (Winter 1968): 5–19.
Schneirov, Richard. "Strikes." In Grossman et al., *Encyclopedia of Chicago*.
"School of Great Promise." *New York Age,* September 21, 1905, 2.
Seinfel, Ruth. "N.J. Negro School Makes Its Own World." *New York Evening Post*, December 31, 1930. A copy is available in MTIS Records.
Sklansky, Jeffrey. "The Work of Class in American History." *Labor: Studies in Working-Class History* 16, no. 4 (2019): 11–28.
Snedden, David. "Pros and Cons of the Gary System." *National Education Association, Proceedings for 1915*: 363–73.
———. "Vocational Education." *New Republic* 2 (May 15, 1915): 40–42. This is Snedden's contribution to the "Two Communications" exchange with John Dewey.
———. "Summation of the Discussion." *NSPIE Proceedings, 1913:* 55–59.
Streator, George. "School in New Jersey Aids Negro Youth." *New York Times,* November 14, 1948. A copy is available in the Harvard Archives.
Thomas, Sheila Gregory. "James Monroe Gregory." In Henry Louis Gates Jr. and Evelyn Brooks Higginbotham, eds., *African-American National Biography*, 1st edition. Volume III. New York: Oxford University Press, 2005, 211–13.
Todd, Helen M. "Why Children Work: The Children's Answer." *McClure's Magazine* 60, no. 6 (April 1913): 68–79.
Valentine, William R., Jr. "Bordentown Prepares for Industry." *Opportunity: The Journal of Negro Life* 17, no. 1 (1937): 11–14.
Vaughan, Kelly. "Progressive Education and Racial Justice: Examining the Work of John Dewey." *Education and Culture* 34, no. 2 (2018): 39–68.
Wells-Barnett, Ida B. *The Reason Why the Colored American Is Not in the Columbian Exposition*. With an introduction by Frederick Douglass. Chicago: Ida B. Wells, 1893.
Werum, Regina. "Sectionalism and Racial Politics: Federal Vocational Policies

and Programs in the Pre-desegregation South." *Social Science History* 21, no. 3 (Fall 1997): 399–453.

Wirth, Arthur. "Charles A. Prosser and the Smith-Hughes Act." *The Educational Forum* 36 (March 1972): 365–71.

Woerdehoff, Frank J. "Dr. Charles McCarthy: Planner of the Wisconsin System of Vocational and Adult Education." *Wisconsin Magazine of History* 41, No. 4 (Summer 1958): 270–74.

Woodward, Calvin. "The Complementary Nature of Manual Training." Address given at the National Education Association, Saratoga, New York, July 1882. In Woodward, *The Manual Training School*.

"The Workshop." *Chicago Inter Ocean*, June 20, 1897, 35.

Wraga, William G. "John Dewey's Idea of the Secondary School." *Education and Culture* 36, no. 2 (2020): 4–28.

Yellin, Eric S. "The (White) Search for (Black) Order: The Phelps-Stokes's First Twenty Years, 1911–1931." *The Historian* 65, no. 2 (Winter 2002): 319–52.

ARTICLES BY ELLA FLAGG YOUNG
(ORGANIZED ALPHABETICALLY BY TITLE)

"Children Should Have Industrial Education If They Don't Go to College." *Journal of Education*, November 16, 1911, 514.

"Educational Notes," *Catholic Educational Review* 5 (1913): 161–62.

"The Educational Progress of Two Years, 1905–1907." *National Education Association, Proceedings for 1907*, 383–405.

"Give Them More Vocational Training." In Idah McGlone Gibson, "What Should We Do for Our Boys and Girls over 14?" *Pittsburgh Press*, September 22, 1912. This was part of a published forum including Gibson, Young, and Jane Addams; Gibson was the chief author.

"Hypothesis in Education." *National Education Association, Proceedings for 1911*, 87–90.

"Industrial Training." *National Education Association, Proceedings for 1915*, 125–27.

"New Demands on Schools." *Journal of Education* 72, no. 17 (November 10, 1910): 453–54.

"The Proper Articulation of Technical Education within the System of Public Education." *National Education Association, Proceedings for 1907*, 1036–41.

"The Public High School." *The School Review* 18, no. 2 (February 1910): 73–83.

"Reciprocal Relations between Subject Matters in Secondary Education." *Educational Bi-Monthly* 2, no. 1 (October 1908): 75–84.

"Review of *Democracy and Education*." *Journal of Education* 84, no. 1 (July 6, 1916): 5–6.

"Scientific Method in Education." In *The Decennial Publications*. Chicago: University of Chicago Press, 1903.

ARTICLES BY JOHN DEWEY
(ORGANIZED BY DATE OF PUBLICATION)

Most of Dewey's writings appear in Jo Ann Boydston, ed., The Collected Works of John Dewey (Carbondale: Southern Illinois University Press); this is a 37- volume collection, published between 1960 and 1993. The volumes are organized chronologically by year of original publication and appear in three series: Early Works, Middle Works, and Later Works. These are given below as, for example, Early Works followed by volume number in that series. In the following list, both the original place of publication and the volume and page number for the Collected Works version are given. (Note that these are organized by year of publication.)

1896. "Interest in Relation to Training of the Will." *National Herbart Society* (1896): 209–46 and University of Chicago Press (1899); *Early Works* 5: 111–46.

1896. "Ethical Principles Underlying Education." *Third Yearbook of the National Herbart Society; Early Works* 5: 54–83.

1896. "The Reflex Arc Concept in Psychology." *Psychological Review* 3 (July): 357–70; *Early Works* 5: 96–109.

1897. "My Pedagogic Creed." *School Journal* 54 (January): 77–80; *Early Works* 5: 84–95.

1897. "Plan for Organization of Work in a Fully Equipped Department of Pedagogy"; *Early Works* 5: 442–47.

1897. "University Elementary School: History and Character." *University Record* 2: 72–75; *Middle Works* 1: 325–34.

1901. "The Place of Manual Training in the Elementary Course of Study." *Manual Training Magazine* 2: 193–99; *Middle Works* 1: 230–37.

1902. "The Educational Situation: Current Problems in Secondary Education." *School Review* 10: 13–28; *Middle Works* 1: 280–99.

1902. "The University of Chicago School of Education." *Elementary School Teacher* 3: 200–203; *Middle Works* 2: 67–71.

1902. "The School as Social Centre." *Elementary School Teacher* 3 (July): 73–86; *Middle Works* 2: 80–95.

1902. *White and Blue*. Brigham Young Lectures, March; *Later Works* 17: 317.

1904. "The Significance of the School of Education." *Elementary School Teacher* 4: 441–53; *Middle Works* 2: 273–84.

1906. "Culture and Industry in Education." *Educational Bi-Monthly* 1, no. 1 (October): 21–23; *Middle Works* 3: 285–93.

1909. "Address to the National Negro Conference." *Middle Works* 4: 156–57.

1913. "An Undemocratic Proposal." *American Teacher* 2: 2–4; *Middle Works* 7: 98–103; later published as "Some Dangers in the Present Movement for Industrial Education," *Child Labor Bulletin* (1913): 69–74.

1913. "What Laws for Vocational Education Should Michigan Adopt: 'Dual' or 'Unit' Control?" *NSPIE Proceedings, 1913*: 27–34; *Middle Works* 7: 85–92.

1914. "A Policy of Industrial Education." *New Republic* 1: 11–12; *Middle Works* 8: 97.

1915. "Education vs. Trade Training–Dr. Dewey's Reply" (part of "Two Communications" exchange with David Snedden). *New Republic* 2: 42–44; *Middle Works* 8: 411–13.

1915. "Industrial Education—A Wrong Kind." *New Republic* 2: 71–73; *Middle Works* 8: 117–22.

1915. "Splitting Up the School System." *New Republic* 2: 283–84; *Middle Works* 8: 123–27.

1916. "The Need of an Industrial Education in an Industrial Democracy." *Manual Training and Vocational Education* 17: 409–14; *Middle Works* 10: 137–43.

1917. "Learning to Earn: The Place of Vocational Education in a Comprehensive System of Public Education." *School and Society* 5, no. 117 (March 24): 331–35.

Unpublished Materials

Full references for theses, dissertations, reports, and other unpublished materials cited in the endnotes are given below, as are the names of archives that hold some of them and the abbreviations used to identify them.

Belfield Papers: Belfield, Henry H., and Belfield Family Papers 1849–1967, Hanna Holborn Gray Special Collections Research Center, University of Chicago Library; abbreviated as Belfield Papers with box and folder numbers.

Blatchford Papers: Blatchford Family Papers, Newberry Library, Chicago.

CMTS Records: Chicago Manual Training School Records, Hanna Holborn Gray Special Collections Research Center, University of Chicago Library. Abbreviated as CMTS Records with box and folder number. Note: catalogs for 1884–1896 are bound together as Series I, Box 2, Folder 2–9; these are referred to as Bound Catalogs.

Du Bois Papers: Special Collections and Archives, University of Massachusetts, Amherst (accessible online).

EHS: Ellendale Historical Society Archives, Coleman Memorial Museum, Ellendale, North Dakota. This material is also on the Internet Archive; the main link is https://archive.org/search.php?query=creator%3A%22Coleman+Museum%22 (accessed October 16, 2023).

ERIC: Education Resources Information Center, U.S. Department of Education, https://eric.ed.gov.

Gregory Papers: James Monroe Gregory Papers, Moorland-Spingarn Research Center, Howard University.

Harvard Archives: Harvard University Archives, Class of 1904 Records (accessible online).

MTIS Records: New Jersey State Archives; materials relating to the Manual Training and Industrial School are all found in SEDMA001, Box 1, unless otherwise noted.

NJSL: New Jersey State Library, Digital Jerseyana Collection.

NYPL: New York Public Library, Main Reading Room, 42nd Street Branch.

RUSC: Rutgers University Special Collections, New Brunswick.
SCRC: University of Chicago, Hannah Holborn Gray Special Collections Research Center.

Adams, Ezola Bolden. "The Role and Function of the Manual Training and Industrial School at Bordentown as an Alternative School, 1915–1955." EdD diss., Rutgers University, 1977; NJSL.
Belfield, Henry Holmes. "Autobiographical Writings, 1891–1903." Belfield Papers, Series I, Box 2, Folder 9.
———. "The New Education." In "Hand and Brain" 2 (May 1885): 1–4. CMTS Records, Series I, Box 3, Folder 2.
———. "Inaugural Address." CMTS Records, Series I, Box 2, Folder 2, Appendix to Sixth Annual Catalog.
Blatchford, E. W. "Annual Report." Delivered June 1886, Chicago Manual Training School Association; CMTS Records, Series I; bound with course catalogs, Box 2, Folders 2–9.
Bordentown School Committee. "Report of the Manual Training and Industrial School, 1909." MTIS Records.
Clark, Jim. "W. E. Hicks, Vocational Education Pioneer, Still Active at 91." Newspaper article, unidentified paper, 1958; EHS.
"Closing Exercises." June 12, 1955; MTIS Records.
"Decade of Progress, A Record of the Recent Growth of the State of New Jersey Manual Training and Industrial School." MTIS Records.
Devore, Wynetta. "The Education of Blacks in New Jersey, 1900–1930: An Exploration in Oral History." EdD diss., Rutgers University, 1980; NJSL.
Donatelli, Rosemary. "The Contributions of Ella Flagg Young to the Educational Enterprise." PhD diss., Faculty of the Social Sciences, University of Chicago, 1971.
Du Bois, W. E. B. "Testimony to the United States Commission on Industrial Education." Du Bois Papers.
Duck, Evelyn Blackmore. "An Historical Study of a Racially Segregated School in New Jersey from 1886–1955." EdD diss., Rutgers University, 1984, NJSL.
"Edwin F. Ladd Memorial Addresses Delivered in Congress, May 9, 1926." Washington, DC: U.S. Government Printing Office, 1927.
Engelbrecht, Lloyd. "The Association of Arts and Industries: Background and Origins of the Bauhaus Movement in Chicago." PhD diss., University of Chicago, June 1973.
Fair, Jean Everhard. "The History of Public Education in the City of Chicago, 1894–1914. MA diss., University of Chicago, August 1939.
Gilpin, Robert H. "Charles A. Bennett: American Pioneer of Industrial Education" (1958). *Plan B. Papers*, 36. The Keep, Eastern Illinois University. https://thekeep.eiu.edu (accessed February 24, 2024).
Goddard, Connie. "Agency and Efficiency: Attitudes toward Industrial Education in Chicago During Ella Flagg Young's Tenure as Superintendent of Schools."

Paper delivered at History of Education Society Annual Conference, November 3, 2022, Baltimore, MD (available upon request to the author).

Goddard, Constance H. "Ella Flagg Young's Intellectual Legacy: Theory and Practice in Chicago's Schools, 1862–1917." PhD diss, University of Illinois at Chicago, 2005. A copy is available at Municipal Reference Library, Chicago, and through University Microfilms.

Gustafson, David. "The Origin and Establishment of the University High School of the University of Chicago." MA thesis, Graduate Faculty, University of Chicago, June 1927. A copy is available at the University of Chicago Library.

"Hand and Brain," February and May 1885. CMTS Records, Box 3, Folder 2. The archive contains only these two issues; it is not known whether there were others.

Hicks, Warren E. "Annual Report of the Public Continuation Schools of Wisconsin," Bulletin of the Wisconsin State Board of Industrial Education, No. 7. Madison: State Board of Industrial Education, 1913. Available in Google Books.

Hoffman, Nancy, and Robert Schwartz. "Gold Standard: The Swiss Vocational Education and Training System." Washington, DC: National Center on Education and the Economy, 2015. Available online through ERIC, U.S. Department of Education.

Moe, Kilmer O., Jr. "Influence of the Hilo Boarding School on Agricultural Education in the Pacific." Master's degree thesis, University of Hawaii, 1953.

Ogren, Christine. "Teachers Grand Tours of Europe." Unpublished paper presented at History of Education Society Annual Conference, November 2020, an online event. Cited with permission of the author.

Oram, Ruby. "Lucy Flower Technical High School." National Register of Historic Places Registration Form, 2016, 2016. OMB No. 1024-0018.

Pillsbury, Nan. "Application for Inclusion for Manual Training and Industrial School." National Register of Historic Places, U.S. Department of the Interior, 1997. NJSL, Digital Jerseyana Collection.

"Princeton University Survey." December 1932. Typescript. Data on student backgrounds and post-graduation plans. MTIS Papers.

Prosser, Charles A., and W. A. O'Leary. "Short-Unit Courses for Wage Earners in Part-Time and Evening Schools." Bulletin of the U.S. Bureau of Labor Statistics, April 1915.

"Public Hearing before the Commission to Investigate the Circumstances Surrounding the Proposed Closing of the Bordentown Manual Training School, May 19, 1955," vol. 1 of 2. NJSL, Digital Jerseyana Collection.

Randall, Ina E. "Industrial Training in the Schools." Oration Delivered upon Graduating from the State Manual Training School, Ellendale, ND, May 17, 1901." EHS.

Rathnau, Joseph N. "The Contributions of Henry Holmes Belfield and the Chicago Manual Training School to the Manual Training Movement." Diss., Faculty of Social Sciences Master of Arts, Department of Education, Chicago,

December 1967. Some excerpts are available at SCRC; the full dissertation is available at the main University of Chicago Library.

Reber, Louis E. "Industrial and Continuation Schools: Their Foundation, Organization, and Adjustment to the Life of the Community." Bulletin of the Wisconsin State Board of Industrial Education, No. 5. Madison: State Board of Industrial Education, 1912, 3–18. Available in Google Books.

Report of the Commission on Industrial Education, Submitted to the Senate and General Assembly of the State of New Jersey in Accordance with Joint Resolution No. 11, Approved April 14, 1909. Trenton: MacCrellish and Quigley, State Printers, 1909. NJSL (not available online).

Report of the Massachusetts Commission on Industrial and Technical Education (also known as the Douglas Commission). Boston, 1906.

Schenck, John P. "Manual Training Schools in America." Unpublished paper by a professor at Northern State University, Aberdeen, South Dakota, 1955. Available from ERIC, ED 391-039.

Schultz, Otto C. "A History of the State Normal and Industrial School at Ellendale, ND." MS thesis, University of North Dakota, August 1947. EHS.

Seinfel, Ruth. "N.J. Negro School Makes Its Own World." *New York Evening Post*, December 31, 1930. Copy available in MTIS Records.

Shine, James E. "The Development of Technical Education in the Chicago High Schools." MA thesis, Loyola University, Chicago, 1933.

Slave Dwelling Project. An organization that maintains records of and rehabilitates former slave quarters in parts of the American South. Accessed October 17, 2023. www.slavedwellingproject.org.

Smith, Ken. "Mind and Hand: Formative Years of a Prairie Town." Dissertation in progress, North Dakota State University, 2023. A copy was made available by the author.

———. "Prospectus." Working paper for a dissertation, 2020. A copy was made available by the author.

Snitcher. Yearbook for the Classes of 1924–1925. EHS.

"Some Results of Bordentown Training." Extension Department, Manual Training and Industrial School, Bordentown, NJ, 1927. MTIS Records.

Streator, George. "School in Jersey Aids Negro Youths." *New York Times*, November 14, 1948. Available from Harvard University Archives, Class of 1904, folder on William Robert Valentine; though a stamp on the article credits it to another newspaper, the byline states the *Times*.

Symes, Arthur L. "A Reflection on Bordentown." DiscoverNJHistory.org. Accessed October 17, 2023. https://discovernjhistory.org/a-reflection-on-bordentown-2/. A member of the class of 1953, Symes was later dean of architecture at Southern University in Louisiana.

"Weekly Letter of the Manual Training and Industrial School." December 1920. MTIS Records.

White, Woody Thomas. "The Study of Education at the University of Chicago, 1892–1958." PhD diss., Division of Social Sciences, University of Chicago, 1977.

Credits

Figure 1. Board of Trustees, University of Illinois.
Figure 2. Courtesy of Google Books.
Figure 3. Ellendale Historical Society; image enhanced by *North Dakota History*.
Figure 4. SCRC, University of Chicago, 74006954 CMTS Records.
Figure 5. SCRC, University of Chicago, 74006954 CMTS Records.
Figure 6. SCRC, University of Chicago, 74006954 CMTS Records.
Figure 7. SCRC, University of Chicago, 74006954 CMTS Records.
Figure 8. Google Books: Cover for *Manual Training* magazine, 1899.
Figure 9. Courtesy of the U.S. Library of Congress, LC-USZ62-49809.
Figure 10. Illinois History and Lincoln Collections, Jonathan Baldwin Turner Papers, University Library, University of Illinois at Urbana-Champaign.
Figure 11. Chicago History Museum, ICHi-183213.
Figure 12. SCRC, University of Chicago: CMTS Records, Series I, Box 3, Folder 7.
Figure 13. SCRC, University of Chicago: CMTS Records, Series I, Box 3, Folder 7.
Figure 14. SCRC, University of Chicago: Image apfe2-00834.
Figure 15. Photo by Kristi Kantorski.
Figure 16. New Jersey State Archives.
Figure 17. New Jersey State Archives.
Figure 18. New Jersey State Archives.
Figure 19. Courtesy of Ellendale Historical Society; image enhanced by *North Dakota History*.
Figure 20. Courtesy of Ellendale Historical Society.
Figure 21. Elmer Thompson, photographer; image digitized by Paul Gronhovd.

Figure 22. Elmer Thompson, photographer; image digitized by Paul Gronhovd.

Figure 23. Elmer Thompson, photographer; image digitized by Paul Gronhovd.

Figure 24. Courtesy of Ellendale Historical Society.

Figure 25. Courtesy of New York Public Library.

Figure 26. DN-0007580, Chicago Daily News Collection, Chicago History Museum.

Figure 27. Wisconsin Historical Society ID# WHI(x3) 9350.

Figure 28. Wisconsin Historical Society ID# Pam, 56-3392.

Figure 29. New Jersey State Archives.

Figure 30. Painting by the late Ladybird Strickland; courtesy of John Medley; photograph by Erik Burro.

Figure 31. Elmer Thompson, photographer; image digitized by Paul Gronhovd.

Index

Addams, Jane, 11, 27, 72–73, 75–76, 108, 169, 174
Adler, Felix, and Workingmen's School, 1, 3–4, 48, 55
African Americans: employment opportunities, 119; ideas about education, 90, 98, 103, 105, 121–22, 124, 160–61; illiteracy and poverty in South, 121–22; industrial education, 118, 123–25, 206–8; Institute for Colored Youth, 93, 103; limited interest in agriculture, 118–19; Lincoln College, 111; manual education and, 111–12; neglected in standard histories, 198; in rural communities, 151–52; Smith-Hughes and, 194; "special education" of, 109; work-related schooling, 197–98. *See also* Hampton Institute; Manual Training and Industrial School (MTIS); racism; Tuskegee Institute; white paternalism
Afro-American Council, 108
agency: after Smith-Hughes Act, 193–96; CMTS, 5; efficiency and, 161, 163–66; MTIS, 91–92; new industrialism and, 60; NI, 127; tools and, 43. *See also* vocational education

agriculture: in college, 29, 32, 38, 42; MTIS, 94–96, 98, 100, 113–20; NI, 132, 148, 154–55, 157; special training needs in rural areas, 180; vocational education and, 159–60, 191
Alridge, Derrick, 117–18, 200
American Association of Educators of Colored Youth, 96
Anderson, Ellen, 136–37, 139, 145
Anderson, James, 116, 207
Anderson, Lewis R.: *History of Manual and Industrial Education*, 31
Andover Seminary band, 28
apprenticeship system, 8–9, 42, 55, 101, 160
architecture, 6–7, 11, 20, 75–78, 90, 152
Armour Institute, 29, 54, 72, 84
Armstrong, Richard, 109, 112–13, 121
Armstrong, Samuel Chapman, 112–13
art and labor, 75, 78, 89–90
Arts and Crafts Movement, 29, 58–60, 72–75, 114

Ball, Frank, 70
Balliet, Thomas, 86
Bamberger, Gabriel, 54–55, 72–73, 76
Bankers Bill, 179–80
Barnes, Albert, 200
Barnett, Ferdinand, 108
Bartlett, A. C., 5, 86, 89

Bartlett, Lorenzo Dow, 128–29, 131–32
Barton, Clara, 92–93
Beecher, Catherine, 36
Beecher, Edward, 28, 34–35, 38
Beecher, Lyman, 36
Belfield, H. H.: "Autobiographical Writings," 69; "Circular to Parents and Guardians," 21–23; on CMTS curriculum, 208; CMTS director, 15–18; CMTS inaugural address, 2–4; on community demand for changes in manual training, 160; Dewey and, 27, 58–60, 63–65, 68–73, 80–86, 160; difficulty of finding faculty, 19–20, 70; eclipsed by Harper and Dewey, 63; education and biography, 11–13; on manual labor in college education, 28–29; on manual training, 144; "Manual Training in the Public School," 26, 59; "My Dear Young Friend" letter, 84; redefining CMTS, 56–58, 71–72; retirement, 88–89. *See also* Chicago Manual Training School (CMTS)
Beman, Solon Spencer, 6–7
Bennett, Charles A., 29–31, 37–38, 43, 70
Bicknell, T. W., 5
Black, R. M., 131, 135, 143, 193–94, 197; *Brief History of North Dakota*, 149; *History of Dickey County*, 133, 154
Blaine, Anita McCormick, 64, 81, 87, 179
Blaine Hall, 81, 84–87
Blair, Francis, 180
Blatchford, E. W.: annual report by, 23; on Belfield, 13; Blatchford Literary Society, 16; chief supporter of CMTS, 11, 112; CMTS as polytechnic, 80, 84; education of, 28–29; at laying of CMTS cornerstone, 5; Newberry Library, 2, 5, 16, 63; president of CMTS board, 2, 9, 15–16, 57
Bobbitt, John Franklin, 189–90
Bordentown (NJ), 91–93. *See also* Manual Training and Industrial School (MTIS)

Boris, Eileen: *Art and Labor: Ruskin, Morris, and the Craftsman Ideal in America*, 74–75
Bradley University (Peoria), 29–30, 122, 144
Brown v. Board of Education (1954), 202–3
Bullock, Henry Allan, 109, 116
Burkholder, Zoë, 200
Burnham, Daniel, 11
Bushnell, Horace, 34
Butler, Nathaniel, 87–88
Butler, Nicholas Murray: *Argument for Manual Training*, 50–51, 65; Blaine Hall dedication, 86; editor of *Educational Monograph* series, 53; Education Day speech, 81; on manual training, 49, 76, 160; NSPIE, 169

Callahan, Raymond E.: *Education and the Cult of Efficiency*, 166
Camp, Katherine and Anna: *The Dewey School*, 65–66
careers of manual training graduates: Tuskegee, 117. *See also* Chicago Manual Training School (CMTS); Manual Training and Industrial School (MTIS); Normal and Industrial School (NI)
Carlyle, Thomas, 43, 58, 76–77
Carnegie, Andrew, 142, 169
Caruthers, J. Thomas, 102
Chicago: architecture, 6–7, 11; Arts and Crafts Movement in, 74–75; "City of the Century," 6–11; coeducating hands and minds in, 53–55; Cooley controversy, 178–81; high schools in, 10, 12–13, 26, 54–55, 171–76, 198; hothouse for ideas about education, 60, 62; industrial growth, 11, 42, 172; population growth, 9–10; "School of Thought," 90; University High School, 84–85, 88–89. *See also* Chicago Manual Training School (CMTS); Chicago Public Schools (CPS); Chicago School of Education

Chicago Architectural Club, 75
Chicago Arts and Crafts Society, 73, 75, 77
Chicago City Club, 179
Chicago Evening High School, 12
Chicago Federation of Labor (CFL), 179
Chicago Institute, 64, 81–84, 86
Chicago Kindergarten Club, 11
Chicago Manual Training School (CMTS), 1–27; absorption by University of Chicago, 57–58, 63; admission requirements, 17–18; alumni banquets, 23–24, 56; annual exhibitions, 23, 80; architectural design, 6–7; attrition, 21–22, 56, 80; in Chicago School of Education, 80, 82–85; chief supporters, 11–16; compared to University Elementary School, 65; course work, 80; curriculum, 16; end of, 79–80, 89; endowments, 57; enrollment, 56–57, 80–81; expectations of students, 21–22; faculty, 19–20, 23; finances, 6–11, 26, 56–58; first board, 9; fundraising, 7, 9; graduates' careers, 22, 56–57, 80; *Hand and Brain* newsletter, 18–19; Laboratory School and, 59; Latin added, 56; lecture series, 23; loss of backers, 56–58; opening of, 16; as polytechnic, 57, 80, 84; preparatory year, 56; public tours, 57; purpose of, 16–24; relocation to Midway, 61–62, 80, 83; scholarships, 8, 17, 19; school building, 6–11, 16, 20, 57, 80–81; shop equipment, 4, 20–21; sports, 56; student body, 17–18; student work, quality of, 23–24; teacher training, 85; three separate programs, 26, 56; tower clock, 57; tuition, 4, 19, 56, 80. *See also* Dewey, John; drawing; history of manual training; manual education/training
Chicago Normal School, 1, 63–64, 88, 166
Chicago Public Schools (CPS): Howland as superintendent, 13, 26; Lane as superintendent, 54–55; manual training in, 12–13, 25–26, 54–55, 62–63, 73; officials attending Dewey's seminar in logical theory, 67; population growth and, 10. *See also* Cooley, Edwin; Young, Ella Flagg
Chicago School of Education, 79–89; administrative responsibilities in, 87–88; beginnings of, 27, 64, 81; Belfield's retirement, 88–89; Blaine Hall, 86–87; CMTS' role in, 82–86; Dewey's and Parker's roles, 83–84; Dewey's leadership, 79–80; Dewey's resignation, 86–87; significance of, 59, 72, 85; uniting teacher training with laboratory method, 85–86
Chicago Teachers Federation, 179
Chicago Tribune, 5, 8, 56, 175, 178–81
Clark, John B., 23
Cleveland: racism in, 198; technical high school, 159; vocational programs in, 128, 143, 177
CMTS. *See* Chicago Manual Training School
Columbian Exposition, 26, 38, 61, 75
Combellick, Neil C., 152–54
Comenius, John Amos, 31–32, 37, 43, 65
Commercial Club (Chicago): CMTS' financial drain on, 26, 57–58; at CMTS graduations, 23; Cooley controversy, 179–80; funding for CMTS, 2, 4–5, 7–8; Kerschensteiner sponsorship, 181, 184; scholarships offered by, 19–20
Commission on Industrial Education (NJ), 115–16
Commission on Industrial Relations (US), 118
Committee on Industrial Education (AFL), 170
common schools: community and, 127, 181; manual work at, 46; meeting societal demands, 51, 162; NI and, 145, 149, 151; purpose of, 33, 167; workshops at, 53

community: building, 104, 123–25; Dewey on, 83; manual training's benefits to, 49, 66–67, 176; schools adapting to needs of, 121, 187; producerism, 130; schools as social centers, 152–53, 165–66
continuation schools, 164, 181–87, 193
Cook County Normal School, 10, 61, 63–64, 79
Cooley, Edwin: controversy over Cooley Bill, 178–81, 185, 189; education of women, 176; European trip, 179, 181; Prussianizing American schools, 181; superintendent of Chicago Public Schools, 174
Cooper Union, 169
Coppin, Fanny Jackson, 93, 96, 103
Coppin, Levi, 103
Corliss engine, 16, 20, 43, 79
Cornell University, 22, 38
correctional facilities, 36–37, 53, 203
Crabtree, Ben, 134
Crabtree, Mattie, 152
Crane, Richard T., 1, 9, 173
Craven, D. Stewart, 102–3, 114
Cremin, Lawrence, 51; *The Metropolitan Experience*, 42; *The Transformation of the School*, 43, 49, 163–64
Crerar, John, 19, 57
The Crisis, 108, 119, 198, 200
Cuban, Larry, 191, 193–95
Currarino, Roseanne, 130

Daughters of the American Revolution (DAR), 76
Della Vos, Victor: Imperial Technical School, 44; Russian method, 8, 31, 44–46; trade school systems, 8
democratization of education: art and labor as means of, 76–79, 89–90; in Chicago, 60–61; *Democracy and Education*, 190; Kerschensteiner and, 181; NI as "living symbol of democracy," 128, 197; as reason for industrial education, 167, 178–79, 204–5. *See also* continuation schools

Dent, George, 34
Dewey, Alice Chipman, 62, 85–86
Dewey, Evelyn, 159, 189; "The School as Social Settlement," 124; *Schools of Tomorrow*, 104, 122–24, 190, 193
Dewey, John, 59–90; advocate for combined academic and industrial training, 59–61; agency and efficiency, 91–92, 160–61, 165–66; Belfield and, 59–61, 69–70; Chicago's educational innovations and, 61–64; "The Child and the Curriculum," 69; *Democracy and Education*, 59, 123, 190; *The Dewey School*, 65–67; Du Bois' and Washington's connection to, 117; "Ethical Principles Underlying Education," 71; exchange with Snedden, 193; failure to address African American education, 124–25, 200; "Industrial Education-the Wrong Kind," 188; instrumental logic, 62; James and *The Metaphysical Club*, 80; Kerschensteiner and, 183–84; logical theory course, 67; manual teacher training at CMTS, 85; on manual training, 69–73; "My Pedagogic Creed," 68; at National Negro Conference, 108; new education meets new industrialism, 73–79; occupations as basis of curriculum, 66; philosophical differences with Parker, 83–84; "The Reflex Arc Concept in Psychology," 68–69; resignation from University of Chicago, 86–88; *The School and Society*, 64, 68, 164; *Schools of Tomorrow*, 104, 122–24, 190, 193; scientific treatment of educational problems, 64–69; "The Significance of the School of Education," 72, 85; on Smith-Hughes Act, 192–93; social aims of school, 66–67, 71; "Two Communications," 188–89; uniting art and labor, 89–90. *See also* Chicago School of Education; Laboratory School; unit versus dual system

Dickey County Leader, 126, 128, 130, 135, 140, 151–52, 194; "To Guide the Hand," 133
Dickey County Teachers Association, 126
Douglas, Paul H., 164, 168, 181, 185, 192–93, 198
Douglas Commission, 167–68, 171
Douglass, Frederick, 93, 106
drawing: Cincinnati curriculum, 37; at CMTS, 4, 6–8, 14, 16–17, 19–22, 24, 80; to develop expressive powers, 51; mechanical arts and, 45; at MTIS, 94; at NI, 136, 139, 149
Drexel Institute, 55
dual versus unit system, *see* unit versus dual system
Du Bois, W. E. B.: "A Choice of Vocation" at MTIS, 120; *Black Reconstruction*, 99; Booker T. Washington and, 106–8, 111; *Crisis* editor, 108; criticism of *Negro Education*, 198; Dewey's connection to, 117; distrust of manual and industrial training programs, 111, 119–21, 123–24; double consciousness, 107, 110; "Education and Work," 198–200; influence on Black education, 161; at MTIS, 92, 125; *The Negro American Artisan*, 118; *Negro Artisan*, 228n74–75; on object of education, 197; "A Rational System for Negro Education," 106; review of *Up from Slavery*, 107; *The Souls of Black Folk*, 107–8; testimony for Commission on Industrial Relations, 109, 118–19
Dunphy, Albert E., 137, 139, 144, 148
Dunwoody Institute, 190, 196

Eastman, Max, 65
Eaton, John, 2, 4–5, 16
economics: Chicago's economy, 6; craftsman ideal, 74, 208; depression of 1893, 39, 134, 171, 187; as escalator, 39–42; industrial education and, 195; literacy and economy, 33; new industrialism, 76–77; political versus economic power, 161, 169–71; social equality and, 106–7, 199
education: adapting to demands of changing economy, 39, 171, 187; compulsory schooling age, 184; controversy over purpose of, 179; educational ideal, 61–62; hands and heads, 27, 32, 39, 144; high schools' responsibilities, 172–73; increases in enrollment, 173; keeping students in school, 160, 170, 181, 183; one-room school houses, 151–54; practice schools and classrooms, 1, 64, 83, 151; urban and suburban opportunity gap, 163; youth employment and family finances, 167–8. *See also* democratization of education; Dewey, John; efficiency; new education
Educational Monographs, 25, 50, 53
Edwards, Anna Camp: *The Dewey School*, 65–67
efficiency, 163–67, 184, 193–96
Eliot, Charles E., 170–71
Ellendale, ND, 126–27, 129–30, 133–34, 155–57. *See also* Normal and Industrial School (NI)
English High and Manual Training School, 26, 173
Ethical Culture Fieldston School, 48
European schools: fostering independence, 10; handicrafts, 48; manual training origins, 29–34, 44; Moravian schools, 31; orphans and pauper children, 36–37; reports on, 15, 101, 179, 181, 183. *See also* Della Vos, Victor

factories, 40–42, 72, 160, 172, 190
Fairbank, N. K., 1, 5, 9
Farmer-Labor Party, 156
Fellenberg, Philipp von, 33–34, 36, 38, 46
feminism, 111, 131, 140, 177. *See also* women's education
Ferris, George Washington Gale, Jr., 38, 75

Field, Marshall, 1–2, 5, 7, 9–10, 61
Fine Arts Building, 64, 76
Fisher, Berenice: *Industrial Education*, 167
Flemington, Alexander, 128–32, 134
Flexner, Abraham, 153–54
Fortune, Thomas T., 98–99, 103, 105, 111–12, 121–22; *Black and White: Land, Labor, and Politics in the South*, 99; "School of Great Promise," 98–99
Franklin, Benjamin, 32–33, 40
Franklin Institute, 37
Fraser, Caroline: *Prairie Fires*, 133
Freedmen's Bureau, 4, 29, 92, 113
Frelinghuysen, Joseph, 103, 114
Froebel, Friedrich, 10, 31–32, 43
Fuller, William A., 9–10

Gale, George Washington, 34
Gardiner Lyceum, 37–38
Gary system, 189–90
Generals, Donald, 117, 123
General Society of Mechanics and Trades, 37
General Trade Union, 41
Gilded Age, 41–42
Gilman, Daniel Coit: "A Plea for the Training of the Hand," 25–26
Goddard, Herbert, 155, 156
Gompers, Samuel, 169–70
Graham, Frederick, 155–57
Graham, Ina Randall, 126, 197–98; "Industrial Training in the Schools," 128, 138–41
Great Dakota Boom, 129–30, 155, 204
Gregory, Fannie, 100, 102, 113
Gregory, James Monroe, 96–100, 102–6, 110–15, 118, 160
Gregory, Montgomery, 111, 114, 196, 203
Grimké, Archibald, 110–11
Grimké, Francis, 103, 110–11, 113
Grimké, Sarah and Angelina Weld, 111
Griscom, John, 34, 36
Groeger, Cristina, 246n163
guild ideal, 72, 74, 89

Haley, Margaret, 179

Haley, Samuel A., 202
Hall, Clyde W., 122–23
Ham, Charles: biography of, 13, 56; on brain's dependence on hands, 74; "The Co-education of Mind and Hand," 53–54; Dewey and, 60, 65–67, 71; on educating women, 36; establishment of CMTS, 5, 11; on European roots of manual education, 31–32; importance of manual training, 28–29; influence on Chicago, 55; "Inventive Genius, or an Epitome of Human Progress," 43–44; on inventors of new technology, 39; lessons from CMTS, 25; *Manual Training: The Solution of Social and Industrial Problems*, 10, 13–15, 43, 49, 153; on opening of CMTS, 16–17; Sennett and, 208; solving social problems with manual training, 47; speeches on manual training, 8–9. *See also* Chicago Manual Training School (CMTS)
Hampton Institute, 92–93, 113, 116, 118; *The Southern Workman*, 99, 200
Hand and Brain, 18–19
handicrafts and handwork, 33, 37, 48, 72–73, 78, 175
Haney, Paul, 169
Harlem Renaissance, 114
Harper, William Rainey: Bradley University and, 122; on Chicago School of Education, 61–64, 90; CMTS acquisition by U of C, 1, 57–58, 80–81; Industrial Art League, 76; philosophical differences with Dewey, 83–84, 86–87
Harris, B. F., 180
Harris, William Torrey: defense of Negro higher education, 198; "Educational Value of Manual Training," 52–53; *Journal of Speculative Philosophy*, 50; on manual training, 76; NSPIE and, 170–71; "Psychology of Manual Training," 50–52; support for traditional education, 160; U.S. commissioner of education, 4, 51, 164

Harrison, Elizabeth, 11, 73
Hastie, William H., 202
hegelianism, 50, 62
Hibbard, William, 7
Hicks, Warren: as assistant superintendent in Cleveland, 177; background, 126–28; *Champion Spelling Book,* 241n76; as deputy superintendent in Wisconsin, 183, 185–87; as "father of industrial education," 162; as head of NEA spelling bee, 241n76; industrial education and, 159–60; Montgomery Gregory and, 196; origins of NI, 134–35; public opinion's effect on NI, 136, 141–42. *See also* Normal and Industrial School (NI)
Hilo Boys Boarding School, 112
Hirsch, Emil, 76
history of manual training, 28–58; broader social context, 43–46; coeducating hands and minds, 53–55; European origins, 29–33, 48; gymnasium or manual labor, 32; Ham's list of manual training programs, 49; Hofwyl to Weld, 33–37; industrial training history, 195–96; labor changes in 19th century, 39–42; psychology and, 50–53; teaching mechanical skills, 46–47; in United States, 28–29, 32–33; Workingmen's School, 48–49. *See also* Della Vos, Victor; European schools; learning by doing
Hitch, Robert, 180
Hodges, Graham: *Black New Jersey,* 109–10, 119
Hofwyl, 33–37, 46
Hogan, David, 168 246n163
home economics, 138, 176–77, 191, 193, 205
Homestead Act, 132
Howard Players, 106, 114
Howland, George, 13, 26
Hudson, John, 129, 157
Hull House, 11, 53–54, 59, 72–76, 104

Illinois Bankers Association, 179

Illinois Industrial University, 38
immigrants, 10–11, 41, 54, 131, 160, 168
Indianapolis, 92, 104, 123–24, 193
Indigenous Americans, 25, 129, 131–32
Industrial Art League, 73–75, 89
industrial arts, 49, 73–77, 89, 100–101, 177, 194
industrial education, 115–25; for African-American students, 123–25, 161, 197–98; benefits from, 171; defined, 115–23; democracy in schools and, 178; economic mobility and, 117; history of, 163–64, 195–96; labor and, 197; "masters of their own industrial fate," 188–89; national movements supporting, 116; nationwide survey of, 101; programs, 47–48; program successes, 162; reform schools, 9, 36–37. *See also* agency; efficiency; unit versus dual system; vocational education
Industrial Education Act (NJ), 93
Industrial Education Association (NY), 25, 50
industrial intelligence, 167, 174
Institute for Colored Youth, 93, 103
Inter Ocean, 5, 13, 56, 72, 74, 178–79
Irish National Land League, 95
Ironsides Echo, 97–100, 114, 202

Jackman, Wilbur, 74, 76, 85–87; "The Future School," 79
Jacobson, Augustus, 8–9, 25, 48, 56
James, Edmund, 179
James, William, 79–80, 89–90, 144, 208
Jefferson, Thomas, 33
Jewish Manual Training School, 29, 53–54, 72
Jim Crow practices, 104–5, 109–10, 122
Johns Hopkins University, 25, 62, 113
Johnson, Willis, 148
Jones, Jenkin Lloyd, 76
Jones, Thomas Jesse: *Negro Education,* 120–22, 198
Jordan, Mildred Rice, 224n1, 240n43, 248n30

Journal of Negro Education, 199
Judd, Charles, 88, 181
Judson, Henry Pratt, 88–89

Kantor, Harvey, and David Tyack: *Work, Youth, and Schooling*, 164
Kean, Carol Judy, 177
Keith, Edson, 5, 9–10
Kendall, Calvin, 102, 104, 119
Kern, Caroline Evans, 148
Kern, O. J., 235n9, 242n94
Kern, W. M., 143–48
Kerschensteiner, Georg, 181, 183–85
Kett, Joseph, 188, 190
kindergarten movement, 10–11, 15, 29, 31–32, 50–51, 60, 65–66
Kingsbury, Susan, 167–68
Kitchen Garden Association, 50, 65
Kliebard, Herbert, 170; *Schooled to Work*, 163–64, 177, 198
Knights of Labor, 41
Knoll, Michael, 189; *Beyond Rhetoric*, 166, 183
Krug, Edward, 170–71, 181, 198; *The Shaping of the American High School*, 164–65
Ku Klux Klan, 107

labor, history of, 39–42
Laboratory School: arts and crafts at, 72; basic idea of, 117; Camp sisters and *The Dewey School*, 65–66; CMTS and, 1–2, 29, 59, 65, 67, 71, 81, 86, 89; community focus of, 67, 71; curriculum and occupations, 123–24; curriculum as trailblazing, 67–68; funding of, 64; history of, 59, 85–87; Michael Knoll on, 166, 183, 189; MTIS and, 104, 117; not mentioned in Ham's book, 71; psychology and, 68–69, 71; self-initiated activity in, 57; similarity to other labs and workshops, 64–66, 70, 89–90. *See also* Dewey, John
Ladd, Edwin, 156
Lane, Albert, 54–55
Lane Technical High School, 173
Lane Theological Seminary, 36

Laurie, Bruce: *Artisans into Workers*, 39–40, 54
Lazerson, Marvin, and W. Norton Grubb: *American Vocationalism*, 164
learning by doing, 31–33, 65, 67, 73–74
Leavitt, Frank, 181
Leiby, Ed, 130
Lewis Institute, 54
Lincoln College, 111
Lloyd, Henry Demarest, 75
Locke, Alain, 103, 113–14
log colleges, 32, 36, 121
Lowden, Frank, 75
Lucy Flower High School, 176, 198
lyceums, 37–38
Lyman, David and Sarah, 112
lynching, 107, 114

MacAlister, James, 55, 66; "The General Question of Manual Training," 49
MacDonald, Neil C., 152
MacNeill, George, 197
Mann, Horace, 33
Manual Arts Press, 122
manual education/training: adaptation to changing needs, 160, 163–64; character and morality as goals of, 121; in colleges, 28–29, 56–58; definition, 91, 115–23; division between manual and mental, 46–47; faculty for, 19–20, 70; hands and heads, 144; importance of, 67–70; labor and, 39–42; psychology of, 50–53, 144; in public schools, 12, 26, 47–49, 51, 54–56, 66–67, 109, 118–19, 175–76, 179, 186; as reform school, 36–37; revitalization of, 73–79; U.S. Bureau of Education survey (1917), 120–21. *See also* Chicago Manual Training School (CMTS); drawing; history of manual training; industrial education; learning by doing; Manual Training and Industrial School (MTIS); Normal and Industrial School (NI); vocational education
Manual Training and Industrial School (MTIS), 91–125; acquisition

and management by state, 92, 94–97; agriculture at, 95–96, 100, 114–16, 118–20; beginnings, 90–94; closing of, 202–3; compared to NI, 206–7; distinctive legacy, 94–96; distinguished visitors to, 202; graduates' careers, 91, 99–100, 102, 119, 123–24; heyday of, 201–2; legacy of, 94–96, 197–208; military training at, 97–98; mission of, 98, 114–15; pupils and programs, 94, 97–100, 114; state pressure on, 101–4. *See also* drawing; Gregory, James Monroe; Valentine, William R.
Manual Training Magazine, 30, 70
Marsh, Florence, 152
Marshall, Thomas, 135, 142
Massachusetts Commission on Industrial and Technical Education, 167–68
Massachusetts Institute of Technology, 1, 38–39, 45
Mayhew, Katherine Camp: *The Dewey School*, 65–67
McCamant, Jane, 223n103
McCarthy, Charles, 182–84
McCaul, Robert, 83
McManis, John, 175
Mead, George Herbert, 179
mechanical skills, 46–47
Meier, August: *Negro Thought in America, 1880 to 1915*, 106, 110, 116
Menand, Louis: *The Metaphysical Club*, 80
Meyner, Robert, 203
Mill, John Stuart, 15
Miller, Donald: *City of the Century*, 6, 60
Miller, Kelly, 103, 113
Milwaukee, 177
Mitchell (John) Committee, 170
model schools, 62, 64, 85–86, 151–54
Mohonk Conferences, 109
Montgomery Ward, 61
morality and character, 53–54, 112, 121
Morrill Act (1862), 38
Morris, George Sylvester, 62
Morris, William, 73–75, 77

Mount Holyoke College, 36
MTIS. *See* Manual Training and Industrial School

National Association for the Advancement of Colored People (NAACP), 108
National Association of Manufacturers (NAM), 169–70
National Education Association (NEA), 5, 9, 43, 48, 50, 169
National Negro Conference, 108
National Society for the Promotion of Industrial Education (NSPIE), 161, 169–71, 181, 185–88, 191, 198
Native Americans. *See* Indigenous Americans
Negro Convention Movement, 93
Negro Education (Thomas Jesse Jones), 120–22, 198
new education: defined, 2–4; fostering equality, 71; kindergarten and manual training, 15; manual training as, 47, 55; new industrialism and, 59, 73–79; old education's deficiencies, 61; postsecondary, 127–28, 141; state support for, 204; union of thought and action, 53
New Harmony Colony, 33–34
new industrialism, 59–60, 73–76, 78–79, 164, 208
New Jersey: Black population in, 109–10, 114, 119; Commission on Industrial Education, 101, 114–15; decision to close MTIS, 202–3; manual education programs in, 115–16; "Mississippi of the North," 105
Newman, Stephan, 103
The New Republic, 161
The New York Age, 98, 102, 111–12, 114
New York College for the Training of Teachers, 53
NI. *See* Normal and Industrial School
Niagara Movement, 108
Nonpartisan League, 130, 155–56
Normal and Industrial School (NI), 126–58, 203–6; curriculum, 137,

Index 279

142–45, 147–49, 154; Demonstration Rural School, 150–54; Domestic Art, 138, 140, 205; Ellendale and, 126–27, 134, 155–57; enrollment at, 135–37, 144–45, 148, 150–51, 157–58; facilities, 150, 153; faculty at, 135–36, 141, 144, 150–51; Fine Arts Department, 136–39, 142, 147–49; *First Annual Catalog*, 137; graduates' careers, 138, 158, 206; Kern and, 143–48; mission, 126–27, 134–51, 206–7; populism and, 154–57, 198; purpose refined, 136–41; state supervision of, 141–43, 148–51, 193–94; Willis Johnson and, 148. *See also* Black, R. M.; Graham, Ina Randall; Hicks, Warren

normal schools, 1, 137, 143, 149, 151–52, 203–4, 206. *See also* Cook County Normal School; Normal and Industrial School (NI); Ogren, Christine

North Dakota: Commissioner of Education Report (1915), 149–50, 154; constitutional convention, 128–32; North Dakota State Teachers Association, 143; populist movement in, 154–57; railroads in, 129–34

Nye, Gerald, 156

Oberlin College (Academy), 36, 93, 96, 103
occupations: idea of, 66–67, 123–24, 189–90; need for skilled laborers, 46–47; training for prevailing, 99, 102, 117, 192, 194. *See also* careers of manual training graduates
O'Fallon Polytechnic Institute, 45–46
Ogren, Christine: *The American State Normal School*, 136–37, 143, 149, 158, 203–4, 206
Omdahl, Lloyd, 155
Oneida Institute (Academy), 34–35, 38, 112
Oram, Ruby, 246n163
Ordway, John, 48
organic circuit process, 68–69
Owen, Robert Dale, 34, 85
Owen, William B., 88

Palmer, Potter and Bertha Honoré, 75
Parker, Francis W.: Chicago Institute, 64; Chicago Normal School, 1, 10–11, 61–62, 79, 88; Chicago School of Education, 27, 81, 83–87; CMTS and, 5; influence on NI, 140–41; on manual training, 15, 71–72; new education and, 73; teacher training, 5; on vocation, 55
Parnell, Charles Stewart, 95, 99
Parnell, Delia Stewart, 95–96, 98
Perry, Hector, 155, 156
Pestalozzi, Johann Heinrich, 33, 36, 43, 52, 117
Phelps-Stokes Fund of New York, 120–21
Philadelphia Centennial Exposition, 31, 44–46, 93
Philadelphia schools, 32, 37, 48–49, 66, 106
Pillsbury, Nan, 94, 96
Pinkney-Sooy, Mary Louise, 146; *Plan Your Own Home*, 145
A Place Out of Time, 202, 206
Plato, 53
Poole, William Frederick, 5, 16
populism, 154–57
poverty and education: Hofwyl, 33–36; manual labor schools, 46, 48, 50; MTIS, 94, 96, 100; NI, 127, 135; poverty as reason for leaving school, 168–69
Prairie School style, 75, 224n132
producerism, 130, 155
Progressive Era, 43, 128–33, 155, 164, 197
Prosser, Charles, 161, 188, 190–91, 193, 196
Prosser Career Academy, 196
Pullman, George, 1–2, 6–7, 9–10, 27, 75

racism, 107–8, 198–99, 202, 207. *See also* African Americans; Jim Crow practices
Randall, Ina. *See* Graham, Ina Randall
Raphael: "Sistine Madonna," 139
Rathnau, Joseph, 12, 217n99, 219n10

Reber, Louis, 185–86
Reconstruction, 99, 104–5, 109
Rensselaer Polytechnic Institute, 29, 38–39
Rice, Joseph Mayer, 61, 63
Rice, Susan, 224n1
Rice, Walter Allan and Ella Mount, 91–93, 96. *See also* Manual Training and Industrial School (MTIS)
Richards, Charles, 169
Richards, Ellen Swallow, 138, 140, 176
Riis, Jacob, 169
Roberts, William, 180
Robinson, Theodore, 180
Rockefeller, John D., 61, 81
Rodgers, David: *The Work Ethic in Industrial America*, 40–42, 164
Roosevelt, Theodore, 107, 169
Rosenwald, Julius, 122, 190
Rosenwald Fund, 151
Rousseau, Jean-Jacques, 43, 65
Runkle, John, 44–47, 65, 140
rural schools, 37, 127, 141, 144, 150–54, 179–80. *See also* Normal and Industrial School (NI)
Rush, Benjamin, 32, 36
Ruskin, John, 58, 73–74, 76–77, 89, 138–39

Sandburg, Carl, 61
School of Mechanic Arts (Boston), 46, 48
schools of technology, 1, 22, 51–52, 56–58, 72
Schultz, Otto C., 142–43
Schutz, Jacob, 149
Sears, Roebuck, and Company, 11, 61
Second Great Awakening, 28, 33
Second Morrill Act (1890), 38, 94
Sennett, Richard: *Culture of the New Capitalism* and *The Craftsman*, 208
senses, learning through, 51–52
skilled labor: changing roles of, 42; combining skillful hands with cultured minds, 46; defined, 8–9; manual training's aim, 44;
preparing students for, 99–101, 119, 201–2; skilled laborers as teachers, 19, 175
sloyd, 48, 52
Small, Albion, 63, 76
Smith, Ken: "'Mind and Hand': Formative Years of a Prairie Town," 128–30, 133, 136, 140, 156
Smith-Hughes Act (1917), 168–71, 191–96
Snedden, David, 161, 185, 193; "Two Communications," 188–89
Social Darwinism, 41
socialism, 41, 74–75, 156
Society for Promoting Manual Labor in Literary Institutions, 28, 35, 93
The Southern Workman, 99, 200
South Side Academy, 81, 84
Spencer, Herbert, 43
Speyer School, 153
Springer, Margaret Warren, 76
Stanton, Elizabeth Cady, 34
Starr, Ellen Gates, 11, 72, 75
State Manual Training School. *See* Normal and Industrial School (NI)
St. George's Fields, 36
St. Louis, 50–52, 176
Stowe, Calvin: *Report on the Elementary Education in Europe*, 36–37
Stowe, Harriet Beecher, 37
Sullivan, Louis, 6, 26, 76
Sumner, Walter, 180

Tappan, Arthur and Lewis, 35, 207
Taylor, Frederick: *Principles of Scientific Management*, 190
teacher preparation (K-12). *See individual normal schools*
teacher preparation (manual training): at Chicago School of Education, 64–70; at CMTS, 19–20, 85; Cook County Normal School, 63; manual training teachers, difficulty finding, 70; at NI, 127, 144, 158, 197; at Teachers College, 50; in vocational education, 174–76
Teachers College, 50, 70–71

Index   281

technology: CMTS becoming school of, 56–58, 80; coeducating hands and minds, 39; history of, 66, 163; impact on labor, 39–42; inventors of, 39; jobs and, 160; programs for, 26, 88–89; schools keeping pace with changes in, 169, 199, 208; schools of, 22, 29, 37–48, 72, 80; technical skills, 40, 88; technological transformation, 40–41. *See also* Ham, Charles

Thompson, Elmer O., 148

Tilden Technical High School, 173

Tingle, Lillian, 136, 138, 140, 145, 205

Toledo Manual Training School, 73

tool instruction: in manual training, 2, 16–17, 26, 65; role of tools, 43–46; Russian method and, 8; shop work, 20, 70, 78; technology and, 89

Trenton School of Industrial Art, 101

Triggs, Oscar Lovell, 75–78, 89

Trotter, William Monroe, 103, 111–12

Turner, Frederick Jackson, 183

Turner, Jonathan Baldwin, 38–39, 208

Tuskegee Institute, 92–93, 104, 106–7, 116–18, 190–91

Twose, George, 73

unions: AFL, 41, 169–70; American Railway Union, 27; Black workers and, 119, 199; Illinois Federation of Labor, 179; industrial education and, 47, 55, 167, 170, 177; Samuel Gompers, 41, 169–70; unionization, 40–42

unit versus dual system, 162, 179, 185–88, 192. *See also* industrial education

University Elementary School, 64–69

University High School, 84–85, 88–89

University of Chicago, 1–2, 57–61, 74. *See also* Chicago School of Education

University of Illinois, 38

University of North Dakota, 128

University Register (1894–1895), 64

U.S. Bureau of Education, 49, 192; survey of Negro education, 119–21. *See also* Eaton, John; Harris, William Torrey

Valentine, Grace, 104

Valentine, William R., 104, 121, 124–25, 193–94, 199, 202

Van Hise, Charles, 183

Van Meter, E. W., 135

Villard, Oswald Garrison, 108

vocation, 55, 115, 120, 123–25, 144. *See also* occupations

vocational education, 159–96; agency and efficiency, 163–66, 193–96; from artisans to factory work, 160; changing economy and school systems, 171–78; Congressional funding, 195; continuation school programs, 181–85; Cooley controversy, 178–81; cost of and enrollment in programs, 176–77; Douglas commission report, 167–68; guiding children into satisfying work, 174–75; high schools, 174–77; industrial intelligence, 167, 174; local needs and national campaigns, 185–87; short-unit courses, 188, 190; Smith-Hughes Bill, 168–71, 191–93; two-year vocational programs in Chicago, 175–76; utilitarian efficiency applied to, 188–91

vocational guidance, 164, 170–71, 180

Washington, Booker T.: anti-Bookerites and Bookerites, 107–8, 111, 113; "Atlanta Compromise," 106, 108; countering illiteracy in South, 122; death of, 111–12; Du Bois and, 106–8, 111; at Hampton school, 113; higher education for Black students, 96; MTIS visit, 99, 102–3; as philosopher of education, 161; as progressive educator, 90, 123; tour of NJ, 119; *Up from Slavery*, 107, 117

Washington University, 1, 9, 45–46

Weld, Theodore, 34–36, 40, 90, 112–13

Wells, Dora, 176

Wells, Ida B., 27, 108

white paternalism, 109, 118–19, 121

Wilder, Laura Ingalls: *The Long Winter*, 133
Wilson, Woodrow, 102
Wirth, Arthur, 39, 43, 124, 188
Wisconsin Idea, 182–87
women's education: equality of sexes, 15; higher education, 36; high school graduation, 173; Lucy Flower High School, 176, 198; preparation for homemaking and workforce, 176–77; at University High School, 88; women's right to vote, 156; at Workingmen's School, 48
Woodward, Calvin: balance between manual and academic, 16; Della Vos and, 44–45; Dewey and, 65–67; director of St. Louis public schools, 176–77; industrial education, defined, 115; manual training programs, 8–9, 90; Manual Training School in St. Louis, 45–46, 163; manual training's value, 160; MTIS and, 92, 143; at NEA, 48; on preparing teachers for manual training programs, 127; "put the whole boy to school," 32; response to "Educational Value of Manual Training," 52–53; speaking at Dickey County Teachers Association, 126; tool use, 46–47, 89
Worcester Polytechnic, 46

Workingmen's parties, 41
"The Workshop" (*Chicago Inter Ocean*), 54–55, 72
Wright, Carroll D.: *Some Ethical Phases of the Labor Question*, 42
Wright, Frank Lloyd, 60, 74, 76–79, 89–90, 208; "Art and Craft of the Machine," 77–78
Wright, Marion Thompson, 202; *Education of Negroes in New Jersey*, 110

Yale College band, 28
Young, Ella Flagg: adapting schools to demands of changing economy, 171–72; agency and efficiency, 159–60, 166; at Chicago School of Education, 86; continuation schools, 183–84; as CPS superintendent, 88, 162–63, 180; democratization of education, 60; on Dewey and Parker, 83; high school for girls, 176; high schools' responsibilities, 172–73; initiator of vocational education programs, 162–63; *Isolation in the School*, 198; as Normal School principal, 88, 174; opposition to Cooley's proposals, 179; Tuskegee Institute visit, 190–91

Zueblin, Charles, 86

CONNIE GODDARD holds a PhD and is a journalist and independent scholar who has coauthored two previous books about Chicago.

The University of Illinois Press
is a founding member of the
Association of University Presses.

———————————————

University of Illinois Press
1325 South Oak Street
Champaign, IL 61820-6903
www.press.uillinois.edu